TRUTH COMMISSIONS AND STATE BUILDING

Truth Commissions and State Building

Edited by

Bonny Ibhawoh,

Jasper Abembia Ayelazuno,

and Sylvia Bawa

McGill-Queen's University Press
Montreal & Kingston • London • Chicago

ISBN 978-0-2280-1898-8 (cloth)
ISBN 978-0-2280-1899-5 (paper)
ISBN 978-0-2280-1963-3 (ePDF)
ISBN 978-0-2280-1964-0 (ePUB)

Legal deposit fourth quarter 2023
Bibliothèque nationale du Québec

Printed in Canada on acid-free paper that is 100% ancient forest free
(100% post-consumer recycled), processed chlorine free

This book has been published with the help of a grant from the Canadian Federation
for the Humanities and Social Sciences, through the Awards to Scholarly Publications
Program, using funds provided by the Social Sciences and Humanities Research
Council of Canada. Funding was also received from McMaster University.

| Funded by the Government of Canada | Financé par le gouvernement du Canada | Canada | Canada Council for the Arts | Conseil des arts du Canada |

We acknowledge the support of the Canada Council for the Arts.
Nous remercions le Conseil des arts du Canada de son soutien.

McGill-Queen's University Press in Montreal is on land which long served
as a site of meeting and exchange amongst Indigenous Peoples, including the
Haudenosaunee and Anishinabeg nations. In Kingston it is situated on the territory
of the Haudenosaunee and Anishinaabek. We acknowledge and thank the diverse
Indigenous Peoples whose footsteps have marked these territories on which peoples
of the world now gather.

Library and Archives Canada Cataloguing in Publication

Title: Truth commissions and state building / edited by Bonny Ibhawoh,
   Jasper Abembia Ayelazuno, and Sylvia Bawa.
Names: Ibhawoh, Bonny, editor. | Ayelazuno, Jasper, editor. |
   Bawa, Sylvia, editor.
Description: Includes bibliographical references and index.
Identifiers: Canadiana (print) 20230466753 | Canadiana (ebook) 20230466842
   | ISBN 9780228018988 (cloth) | ISBN 9780228018995 (paper)
   | ISBN 9780228019633 (ePDF) | ISBN 9780228019640 (ePUB)
Subjects: LCSH: Truth commissions—Africa. | LCSH: Nation-building—Africa.
   | LCSH: Transitional justice—Africa. | LCSH: Restorative justice—Africa.
Classification: LCC DT30.5.T78 2023 | DDC 960.3/2—dc23

This book was typeset in 10.5/13 Sabon Pro.

To all survivors who, at the risk of re-traumatization,
bear witness to atrocities

Contents

Table and Figures   ix
Acknowledgments   xi
Abbreviations   xiii

Introduction: Truth Commissions and the Politics of State Building   3
Bonny Ibhawoh, Sylvia Bawa, and Jasper Abembia Ayelazuno

SECTION ONE: CONCEPTUAL AND THEORETICAL ENGAGEMENTS
1   Truth Commissions, Civic Participation, and State Building   35
Jennifer Wallace and Bonny Ibhawoh
2   Truth-Seeking Processes as Redress for Victims of Conflict-Related
Sexual Violence   58
Jean de Dieu Sikulibo
3   The African Human Rights and Transitional Justice Architecture:
An Analytical Outline   75
Obiora C. Okafor and Uchechukwu Ngwaba
4   Decolonization, Gender, and Transitional Justice in
Post-Colonial Africa   99
Sylvia Bawa

SECTION TWO: METHODS AND PROCESSES
5   Whites and the South African Truth and Reconciliation
Commission   121
Roger Southall
6   Truth, Reconciliation, and Peace: Building a National Infrastructure
for Peace in Sierra Leone   143
Teddy Foday-Musa

7   Truth, Justice, and National Reconciliation: The Dilemmas of
    Transitional Justice in Burkina Faso   163
    Aboubacar Dakuyo

8   Mali's Truth, Justice, and Reconciliation Commission: Truth Seeking
    and Peacebuilding across Borders   186
    Janine Lespérance

9   Post-Authoritarianism, Truth Seeking, and the Judicial Accountability
    Gap: Lessons from Nigeria   208
    Hakeem Yusuf

    SECTION THREE: DOCUMENTS AND ARCHIVES

10 TRCs and the Archival Imperative   239
    Abena Ampofoa Asare

11 Nation and Narration: Creative Imaginaries of Truth and
    Reconciliation   256
    Paul Ugor

12 The South African Truth and Reconciliation Commission and
    Access to its Documentation   281
    Proscovia Svärd

13 The Gambian TRRC: Toward a "Comprehensive Model" of
    Truth Commissions   295
    Baba G. Jallow

    SECTION FOUR: OUTCOMES AND LEGACIES

14 Ghana's National Reconciliation Commission: A Retrospective   315
    Robert K. Ame and Seidu M. Alidu

15 The Long-Term Legacies of Transitional Justice:
    Understanding the Paradox of Peace in Sierra Leone   341
    Gearoid Millar

16 Rebuilding Social Cohesion in Post-Genocide Rwanda   358
    Jean Nepo Ndahimana

    Conclusion: Assessing Truth Commission Impacts and Legacies   373
    Bonny Ibhawoh

    Contributors   379
    Index   387

Table and Figures

TABLE

6.1 Sierra Leone TRC sensitization messages.
     Credit: Teddy Foday-Musa 151

FIGURES

0.1 Global map of national and regional truth commissions.
     Credit: Bonny Ibhawoh. Adapted from Saskia Nauenberg,
     "Spreading the Truth: How Truth Commissions Address Human
     Rights Abuses in the World Society," *International Sociology* 30,
     no. 6 (2015). 10
0.2 National and regional truth commissions established per year.
     Credit: Bonny Ibhawoh. Adapted from Saskia Nauenberg,
     "Spreading the Truth: How Truth Commissions Address Human
     Rights Abuses in the World Society," *International Sociology* 30,
     no. 6 (2015). 11
14.1 Detention violations over the period. Credit: Robert K. Ame
     and Seidu M. Alidu 319
14.2 Perpetrator responsibility for all violations. Credit: Robert K. Ame
     and Seidu M. Alidu 319
14.3 Reasons for making statements to the commission.
     Credit: Robert K. Ame and Seidu M. Alidu 321

Acknowledgments

Most of the chapters in this volume were first presented at an international conference on truth commissions organized by the Confronting Atrocity Project at McMaster University's Centre for Human Rights and Restorative Justice. We are grateful for the generosity and support of the funders of the conference and project, including the Social Sciences and Humanities Research Council of Canada, McMaster University, and the University for Development Studies, Ghana. We are indebted to faculty colleagues and student research assistants who helped organize the Truth and Reconciliation Commission conference at the University of Ghana, especially Noble Gati. We thank the staff of the University of Ghana Guest House for hosting us and for their warm hospitality.

We are grateful to researchers involved with the Confronting Atrocity Project whose research on truth commission records was helpful to framing the themes in this volume: Adebisi Alade, Chelsea Barranger, Melike Yilmaz, Mesut Yilmaz, in Canada; Benjamin Freeman in Liberia; Abubakar Koroma in Sierra Leone; and Leonardo Torres in Colombia.

We conceived this book as a dialogue between academics, policymakers, and practitioners who are interested and involved in the work of truth commissions not only as a transitional justice measure but also as a mechanism for post-conflict and post-authoritarian state (re)building. We are grateful to the practitioners and policymakers who participated at various phases of this project and facilitated our conversations on the important questions this book addresses: Baba Jallow, executive secretary of the Gambia Truth, Reconciliation and Reparations Commission; Christopher Till, founding executive

director of the Apartheid Museum, South Africa; Janine Lespérance
of Avocats sans frontières (Lawyers without Borders); Jean Nepo
Ndahimana of Aegis Trust, Rwanda and the Kigali Genocide
Memorial; Abubakarr Koroma of the Sierra Leone Peace Museum,
which holds the archives of the Sierra Leone Truth Commission. We
are also grateful to Jerome Verdier, who chaired the Liberian Truth
and Reconciliation Commission, for sharing his unique insights into
the workings of the Liberian TRC in conversations that helped frame
this book. We thank Benedict Inedia for painting the cover image
for this book.

The ongoing dialogue between academics, policymakers, and practitioners has enriched our understanding of the processes, impacts,
and legacies of truth commissions as mechanisms for transitional
justice, restorative justice, and state (re)building.

Abbreviations

ACHPR African Charter on Human and Peoples' Rights
AfCHPR African Court on Human and Peoples' Rights
AFRC Armed Forces Revolutionary Council
ANC African National Congress
APC All People's Congress
APRM African Peer Review Mechanism
APSA African Peace and Security Architecture
ASFC Avocats sans frontières Canada (*also* Lawyers without Borders Canada)
AU African Union
AUTJP African Union Transitional Justice Policy
CDIPH Université Laval's Clinique de droit international pénal et humanitaire (International Criminal and Humanitarian Law Clinic)
CEDAW Convention on the Elimination of All Forms of Discrimination Against Women
CEI Commission d'enquête indépendante
CHRAJ Commission on Human Rights and Administrative Justice
CMA Coordination des mouvements de l'Azawad (Coordination of Azawad Movements)
CNLG National Commission for the Fight against Genocide (Commission nationale de lutte contre le génocide)
CNR Commission for National Reconciliation (Burkina Faso; precursor to CNRR)
CNRR Commission for National Reconciliation and Reforms (Burkina Faso)
CNT Conseil national de la transition

CPIJ Canadian Partnership for International Justice
CSOs Civil Society Organizations
CTF Commission of Truth and Friendship
    Indonesia – Timor-Leste)
CVJR Commission Vérité, Justice et Réconciliation
    (Truth, Justice, and Reconciliation Commission) (Mali)
DDR Disarmament, Demobilisation and Reintegration
    (Sierra Leone, ch 15)
DOJ Department of Justice
ECOWAS Economic Community of West African States
EPR Ethnographic Peace Research
FSC Federal Supreme Court
GIZ German Agency for International Cooperation
GTRC Greensboro Truth and Reconciliation Commission (US)
HCRNU High Council for Reconciliation and National Unity /
    Haut Conseil pour la Reconciliation et l'Unité Nationale
HRSA Human Rights Strategy for Africa
HSRC Human Sciences Research Council
ICC International Criminal Court
ICTJ International Center for Transitional Justice
ICTR International Criminal Tribunal for Rwanda
ICTY International Criminal Tribunal for the Former Yugoslavia
IGAD Intergovernmental Authority on Development
IGP inspector general of police
IMF International Monetary Fund
NCTR National Centre for Truth and Reconciliation, Canada
NGOs non-governmental organizations
NP National Party
NPP National Patriotic Party, Ghana
NRC National Reconciliation Commission (Ghana)
NSGC National Service of Gacaca Courts
NURC National Unity and Reconciliation Commission (Rwanda)
OAU Organisation of African Unity
PCRD [AU] *Policy Framework for Post-Conflict Reconstruction
    and Development*
PNDC Provisional National Defense Council, Ghana
REC Regional Economic Communities
REMHI Project for the Recovery of Historical Memory
    (Guatemalan Truth Commission)
REN-LAC Le Réseau national de lute anti-corruption

RRC Reparations and Rehabilitation Committee
RSPs Regional Selection Panels
RUF Revolutionary United Front
SAHA South African History Archive
SAPs Structural Adjustment Programs
SCSL Special Court for Sierra Leone
SLPP Sierra Leone People's Party
TIA Tribunals of Inquiry Act
TJRC Truth, Justice, and Reconciliation Commission (Kenya)
TRC South African Truth and Reconciliation Commission
TRRC Truth, Reconciliation and Reparations Commission
  (The Gambia's)
UN United Nations
UNDP UN Development Programme

TRUTH COMMISSIONS AND STATE BUILDING

INTRODUCTION

Truth Commissions and the Politics of State Building

Bonny Ibhawoh, Sylvia Bawa,
and Jasper Abembia Ayelazuno

At the presentation ceremony of the South African Truth and Reconciliation Commission's (TRC) final report in 2003, its chair, Archbishop Desmond Tutu, hailed the TRC's work as a significant step in
the country's journey toward healing and reconciliation. An ardent
proponent of restorative justice, Tutu proclaimed enthusiastically:
"We are celebrating our freedom today from the ghastly shackles
and vicious injustice of an awful [apartheid] system. We scored a
spectacular victory over an evil system."[1] He added that the South
African TRC has become a "benchmark against which others are
measured as something to emulate." The final volume of the TRC
report that Tutu presented centred on reparations for the victims
of apartheid, including recommendations for a "wealth tax" on
the "beneficiaries of apartheid" to fund reparations payments. The
nation, Tutu stated, had a legal and moral obligation to honour
long overdue reparations to victims. He acknowledged, however,
one of the most serious flaws of the TRC: although it had the power
to *grant* amnesty to perpetrators, it could only *recommend* reparations for victims.[2]

This limitation raised several questions. Since the TRC could
only recommend reparations, not grant them, how could it ensure
restitution and justice to victims? How could it ensure that the
"beneficiaries of apartheid" fulfilled the obligation to make reparations? Moreover, white South African elites – the main beneficiaries
of apartheid and still among the wealthiest people in the country –
had largely refused to participate in the TRC process. P.W. Botha,
who was president during the worst years of apartheid oppression in

the 1980s, refused to appear before the TRC, despite several subpoenas and requests from the commission. A defiant Botha stated that his white Afrikaner minority would bow only to God, and he would not appear in person before what he described as Archbishop Tutu's "circus."[3] Given these fraught realities, hadn't the TRC fallen short of its truth-finding and reconciliation objectives? Tutu's response was more subdued. He reiterated his belief that the TRC was a "victory" for the country and a defining step in the nation's healing process. He conceded though that on matters of truth and reconciliation, "You can't hold a pistol to somebody's head."[4] Tutu's optimism and resignation convey a central theme of this book: the paradoxes of hopefulness and despair, triumphs and limitations of truth commissions in nation building.

This volume examines truth commissions as mechanisms for civic inclusion, identity formation, institutional reform, and nation (re)building in post-conflict and post-authoritarian societies. It explores truth commissions' mandates, methods, outcomes, and legacies and how they shape state-building processes in transitional and restorative justice contexts. Wide-ranging contributions from expert scholars, practitioners, and policymakers, offer multidisciplinary and cross-sectoral perspectives on the complex role of truth commissions as mechanisms for addressing grave and mass human rights violations.

Since the 1980s, the world has witnessed a proliferation of truth commissions as models of transitional and restorative justice. As of 2023, over fifty state-sponsored or civil society led truth commissions have been established worldwide. As a method of transitional justice, truth commissions are a vital element of the repertoire of strategies for peacebuilding and state building after countries have been torn apart by conflict and authoritarian rule. They continue to be employed amid democratic transitions and in the aftermath of deadly civil wars characterized by gross human rights violations. Apart from the traditional truth-seeking mandate, many of these commissions have explicit reconciliation mandates, making them Truth and Reconciliation Commissions (TRCs).

Most truth commission have been established in transitional states in Latin America and Africa, with nearly half of the total number implemented on the African continent between 1995 and 2001. In terms of number, Africa has become the main regional site of truth commissions, with a variety of iterations of such processes developed in almost twenty countries. African truth commissions have taken various forms, including international bodies, national commissions, local judicial and non-judicial processes, and community-based justice practices.[5] Drawing on a broad scope of case studies from Africa and beyond, this volume offers insights into the mandates, processes, outcomes, and legacies of truth commissions and how they have shaped or failed to shape state (re)building, particularly in post-conflict and post-authoritarian rule contexts.

Although the scholarship on truth commissions as mechanisms for transitional justice is rich and diverse, the Truth Commission model is relatively new, hence the need for iterative evaluation and interpretations of the model as it has evolved in different countries and regions of the world. Moreover, beyond the context of transitional justice, few studies have examined truth commissions within the specific framework of state building. Even though state building is often not an explicitly stated goal of truth commissions, it is implied in their mandates and evident in their processes, recommendations, and outcomes. Indeed, state building is integral to transitional justice.

Transitional justice is typically associated with periods of political change, characterized by legal responses to confront violations arising from conflict or the wrongdoings of repressive predecessor regimes. However, transitional justice can also be associated with the *transition* of society from the oppressive legacies of historical atrocities and exclusion toward justice, inclusion, and reconciliation. Pursuing justice in normal situations poses enormous difficulties. Doing so in countries undergoing transitions intensifies these difficulties because it requires the delicate balance of two imperatives: "On the one hand, there is the need to return to the rule of law and the prosecution of offenders. On the other hand, there is a need for rebuilding societies and embarking on the process of reconciliation."[6] The goals of transitional justice measures are therefore often to repair and rebuild fractured states and societies. This typically involves balancing transitional justice measures and *realpolitik*.

The contributions to this volume constitute a wide range of disciplinary perspectives on truth commissions and state building. In conceptualizing this book, our goal was to produce a text that blends the valuable insights of academic theory and analyses with praxis in the field. For this reason, some of the chapters deviate from the model of typical scholarly pieces. These practice-oriented and

evidence-based chapters are fascinating narratives from those working in the fields of transitional and restorative justice, enriched with
practical lessons about how TRCs work.

This introductory chapter formulates the conceptual and analytic
framework of the book and outlines its thematic coherence. First, we
engage critically with the literature on the state and its building, flesh-
ing out the core qualities and dynamics of state building to foreground
the political context in which truth commissions are established and
why they constitute part of the strategies of state (re)building. Second,
we provide brief outlines of the chapters' arguments, demonstrating
their connections and how they address the book's broader themes.
Third, we outline the rationale of the book's organization.

THE GLOBALIZATION OF TRUTH COMMISSIONS

Several chapters in this volume take up the debate over the definition
of truth commissions (see chapters 1 and 2). Our limited goal here is
to broadly map the expanding global appeal and dimensions of truth
commissions as a model of transitional state building. Truth commissions have become a popular way of addressing human rights
violations and historical atrocities. Since they first appeared in Latin
America in the 1980s, truth commissions have been established in
over fifty countries. While most of these are national truth-seeking
projects, a few are grassroots community-led or regional truth commissions. Although truth commissions have been established for
varied purposes, their primary mandate is to investigate past human
rights abuse with the aim of finding the "truth" about the causes,
patterns, and consequences of political violence. Truth commissions
are also often charged with providing redress for victims through
recommendations for prosecution, amnesty, institutional reforms,
and reparation programs of apologies, memorials, and compensation. In all, truth commissions represent the hope that collective
acknowledgment of past atrocities, reflection, and repair can help
build less violent and more equitable and inclusive societies.

In the past two decades, the focus of truth commissions has expanded
to cover more types of human rights violations, going beyond crimes
against physical integrity to include an extensive array of violations
of economic, social, and cultural rights. Truth commissions have also
become targeted for addressing the abuses suffered by specific victim
groups, including women, children, minority groups, and Indigenous

peoples. National truth commissions have been established to investigate state repression (Chile), and they have been deployed across the world as a mechanism for investigating racial injustice (South Africa), slavery and indentured servitude (Mauritius), genocide (Rwanda), war crimes (South Korea), and state abuses (Morocco). Truth Commissions have also been used in democratic transition processes (Ghana), as a means of addressing government corruption (Philippines), and for redressing historical injustices against Indigenous peoples (Canada, Greenland).

Truth commissions differ in terms of the specific goals they prioritize. For example, national reconciliation was at the fore of the work of the South African TRC. In contrast, Argentina's National Commission on the Disappeared sought primarily to uncover the facts about disappeared persons through public hearings and trials; reconciling perpetrators and victims was less of a focus.[7] The Liberian TRC postulated economic crimes as a critical driver of conflict.[8] Similarly, The Gambia's Truth, Reconciliation and Reparations Commission focused much of its work on economic rights violations and reparations for victims. In Rwanda, the National Unity and Reconciliation Commission focused on reunifying communities fractured by genocide through the Gacaca courts. The diverse structures and mandates of these commissions limit precise definition of what constitutes a truth commission.

The establishment of the South African TRC in 1995 by the government of Nelson Mandela to investigate apartheid-era crimes brought renewed international visibility to truth commissions as transitional and restorative justice mechanisms. The South African TRC popularized many attributes now associated with truth commission processes, such as public hearings, reconciliation, and "amnesty for truth" provisions. Through publicly televised TRC proceedings, perpetrators came face to face with survivors and victims' families. The amnesty provisions and reconciliation mandates of the South African TRC also set it apart from most previous truth commissions.

The Canadian TRC was inspired by the South African example, modelling its public hearings after those of the South African TRC. The leaders of the Canadian TRC acknowledged that their understanding of the purpose and value of truth telling and reconciliation was based on the South African TRC. Justice Murray Sinclair, who chaired the Canadian TRC, stated: "We learned a great deal from the South African commission in terms of how to engage with survivors of atrocities, how to provide support to them in the course of their testimony, how to ensure that their sense of story was validated, and how to ensure that they understood the importance of not only truth-telling, but the importance of making a contribution to reconciliation."[9] However, the Canadian TRC also had unique elements grounded in Indigenous knowledge and dispute-resolution practices that have been adopted in other truth-seeking processes.

Since the establishment of the South African TRC, truth commissions have become a global project. Once confined to transitional states in the Global South, truth commissions have now spread to the advanced democracies. In 2008, Canada established a TRC to document the history of the Indian Residential School system and its impacts on Indigenous communities. Since then, several Western countries have adopted, or are in the process of establishing, truth commissions to address historical injustices against racial and ethnic minorities or political groups.

There are long-standing debates in Australia and New Zealand about adopting a Canadian-style TRC to address the state's historical relations with Aboriginal peoples. Both countries have previously established truth commission–like bodies to address these issues. In 2020, the government of the Australian state of Victoria announced it would launch a truth and justice process to "recognize historic wrongs and address ongoing injustices for Aboriginal Victorians."[10] Following widespread protests for racial justice in the United States in 2019, political leaders there introduced congressional proposals to establish a "United States Commission on Truth, Racial Justice, Healing and Transformation."[11]

Similarly, some Nordic countries, building on the Canadian and Greenlandic reconciliation process, are embracing Truth and Reconciliation Commissions. Norway, Sweden, and Finland have drawn on the TRC model to address the effects of historical assimilation policies directed at the indigenous Sámi population and Finnish-speaking minorities.[12] In Norway, a TRC was established in 2018 to examine the Norwegian state's past injustices committed against the Sámi and Kven peoples. In Finland, the main Sámi political bodies approved the proposal for a commission in 2019, while in Sweden, public debates are ongoing about the truth and reconciliation process.[13] In 2018, Spain announced its own truth commission to unveil the crimes committed during the civil war and Franco's dictatorship, more than forty years after his death. The Council of

Europe has also called for truth commissions to be established in several European countries to unravel the truth about mass atrocities against persecuted European minorities such as the Roma people. The council specifically calls for a full accounting of the atrocities committed against the Roma people by the Nazis and other fascist regimes, believing that a complete account and recognition of these crimes through truth commissions might restore trust among the Roma toward the wider society.[14]

The map (figure 0.1) and graph (figure 0.2) illustrate the global spread of truth commissions both at national and regional levels. The figures only take into account official truth commissions. When unofficial or grassroots truth commissions are included, the popularity of these commissions becomes even more apparent.

The growing popularity of truth commissions has coincided with the resurgence of memory politics and a period of increasing challenge of the nation-state's hegemony over history. As official narratives are challenged by societal demands for accurate and truthful representations of the past, truth commissions have become public spaces for policing the boundaries of truth and falsehood, fact and opinion, and past and present.[15] With roots in the post-colonial states of Latin America and Africa, the truth commission model also represents a normative contribution of the Global South to international human rights and justice. While the use of truth commissions as transitional justice mechanisms in the Global South has been relatively well studied, much less work has been done on the growing adoption of the truth commission model to address historical atrocities and injustices in the Global North.

Evidently, the mandates, processes, and outcomes of truth commissions established to address contemporary human rights violations in transitional states in the Global South differ from those established to address the legacies of historical abuses and injustices in Western democracies. These differences in historical, social, and political contexts complicate the conceptualization and theorization of truth commissions. However, because truth commissions have had the longest history in the Global South, case studies from Africa and Latin America offer unique insights into their development as models of transitional and restorative justice. The contributions in this volume reflect the complexities of truth commission processes as mechanisms for transitional justice, as traditionally framed, and as deliberative processes in civic engagement and state (re)building.

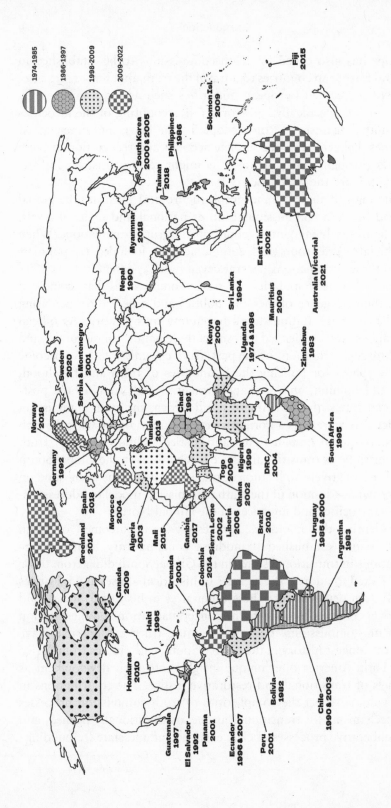

Figure 0.1 | Global map of national and regional truth commissions

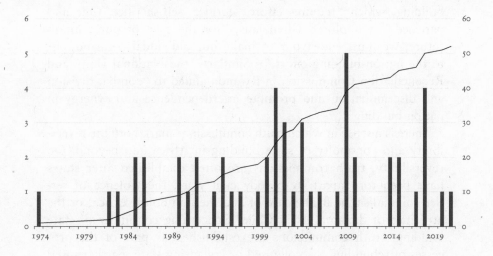

Figure 0.2 | National and regional truth commissions established per year

TRUTH COMMISSIONS AND
STATE BUILDING IN AFRICA

State building is a continuous, albeit non-linear process shaped by socio-historical contexts. In Africa, as in most post-colonial societies, state-building processes are characterized by incompletion, fragility, and reversibility.[16] This book examines truth commissions not only as transitional justice mechanisms but also as part of the core processes of state building or nation building in post-conflict and post-authoritarian political situations in Africa.[17] Our foundational premise is that truth commissions are inherently state-building projects, even when this is not apparent from their mandates. For example, Nigeria's Human Rights Violations Investigation Commission found it expedient to go beyond its investigation mandate to explore pathways for promoting nation building. It noted that the commission was "uniquely the best opportunity that Nigerians have had in several years to forge an informed understanding of their country's past and to put in place the necessary foundational building blocks on which a new Nigerian nation would rest."[18] Ghana's National Reconciliation Commission urged collective commitment to nation building, which "requires effort, sacrifice, self-sacrifice, time and patience." It implored Ghanaians, "for the sake of our nation's future, we must endeavour to make our individual contributions to the nation-building effort."[19] Similarly, the National Unity and Reconciliation Commission in Rwanda aimed to "combat division and discrimination and promote interdependence and synergy in nation-building."[20]

There is a sense in which truth commissions mark both the reversibility and continuity of state building in Africa and beyond. On reversibility, truth commissions are often established after states have been torn apart by bloody civil wars, the violence of settler colonialism as in the case of apartheid in South Africa, or the atrocities of dictators as in Chile. Concerning continuity of state building, truth commissions are established as part of the processes of rebuilding the collapsed or collapsing state, partly caused by nationalist tensions and conflicts between different nations within the state, as the cases of Rwanda, Liberia, and Sierra Leone illustrate. Logically, these assertions about the reversibility and continuity of state building foreground three related questions: First, how do we conceptualize state building and nation building within the work of truth commissions? Second, how do state power and the state-building agendas mediate truth commission mandates and processes? Here, we consider issues of inclusivity and marginalization in state- and nation-building discourses and practices. Third, how do truth commissions figure in the power structures that the state constructs and reinforces in the era of neo-liberal democracy and post-conflict peacebuilding?

In conceptualizing the state and state building, we recognize that a state is different from a nation, with the latter more socially complex than the former. Our conceptualization draws on the Weberian definition of the state that centres the monopoly of the legitimate use of force in the enforcement of the ruling order and investment with authority to make and implement binding decisions for people and organizations juridically located in a particular territory.[21] A key element in this Weberian conception of the state is political legitimacy centred on administrative, legal, extractive, and coercive organizations.[22] Historically, the emergence of states has preceded the emergence of nations, and this sequential development of the state and nation has much to do with the unique characteristics of a nation.[23] The people who constitute a nation typically have a shared culture or shared recognition of belonging to that nation.²⁴ The underlying quality of a nation, therefore, is the sense of oneness that ties members together through their shared history, cultures, convictions, loyalties, and solidarities.²⁵ The nation represents a community whose members believe that the "political and the national unit should be congruent."²⁶

This more profound sense of belonging to a nation is captured by Benedict Anderson's conceptualization of a nation as an imagined political community.²⁷ Forging a nation into a state – what is conceptualized as a nation-state – typically involves transforming an existing shared sense of nationhood to a new, expanded shared understanding of a nation-state based primarily on political solidarities. While the process of state building may have an end date, nation building remains a continual and aspirational project due to the dynamic constitution of the nation over time in terms of people, values, and norms. This is particularly true of multinational states with diverse constituent nations that are susceptible to threats of sub-national factionalism.²⁸

State failure is central to the work of truth commissions, which are often established in the aftermath of spectacular weakening or failure of state apparatus, as in the post-conflict contexts of Liberia, Sierra Leone, and Mali (chapters 6 and 8), or the post-authoritarian context of Burkina Faso and Gambia (chapters 7 and 13). In many African countries where truth commissions have been established, state failure is directly linked to political instability. The post-authoritarian context in which truth commissions emerge equally reflects a threat to or weakening of the state. Authoritarian and apartheid regimes, as the cases of The Gambia and South Africa illustrate, are often characterized by regime leaders' systematic and horrific abuses of the human rights of specific segments of citizens for various reasons. These abuses threaten the political legitimacy and collective loyalty of citizens to the state, as the victims feel excluded and unjustly treated as citizens. The Gambian Truth and Reconciliation and Reparations Commission, for example, was established specifically to investigate the egregious human rights abuses by the former authoritarian government of the deposed president Yahya Jammeh.

The African state that provides the backdrop for our study of truth commissions has been shaped by the specific colonial and post-colonial socio-historical conditions under which it emerged and evolved. As several scholars have noted, the African state was built on the colonial logic of economic exploitation and "divide and rule" rather than socio-political cohesion.[29] For the European states-men who gathered in Berlin in 1884 to carve up African territories among European powers, the goals were not to create nations bound together or ethnolinguistic affinities or geographical contiguity. The driving economic and political considerations in creating colonial states in Africa were external, not internal to the indigenous nations that were to constitute the state. These antecedents have shaped the functioning of the post-colonial states, impacting the political and economic structures, and the social order.

In many parts of Africa, the legacy of the colonial state "decanted into a patrimonial autocracy which decayed into crisis by the 1980s, bringing external and internal pressures for economic and political state reconfiguration."[30] As political scientist Crawford Young has noted, the spread of civil conflict and political instability in Africa in the 1990s stood as a metaphor for a weakened state.[31] Post-colonial state building efforts were constrained by the failures of politi-cal leadership and the neo-liberal economic and political reforms imposed on several insolvent African countries as lending condi-tionalities by Bretton Woods Institutions such as the International Monetary Fund (IMF) and the World Bank. Prescribed austerity mea-sures and Structural Adjustment Programs (SAPs) aimed at reducing government expenditure resulted in the removal of subsidies for social services such as education and health, trade liberalization, and currency devaluation, which reduced the economic and political control the state exercised. Several studies have linked SAPs to polit-ical repression, authoritarianism, and human rights violations in the developing countries where they were implemented.[32] Because these programs created economic difficulties for people and were unpop-ular, they triggered civil unrest. This predisposed weak governments that already had problems of legitimacy to resort to excessive repres-sion and coercion to enforce mandated economic austerity measures. By the 1990s, the weakening of state control and legitimacy, and the erosion of national cohesion in many African countries limited the scope for effective reform, ushering in a complex web of divisive politics, separatist agitations, and civil conflicts. These political and economic challenges rooted in colonial rule and the post-colonial crises of governance are the immediate precipitators of the con-flicts and violations that most African truth commissions have been tasked with investigating and redressing.

The centrality of post-colonial state failure to the work of African truth commissions is evident in their findings and recommendations. Kenya's Truth, Justice, and Reconciliation Commission attributed the political conflicts in the country to distrust and division along ethnic and regional lines. The commission noted that inter-communal distrust had festered mainly because "a myriad of issues which are at the core of nation-building have largely remained unresolved."[33] These lingering issues include conflicts over land, inequality and regional imbalances, and impunity combined with a lack of transparency and accountability that eroded a sense of belonging, nationhood, and public trust in political and governance institutions. Mauritius's Truth and Justice Commission attributed the political crisis in the country partly to the lack of a road map for nation building and the weak efforts to encourage a national identity and secure "economic democracy." As stated in its final report: "Not enough has been done to encourage a national spirit in the minds of the people."[34]

Given the centrality of state failure to the work of truth commissions, we need to understand better their role in state (re)building processes. State building in these contexts goes beyond the traditional benchmarks of expanding and consolidating exclusive control over a territory and its population, maintaining domestic order, and extracting resources.[35] It also includes restoring or enhancing state legitimacy by democratizing state institutions; rebuilding trust between citizens and the state and among citizens; and fostering national cohesion through justice, reconciliation, and restitution. Several chapters in this volume delineate the ways in which truth commissions intervene in the rebuilding process of national identities and state institutions disintegrated by civil war or fractured by authoritarian rule.

A discussion of state building is incomplete without reference to citizens, who are central to building and sustaining the state. As several contributions in this book show, a great deal of the work of truth commissions focuses on citizens (victims, perpetrators, collaborators, and bystanders), the relationships between citizens, and the relationship between citizens and the state. The fundamental *problematique* of society, for which the state was conceived as a solution, revolves around citizens and their relationship with each other: how to preserve law and order for peaceful coexistence.[36] The nature of this relationship between the state and its citizens is critical

to political legitimacy. It is a crucial factor that influences the formation and enduring existence of the state. The chapters in this volume
illustrate both the power and vulnerabilities of citizens in relation
to the state. In revealing the extent of abuse suffered by victims,
truth commissions reveal the vulnerabilities of citizenship. Through
their investigations and public hearings, they provide a forum for
victims to confront perpetrators, narrate their stories, and demand
justice. Truths Commissions also reveal the possibilities for engaged
citizenship and state accountability. This book offers insights into
the contestations and vulnerabilities of citizenship, illustrating the
power of citizens within and outside the state's territorial borders,
non-governmental organizations, and civil societies to wield power
in the affairs of the state through truth commission processes.

COLONIAL ANTECEDENTS

Even where their mandates centre on contemporary human rights violations, historical contexts are always in the foreground of truth commission processes. Although most African truth commissions focus
on contemporary abuses, many also have the mandate to investigate
the "root causes" of conflict and abuse.[37] Often, this centres on the
colonial origins of the state. One global study of the mandates and
final reports of truth commissions found that histories of colonialism
and imperialism were dominant themes.[38] For example, the Kenyan
Truth, Justice, and Reconciliation Commission linked contemporary
political conflicts and violence in the country to the "unspeakable and
horrific gross violations of human rights perpetrated by the British
colonial government between 1895 and 1963."[39] The commission referenced practices that had been institutionalized under British colonial
rule, including racial segregation, detention camps, torture, collective
punishment, massacres, and unlawful killings. It found that incidents
of extrajudicial killings going back to the colonial period continued
into the post-colonial period.

Similarly, Morocco's Equity and Reconciliation Commission
received several petitions from persons who requested investigation
and compensation for injuries they had been subjected to as a result
of violations committed by the French or Spanish colonial authorities. The commission could not investigate these cases because its
mandate was limited to grave violations committed by public officers of the Moroccan state or individuals or groups acting in its

name. Nonetheless, the commission noted that it had an obligation to help Moroccans uncover the truth.[40]

The most extensive investigation into colonial abuses by an African truth commission so far has been undertaken by the Truth and Justice Commission of Mauritius. Its mandate included assessing the consequences of slavery and indentured labour during the colonial period up to the commission's establishment. The commission, therefore, focused on the continuities in the history of human rights violations in the country. It found that for over a century, many Mauritians suffered gross human rights violations under Dutch, French, and British colonial rule, including the violence and indignities of enslavement; forced labour; arbitrary killings; social, political, and economic discrimination; and other forms of injustices that would today be considered crimes against humanity. The decision to eventually grant freedom and independence to colonial territories, the commission found, was not an altruist choice motivated by human rights considerations but rather by political and economic calculations. The commission concluded in its report that however substantial its recommendations, it could not adequately respond to the hurt, suffering, and loss of dignity that many Mauritians experienced under colonial rule: "We cannot bring back the dead, but if the measures we propose are implemented, it will markedly improve the quality of life for descendants of both slaves and indentured labourers who have suffered during the colonial period."[41]

Such investigations into the histories and legacies of colonial abuses are not limited to African truth commissions. Much of the work of the Canadian and South Korean truth commissions centred on colonial atrocities. While the Canadian TRC highlighted abuses against Indigenous children in colonial residential schools, the Korean TRC drew attention to the abuses under Japanese imperial rule. Some chapters in this volume explore further how truth commissions address colonialism and its legacies in their investigations and recommendations in post-colonial contexts (chapters 2 and 8).

AFRICAN LESSONS AND PERSPECTIVES

This book is concerned with the role of the truth commission as a mechanism for state building in post-authoritarian and post-conflict transitional countries in Africa. One of the most well-known truth commissions to have been established in Africa, the South African

Truth and Reconciliation Commission (TRC), placed great emphasis on the potential for the TRC to contribute to state building, beginning with the commission mandate. The Promotion of National Unity and Reconciliation Act of 1995, which established the TRC, laid out the objectives of the process. The act emphasized that truth telling was necessary to achieve the ultimate TRC objective of promoting "national unity and reconciliation in a spirit of understanding which transcends the conflicts and divisions of the past."[42] The stated objective was to establish national unity in South Africa and create a stable and fair society.[43] Thus, state building as an expected outcome was embedded in the work of the TRC from the creation of the commission.

Since the establishment of the South African TRC, truth commissions and state building have become increasingly favoured as complementary processes. Rwanda's post-genocide National Unity and Reconciliation Commission (NURC), established in 1999, was mandated "to promote unity, reconciliation, and social cohesion among Rwandans and build a country in which everyone has equal rights and contributes to good governance."[44] The discourse embedded in NURC's documentation and practices focused on state building through the creation of a culture of peace, which was deemed necessary to establish as the groundwork for the country to rebuild and reunify after the 1994 genocide.

Similarly, the Liberian TRC positioned nation building as an objective of its mandate to promote national peace, security, unity, and reconciliation.[45] This discourse of state building continues to be embedded in more recent truth commission processes, such as Mali's Truth, Justice, and Reconciliation Commission, which aims to consolidate national unity and democratic values to ensure lasting peace (chapter 8)[46] and The Gambia's Truth, Reconciliation and Reparations Commission (TRRC) (chapter 13).

Although there is a role, or at the very least an expected role, for truth commissions in state-building efforts, prevailing political and socio-economic conditions influence their interventions in these efforts. Several contributions in this volume explore the political and societal factors that shape or constrain truth commissions' state-building interventions, as well as the kind of state that emerges in their aftermath. Reflecting on the role of truth commissions in state building requires assessments not only of real-time processes and methods but also of long-term outcomes and legacies. State building is rarely a linear process of relentless progress. It is often a more complex and ongoing process of negotiation and consensus building across political, factional, and ideological lines. As such, the comparative examination of diverse truth commissions at various intervals provided in this book helps to elucidate the commissions' immediate and long-term state-building goals.

The varied and unique insights of scholars and practitioners on truth commission processes and state building compiled in this volume address the growing need for better understanding of the truth commission model. As more countries and societies adopt this model to address historical injustices and contemporary abuses, we need to know what works and under what conditions. The chapter by Baba Jallow details how more recent truth commissions such as Gambia's TRRC have sought lessons from research on past truth commissions, even as they grapple with the challenges we highlight in this volume.[47] Jallow, who as executive secretary of the TRRC, brings both academic and policy-making perspectives to the debate, argues that truth commissions engender narratives that help societies come to terms with their painful past and cement their determination to build a better future, despite their very practical limitations and the persistent controversy surrounding their existence and mandates. Truth commissions, therefore, remain a viable option for societies seeking to transition from conflict, dictatorship, or legacies of historical injustice toward peace, democracy, and reconciliation.

Several chapters in this volume frame truth commissions in terms of political rights and democratic participation. Reinforcing the central argument of this volume, Wallace and Ibhawoh (chapter 1) examine truth commissions as participatory state-building projects. They question the claims that the nation-building interventions of truth commissions undermine their primary mandates of truth-seeking and victim-centred justice, thereby blunting their effectiveness. They argue instead that truth commissions are inherently state-building ventures and should be assessed as such because they can help divided societies rebuild civic trust, forge inclusive identity, and restore fractured state institutions. Further, they analyze the effectiveness of truth commissions as deliberative mechanisms for participatory nation building. They acknowledge the point, repeatedly made, that transitional justice measures can be politically instrumentalized to advance statist and factional agendas. While they concede that statist agendas can conflict with the primary truth-finding and justice mandates of truth commissions, they argue that we can better understand, utilize, and evaluate truth commissions by framing them not just as transitional justice mechanisms but also as veritable state-building projects.

Janine Lespérance (chapter 8) similarly addresses the ongoing work and challenges of the Truth, Justice, and Reconciliation Commission in Mali (CVJR). Lespérance reflects on how the CVJR has incorporated aspects of other African truth commissions into the local Malian context.[48] As Lespérance's chapter exemplifies, the comparative studies in this book contribute to developing a better understanding of the connections between truth commissions within Africa and worldwide. Policymakers and practitioners involved in truth commission design and implementation can learn from studies and reflections on earlier truth commissions and, most importantly, can localize these lessons.

Robert Ame and Seidu Alidu (chapter 14) demonstrate why the assessment of truth commissions must go beyond final reports and immediate outcomes. The authors reflect on the impacts of Ghana's National Reconciliation Commission (NRC) fifteen years after its completion. Ame and Alidu illustrate that those in political power considered the NRC's short-term goals to have been achieved; however, the assessment of medium- and long-term impact tells a different story. Human rights violations by state security forces, which the NRC was tasked with investigating and addressing, are still prevalent, indicating that the long-term goal of reconciliation and systemic change has yet to be fulfilled.[49]

In chapter 7, Aboubacar Dakuyo similarly finds that in the few years following completion of the work of Burkina Faso's Commission for National Reconciliation and Reforms (CNRR), a "revolutionary" feeling in the country gave an illusion that the commission's goals had been met.[50] Reconsidering state-building efforts in more recent years, Dakuyo reveals this may not be the case in the long term, as the current regime remains hesitant to disrupt the apparent peace by implementing the human rights accountability measures the CNRR recommended.

Interestingly, studies such as Gearoid Millar's (chapter 15) seemingly arrive at the opposite conclusion to Ame and Alidu and Dakuyo. Millar notes that scholarship on Sierra Leone's TRC in the immediate aftermath of the commissions' work did not perceive a realistic lasting peace in the country. The prevalent assumption was that the TRC had fallen short of both its justice and peacebuilding goals. In re-evaluating state-building efforts approximately twenty years since the civil war, Millar argues that peace has largely been sustained.[51] This finding reinforces the point about the inevitability of changes in public attitudes and shifts in scholarly assessments of truth commissions over time. Outcomes and legacies that are not immediately evident might become apparent over time. Truth commission scholars must therefore remain open to re-evaluating their assumptions and conclusions as Millar does in this volume. The chapters in this book assess truth commissions in assorted contexts and from differing perspectives. They show the relevance and impacts of truth commissions during and long after they complete their work. The impacts of truth commissions on state building can be influenced by a myriad of shifting factors, such as truth commission priorities, changing public attitudes, and the dynamics of political power and social forces.

In reflecting on the short- and long-term impacts of truth commissions on state building, many contributors to this book make policy recommendations, suggesting ways to design, implement, and execute truth commission processes. Jean de Dieu Sikulibo (chapter 2) notes the need for truth commissions to better integrate community-based truth-telling methods into their work, especially in commissions addressing gender-based violence and sexual violence.[52] Such methods involve a more holistic approach to addressing structural violence, which is necessary for effective long-term peacebuilding. The theme of gender is carried on in chapter 4, where Sylvia Bawa explores gendered experiences of truth commissions through the portrayal and treatment of Winnie Mandela during the South African TRC. Bawa finds that truth commissions often neglect to address gendered crimes and tend to focus on individuals in their practices. This results in a failure to address systemic issues and the sidelining of women's experiences. When women's experiences are sidelined in truth commission processes, they continue to be relegated to state-building efforts afterward; therefore, truth commissions should approach their work through an explicitly gendered lens for effective state building.[53]

Several chapters in this volume show how prevailing political, social, and economic conditions define the potentials and limitations of truth commission interventions in state building. For truth commissions to be effective mechanisms for state building in transitional societies, their processes must be transparent and unencumbered by agendas of sponsoring governments. The records and documents they produce must also be readily accessible to the public. Truth commissions typically deal with two types of records. The first are *open records* gathered through investigations, unclassified statements, and public hearings culminating in a final report. The second are *closed records*, classified and confidential records that cannot be immediately made public, usually to protect the interests and safety of participating victims-survivors.

Most truth commissions aspire to make their open records publicly accessible. The assumption is that the more accessible truth commission records are, the better the chances of exposing the truth about abuses, holding perpetrators accountable, and ensuring justice for victims; however, access to these open records is not always guaranteed. Governments and political leaders might not be keen on preserving truth commission records where they indict government officials or reach conclusions that influential actors find adverse to their interests. Access to truth commission records is also impeded by lack of resources and required expertise in resource-constrained developing states where most truth commissions have been established. South Africa's Apartheid Museum and TRC Collection at the National Archives, Sierra Leone's Peace Museum, Chile's Museum of Memory and Human Rights, and Canada's National Centre for Truth and Reconciliation represent different models of truth commission record-keeping.

In chapter 12, Proscovia Svärd, an information science scholar who studies truth commission records, argues that despite the South African TRC's reputation as the model truth commission, the country has yet to accomplish one of its key recommendations of making TRC documentation easily accessible.[54] Svärd outlines some of the obstacles impeding public access to truth commission records in South Africa and how they might be addressed. In chapter 10, Abena Asare explores further the challenges of public access to truth commissions. She argues that citizens need access to the full truth commission archive, not simply the final report, for the documentation to contribute to truth finding and state building. Asare calls for truth commissions to plan ahead to build archives to house their records because ongoing state-building processes can easily be undermined by governments working to disappear documentation.[55]

Archives and documentation are crucial aspects of the work of truth commissions. The United Nations (UN) *Principles for the Protection and Promotion of Human Rights through Action to Combat Impunity* highlights the importance of preserving truth commissions' archives. The UN recommends that at the outset of the work truth commissions should clarify the conditions that will govern access to their documents, including conditions aimed at preventing disclosure of confidential information while facilitating public access to their archives. The UN principles also stress that "the right to know implies that archives must be preserved. Technical measures and penalties should be applied to prevent any removal, destruction, concealment, or falsification of archives, especially for the purpose of ensuring the impunity of perpetrators of violations of human rights and humanitarian law."[56]

Recent truth commissionns have paid more attention to archiving and documentation than earlier commissions. In chapter 8, Lespérance notes that the Malian Truth Commission, having learned from other countries' struggles to archive truth commission documents, is working toward creating a permanent institution to support the ongoing nature of the truth commission work. Documentation of truth commission processes is not limited to the record of archives and formal institutions. It is also reflected in media and literary cultures that narrate and interpret the work of truth commissions. In chapter 11, Paul Ugor demonstrates the usefulness of literary studies and critical discourse analysis approach in revealing the intricacies of how truth commission discourse is maintained in the state-building aftermath of transitional justice.[57]

Some contributors in this volume suggest developing robust "peace infrastructure" to sustain the state-building interventions of truth commissions in the long term. In chapter 6, Teddy Foday-Musa argues that fulfilling the recommendations of truth commissions and meeting their goal of national reconciliation requires the establishment of independent national peacebuilding infrastructure. Foday-Musa provides a case study of post-conflict Sierra Leone, which reveals that although the country has not met many of the TRC's recommendations due to a lack of institutional infrastructure, the inauguration of a national deliberative conference – Bintumani-III – is a sign that the process of peace infrastructure development has begun more formally.[58]

In chapter 16, Jean Nepo Ndahimana provides a similar overview of the Rwandan transitional justice experience, highlighting

the many organizations established and practices developed
throughout the process, such as the Gacaca courts, the Genocide
Survivors Support and Assistance Fund (FARG), memorialization
efforts, changes to the school curriculum, and state security sector
reforms.[59] Ndahimana's chapter highlights the range of institutions, commissions, and projects that all assisted in state rebuilding
in post-genocide Rwanda. This further supports the argument for
developing governance institutions and infrastructure outside of
TRCs to sustain post-conflict peace.

This volume aims at fostering dialogue between academics, policymakers, and practitioners interested and involved in the work of
truth commissions. The unique perspective that practitioners bring
to our understanding of the processes and impacts of the truth
commission is evident in the contributions by practitioners and policymakers to this volume, such as chapter 8, Lespérance on Mali's
Truth, Justice, and Reconciliation Commission and chapter 13,
Baba Jallow on the Gambian Truth, Reconciliation and Reparations
Commission. In many countries, the ongoing work of truth-seeking,
peacebuilding, and reconciliation efforts of truth commissions that
should be shared across different organizations and groups that constitute a system of peace infrastructure is too frequently shouldered
by only a few civil society organizations (CSOs). Therefore, a more
robust peace infrastructure is necessary to sustain state-building
efforts post–truth commission.

Ultimately, the success of truth commissions may be measured
in terms of public perceptions of the completeness of the "truth"
they find, and the relevance and impact of their recommendations
for justice, restitution, reconciliation, and state (re)building. Ideally,
post–truth commission implementation and reconstruction work
should involve a myriad of state, inter-state, and non-state apparatuses, including government agencies, local and international
non-governmental organizations; CSOs; media, international law,
and the international human rights community. This infrastructure and assemblage speak to the complexities of state rebuilding in
post-conflict and post-authoritarian transitional societies. In effect,
the real work of state reconstruction and reconciliation comes after
the conclusion of the work of truth commissions. Truth commissions then, have the additional task of envisioning the infrastructure
required to ensure that the work of rebuilding continues after its
more formal role ends.

APPROACHES AND METHODOLOGIES

If we have established that truth commissions contribute to state building, albeit in varying and sometimes contradictory ways depending on local circumstances, how do we measure the impacts of truth commissions on state building? The chapters presented in this book offer some suggestions for assessing this connection. The volume contributors draw on primary source material from truth commission databases such as the Global Truth Commission Index, various truth commission archives and digital repositories, media records, surveys, and interviews.

In exploring the nexus between the work of truth commissions and state building, this book makes salient interventions in current academic debates. First, the book analyzes truth commissions from diverse disciplinary and thematic frameworks: human rights, transitional justice, restorative justice, peacebuilding, democratic participation, archives and information science, and literary cultures. This range is significant because the volume demonstrates that the work of truth commissions has far-reaching ramifications for almost all sectors of society. Rather than conceptualizing state building as extraneous to the work of truth commissions or an accidental by-product (as many extant studies have done), we analyze the effectiveness of truth commissions as deliberative mechanisms intrinsic to state building in the aftermath of conflict or authoritarian rule.

The second intervention this book makes is in the discourse on truth commissions as a mechanism for civic inclusion and democratic participation. While scholars have paid some attention to understanding truth commissions as transitional justice mechanisms, relatively little attention has been given to understanding them as civic participatory processes. Civic engagement and public participation are critical goals of many truth commissions. They confer legitimacy on truth-finding processes. The objectives of truth finding, victim-centred justice, and reconciliation are contingent on civic engagement, which truth commissions seek through public hearings and outreach campaigns to elicit public participation. Several chapters in this volume examine the extent to which truth commissions provide spaces for civic engagement and public participation in governance.

The third intervention of this book is in the broader debate over assessing the effectiveness of truth commissions and proffering policy recommendations. Transitional justice scholars have offered various frameworks for evaluating the impact of truth commissions beyond categorizing them simply as strong or weak, successes or failures. These frameworks assess direct and indirect political impact through civil society, governance transparency and accountability, social norms, and judicial impacts. While these frameworks decentre political impacts and allow for a greater examination of the multitude of ways truth commissions can influence societies, "an assumption of temporal permanence remains embedded in the question of a truth commission's effectiveness."[60] As Jennifer Wallace and Bonny Ibhawoh note in chapter 1, this can be problematic because the work of truth commissions is often an ongoing process that does not end with publishing a final report. This volume contributes to these discussions by presenting a range of methods and approaches for assessing the impacts of truth commissions on state building from diverse political, social, economic, cultural, pedagogical, and temporal perspectives.

Obiora Okafor and Uchechukwu Ngwaba's chapter 3 provides an important reminder that studies of truth commissions must go beyond the commissions and associated state actors since many policies, organizations, and individuals significantly influence the ways Truth Commissions enhance or hinder state-building processes.[61] In chapter 15, Gearoid Millar also suggests that in assessing truth commissions, scholars examine a more comprehensive range of impacts on diverse communities. Many previous studies exclusively presented the experiences of the individuals deeply connected to the truth commission, which constituted the elite of society in Millar's studies of the Sierra Leonean TRC.[62] In chapter 5, Roger Southall reflects on gauging the response of white South Africans to the TRC. He argues that even though there was very little engagement in the TRC from the white South African community, it plays a significant role in the trajectory of reconstruction in the country and, therefore, needs to be included in any examination of the outcome of the TRC process.[63] The lesson here is that in assessing the impact of truth commissions, the stories of those not directly involved with the process are as relevant as the stories of those who participated. Many of these case studies suggest that to better understand the complex nature of the state building during and after truth commission processes, we must broaden our scope and assessment criteria.

As we expand the scope of truth commission studies, the picture becomes more complicated. Many chapters in this volume challenge and extend long-practised research methodologies in transitional justice that have insufficiently accounted for these complexities. As mentioned, truth commissions are relatively new mechanisms of transitional justice and models of restorative justice. Add to this our argument in this volume that they are also implicit and explicit mechanisms for state (re)building. Our understanding of truth commissions within these various frameworks will continue to evolve as more countries and communities adopt this model, and we learn more about the processes and outcomes.

Millar's self-critical essay in this volume is an example of the benefits of this pragmatic approach to truth commission studies (chapter 15). Millar revisits his earlier work on the Sierra Leone Truth Commission, which he had argued was an "actively provocative and potentially re-traumatizing event." In his revisionist reflections, he explores the inconsistencies of these findings and argues that they are rooted in the programmatic nature of the research he conducted. The program-specific and temporally bounded nature of his previous evaluative research ignored the complex interactions between the many parallel projects administered in cases of comprehensive post-conflict intervention. In response, he proposes an innovative model of Ethnographic Peace Research (EPR) that can be used to examine the legacy of TRCs as one component of complex and long-term post-conflict interventions. EPR, Millar contends, offers a better way forward in assessing the enduring legacies of truth commissions, as it centres around lived experiences and nuances.[64]

ORGANIZATION

This book is divided into four sections that emphasize the processes, outcomes, and legacies of truth commissions in the contexts of transitional justice, restorative justice, and state building. The first section on *conceptual and theoretical engagements* examines conceptual and theoretical debates about truth commission. Chapters explore the discourse on truth commissions within transitional and restorative justice scholarship, as mechanisms for truth seeking, civic engagement, and state building.

The second section considers the *methods and processes* of truth commissions. Chapters examine the social, political, and legal complexities arising from the work of truth commissions. The section focuses on how truth commissions shape nation-building efforts

and how state-building agendas, in turn, influence truth and reconciliation processes. This section includes insights from countries
that experienced a truth commission decades ago, such as Burkina
Faso, Sierra Leone, and South Africa, and from countries with truth
commissions currently underway, such as Mali. While each chapter
presents the unique challenges in different countries, combined, they
reveal that even when state-building goals are built into the design,
practice, and recommendations of truth commissions, various societal and political factors can alter state-building endeavours.

The third section addresses the important question of *documenting and archiving* truth commission records. It positions truth
commission documentation, archiving, and literacy cultures as
part of state-building efforts. Chapters examine literary, creative
narrativization of truth commissions, archiving, and memorialization in museum exhibits. Contributors in this section emphasize
the need for ongoing documentation after the completion truth
commissions' work. Practitioners in the museum field working to
educate visitors on truth commission processes provide insights
alongside critical analyses from scholars concerned with the state
of truth commission documentation and public discourse. This section includes a chapter that proposes a new comprehensive model
of truth commissions.

The fourth and final section focuses on the *outcomes and legacies*
of truth commissions with case studies on their long-term legacies
and implications for social cohesion. The chapters explore how and
why post–truth commission political landscapes influence truth
commission goals relating to justice, human rights accountability,
and reconciliation.

NOTES

1 Jan Hennop, "Tutu Hands over South Africa's Truth Commission
   Report," Agence France-Presse, 21 March 2003.
2 Graeme Hosken, "Tutu Concedes TRC Flaw," *Times* (South Africa),
   29 November 2013.
3 Reuters News Agency, "Tutu Lays Charges against Defiant Botha, Former
   South African President's Absence from Truth Commission Anger
   Officials," *Globe and Mail* (Canada), 20 December 1997.
4 Hennop, "Tutu Hands over South Africa's Truth Commission Report."

5 See chapter 3 in this volume for details on all the different approaches to truth commissions established in Africa. Okafor and Ngwaba, "The African Human Rights and Transitional Justice Architecture," this volume.

6 Alexander Boraine, "Transitional Justice: A Holistic Interpretation," *Journal of International Affairs* 60, no. 1 (2006): 17–27.

7 United States Institute of Peace, "Truth Commission: Argentina," accessed 23 July 2021, www.usip.org/publications/1983/12/truth-commission argentina.

8 Carla De Ycaza, "A Search for Truth: A Critical Analysis of the Liberian Truth and Reconciliation Commission," *Human Rights Review* 14, no. 3 (2013): 202.

9 Canadian Broadcasting Corporation, "Canada's Truth Commission Learned from Mandela, Says Head," CBC News, 9 December 2013, www.cbc.ca/news/canada/manitoba/canada-s-truth-commission-learned-from-mandela-says-head-1.2454851.

10 Daniel Andrews, "Delivering Truth and Justice for Aboriginal Victorians," www.premier.vic.gov.au/delivering-truth-and-justice-aboriginal-victorians.

11 H.Con.Res.19 – 117th Congress (2021–2022): Urging the establishment of a United States Commission on Truth, Racial Healing, and Transformation, 25 February 2021, www.congress.gov/bill/117th-congress/house-concurrent-resolution/19/text.

12 Astrid Nonbo Andersen, "The Greenland Reconciliation Commission: Moving Away from a Legal Framework," *The Yearbook of Polar Law Online* 11, no.1 (2020): 214–44.

13 Rauna Kuokkanen, "Reconciliation as a Threat or Structural Change? The Truth and Reconciliation Process and Settler Colonial Policy Making in Finland," *Human Rights Review* 21, no. 4 (2020): 293.

14 Commissioner for Human Rights, Council of Europe, *Human Rights of Roma and Travellers in Europe* (Strasbourg: Council of Europe Publishing, 2010), 8–9.

15 Onur Bakiner, *Truth Commissions: Memory, Power, and Legitimacy* (Philadelphia: University of Pennsylvania Press, 2016), 8.

16 Thomas Bierschenk and Jean-Pierre Olivier de Sardan, "Studying the Dynamics of African Bureaucracies: An Introduction to States at Work," in *States at Work: Dynamics of African Bureaucracies*, ed. Thomas Bierschenk and Jean-Pierre Olivier de Sardan (Leiden: Brill, 2014), 7.

17 We use the concepts of state building and nation building interchangeably in this volume for reasons outlined by Wallace and Ibhawoh in chapter 1.

18 *Synoptic Overview of the Human Rights Violation Investigation Commission (HRIVC) Report: Conclusions and Recommendations*, section 32, 23.

19 *National Reconciliation Commission Report* vol. 1 (Accra, 2004), 182.

20 *Unity and Reconciliation Process in Rwanda* (National Unity and Reconciliation Commission: Kigali, 2016) 36.

21 Juan J. Linz, "State Building and Nation Building," *European Review* 1, no.4 (1993): 358; and D. Rueschemeyer and P.B. Evans, "The State and Economic Transformation: Toward an Analysis of the Conditions Underlying Effective Intervention," in *Bringing the State Back In*, ed. P.B. Evans, D. Rueschemeyer, and T. Skocpol (Cambridge: Cambridge University Press, 1985), 47.

22 Theda Skocpol, "Bringing the State Back In: Strategies of Analysis in Current Research," in *Bringing the State Back In*, ed. P.B. Evans, D. Rueschemeyer, and T. Skocpol (Cambridge: Cambridge University Press, 1985); and Peter B. Evans, *Embedded Autonomy: States and Industrial Transformation* (Princeton: Princeton University Press, 1995).

23 Linz, "State Building and Nation Building," 355.

24 Ernest Gellner, *Nations and Nationalism: New Perspectives on the Past* (Ithaca: Cornell University Press, 1983).

25 Gellner, 7.

26 Ibid., 1.

27 Benedict Anderson, *Imagined Communities: Reflections on the Origin and Spread of Nationalism* (London: Verso Books, 2006).

28 Linz, "State Building and Nation Building."

29 Mahmood Mamdani, *Citizen and Subject: Contemporary Africa and the Legacy of Late Colonialism* (Princeton: Princeton University Press, 1996).

30 Crawford Young, "The End of the Post-Colonial State in Africa? Reflections on Changing African Political Dynamics," *African Affairs* 103, no. 410 (2004): 46.

31 Young, 46.

32 See, for example, M. Rodwan Abouharb and David Cingranelli, *Human Rights and Structural Adjustment* (Cambridge: Cambridge University Press, 2007).

33 *Report of the Truth, Justice and Reconciliation Commission*, vol. 1 (Nairobi: TJRC, 2013), xix.

34 *Report of the Truth and Justice Commission [Mauritius]*, vol. 1 (Government Printer, 2011), 11.

35 Martha C. Johnson and Meg Smaker, "State Building in De Facto States: Somaliland and Puntland Compared," *Africa Today* 60, no.4 (2014): 3–23.

36 Gellner, *Nations and Nationalism*, 4.
37 Chelsea Barranger, "References to Colonialism, Colonial, and Imperialism in Truth Commissions" (Hamilton: Centre for Human Rights and Restorative Justice, McMaster University, 2019).
38 Barranger, "References to Colonialism, Colonial, and Imperialism."
39 *Report of the Truth, Justice and Reconciliation Commission*, vol. 1 (Nairobi: TJRC, 2013), ix.
40 Kingdom of Morocco, *Equity and Reconciliation Commission: Final Report* (2006). See *Justice and Reparations for Victims* vol. 3, 79; and *Establishing Truth and Responsibility Regarding Human Rights Violations*, vol. 2, 95.
41 *Report of the Truth and Justice Commission [Mauritius]*, vol. 1, 10.
42 Promotion of National Unity and Reconciliation Amendment Act 34 of 1995 (South Africa), "Truth and Reconciliation Commission: Objectives of Commission," 4, www.ihl-databases.icrc.org/en/national-practice/promotion-national-unity-and-reconciliation-act-act-34-1995.
43 Promotion of National Unity and Reconciliation Amendment Act 34 of 1995(South Africa), "Truth and Reconciliation Commission: Functions of Commission," 6, www.ihl-databases.icrc.org/en/national-practice/promotion-national-unity-and-reconciliation-act-act-34-1995.
44 National Unity and Reconciliation Commission, Rwanda, "Mission," www.truthcommissions.humanities.mcmaster.ca/wp-content/uploads/2021/03/unity-and-reconciliation-process-in-rwanda.pdf.
45 Liberian TRC, Truth and Reconciliation Commission Act, 12 May 2005, www.refworld.org/pdfid/473c6b3d2.pdf.
46 Ordinance no. 2014-003, 15 January 2014. *Portant Creation de la Commission Vérité, Justice et Réconciliation.*
47 See chapter 13, Jallow, "The Gambian TRRC," this volume.
48 See chapter 8, Lespérance, "Mali's Truth, Justice, and Reconciliation Commission," this volume.
49 See chapter 14, Ame and Alidu, "Ghana's National Reconciliation Commission: A Retrospective," this volume.
50 See chapter 7, Dakuyo, "Truth, Justice, and National Reconciliation," this volume.
51 See chapter 15, Millar, "The Long-Term Legacies of Transitional Justice," this volume.
52 See chapter 2, de Dieu Sikulibo, "Truth-Seeking Processes as Redress for Victims of Conflict-Related Sexual Violence," this volume.
53 See chapter 4, Bawa, "Decolonization, Gender, and Transitional Justice in Post-Colonial Africa," this volume.

54 See chapter 12, Svärd, "The South African Truth and Reconciliation and Access to its Documentation," this volume.

55 See chapter 10, Asare, "TRCs and the Archival Imperative," this volume.

56 United Nations (UN), *Principles for the Protection and Promotion of Human Rights through Action to Combat Impunity* (Geneva: UN, 2005), principles 8(f) and 14.

57 See chapter 11, Ugor, "Nation and Narration," this volume.

58 See chapter 6, Foday-Musa, "Truth, Reconciliation, and Peace," this volume.

59 See chapter 16, Ndahimana, "Rebuilding Social Cohesion in Post-Genocide Society," this volume.

60 See chapter 1, Wallace and Ibhawoh, "Truth Commissions, Civic Participation, and State Building," this volume.

61 See chapter 3, Okafor and Ngwaba, "The African Human Rights and Transitional Justice Architecture," this volume.

62 See chapter 15, Millar, "The Long-Term Legacies of Transitional Justice."

63 See chapter 5, Southall, "Whites and the South African Truth and Reconciliation Commission," this volume.

64 See chapter 15, Millar, "The Long-Term Legacies of Transitional Justice."

Conceptual and Theoretical Engagements

Truth Commissions, Civic Participation, and State Building

Jennifer Wallace and Bonny Ibhawoh

The growing popularity of truth commissions calls for a deeper and systematic understanding of how they work as mechanisms for civic participation and state (re)building in the aftermath of conflict or authoritarian rule. Four decades after the first well-known truth commissions were established in Latin America in the 1980s, we now have enough data on their processes in almost every region of the world to map the common patterns and unique characteristics of these truth commissions. Enough time has passed to allow us to go beyond evaluating the immediate impacts of truth commissions, as earlier studies did, in order to assess their long-term implications for participants, states, and societies at large.

Although scholars have paid some attention to understanding truth commissions as transitional justice mechanisms, relatively little attention has been given to understanding them as civic participatory processes within state-building agendas. State building is not often an explicitly stated goal of truth commissions. Most truth commissions focus on investigating the root causes and societal consequences of past human rights violations to bring justice to victims and, in some cases, foster reconciliation. However, civic engagement and public participation are critical goals of many truth commissions. Implicit in the truth-finding, justice, and reconciliation mandates of truth commissions is the task of rebuilding states fractured by conflict and human rights abuses. Truth commission processes and recommendations have implications for state-building processes regarding public participation in terms of investigations and hearings, institutional reforms, and restitutive strategies to redress abuses, prevent reoccurrence, and foster reconciliation. Truth commissions are inherently state-building projects because they aim to provide the foundations for divided societies to rebuild civic trust and reform state institutions.

Critics contextualize the emergence of truth commissions within the post–Cold War wave of democratization that prioritized the adoption of neo-liberal economic policy over meaningful accountability for human rights violations and historical injustice.[1] For many post-authoritarian and post-communist states transitioning to democracy, truth commissions emerged in the 1980s and 1990s as a popular alternative to criminal trials in dealing with past atrocities. This has prompted skepticism toward truth commissions that are yoked to statist agendas and government aims.[2] Truth commissions are regarded more as instruments of statist legitimization than as mechanisms for justice and accountability for human rights violations. Certainly, the pursuit of state-building goals can undermine the truth-seeking and justice mandates of truth commissions. For example, with the South African Truth and Reconciliation Commission (TRC), critics have argued that the government's interest in nation building through reconciliation undermined accountability for apartheid-era human rights abuses. Human rights, one critic argues, were "dragooned by an emergent bureaucratic elite into the service of nation-building."[3] The constitutional right of victims to seek justice and pursue civil claims against perpetrators was taken away by the TRC's amnesty provisions, which precluded both criminal and civil prosecutions. In short, the political design and sociological function of South Africa's TRC were to legitimate the post-apartheid state.[4]

Similarly, in some Latin American countries the political constraints created by a negotiated settlement curtailed the search for truth and justice and ultimately led to the erosion of truth commissions' legitimacy.[5] Peru's TRC is said to have been used to promote the government's neo-liberal agenda. In its focus on reconciling perpetrators and victims, the Peruvian TRC placed limits on exploring the extent to which the ideal of integration with national institutions may itself be implicated in violence and injustice.[6] Chile's National Commission for Truth and Reconciliation faced similar criticism. Government influence over the commission has restricted opportunities for truth seeking and bringing justice to victims. The government denied the commission power to subpoena witnesses or name perpetrators and limited the duration of the commission to less than one year. As a result, the commission could not complete its most pertinent task of identifying all victims by name and determining their fate and whereabouts.[7]

We intervene in these debates by examining truth commissions as participatory state-building projects. Rather than conceptualizing state building as extraneous to the work of truth commissions or as random by-product, we analyze the effectiveness of truth commissions as deliberative mechanisms for state building. We examine the extent to which truth commissions provide spaces for civic engagement and public participation in ways that promote cohesion and inclusive governance and strengthen state institutions. We recognize that statist agendas can conflict with the truth-finding and justice mandates of truth commissions. This is particularly true when the interests of sponsoring governments are conflated with the public interest. In such circumstances, the framework for public participation in truth commission processes can be circumscribed by government interests and interventions. Nevertheless, given the crucial role that truth commissions increasingly play in institutional reforms, it is necessary to understand and evaluate them as mechanisms for state building. This is relevant to both post-conflict and post-authoritarian transitional contexts. Our discussion is framed around two key questions: Where does state building fit within the mandates, processes, and outcomes of truth commissions? How effective are truth commissions as civic engagement mechanisms and democratic participation in transitional states and societies?

In addressing these questions, we offer a framework for understanding the intersections between the explicit truth-finding, justice, and reconciliation mandates of truth commissions, and implicit state-building goals. We argue that in both post-conflict and post-authoritarian contexts, state building is integral to truth commission goals. The primary objectives of truth finding, victim-centred justice, institutional reform, and reconciliation are foundational to the secondary goals of state building. In assessing the effectiveness of truth commissions, we should consider their implicit role as mechanisms for civic engagement, public participation, and state building rather than see them simply as transitional justice mechanisms "dragooned" to serve nation-building agendas. By framing truth commissions as both transitional justice instruments and participatory state-building projects, we can better assess their effectiveness and evaluate their impact.

Our analysis draws on data from two related projects: the Confronting Atrocity Project, which documents and analyzes truth commission records, and the Global Truth and Reconciliation Commission Collection of Participedia, a database of case studies of public participation initiatives and democratic innovations.[8] Participedia analyzes truth commissions as innovative deliberative and dialogic processes.[9] These processes are framed as democratic innovations in the sense that they are practices that depart from, or supplement, the traditional institutional architecture we usually attribute to the developed democracies. Functionally, truth commissions as democratic innovation empower inclusions; develop collective agendas; and increase the capacities of peoples to collectively address questions of justice, citizenship, and governance for themselves. To be sure, truth commissions do not always serve these functions.

Truth commissions are weakened when the sponsoring governments push a narrow and politically expedient notion of reconciliation (e.g., Chile and South Africa) or where a government intentionally deprives the commission of resources to curb its influence and authority (e.g., Guatemala and Nigeria).[10] However, where truth commissions have the autonomy and support of sponsoring authorities to implement their mandates, they increase one or more of these functions, usually in concert with or in opposition to other features of political systems. Normatively, truth commissions as democratic innovations have the potential to increase collective support for self-development and self-empowerment.[11]

Although we frame our discussion around state building, we recognize the parallels and distinctions with the related concept of nation building, which is typically defined as actions undertaken by national actors to forge a sense of common nationhood, usually to overcome ethnic, sectarian, or communal differences. Nation-building interventions seek to counter alternate sources of identity and loyalty and mobilize a population behind parallel state-building projects. We conceptualize *state building* as encompassing aspects of *nation building* that in turn encompass efforts to build state capacity and accountability, including actions to strengthen state institutions, enhance service delivery, promote civic engagement, and foster national cohesion.[12]

TYPOLOGIZING TRUTH COMMISSIONS

There is lingering ambiguity surrounding what constitutes a truth commission. There is also uncertainty over methodologies for interpreting and assessing truth commission mandates, processes, and outcomes. Scholarship on truth commissions adopts a spectrum of broad and narrow definitions. The broad definitions centre on officiality, temporality, and outcome, describing truth commissions as temporary *official* bodies established to investigate a pattern of human rights abuses that culminate their work in a report.[13] Their mandate is typically to investigate past human rights violations, identity patterns and causes of violence, and publish a final report through a politically autonomous procedure.[14] Most truth commissions are indeed official, non-judicial bodies of a limited duration, established to determine the facts, causes, and consequences of past human rights violations.[15] However, definitions of truth commissions centred on official mandates and temporality exclude non-official grassroots truth commissions and open-ended truth-seeking processes.

Narrower definitions of truth commissions differentiate between standard commissions of inquiry and "socio-historical commissions." Some scholars argue that socio-historical inquiries addressing historical wrongs that occurred at least a generation prior are not truth commissions. The Canadian Truth Commission, despite its name, has been described as a "socio-historical commission" rather than a truth commission.[16] Indeed, a critical difference between standard government-appointed inquiry commissions and truth commissions is the level of autonomy the latter have to do their work. While inquiry commissions are typically constituted as direct arms of the government, truth commissions, though officially sanctioned, are not entirely under the jurisdiction of the sponsoring political authority.

It matters if an official investigatory body counts as a truth commission because conceptual vagueness hinders our ability to assess truth commissions as transitional justice mechanisms. It is helpful to set conceptual and analytical parameters. We disagree with the arbitrary and impractical distinction between truth commissions and socio-historical commissions, since most truth commissions have a mandate to investigate the historical or root causes of abuse, which often transcend a single generation.

Irrespective of their temporal mandates, many truth commission reports scrutinize the past, across several generations, to examine the historical antecedents of the conflicts and human rights abuses they are charged to investigate.

Our definition of truth commissions is broad, encompassing the wide range of non-judicial and quasi-judicial truth-seeking bodies established to investigate and report on contemporary human rights abuses and historical injustices. These may be officially sanctioned or established outside state apparatus since this distinction is not always clear-cut. For example, the Guatemalan Truth Commission, the Project for the Recovery of Historical Memory (REMHI), started as a grassroots effort run by the Catholic Church before the government adopted it.[17] It was a truth commission even before it received official state sanction.

Another defining attribute of truth commissions is their *restorative justice* mandate. Truth commissions are generally considered a form of restorative justice nested under the umbrella of transitional justice. Although even this categorization remains unsettled. Transitional justice processes are typically considered either *restorative* or *retributive* measures aimed at achieving justice in societies moving from authoritarian rule or conflict toward democracy or stability. Retributive justice revolves around the punishment of perpetrators and often involves trials and the deployment of the criminal justice system. Retribution in this context is "vengeance curbed by the intervention of someone other than the victim," who then decides on a punishment that is proportional to the harm done.[18] The classic reference point for retributive justice in international law is the Nuremberg and Tokyo war crimes tribunals established after the Second World War.

Alternatively, restorative justice is not primarily concerned with the punishment of the perpetrator; instead, restorative justice processes focus on repairing the relationship between perpetrator and victim. The contemporary restorative justice movement began in the early 1990s as a reaction to the perceived failures of "retributive" approaches to criminal justice common in liberal democratic societies.[19] Rather than seeking the punishment of perpetrators and their separation from society through penal and carceral systems, the restorative approach proposes rebuilding and strengthening the relationships between all individuals involved. While restorative justice does not preclude perpetrator punishment, this is not the central objective. In transitional justice contexts, restorative justice requires work to restore victims, offenders, and communities who have been fractured by abuse and violations.[20] The establishment of truth commissions is often born out of the need to rebuild trust and restore proven relationships after abuse or conflict. Given the reconciliation mandate of most truth commissions, they have become synonymous with the restorative justice model at national and broader societal levels.

Our analysis locates truth commissions at the intersection of restorative and transitional justice. We take an expanded view of *transitional justice* that goes beyond the efforts to address systematic human rights violations in societies emerging from periods of conflict or repression.[21] Within the transitional justice framework, we include socio-historical transitions in countries seeking to address past injustices through collective acknowledgment and restitution. Even in advanced liberal democracies like Canada, where a truth commission was established to investigate historical atrocities committed against Indigenous peoples, the goal is to *transition* society from the legacies of injustice and exclusion toward justice and reconciliation. As Ruti Teitel has argued, the conception of justice in periods of political change is constructivist. It is alternately constituted by, and constitutive of, the transition. The conception of justice that emerges is contextualized and contingent on the nature of prior injustice.[22]

TRUTH COMMISSIONS AND RESTORATIVE JUSTICE

The restorative justice aspirations of truth commissions have attracted both praise and criticism. One advocate of truth commissions as restorative justice mechanisms is Desmond Tutu, who, as chair of the South African TRC, argued that rebuilding fractured relationships is central to this form of justice. Because human rights violations rupture the relationship between perpetrator, victim, and society, justice should centre on healing, repairing, and restoring broken relationships. Tutu asserted that for justice to be considered served, the perpetrator must extend efforts to heal the relationship that can then be optionally received by the victim, should they want to engage in "drawing out the sting in the memory," to allow the relationship to begin healing.[23] For proponents, restorative justice reflects the implicit nation-building agenda of truth commissions, because what they aspire to restore is not just rebuilding individual relationships but also mending societal fissures.

But how effective is the restorative justice that truth commissions advance? How does it align with truth commissions' explicit truth-seeking and victim-centred justice mandate? With the South African TRC established in 1995 to investigate apartheid-era human rights violations, critics claim that the political elite used the discourse of restorative justice to "manufacture legitimacy" in state institutions. The TRC, critics argue, was guided by the new political power to produce a "truth" that legitimated the authority of the new government of the African National Congress (ANC) and allowed it to maintain its political goals.[24] Therefore, the discourse of restorative justice was instrumentalized to serve the nation-building agenda at the expense of truth and justice.[25] The government presented the TRC as a necessary compromise for the democratic transition. Human rights became the language of political compromise rather than of principle and accountability.[26]

The achievements and limitations of the South African TRC have been well analyzed elsewhere, and these details are not our primary concern here.[27] Instead, we focus on a key assumption in the critiques: the claim that state-building goals are extraneous to truth commission objectives and inherently undermine their truth-finding and justice mandates. Underlying these critiques is a tendency to link restorative justice dialectically to nation building in ways that traditional retributive justice is not. Truth commissions dispensing restorative justice are no more tools of nation building than regular courts dispensing retributive justice. For transitional states, there are obvious benefits in combining retributive measures within restorative justice processes and vice versa. However, both restorative and retributive measures need to be aligned with the broader transition goals of accountability through truth-finding and victim-centred justice.[28] If we conceptualize state building in terms of building state capacity; strengthening administrative, judicial, and accountability systems; promoting civic engagement; and fostering national cohesion, the complementarity between retributive and restorative measures becomes obvious. Countries recovering from conflict or authoritarian rule are confronted with the challenges of rebuilding national institutions and civic trust. In societies fractured by ethnic and sectarian violence, the establishment of truth commissions is driven as much by the need to foster national cohesion through reconciliation as by the quest for truth and justice.

While retributive justice dispensed through criminal justice processes can enhance accountability for abuse and strengthen legal and judicial capacities, truth commissions as restorative justice mechanisms can promote civic engagement and institutional reform in fractured transitional societies. Admittedly, civic engagement is not often an explicit mandate of truth commissions. However, the goals of truth finding, victim-centred justice, and reconciliation are congruent with civic engagement, which truth commissions seek through investigations, public hearings, and information campaigns to elicit public participation. Truth commissions can serve as mechanisms for fostering civic engagement and public participation in transitional societies characterized by distrust of government and public institutions. Although this aspect of truth commissions' work has received little attention, public participation in truth commission processes has profound implications for accountability, justice, and administrative service delivery that are crucial to state building.

PARTICIPATION AND TRANSITIONAL JUSTICE

Civic engagement and political participation are essential to transitional societies, especially during democratic transitions. Civic engagement is crucial for conferring legitimacy on elected governments, monitoring governments, and holding them accountable for their actions while giving voice to citizens so that their perspectives are included in public decision-making. Given declining levels of political and civic engagement, even in established democracies, there has lately been an emphasis on nurturing increasing participation as an intellectual and normative theme in contemporary democratic theory. Interest in participatory forms of governance has been driven by the assumption that public deliberation about common purposes is crucial for sustainable public policies and stable societies. The conventional wisdom is that participatory politics helps to improve the chance of a sustainable outcome by associating all the relevant stakeholders in the policy-making process. The more that relevant participants are incorporated into a policy-making process, the greater the chance that the measures will be voluntarily accepted and effectively implemented. Hence, the greater the expectation that the policies agreed on will be sustainable. This reasoning underpins the normative need to create and deepen citizen participation in decision-making.

Political theorists have noted the intrinsic value of participation in empowering citizens by increasing their political efficacy and understanding their interests and responsibilities.[29] But to enhance citizen participation, it is necessary to understand the underlying factors and processes that facilitate or hinder political and civic engagement so that these can be harnessed or redressed through appropriate actions and policy interventions.[30] Enhancing political and civic engagement requires understanding the merits and limits of participatory governance initiatives and interventions in specific political and social contexts. The form and extent of civic participation in governance are shaped by historical trajectories, the configuration of power, the balance of social forces in society, and the pressure that marginalized groups exert on the political system.

Truth commission studies can illuminate our understanding of participatory governance processes in developing transitional societies. The discourse on deliberative and participatory politics has, for the most part, centred on advanced democracies and the new techno-policy instruments and strategies being conceptualized and operationalized by planners, activists, and entrepreneurs.

The scholarship on deliberative democracy has been dominated by discussion of so-called deliberative mini-publics prevalent in Western democracies, such as citizens' juries, citizens' assemblies, consensus conferences, deliberative polls, and participatory budgeting fora.[31] In many new and emerging democracies, discussions of deliberative politics and participatory governance have centred on transitioning from authoritarian institutions and processes to democratic channels for public participation in governance. Participatory governance in these contexts includes establishing transitional justice mechanisms and facilitating public participation within them. Another limitation of participatory governance scholarship is that it has mostly been framed in terms of *good governance* and *poverty reduction*. However, there is growing recognition that conflict resolution, human security, and post-conflict peacebuilding are central to participatory governance in post-conflict and politically fragile societies. In emerging democracies with constrained civic spaces, truth commissions are integral to the conflict resolution and peacebuilding aspects of civic participation and participatory governance.

If truth commissions are so central to participatory governance in transitional societies, how do we assess their impacts? Transitional justice scholars have offered various frameworks for assessing the impact of truth commissions beyond categorizing them simply as strong or weak, successes or failures. These frameworks assess direct and indirect political impact through civil society, governance transparency and accountability, social norms, and judicial impact.[32] These frameworks rightly decentre political impacts and allow for a greater examination of the multitude of ways truth commissions can influence societies. However, an assumption of temporal permanence remains embedded in the question of a truth commission's effectiveness. This can be problematic since the work of truth commissions is often an ongoing process that does not end with publishing a final report. Moreover, public attitudes toward truth commissions are bound to change over time among various groups involved with the process. Scholarly assessment of the effectiveness of truth commissions also shifts as new information comes to light, especially regarding long-term impacts on political culture and social attitudes. Therefore, any evaluation of truth commissions is, at best, a snapshot of prevailing attitudes at a particular place and time.

TRUTH COMMISSIONS AND CIVIC PARTICIPATION

Civic engagement and public participation resonate in truth commissions' mandate, processes, and outcomes. A Truth Commission process is by nature a public process, and its success depends on public participation. Truth commissions recognize the need for public ownership and participation in the commission's activities.[33] Because public participation confers legitimacy, many truth commissions seek to develop partnerships with civil society organizations (CSOs) for public education and involvement in different phases of their work. There is also recognition that the implementation of the TRC recommendations depends on how civil society engages the government and other state institutions. The United Nations (UN) *Principles for the Protection and Promotion of Human Rights through Action to Combat Impunity*, which prescribes a framework for the establishment of truth commissions, emphasizes the centrality of public participation. It states: "To the greatest extent possible, decisions to establish a truth commission, define its terms of reference and determine its composition should be based upon broad public consultations in which the views of victims and survivors especially are sought."[34]

One of the most challenging issues faced by the framers of Truth Commissions is how to design terms of reference that can encourage willing and active participation by ordinary citizens as part of the effort to procure accurate information.[35] Since most truth commissions are non-judicial mechanisms that have no subpoena powers, they are limited in their ability to compel participation. The South African TRC briefly considered compelling the participation of accused perpetrators who declined its invitation through subpoenas. It ultimately decided that voluntary participation would best serve its goal of reconciliation.[36] Similarly, the mandate of the Canadian TRC stipulated that the commission had no powers of subpoena, and could not "name names" of perpetrators.[37] Given these procedural restrictions, truth commissions must rely on the soft power of persuasion and relevance to encourage participation.[38]

Public participation, particularly of perpetrators and victim-survivors, also serves a pedagogical purpose. Victim testimonies conveyed through statements, petitions, and public hearings are used to educate and sensitize a broader public about periods of gross and systematic human rights violations. Additionally, participation is an essential component of justice and restitution, which are the critical goals of truth commissions. For many victim-survivors, their participation in truth commission processes is the first time they receive recognition from a state entity and are treated with interest and respect by the public.[39]

Most truth commissions are expressly tasked with fostering public participation and civic engagement. Peru's TRC has a mandate to "establish appropriate communication channels and promote the population's participation, particularly of [those] most affected by political violence."[40] The South African TRC aimed at "openness to public participation and scrutiny." Its goal was to transcend past divisions by listening carefully to the complex motives and perspectives of all those involved.[41] Tunisia's Truth and Dignity Commission, established to investigate government abuses, aimed to "provide public spaces that allow everybody's participation in the debate and that ensure the credibility of the process, as well as their public ownership, as dialogue processes about the past."[42]

Apart from their mandates, truth commission *processes* are also structured to enhance the participation of diverse stakeholders through public hearings, statement taking, and other civic engagement activities targeted at specific groups such as victims-survivors, women, youth, and children. The South African TRC, given its ambitious scale and international prestige, is often considered the model truth commission to which others are compared.[43] The commission took testimony from over 21,000 victims and witnesses, 2,000 of whom also appeared in public hearings. Public participation was reflected in extensive media coverage of the commission. Four hours of hearings were broadcast live daily over national radio and television. Televised truth commission hearings became the most-watched news show in the country.[44] The work of the Liberian TRC, established to investigate human rights abuses committed during the country's decade-long civil war, involved three years of investigations and public hearings that elicited over 20,000 statements from within Liberia and its diaspora communities. Similarly, the Ghanaian Truth Commission process spanned three years of investigations and public hearings in which more than 100 people testified, and over 40,000 statements were submitted.

The depth of the public outreach work of truth commissions is reflected in the activities targeted at specific groups. For example, the Liberian TRC established specialized outreach committees on gender, youth, children, and the diaspora to ensure broad-based participation of these groups in the TRC process. The goal of the gender committee was to ensure that women's concerns were adequately expressed and addressed, while the diaspora objectives were to create awareness and encourage participation in Liberia's large diaspora communities.[45] Statistical data indicate that these public engagement initiatives were partly successful. Over 50 per cent of statements gathered during the Liberia TRC's statement-taking exercise are attributed to women.[46] Even so, some Liberians complained that opportunities for public participation, particularly of diaspora communities, were inadequate.[47]

Like the Liberian TRC, the Kenyan Truth, Justice, and Reconciliation Commission (TJRC) was founded on the premise that "the success of a Truth Commission partly depends on a nation's awareness and level of its people's participation in its processes."[48] Its work was guided by the recognition that vulnerable groups are a central pillar of any comprehensive and inclusive truth-seeking process. Its Civic Education and Outreach Department organized several activities, including training stakeholders, hosting workshops and meetings, and participating in community events.[49] In particular, the commission sought the involvement of victims in the process of design,

implementation, and monitoring of the reparations program it recommended to address human rights abuses.[50] Despite these efforts,
critics questioned the extent of public participation, noting the
refusal of key government officials accused of abuses to participate
in the truth commission process.[51]

Public participation in the Tunisian Truth and Dignity Commission
processes took the form of both support and opposition. Civil society
groups participated actively in the Truth and Dignity Commission
established by the government in 2013 to investigate gross human
rights violations committed by the state and provide compensation and rehabilitation to victims. They resisted the government's
attempts to grant amnesty to former regime officials accused of corruption and abuse. They also resisted attempts to remove the issue
of corruption and transitional economic justice from the responsibilities mandated by the Truth and Dignity Commission.[52]

In their final reports, many truth commissions have noted that
political marginalization and lack of participation in governance lie
at the root of the conflicts and human rights abuses they investigate.
The Peruvian TRC report stressed that pervasive fear and distrust
debilitate Peruvian communities affected by the violence, undermining its members' civic and social participation.[53] The Sierra
Leonean TRC heard submissions from various authoritative sources
that the protracted war in that country was primarily the result of
failures in governance and the lack of democratic participation in
decision-making processes. Significantly, it also noted that institutional reforms and reconciliation could not move forward without
the broader political participation in governance.[54]

Recognizing that political exclusion is a root cause of conflict
and abuse, Truth Commissions have made *recommendations* to
enhance civic inclusion and participation in governance. The recommendation of the Timor-Leste and El Salvador Truth Commission
centred on civic inclusion and democratic participation. The recommendations of the Commission of Truth and Friendship (CTF)
Indonesia – Timor-Leste are based upon three principles intended to
promote restorative justice: recognition of full rights of individuals
as citizens with dignity and honour as humans; building civic trust
through *public participation* to restore people's confidence in the
government, legal system, police, and military; and social solidarity
that demands interest and willingness of the people to empathize
with others.[55] The commission noted that a key cause of conflict

in the country was the perception by some Timorese that they were being excluded from full participation in governance.[56] Similarly, the recommendation of the El Salvador TRC was based on the principles of *democracy*, which leave the fundamental decisions as to the destiny of society in the hands of the people; *participation*, which integrates minorities with the majority and centres democracy as a model of human coexistence; *the rule of law*, which guarantees equality; and *respect for human rights* as a basis for freedom and dignity.[57]

Although public participation and civic engagement are dominant themes in truth commission discourses, the extent to which they foster participatory democracy and enhance human rights democracy remains uncertain. One cross-national analysis of the impact of truth commissions in South Africa, El Salvador, Chile, and Uganda indicates that truth commissions tend to have appreciable effects on human rights in the longer term but more limited impact on democratic development.[58] Another study suggests that the "publicness" of a truth commission – defined by whether it has public hearings, releases a public report, and names perpetrators – contributes to democratization. In short, the more public and participatory a truth commission is, the more it will contribute to democratization.[59] An analysis of sixteen Latin American nations found that trials and a successful truth commission provoked macro-social benefits and reinforced respect for human rights.[60] Ethnographic studies in South Africa also suggest that civic engagement and public participation in truth commission activities fostered ownership of both transitional justice processes and governance at local levels.[61]

Despite evidence that suggests a correlation between truth commissions, democracy, and human rights, public participation does not always yield the desired outcomes. While some participants in a truth commission process view it as a positive and empowering experience, others have experienced it as a "painful and disempowering process filled with unmet expectations and promises."[62] There is always the risk that victims and other participants in truth commission processes will view their participation as a mere data collection exercise or a disingenuous means of legitimizing statist agendas, if they see no concrete benefits in their own struggle for recovery and justice. In raising expectations and leaving participant aspirations unmet, truth commissions can cause harm by leaving victim-survivors with a deeper sense of deception and neglect. Participants could become disillusioned with a transitional justice project and may cease to participate in the political struggle needed to continue the transition started by the TRC. They may stop demanding their rights, including the implementation of political and institutional reforms.[63] In this situation, participation in the truth commission process could have the undesirable long-term effect of undermining rather than enhancing democracy. We have anecdotal evidence of this.

In South Africa, the government's failure to pay or institute timely and adequate reparation to victims has created renewed political tensions that threaten to undermine the work and legacy of the truth commission.[64] Many South Africans still feel the TRC's work was never fully completed. It delivered minimal accountability or restitution, and the promised healing never materialized.[65] As TRC Chairman Desmond Tutu put it: "I cannot explain how a black person living in a squalid ghetto, nearly 10 years after freedom ... [who] get[s] up and work[s] in town, which is still largely white, in palatial homes and then return[s] at night to the squalor, does not say: 'To hell with Tutu and the Truth Commission, with Mandela and all these people and go on the rampage.'"[66] In Peru, there was a high level of disappointment after the publication of the TRC's report due to the government's failure to implement the TRC recommendations. Among the most disappointed were victim-survivors who believed their participation and testimony would result in prompt compensation for their suffering.[67]

In some cases, truth commissions have failed to elicit public participation due to the political circumstances under which they emerged. One such example is the Greensboro Truth and Reconciliation Commission (GTRC) in the United States, established by civil society groups in 2004 to investigate a skirmish in 1979 between political protesters and the Ku Klux Klan that led to the death of some protesters. Unlike most truth commissions, the GTRC received no official support or recognition. Throughout its truth-seeking process, government officials, including the mayor and city council of Greensboro, publicly opposed the commission. The Greensboro City Council voted 6–3 along racial lines to openly oppose the GTRC, making it impossible for the commission to work with local law enforcement or local prosecutors in any official capacity.[68] The commission noted with frustration in its final report: "We are profoundly disturbed by the absence of broad participation of Greensboro citizens in these proceedings and believe that this is

rooted in the growing tendency of the American people to be pre-
occupied with material accumulation rather than the well-being of
our community and country."[69] To address this civic apathy, the
commission proposed sponsoring grassroots discussions of the TRC
in the public square, community organizations, and neighbourhood
groups, and including community building in the school curriculum
for our children K–12.

The Greensborough Truth Commission might be an exceptional case because it was not state-sponsored. In most cases, truth
commission investigations and public hearings provide spaces for
civic engagement and participatory deliberations among stake-
holder groups. Such spaces, however constrained, are crucial for
trust building and institutional reforms in fragile or fragmented
transitional societies. Ethnographic studies of truth commission
hearings point to the healing value of public truth telling through
the opportunity it offers victims' voices in a justice-seeking process.
For example, the highly participatory nature of public hearings
in the truth commissions in the Solomon Islands and Timor-Leste
allowed individuals to express their perspectives. By creating
a space for victims to voice their experiences in a public forum,
the truth-seeking hearings allowed individuals to reclaim their
narratives and dignity.[70] It also provided an official platform for
collective acknowledgment of their victimhood.

CONCLUSION

We return to the questions that frame our discussion. Where does
state building fit within the work of truth commissions, and how
effective are truth commissions as mechanisms of civic engagement
and democratic participation in transitional societies? We conclude
that although state building is often subsumed in the discourse of
truth finding, justice, and reconciliation, it is central to the work of
truth commissions. Framing truth commissions as both transitional
justice mechanisms as well as state-building projects allows for a
more comprehensive evaluation of their impacts and legacies.

Despite the instrumentalization of truth commissions to further
statist agendas, there is evidence to suggest that if done properly,
truth commissions can be effective mechanisms for civic engagement
and participatory democracy in transitioning states. Truth commissions can assist divided societies in overcoming cultures of exclusion

and distrust through civic participation aimed at addressing human rights violations and institutional reforms needed to prevent new violations.[71] For example, the South African TRC process, despite its shortcomings, was instrumental in facilitating public participation and civic engagement in the country's democratic transition process. Even critics acknowledge that public recognition of repressed narratives brought together populations that had been separated by the racialized boundaries of apartheid. This created a baseline for shared understanding that "allowed for a fusion of horizons and defined the parameters for discussion of the past."[72]

A UN study of truth commissions found that they function most successfully when they give voice to victims in the public sphere, foster social integration by officially acknowledging atrocities, and validate victimhood. This can help to end the cycles of resentment and mistrust and aid the process of institutional reforms and redress through prosecutions and reparations programs.[73] Assessment of truth commissions' impact on democracy, human rights, or state building should not be limited to immediate or short-term outcomes. Instead, assessing social and political impact should take comprehensive and sustained short-, medium-, and long-term perspectives. For example, the records and archives of truth commissions can have enduring impacts on democracy long after a commission's work has ended.[74] The diverse public voices and perspectives captured in these archives can provide grounds for ongoing democratic and human rights claims and reforms. TRC processes, recommendations, archives, and memorialization projects should therefore be considered deliberative democratic spaces that could be designed and implemented to invite and include the population in the decision-making process of shaping the future. This would represent an enhancement of the role truth commission archives can play in deepening democratic processes and protecting human rights.

NOTES

1 Kerry Bystrom, "Reassessing South African Truth and Reconciliation," in *Truth Commissions and the Culture of Dissenting Memory: The Global South*, ed. Véronique Tadjo (New York: Routledge, 2019), 2.

2 Sarah Zwierzchowski, "Incomplete Truth, Incomplete Reconciliation," in *Flowers in the Wall: Truth and Reconciliation in Timor-Leste, Indonesia,*

and Melanesia, ed. David Webster (Calgary: University of Calgary Press, 2018), 23.

3 Richard Wilson, *The Politics of Truth and Reconciliation in South Africa: Legitimizing the Post-Apartheid State* (Cambridge: Cambridge University Press, 2008), 28.

4 Wilson, 224.

5 Ibid., xvi.

6 Jeff Corntassel and Cindy Holder, "Who's Sorry Now? Government Apologies, Truth Commissions, and Indigenous Self-Determination in Australia, Canada, Guatemala, and Peru," *Human Rights Review* 9, no. 4 (2008): 465–89.

7 Mark Ensalaco, *Chile Under Pinochet: Recovering the Truth* (Ann Arbor: Philadelphia University of Pennsylvania Press, 2010), 188.

8 Confronting Atrocity through Truth Commissions (CATC), https://truthcommissions.humanities.mcmaster.ca/; Participedia network https://participedia.net/; Participedia Global Truth and Reconciliation Commission Collection. https://participedia.net/collection/8015. The authors are members of the CATC and Participedia research networks.

9 See, for example, "Women's Radio Listening Groups in Kenya," https://participedia.net/case/4949; Truth and Reconciliation Commission of Liberia, https://participedia.net/case/7756.

10 Onur Bakiner, "One Truth among Others? Truth Commissions' Struggle for Truth and Memory," *Memory Studies* 8, no. 3 (2015): 356.

11 For a discussion of democratic innovation, see Graham Smith, *Democratic Innovations: Designing Institutions for Citizen Participation* (Cambridge: Cambridge University Press, 2009).

12 Organization for Economic Co-operation and Development (OECD), "Concepts and Dilemmas of State Building in Fragile Situations: From Fragility to Resilience," discussion paper, 2008, 13, www.oecd.org/dac/conflict-fragility-resilience/docs/41100930.pdf.

13 Priscilla B. Hayner, *Unspeakable Truths: Transitional Justice and the Challenge of Truth Commissions*, 2nd ed. (York & London: Routledge, 2011), 4, 11.

14 Onur Bakiner, *Truth Commissions: Memory, Power, and Legitimacy* (Philadelphia: University of Pennsylvania Press, 2016), 24.

15 "International Centre for Transitional Justice Truth Seeking: Elements of Creating an Effective Truth Commission," https://ictj.org/sites/default/files/ICTJ-Book-Truth-Seeking-Chapter2-2013-English.pdf.

16 Eric Wiebelhaus-Brahm, "What Is a Truth Commission and Why Does it Matter," *Peace & Conflict Review* 3, no. 2 (2009): 12.

17 REMHI's 1998 report *Guatemala, Nunca más*, served as a precursor to the work of Guatemala's formal Truth Commission.

18 Martha Minow, *Between Vengeance and Forgiveness: Facing History after Genocide and Mass Violence* (Boston: Beacon Press, 1998), 12.

19 Howard Zehr, "Journey to Belonging" in *Restorative Justice: Theoretical Foundations*, ed. Elmar G.M. Weitekamp and Hans-Jürgen Kerner (New York: Routledge, 2011), 21.

20 Elmar Weitekamp and Hans-Jürgen Kerner, eds, *Restorative Justice: Theoretical Foundations* (New York: Routledge, 2011).

21 International Centre for Transitional Justice, "What is Transitional Justice?," www.ictj.org/about/transitional-justice.

22 Ruti Teitel, *Transitional Justice* (Oxford: Oxford University Press, 2000), 6.

23 Desmond Tutu, *No Future without Forgiveness* (New York: Doubleday, 1999), 271.

24 Mahmood Mamdani, "The Truth According to the TRC," in *The Politics of Memory: Truth, Healing, and Social Justice*, ed. Ifi Amadiume and Abdullahi An-Na'im (London: Zed, 2000), 177–8.

25 Wilson, *The Politics of Truth and Reconciliation in South Africa*, 28.

26 Richard Wilson, "Challenging Restorative Justice," *Human Rights Dialogue* (2002): 15.

27 See, for example, Paul Gready, *The Era of Transitional Justice: The Aftermath of the Truth and Reconciliation Commission in South Africa and Beyond* (London: Routledge, 2012); Hugo van der Merwe and Audrey Chapman, eds, *Truth and Reconciliation in South Africa: Did the TRC Deliver?* (Philadelphia: University of Pennsylvania Press, 2008); Wilmot Godfrey James and Linda Van de Vijver, *After the TRC: Reflections on Truth and Reconciliation in South Africa* (Athens: Ohio University Press, 2001); Charles Villa-Vicencio and Wilhelm Verwoerd, *Looking Back, Reaching Forward: Reflections on the Truth and Reconciliation Commission of South Africa* (London: Zed, 2000).

28 Minow, *Between Vengeance and Forgiveness*, 50.

29 Geraint Parry and Bryce Anderson, *Participation in Politics* (Manchester: Manchester University Press, 1972), 26.

30 Martyn Barrett and Bruna Zani, *Political and Civic Engagement: Multidisciplinary Perspectives* (New York: Routledge, 2015), 9.

31 For example, these cases of deliberative democracy dominate the Participedia database of global democratic innovations; see https:// participedia.net/.

32 Bakiner, *Truth Commissions: Memory, Power, and Legitimacy*, 105.

33   *Witness to Truth: Report of the Sierra Leone Truth and Reconciliation Commission*, vol. 1 (Accra: GPL Press, 2004), 143.

34   United Nations, *Principles for the Protection and Promotion of Human Rights through Action to Combat Impunity* (Geneva: United Nations, 2005), principle 6.

35   Joanna R. Quinn and Mark Freeman, "Lessons Learned: Practical Lessons Gleaned from Inside the Truth Commissions of Guatemala and South Africa," *Human Rights Quarterly* 25, no. 4 (2003): 1129.

36   Hayner, *Unspeakable Truths*, 107.

37   Rosemary Nagy, "Truth, Reconciliation and Settler Denial: Specifying the Canada-South Africa Analogy," *Human Rights Review* 13 (2012): 355.

38   Ronald Slye, *The Kenyan TJRC: An Outsider's View from the Inside* (Cambridge: Cambridge University Press, 2018), 81.

39   Lisa Laplante and Kimberly Theidon, "Truth with Consequences: Justice and Reparations in Post-Truth Commission Peru," *Human Rights Quarterly* 29, no. 1 (2007): 238.

40   Decreto Supremo No. 065-2001-PCM, Section 6(f), (4 June 2001). Cited in Laplante and Theidon, "Truth with Consequences," 238.

41   *Truth and Reconciliation Commission of South Africa Report,* vol. 1 (2006), 113.

42   *Truth and Dignity Commission [Tunisia]: The Final Comprehensive Report* (Avocats sans Frontières, 2019), 500.

43   Hayner, *Unspeakable Truths*, 27–8. See also Lyn S. Graybill, *Truth and Reconciliation in South Africa: Miracle or Model?* (Boulder: Rienner, 2002).

44   Hayner, *Unspeakable Truths*, 28.

45   *Final Report of the Truth and Reconciliation Commission of Liberia*, vol. 1: *Findings and Determinations* (Monrovia: Truth and Reconciliation Commission, 2008), 144–5.

46   *Final Report of the Truth and Reconciliation Commission of Liberia*, vol. 1, 144.

47   Laura Young and Rosalyn Park, "Engaging Diasporas in Truth Commissions: Lessons from the Liberia Truth and Reconciliation Commission Diaspora Project," *International Journal of Transitional Justice* 3, no. 3 (2009): 341–61.

48   *Report of the Truth, Justice and Reconciliation Commission*, vol. 1 (Nairobi: TJRC, 2013), 111.

49   *Report of the Truth, Justice and Reconciliation Commission*, vol. 1, 82.

50   *Report of the Truth, Justice and Reconciliation Commission*, vol. 1, 121.

51   Slye, *The Kenyan TJRC*, 176.

52 Manich Msamah (Manich Msema7), Tunisia, Participedia, https://\
    participedia.net/case/6252.
53 Laplante and Theidon, "Truth with Consequences," 233.
54 *Witness to Truth: Report of the Sierra Leone Truth and Reconciliation
    Commission*, vol. 2 (Accra: GPL Press, 2004), 7.
55 *Per Memoriam ad Spem: Final Report of the Commission of Truth and
    Friendship (CTF) Indonesia - Timor-Leste* (Denpasar: Commission of Truth
    and Friendship, 2008), 21.
56 *Per Memoriam ad Spem*, 43.
57 Commission on the Truth for El Salvador, *From Madness to Hope:
    The 12-year War in El Salvador. Report of the Commission on the Truth
    for El Salvador* (New York: United Nations, 1993).
58 Eric Wiebelhaus-Brahm, *Truth Commissions and Transitional Societies:
    The Impact on Human Rights and Democracy* (New York: Routledge,
    2010).
59 Laura Taylor and Alexander Dukalskis, "Old Truths and New Politics:
    Does Truth Commission 'Publicness' Impact Democratization?" *Journal
    of Peace Research* 49, no. 5 (2012): 671–84.
60 Carlos Martín-Beristain, Darío Páez, Bernard Rimé, and Patrick
    Kanyangara, "Psychosocial Effects of Participation in Rituals of
    Transitional Justice: A Collective-Level Analysis and Review of the
    Literature of the Effects of TRCs and Trials on Human Rights Violations in
    Latin America," *International Journal of Social Psychology* 25, no. 1
    (2010): 47–60.
61 See D. Skinner "An Evaluation of a Set of TRC Public Hearings in
    Worcester: A Small Rural Community in South Africa," *Psychology,
    Health & Medicine* 5, no. 1 (2000): 97–106.
62 Brandon Hamber and Patricia Lundy, "Lessons from Transitional Justice?
    Toward a New Framing of a Victim-Centered Approach in the Case of
    Historical Institutional Abuse," *Victims & Offenders* 15, no. 6 (2020):
    744–70.
63 Laplante and Theidon, "Truth with Consequences," 241.
64 Kitty Dumont and Sven Waldzus, "Reparation Demands and Collective
    Guilt Assignment of Black South Africans," *Journal of Black Psychology*
    43, no. 1 (2017): 27–49.
65 Christopher Torchia, "A Tense Exchange Highlights Unsettled Part of
    Tutu's Legacy," Associated Press, December 31, 2021.
66 Jan Hennop, "Tutu Hands over South Africa's Truth Commission
    Report," Agence France-Presse, 21 March 2003.
67 Laplante and Theidon, "Truth with Consequences," 241.

68 Joshua Inwood, "The Politics of Being Sorry: The Greensboro Truth
    Process and Efforts at Restorative Justice," *Social & Cultural Geography*
    13, no. 6 (2012): 6–12. Also see David Androff, "'To not Hate':
    Reconciliation among Victims of Violence and Participants of the
    Greensboro Truth and Reconciliation Commission," *Contemporary
    Justice Review* 13, no. 3 (2010): 269–85.

69 *Greensboro Truth and Reconciliation Commission Report* (Greensboro:
    GTRC, 2006), 467.

70 Holly Guthrey, *Victim Healing and Truth Commissions: Transforming
    Pain Through Voice in Solomon Islands and Timor-Leste* (New York:
    Springer, 2015), 4.

71 "International Centre for Transitional Justice Truth Seeking: Elements of
    Creating an Effective Truth Commission."

72 Wilson, "Challenging Restorative Justice," 16.

73 UNCHR, "The Right to Truth and Challenges Faced by Truth
    Commissions. Report of the Special Rapporteur on the Promotion of
    Truth, Justice, Reparation and Guarantees of Non-recurrence" (28 August
    2013) UN Doc AJHRC/24/42 (hereafter "Right to Truth Report"); Anna
    Vrdoljak, "Cultural Heritage, Transitional Justice and the Rule of Law,"
    in *The Oxford Handbook of International Cultural Heritage Law*, ed.
    Francesco Francioni and Ana Vrdoljak (Oxford: Oxford University Press),
    182.

74 Briony Jones and Ingrid Oliveira, "Truth Commission Archives as 'New
    Democratic Spaces,'" *Journal of Human Rights Practice* 8, no. 1
    (2016), 6–24.

2

Truth-Seeking Processes as Redress for Victims of Conflict-Related Sexual Violence

Jean de Dieu Sikulibo

Many countries afflicted by conflicts also experience conflict-related sexual violence against their citizens. These crimes are often deployed as a tactic of war and terrorism.[1] Over recent years, improving the understanding of these crimes in conflict settings has significantly progressed: a growing body of empirical studies reveal how these criminal practices have become a viable part of military strategies.[2] The United Nations (UN) Security Council has recently passed several resolutions that seek to prevent sexual violence in conflict situations and raise awareness of the scourge of these crimes.[3] This prompted the UN to adopt resolution 2467 (2019) in April 2019, emphasizing the need for a "survivor-centred approach" to inform all measures aimed at addressing these crimes in post-conflict settings.[4]

Further, a milestone has been registered in the international criminal prosecution of these crimes.[5] More significantly, building on the progress made by the International Criminal Tribunal for the Former Yugoslavia (ICTY) and its "sister" for Rwanda (ICTR), the Statute of the International Criminal Court (ICC) provides a broader basis upon which conflict-related sexual violence can be prosecuted.[6] The ICC has issued judgments confirming rape and other acts of sexual violence as war crimes and crimes against humanity.[7] These crimes, often systematically used as a warfare tactic, not only destroy individual lives but also fracture communities.[8] Their uniquely destructive nature adds a new layer of challenge to carry out effective redress for the victims in order to lay solid foundations for rebuilding affected communities.

This study focuses on the grim legacy of conflict-related sexual violence. It examines the contribution of quasi/non-judicial transitional justice mechanisms in ensuring recognition and validation of victims' experiences to promote societal level transformation. Considering the heinous nature of such crimes, the study makes a positive contribution to enhance understanding of how a holistic approach is vital to cover all dimensions of these crimes, such as pre-existing structural conditions that often facilitate these crimes in war. Drawing from the experiences of various transitional societies that have included this violence in the design and implementation of truth-seeking processes, the analysis highlights the critical role of such processes in ensuring structurally transformed societies, which in turn makes vital contributions to the whole of state (re)building.

TRUTH COMMISSIONS AND REDRESS FOR VICTIMS OF CONFLICT-RELATED SEXUAL VIOLENCE

Many transitional societies have faced significant challenges in addressing mass violence, often resorting to truth-seeking processes to help affected communities understand and acknowledge the scope of abuses committed. It has become widely recognized that mechanisms such as truth commissions and other community-based approaches to accountability and reconciliation can play a critical role in rebuilding societies emerging from large-scale violence.[9] As explained in the introduction of this book, the fundamental justifications for these processes are construed around the need to establish the truth about past human rights violations and thereby advance public comprehension of the affected countries' dark past. However, despite the prevalence of sexual violence in conflict situations, recent studies emphasize how these crimes are generally neglected or marginalized in the work of truth-seeking processes.[10] Integrating these crimes in quasi/non-judicial transitional justice initiatives after periods of mass atrocities remains a highly complex challenge.

In addition to a lack of specific reference to sexual violence in many truth commissions' mandates, the marginalization of these crimes in such processes is also often due to a lack of appropriate measures to facilitate adequate participation of victims. Mayesha Alam explains that due to the general lack of sensitive approaches to the harms suffered by victims of sexual violence in the operational structure of truth-seeking processes, most victims engaging with those

processes choose to focus on other crimes.[11] A field study on Truth
and Reconciliation Commissions (TRCs) conducted by the Coalition
for Women's Human Rights in Conflict Situations found that they
have generally failed to devote adequate attention to sexual violence in conflicts and its consequences for victims.[12] This view aligns
with the UN High Commissioner for Human Rights recent report
submitted to the UN General Assembly on gender-based and sexual
violence in relation to transitional justice, underlining that attention
to such violence is often absent from the work of TRCs.[13] The failure
of many commissions to adequately address sexual violence arises
from various factors, including the lack of gender sensitivity within
commissions' design and implementation processes as well as the
outcomes of such commissions.[14]

The inclusion of gender sensitivity in the design and conduct of
truth processes, therefore, determines the extent to which such processes can successfully address women's experience of sexual violence
in war.[15] Specially tailored measures for ensuring the victims' participation without the risk of re-traumatization are essential elements of
the gender-sensitive approach in the work of truth-seeking processes.
These measures include, for instance, integrating a sufficient number
of women and staff well-trained on gender issues, and adopting appropriate victims-sensitive protocols to support vulnerable victims.[16] A
safe and enabling environment for victims to discuss their traumatic
stories is central to enhancing positive outcomes for women.

In South Africa, for instance, crimes of sexual violence were substantially overlooked in the mandate of the South African TRC.
Despite the prevalence of sexual violence during the apartheid
years,[17] these crimes were not included as a separate gross violation
in the mandate of the commission. The TRC was created after apartheid in South Africa ended.[18] The Promotion of National Unity and
Reconciliation Act made no specific reference to crimes of sexual
violence. Interventions by women's activists led to the commission
addressing these crimes in special hearings and exploring some
unique mechanisms to facilitate victims' testimony.[19] Despite efforts
to integrate these crimes in the truth-gathering process, the lack of
a gender perspective in the mandate of the commission impeded its
ability to fully account for the experiences of victims of sexual violence under apartheid.[20] The TRC itself acknowledged its inability
to account for the myriad forms of harms women suffered under

apartheid, particularly sexual violence, by stressing in its report that to fully address their experiences during this period would have required an amended TRC mandate and definition of gross human rights violations.[21]

Furthermore, the lack of gender-sensitive measures in the TRC's mandate resulted in the commission's failure to engage with women who suffered sexual violence under apartheid.[22] Studies indicate that women were unwilling to talk about their experiences to the extent that only 140 explicitly mentioned rape in over 21,000 testimonies given in hearings for women.[23] Tristan Anne Borer explains that, although the commission's final report noted women were victims of sexual violence in South Africa, the commission failed to provide details on the political dimension of these crimes during apartheid.[24] Scholars often tout the South African TRC as a success. Still, its inability to establish a comprehensive portrayal of the nature and extent of sexual violence, including the political function of these crimes during the apartheid era, is one of its significant flaws.

Similarly, many other truth commissions neglected or failed to apply due diligence regarding acts of sexual violence.[25] In David Tombs's study of the functioning of TRCs in El Salvador and Guatemala, he found that in El Salvador, the commission's final report referred only cursorily to sexual violence, relegating several similar sexual violence–related cases to unpublished attachments.[26] This, even though state forces frequently committed rape and other acts of sexual violence during the civil war in El Salvador, including sexual torture for male political detainees and women in detention.[27] In conflict situations, many women are systematically raped before being killed. Although this was the case during the El Salvador civil war from 1981 to 1991,[28] the TRC ignored these occurrences in detention camps and emphasized other crimes victims suffered.[29]

Although many truth commissions have been attributed with shortcomings by a failure to integrate sexual violence in the quest for truth or include a gender-sensitive perspective in their work,[30] some commissions, such as in Peru,[31] Guatemala,[32] Timor-Leste,[33] and Sierra Leone[34] have addressed issues of sexual violence. Also, the relatively recent community-based transitional justice approach to accountability and reconciliation in post-genocide Rwanda, known as Gacaca, was proactive in addressing complex issues of systematic sexual violence against Tutsi women during the genocide. More recent truth commissions incorporated gender-sensitive approaches into their operational structure in an attempt to overcome the challenges to documenting a comprehensive account of their victims' experiences.

TRUTH-SEEKING PROCESSES, CONFLICT-RELATED SEXUAL VIOLENCE, AND VICTIM EMPOWERMENT

Important lessons can be drawn from some recent truth-seeking processes that have addressed the victims' experiences of conflict-related sexual violence. The following analysis serves to substantiate the argument that the increasing truth-telling initiatives can help ensure transformative responses to the structural dynamics and complex effects of sexual violence as a weapon of war.

Addressing Sexual Violence through Truth-Telling Processes in Liberia and Sierra Leone

In addition to the Peruvian TRC,[35] often hailed as the first to extensively cover the crimes of sexual violence,[36] other notable examples of truth-seeking processes that broadly addressed these issues include the Commission for Historical Clarification in Guatemala,[37] the Commission for Reception, Truth and Reconciliation in Timor-Leste,[38] and the TRCs in Sierra Leone[39] and Liberia.[40] Although sexual violence has become an integral aspect of warfare, these crimes are perpetrated with significant variation in scale and character.

Rape has been used as a tactic of war and terrorism in many regions, including Africa, where these crimes affected millions of women and men during armed conflicts in Sierra Leone and Liberia. Studies indicate that throughout the armed conflict in Sierra Leone from 1991 to 2001, thousands of women were subjected to widespread and systematic sexual violence, including gang rape and rape with objects such as weapons.[41] Rape in Sierra Leone became a spectacle, as much of this violence took place in public settings or using media coverage.[42] Carroll Bogert and Corinne Dufka found that sexual violence was the most prevalent human rights abuse during the conflict.[43] Similarly, in Liberia, some studies suggest many women and girls were victims of war-related sexual violence in the wake of the country's fourteen-year civil war.[44] After the war, the country faced an enormous task to address the legacy of these crimes in

Liberian communities. For instance, Doctors without Borders in Liberia observed that the country faced a pressing need for "rehabilitating and detraumatising people, both victims and perpetrators."[45]

After such tragic periods, Sierra Leone and Liberia have witnessed several developments in transitional justice, including the establishment of truth-seeking processes for addressing the goals of justice and reconciliation. These processes commonly incorporated gender-sensitive approaches into their operational structure. This resulted in the commissions' final reports spotlighting the horrific sexual atrocities endured by victims in the respective communities.

In Sierra Leone, the TRC was used alongside the Special Court for Sierra Leone (SCSL), created in partnership with the UN.[46] Cases of sexual violence were included in the work of both the SCSL and the TRC. While the SCSL made significant strides in addressing sexual violence, it left a conflicting legacy in providing a sense of justice and redress for the victims, mainly due to a lack of sensitivity among the majority of judges toward sexual offences.[47] In Lotta Teale's empirical study in Sierra Leone, she found that a lack of understanding of the SCSL's work for victims also contributed to its limited response in addressing the needs of victims of conflict-related sexual violence.[48] Due to the nature of the criminal justice process, a number of these victims lamented the SCSL's failure to give space to their stories, especially in cases where counts of sexual violence were not included in indictments.[49]

In contrast to the proceedings of the SCSL, the TRC process endeavoured to accommodate victims of rape, sexual slavery, enforced prostitution, forced pregnancy, and any other form of sexual violence committed during Sierra Leone's eleven-year civil war to ensure their stories were heard. The commission's establishing act called for efforts to help restore victims' dignity with particular attention to the subject of sexual abuse.[50] To encourage women's participation in the commission's proceedings, considerable efforts were made to facilitate the telling of their traumatic stories.[51] These included comprehensive explanations to victims of sexual violence about the commission's process and why their testimonies were important.[52]

Notably, during the TRC's proceedings in Sierra Leone, women and girls who were to testify before the commission were treated with extreme sensitivity. Significant efforts were made to ensure privacy and confidentiality and create an enabling environment. For

instance, as Samantha Lakin describes, special hearings were organized for victims of sexual violence, during which counsellors would
sit beside those willing to share their stories to provide support and
assistance, and the commission would reschedule a hearing if some
victims were not comfortable speaking about their experiences.[53] The
final report established that brutal acts of sexual violence, including
rape, sexual slavery, enforced prostitution, forced pregnancy, and
enforced sterilization were the most prevalent crimes that women
suffered during the civil war.[54]

Similarly, in the wake of Liberia's fourteen-year civil war, during
which rape was leveraged as a weapon to instill terror and humiliate whole communities,[55] the Act to Establish the Truth and
Reconciliation Commission of Liberia, adopted in 2005, specifically stressed the need for measures to protect the dignity and
safety of the victims and avoid their re-traumatization.[56] The commission's work contributed to exposing how gruesome acts of
sexual violence were inflicted on women and men as a means of
destroying families and the country's social values.[57] These include,
for instance, forced incest, such as the forced rape of women by
their sons or brothers. In Liberia, as in Sierra Leone, the commission's work not only provided a detailed account of the traumatic
experiences of victims of sexual-related atrocities in the country's
civil war but also contributed significantly to address the lasting
effects of these crimes, particularly the need for a change in negative societal attitudes toward the victims.

In the context of Sierra Leone, one study found that the commission addressed the need for social reconstruction and recommended
sensitivity toward the status of women in the community, particularly those who were victims of systematic sexual violence during the
civil war.[58] The commission made a wide range of recommendations
intended to address the effects of these crimes in Sierra Leone's communities and promote societal changes, including measures aimed
at changing negative attitudes toward victims of sexual violence.[59]

Although many TRCs generally tend to provide little regard for
conflict-related sexual violence, and they often fail to account for
the complex experiences of victims, recent developments have provided some lessons as to how these processes can be instrumental in
addressing the often deep-rooted structural conditions that enable
this violence in war, and which in turn lay foundations for structurally changed societies.

In Sierra Leone, for example, testimonies of victims of sexual violence enabled the commission to expose the close ties between the pre-existing gender norms in Sierra Leonean communities and the nature and extent of violence that women and girls endured during the country's civil war.[60] Accordingly, in its recommendations for redress, the commission's report pointed to the country's pressing need to address the gender inequalities in these communities, emphasizing the existing laws and practices that marginalize females.[61] Moreover, the analysis of transitional societies that included these crimes into mandates of truth-seeking processes indicates the critical role these processes play in aiding societal recognition and validation of the victims' experiences, which is a key aspect of state (re)building in the wake of mass atrocities.

However, as is discussed below in reference to Rwanda, the engagement of victims of sexual violence in the quest for truth is by no means an easy process. Although it is essential to integrate these crimes into the mandates of truth-seeking processes, mechanisms aimed at facilitating the victims' participation are vital to ensure their experiences and interests are appropriately considered during such processes' activities and outcomes.

REDRESS FOR THE VICTIMS OF SEXUAL VIOLENCE THROUGH THE GACACA COURTS IN RWANDA

One of the crucial elements of the genocide against Tutsi in Rwanda was the systematic use of rape and other brutal acts of sexual violence.[62] René Degni-Segui, the UN Special Rapporteur of the Commission on Human Rights on Rwanda, estimated that between 250,000 and 500,000 Rwandan Tutsi women were raped as part of broader strategies to wipe out the Tutsi group in Rwanda in 1994.[63]

Throughout the genocide against Tutsi in Rwanda, Tutsi women were individually or gang raped. Several accounts emphasize how many victims were raped or sexually mutilated in front of their families, friends, and other community members. Thousands of Tutsi women were, for instance, raped on the streets and sexually mutilated with sharp sticks, machetes, knives, and boiling water.[64] Indeed, the strategic use of sexual violence against Tutsi women was intended to humiliate and dehumanize victims. The experiences of victims of mass sexual violence during the genocide in Rwanda were so profoundly destructive that some researchers have described survivors as the "living dead."[65] Thousands of Tutsi women were raped to death with objects or raped before being killed "as a way of making death more gruesome."[66] These complex and grave lived experiences have devastatingly shattered victims' lives and their communities in myriad ways.

In addition to challenges and barriers to accountability for perpetrators of genocide against Tutsi, Rwanda was faced with the arduous task of rebuilding the country's shredded social fabric. Even though Rwandan ordinary courts were overwhelmed, given the sheer number of people involved in the genocide (victims and perpetrators), there was also a pressing need for reconciliation.[67] To combine the desire for justice and the need for reconciliation in addressing genocide cases, Rwanda introduced a participatory justice process known as the Gacaca courts, built upon the Rwandan traditional dispute-resolution mechanisms.[68]

The rationale for the Gacaca courts was to deal with an influx of genocide cases, promote communal healing and reconciliation, and restore social cohesion.[69] As Phil Clark explains, the Gacaca court's primary aim was to restore social harmony among Rwandans by involving "the people who experienced the genocide first-hand at every stage."[70] Community members were therefore required to provide testimony and evidence against suspects and participate in public hearings. Given the societal stigmatization and other deep-rooted culturally imposed taboos about rape in the Rwandan context,[71] the public nature of the Gacaca processes would have certainly impeded the ability of victims of sexual violence to share their traumatic experiences. To address this concern, several procedural protections for victims of sexual violence were adopted to create an enabling environment for victims to share their experiences.[72]

The Gacaca courts, which closed in 2012, significantly contributed to truth recovery and brought to light the complexity of Tutsi victims' experiences of the strategic use of rape during the genocide against Tutsi in Rwanda. Despite the prevalence of acts of sexual violence during the genocide against Tutsi people in Rwanda, only a small number of cases involving sexual violence have been dealt with by ordinary courts and the ICTR. Studies indicate, for instance, that in over a thousand genocide cases that were heard in regular court, very few included rape charges, and many other rape charges were dropped due to lack of evidence.[73] Creating a comfortable and enabling environment for victims and implementing a range of measures to ensure victims' privacy and confidentiality significantly enabled survivors to share their stories during the Gacaca processes. Several accounts suggest the Gacaca processes served to empower the victims of sexual violence, countering their isolation and especially addressing the multifaceted social dimensions of these crimes in the Rwandan community.

It is important to stress that rape as a tool of genocide in Rwanda was also facilitated by dehumanizing stereotypes for Tutsi women in Rwanda pre-genocidal media, such as the prohibition for Hutu men to marry Tutsi women.[74] The Gacaca processes provided an opportunity for victims and perpetrators to engage in collective debate about the nature and root causes of this violence. This was instrumental in facilitating the transformation of the Rwandan society, not least in terms of empowering women and enabling much-needed change of the discriminatory attitudes toward the victims. This, in turn, paved the way for collective healing and rebuilding of Rwandan communities.

CONCLUDING REMARKS

Wartime sexual violence is a multifaceted phenomenon, increasingly used by warring parties with strategic objectives. This violence is often deeply rooted in local contexts with far-reaching destructive implications for the victims and societal cohesion. The analysis in this chapter argues that to effectively redress sexual violence as a weapon of war, it is crucial to consider the broadest spectrum of impact of these crimes, at both individual victim and community levels. Drawing on a variety of truth-seeking processes, this study argues that enhancing victims' engagement with such processes, whereby their experiences of sexual violence and their interests are appropriately considered during all truth commissions' activities and outcomes, can empower victims and enable the much-needed societal transformation. The critical role of gender sensitivity within truth commissions' design and implementation processes must be stressed to enhance positive and comprehensive outcomes for the victims of sexual violence.

Significantly, integrating these crimes into the design and conduct of these truth-seeking processes and ensuring an enabling environment for women to discuss their traumatic experiences can provide opportunity for the moral condemnation of these crimes in affected societies. Moreover, the potential transformative effects of such processes on the often-challenging social dimension of these crimes would be vital to the state (re)building process because they have the potential to promote necessary changes to existing conditions affecting women in many societies. Addressing entrenched and damaging attitudes toward women is a key element in ensuring structurally transformed societies, particularly in countries enduring the harrowing legacy of conflict-related sexual violence.

NOTES

1 See, for instance, the following reports by the UN Secretary-General: *Conflict-Related Sexual Violence: Report to the Secretary-General*, (S/2022/272) (New York: UN, 29 March 2022); *Conflict-Related Sexual Violence: Report to the Secretary-General*, (S/2021/312) (New York: UN, 30 March 2021); and *Conflict-Related Sexual Violence: Report to the Secretary-General*, (S/2020/487) (New York: UN, 3 June 2020).

2 See, for instance, Ragnhild Nordås and Dara Kay Cohen, "Conflict-Related Sexual Violence," *Annual Review of Political Science* 24 (2021): 193–211; Allison R. Reid-Cunningham, "Rape as a Weapon of Genocide," *Genocide Studies and Prevention* 3, no. 3 (2008): 279; Kelly D. Askin, "Prosecuting Wartime Rape and Other Gender-Related Crimes under International Law: Extraordinary Advances, Enduring Obstacles," *Berkeley Journal of International Law* 21, no. 2 (2003): 10.

3 See, for instance, Resolution 1888 (2009), Adopted by the Security Council at its 6195th meeting, 30 September 2009, § 6 S/RES/1888 (2009); Resolution 2106 (2013), Adopted by the Security Council at its 6984th meeting, 24 June 2013, § 2 S/RES/2106 (2013); Resolution 2122 (2013), Adopted by the Security Council at its 7044th meeting, 18 October 2013, §10 S/RES/2122 (2013).

4 See the UN Security Council Resolution 2467 (2019), Adopted by the Security Council at its 8514th meeting, 23 April 2019, S/RES/2467 (2019).

5 See Jean de Dieu Sikulibo, "The Evolving Status of Conflict-Related Rape and other Acts of Sexual Violence as Crimes under International Law," *Journal of International Law of Peace and Armed Conflicts* 27, no.2 (2014).

6 ICC, Rome Statue of the International Criminal Court, art. 7(1) (g) and 8(2) (b) (xxii); (e) (vi), Adopted in Rome, 17 July 1998.

7 See for instance, the Prosecutor v. Bosco Ntaganda, case No. ICC-01/04-02/06, Judgement of 7 November 2019.

8 See Kjeld van Wieringen, "To Counter the Rationality of Sexual Violence: Existing and Potential Policies against the Genocidal Use of Rape as a Weapon of War in the Democratic Republic of Congo," *Journal of International Humanitarian Action* 5, no.8 (2020).

9 See, for example, John Perry and T. Debey Sayndee, *African Truth Commissions and Transitional Justice* (Lanham, MD: Lexington Books, 2015); Alison Bisset, *Truth Commissions and Criminal Courts* (Cambridge: Cambridge University Press, 2012); Rosalind Shaw, Lars Waldorf, and Pierre Hazan, eds, *Localizing Transitional Justice: Interventions and Priorities after Mass Violence* (Redwood City, CA: Stanford University Press, 2010); Nina Schneider and Marcia Esparza, eds, *Legacies of State Violence and Transitional Justice in Latin America: A Janus-Faced Paradigm?* (Lanham, MD: Lexington Books, 2015).

10 See, for instance, Natalia Szablewska and Clara Bradley, "The Nexus between Sex-Work and Women's Empowerment in the Context of Transitional Societies of Southern Asia," in *Current Issues in Transitional Justice: Towards a More Holistic Approach*, ed. Natalia Szablewska and Sascha-Dominik Bachmann (Switzerland: Springer, 2015), 235–60; see L.C. Turano, "The Gender Dimension of Transitional Justice Mechanisms," *New York University Journal of International Law and Politics* 43, no. 4 (2011): 1082.

11 See Mayesha Alam, *Women and Transitional Justice: Progress and Persistent Challenges in Retributive and Restorative Justice* (London: Palgrave Macmillan, 2014), 93.

12 See Coalition for Women's Human Rights in Conflict Situations, "Women's Right to Reparation: Background Paper for the Nairobi Meeting from 19 to 21 of May, 2007."

13 See the UN Human Rights Council, *Analytical Study Focusing on Gender-Based and Sexual Violence in Relation to Transitional Justice, Report of the Office of the UN High Commissioner for Human Rights* 30 June 2014, (A/HRC/27/21), § 16.

14 See Jeremy Sarkin and Sarah Ackermann, "Understanding the Extent to which Truth Commissions are Gender Sensitive and Promote Women's Issues: Comparing and Contrasting these Truth Commission Roles in South Africa, Guatemala, Peru, Sierra Leone and Liberia," *Georgetown Journal of International Law* 50, no.2 (2019): 463–516.

15 See Kimberly Theidon, "Gender in Transition: Common Sense, Women and War," *Journal of Human Rights* 6, no. 4 (2007): 453–78. See also Fiona C. Ross, "An Acknowledged Failure: Women, Voice, Violence, and the South African Truth and Reconciliation Commission" in *Localizing*

Transitional Justice: Interventions and Priorities after Mass Violence (Redwood City, CA: Stanford University Press, 2010), 69–91.

16 See Luke Moffett and James Gallen, *From Truth to Repair: Implementing Truth Commissions' Recommendations on Reparations: Reparations, Responsibility and Victimhood in Transitional Societies* 2020, 11. See also Jeremy Sarkin and Sarah Ackermann, *supra* note 14 at 476.

17 Sue Armstrong, "Rape in South Africa: An Invisible Part of Apartheid's Legacy," *Focus on Gender* 2, no. 2 (1994): 35–9.

18 See the Promotion of National Unity and Reconciliation Act, No. 34 of 1995, accessed 16 September 2019, www.gov.za/documents/promotion-national-unity-and-reconciliation-act.

19 See B. Russell, "A Self-Defining Universe? Case Studies of the Special Hearings: Women of South Africa's Truth and Reconciliation Commission," *African Studies* 67, no. 1 (2008): 49; Hayli Millar, "Facilitating Women's Voices in Truth Recovery," in *Listening to the Silences: Women and War*, ed. Helen Durham and Tracey Gurd (Brill NV: Leiden, 2005), 180.

20 See Tristan A. Borer, "Gendered War and Gendered Peace: Truth Commissions and Post-conflict Gender Violence: Lessons from South Africa," *Violence against Women* 15 (2009): 1169–93.

21 See Truth and Reconciliation Commission in South Africa, Report of 1999, vol. 4, 287.

22 See R. Rubio-Marín, "Reparations for Conflict-Related Sexual and Reproductive Violence: A Decalogue," *William & Mary Journal of Women and the Law* 19, no. 1 (2012): 76.

23 See The South African Truth and Reconciliation report, 1998, 296, cited by T.A. Borer, "Gendered War and Gendered Peace, Truth Commissions and Post conflict Gender Violence: Lessons from South Africa," *Violence against Women* 15 (2009): 1173.

24 See Borer, *supra* note 20, 1179.

25 See Vasuki Nesiah et al., *Truth Commissions and Gender: Principles, Policies, and Procedures* (International Center for Transitional Justice, Gender Justice Series, 2006), www.ictj.org/publication/truth-commissions-and-gender-principles-policies-and-procedures.

26 See David Tombs, "Unspeakable Violence: The UN Truth Commission in El Salvador and Guatemala," in *Reconciliation, Nations and Churches in Latin America*, ed. Iain S. Maclean (Farnham: Ashgate, 2013).

27 See Adrienne Aron et al., "The Gender-Specific Terror of El Salvador and Guatemala: Post-Traumatic Stress Disorder in Central American Refugee Women," *Women's Studies International Forum* 14, no.1–2 (1991): 39.

28 See M. Eriksson, *Defining Rape: Emerging Obligations for States under International Law?* (Martinus Nijhoff Publishers, 2011), 130.

29 See Tombs, *supra* note 26.

30 See UN Human Rights Council, *Analytical Study Focusing on Gender-Based and Sexual Violence in Relation to Transitional Justice*, § 16.

31 The truth commission in Peru was established in June 2001 and concluded its activities in 2003.

32 The truth commission in Guatemala was set up in 1997 and concluded its activities in 1999.

33 The Commission for Reception, Truth and Reconciliation in East Timor was set up in 2001 as the first of two truth commissions set up by Timor in order to inquire into the human rights violations committed during the twenty-five years of civil war, and the Timor-Leste Commission of Truth and Friendship was established in 2005 following widespread and extreme violence during the Indonesian occupation of East Timor.

34 Sierra Leone's TRC was established by the Lomé Peace Agreement of 7 July 1999 between the government and the rebel Revolutionary United Front after the nine-year civil war in Sierra Leone, marked by the systematic use of rape and other acts of sexual violence as weapons.

35 The TRC in Peru was established in June 2001, under the transitional government of Valentín Paniagua Coazao through the Supreme Decree No. 065-2001-PCM.

36 See Jelke Boesten, *Sexual Violence During War and Peace: Gender, Power, and Post-Conflict Justice in Peru* (New York: Palgrave Macmillan, 2014), 17.

37 The Guatemala Commission for Historical Clarification was established as part of the UN-brokered peace agreement between Guatemala and the *Unidad Revolucionaria Nacional Guatemalteca* to investigate human rights violations during the civil war from 1962 to 1996.

38 Established in 2000 by the UN and the government of Timor-Leste to inquire into human rights violations committed between April 1974 and October 1999. The commission delivered its report on 31 October 2005.

39 Established by the Lomé Peace Agreement of 7 July 1999.

40 Established by Liberia's Peace Agreement in 2003 after fourteen years of civil war.

41 See Megan Gerecke, "Explaining Sexual Violence in Conflict Situations," in *Gender, War, and Militarism: Feminist Perspectives*, ed. Laura Sjoberg and Sandra Via (Santa Barbara, CA: Praeger, 2010).

42 Gerecke, 149.

43 Carroll Bogert and Corinne Dufka, "Sexual Violence in Sierra Leone,"
The Lancet 357, no. 9252 (2001): 304.

44 See L. Piwowarczyk, "Speaking With Post-War Liberia: Gender-Based
Violence Interventions for Girls and Women," in *Women, War, and
Violence: Personal Perspectives and Global Activism*, ed. Robin M.
Chandler, Lihua Wang, and Linda K. Fuller (New York: Palgrave
Macmillan, 2010), 32.

45 See Almudena Toral, "History of Violence: Struggling with the Legacy of
Rape in Liberia," *Time* magazine, 30 April 2012, http://world.time.
com/2012/04/30/history-of-violence-struggling-with-the-legacy-of-
rape-in-liberia/.

46 The UN Security Council Resolution 1315 (2000), adopted at its 4186th
meeting, 14 August 2000 provided the UN Secretary-General with a mandate to negotiate an agreement with the government of Sierra Leone to set
up a mixed jurisdiction to address serious crimes committed during the
country's decade-long civil war from 1991 to 2001. The agreement
between the UN and the government of Sierra Leone was signed in
Freetown on 16 January 2002. The parliament of Sierra Leone ratified this
agreement in March 2002.

47 See Lotta Teale, "Addressing Gender-Based Violence in the Sierra Leone
Conflict: Notes from the Field," *African Journal on Conflict Resolution* 9,
no. 2 (2009): 73.

48 Teale, 74.

49 The Prosecutor v. Sam Hinga Norman, Moinina Fofana and Allieu
Kondewa, Case No SCSL-04-14-T, The SCSL, Decision on Prosecution
Request to Leave to Amend the Indictment, 20 May 2004.

50 See the Sierra Leone Truth and Reconciliation Commission Act (2000)
Part III, art. 2(b).

51 See Hayli Millar, "Facilitating Women's Voices in Truth Recovery: An
Assessment of Women's Participation and the Integration of a Gender
Perspective in Truth Commissions," in *Listening to the Silences: Women and
War*, ed. Helen Durham and Tracey Gurd (Leiden: Nijhoff, 2005), 171–222.

52 See Samantha Lakin, "Keeping the Focus on Responding to Victims:
Response to HSR 2012," World Peace Foundation, 19 March 2013, http://
sites.tufts.edu/reinventingpeace/2013/03/19/keeping-the-focus-
on-responding-to-victims-a-response-to-the-hsr-2012/.

53 Lakin, 52.

54 See Christine Evans, *The Right to Reparation in International Law for
Victims of Armed Conflict* (New York: Cambridge University Press,
2012), 176.

55 See the Republic of Liberia Truth and Reconciliation Commission, Final Report, *Volume 1: Preliminary Findings and Determinations*, 19 December 2008, http://trcofliberia.org/resources/reports/final/volume-one_layout-1.pdf.

56 See *Liberia: An Act to Establish the Truth and Reconciliation Commission (TRC) of Liberia*, approved 10 June 2005, www.refworld.org/docid/473c6b3d2.html.

57 See Rashida Manjoo and Calleigh McRaith, "Gender-Based Violence and Justice in Conflict and Post-Conflict Areas," *Cornell International Law Journal* 44 (2011): 29.

58 See Samantha Lakin, *supra* note 52.

59 See Sierra Leone Truth and Reconciliation Commission Final Report, vol. 2, chapters 3 and 4, http://sierraleonetrc.org/index.php/view-the-final-report.

60 See Sierra Leone Truth and Reconciliation Commission Final Report, vol. 3B, chapter 3. See also UN Human Rights Council, *Analytical Study Focusing on Gender-Based and Sexual Violence in Relation to Transitional Justice*, § 15.

61 See Sierra Leone Truth and Reconciliation Commission Final Report, vol. 3B, chapter 3.

62 See Christopher W. Mullins, "'We Are Going to Rape You and Taste Tutsi Women': Rape During the 1994 Rwandan Genocide," *British Journal of Criminology* 49, no. 6 (2009): 719–35.

63 See Rene Degni-Segui: The UN Special Rapporteur of the Commission on Human Rights, *Report on the Situation of Human Rights in Rwanda*, (UN Doc. E/CN.4/1996/68), 29 January 1996, § 16.

64 Binaifer Nowrojee, "'Your Justice is Too Slow': Will the ICTR Fail Rwanda's Rape Victims?" *United Nations Research Institute for Social Development* (2005): 7.

65 See Catherine Newbury and Hannah Baldwin, "Aftermath: Women in Post-genocide Rwanda," Center for Development Information and Evaluation, Working Paper no, 303 (2000): 4, http://pdf.usaid.gov/pdf_docs/pnacj323.pdf.

66 Samuel Totten, "The Plight and Fate of Females during and Following the 1994 Rwandan Genocide," in *Genocide: A Critical Bibliographic Review*, ed. Samuel Totten (Piscataway, NJ: Transaction Publishers, 2012), 192.

67 See Phil Clark, *The Gacaca Courts and Post-Genocide Justice and Reconciliation in Rwanda: Justice without Lawyers* (Cambridge: Cambridge University Press, 2010).

68 See the Organic Law of 26 January 2001 Setting Up Gacaca Jurisdictions

and Organizing Prosecutions for Offences Constituting the Crime of Genocide or Crimes Against Humanity Committed between 1 October 1990 and December 31, 1994. The Gacaca courts were officially closed in 2012.

69 See Human Rights Watch, "Law and Reality: Progress in judicial reform in Rwanda," July 2008, www.hrw.org/sites/default/files/reports/rwanda0708webwcover.pdf. See also William A. Schabas, "The Rwandan Courts in Quest of Accountability: Genocide Trials and *Gacaca* Courts," *Journal of International Criminal Justice* 3 (2003): 880.

70 See Phil Clark, "How Rwanda Judged its Genocide," *Africa Research Institute: Counterpoints* (2012): 3.

71 See M. Zraly, S.E. Rubin, and D. Mukamana, "Motherhood and Resilience among Rwandan Genocide-Rape Survivors," *Ethos* 41, no. 4 (2012): 420.

72 See Art. 38 of the Organic Law No. 16/2004 of 19/6/2004, establishing the organisation, competence and functioning of Gacaca courts charged with prosecuting and trying the perpetrators of the crime of genocide and other crimes against humanity, committed between 1 October 1990 and 31 December 1994.

73 Art. 38 of the Organic Law No. 16/2004 of 19/6/2004.

74 See Nicholas A. Robins and Adam Jones, *Genocides by the Oppressed: Subaltern Genocide in Theory and Practice* (Indiana University Press, 2009), 17.

3

The African Human Rights and Transitional Justice Architecture: An Analytical Outline

Obiora C. Okafor and Uchechukwu Ngwaba

The critical drivers and triggers of conflicts on the African continent include legitimate governance deficits, human rights violations, and a lack of respect for the rule of law and constitutionalism.[1] Transitional justice in the African context takes on a special character and orientation beyond the traditional focus on retributive justice to encompass restorative, redistributive, and transformative justice.[2] Thus, while the core objective of transitional justice praxis in Africa should, and does, remain similar to transitional justice orthodoxy in the international context – namely, the fight against impunity and the push for accountability and post-conflict reconstruction and development[3] – the emerging consensus points to the "effective realization of socio-economic justice, gender justice, and the right to development" as equally critical, if not central, to the redress of past injustices.[4] Instrumental to the successful delivery of this broadened set of objectives is a combination of traditional and non-traditional frameworks embedded in a wide range of laws, policies, institutions, and community norms and customs. In combination, they present the rough contours of "an African model and mechanism for dealing with not only the legacies of conflicts and violations but also governance deficits and developmental challenges" in line with the African Union's (AU) *Agenda 2063*.[5]

Against this backdrop, this chapter analytically outlines the field of the human rights and transitional justice architecture that has emerged on the African continent. The nature of the full range of the AU's transitional justice laws, policies, institutions, and mechanisms is mapped. The strengths and weaknesses of the architecture deciphered in the result are parsed. In the end, the chapter suggests that a rather odd combination of strong laws and weak institutions have all too often stymied the attainment of transitional justice objectives on the African continent.

First, the chapter discusses the African human rights system and delineates the broad framework of that system as relevant to the objectives of transitional justice. Next, the chapter surveys the contours of the institutional landscape of transitional justice in Africa, drawing attention to the various forms and approaches adopted to offer redress for human rights abuses and violations in the transitional justice context. Third, the chapter analyzes the relative strengths and weaknesses of the African human rights and transitional justice architecture that has been discussed in the previous sections. The concluding section reflects on the prospects for strengthening human rights and transitional justice in Africa.

THE AU HUMAN RIGHTS SYSTEM AND THE SHARED VALUES INSTRUMENTS

Although the African transitional justice architecture is significantly more extensive than its human rights system, it is suggested that the Constitutive Act of the AU (Constitutive Act), the African Charter on Human and Peoples' Rights (ACHPR) and its protocols, together with the AU shared values instruments provide the "guidelines and impulses,"[6] which radiate through the transitional justice architecture that has evolved across the continent. The "radiating effect" theory is owed to the work of the Federal Constitutional Court of Germany, which was cited with approval by Robert Alexy in the development of his treatise on the impact of constitutional rights norms on other areas of law. Alexy suggests that constitutional rights norms "embody an objective order of values, which apply to all areas of law ... and provide guidelines and impulses for the legislature, administration and judiciary."[7]

Borrowing from this line of reasoning, with modifications to account for the specific nuances of the AU human rights system, we suggest that although the character and tenor of constitutions in domestic law systems differ significantly from those of international law systems (like the AU's), there is a clear sense in which the AU's Constitutive Act, the ACHPR and its protocols, as well as AU's shared values instruments, can, as a collective body of norms, serve similar functions to constitutions in domestic law systems (depending, of course, on the system of reference). This is certainly the case with regard to the Constitutive Act (in relation to the AU as a whole) and the ACHPR (in relation to the African human rights system as a whole). In the context of transitional justice, these texts can provide guidelines and impulses that radiate across the entire AU system. This radiating effect becomes more significant when account is taken of how these legal instruments shape the trajectories of transitions that the transitional justice field in Africa overtly, but also covertly or unintentionally, promotes.

By understanding the primacy of the Constitutive Act, the ACHPR and its protocols, and the AU shared values instruments in shaping the landscape of transitional justice in Africa, we are better situated to interpret and appreciate the vast field of transitional justice on the continent. In turn, we also become better equipped to clearly identify areas of strengths and weaknesses in the resulting architecture. As noted in Objective 9 of the African Union Transitional Justice Policy (AUTJP) adopted in February 2019: "The overall objective of the AUTJP is to provide the policy parameters on holistic and transformational Transitional Justice in Africa, drawn from – amongst others – the AU Constitutive Act, *Agenda 2063*, the ACHPR and the shared values instruments. The policy offers guidelines, possible benchmarks and practical strategic proposals for the design, implementation, monitoring and evaluation of African TJ processes."[8]

For a better mapping of the specific contributions of each of these legal instruments to the radiating effect, closer scrutiny of each instrument is required. This inquiry focuses on relevant legal instruments (hard law and soft law) that inspire, inform, and shape transitional justice praxis in Africa. The section titled "Mapping the Institutional Landscape of Transitional Justice in Africa" explores the contours of the transitional justice landscape, examining the relevant institutions and mechanisms.

The AU's Hard Law Human Rights Instruments
Relevant to Transitional Justice

The hard law instruments considered in this section cover a wide range of subjects but can be linked by their shared commitment to advancing human and peoples' rights, democratic rights, constitutionalism, and respect for the rule of law, as well as to offering redress for grave human rights abuses and violations, among other such values. These instruments include the Constitutive Act, the ACHPR, the Protocol to the ACHPR, and a number of other related treaties. Each of them is listed briefly here for their pertinent content.

A) THE CONSTITUTIVE ACT
Given Africa's long (though not at all unique) history of dealing with the legacies of violent conflicts and violations of human rights and dignity, it comes as no surprise that, as on other continents, African societies have long been exposed to transitional justice processes in their quest to heal from the trauma brought about by conflicts and violations of human rights.[9] It is thus meaningful that Article 4(e) of the Constitutive Act of the AU calls for peaceful resolution of conflicts among its member states through appropriate means decided upon by the assembly. Furthermore, Article 4(o) of this same act urges respect for the sanctity of human life and condemnation and rejection of impunity. Significantly, Article 4(h) confers enormous powers on the AU to intervene within its member states in cases of mass atrocities, grave human rights abuses, crimes against humanity, and genocide.[10]

B) THE AFRICAN CHARTER ON HUMAN
AND PEOPLES' RIGHTS
The AU's predecessor body, the Organisation of African Unity (OAU), established in 1963, was more focused on state sovereignty, territorial integrity, and non-interference in the affairs of states than on human rights. While it was not unconcerned with human rights (as is reflected in its deep focus on ending colonialism, apartheid, and the detrimental foreign economic exploitation of Africa's resources), issues about the internal civil and political rights situations in member states tended to be kept at the fringes and treated as matters within the exclusive purview of states.[11] Nonetheless, the normative framework of the African human rights system was established during this period with the promulgation of the ACHPR by the OAU's Assembly of Heads of States in 1981, the African (Banjul) Charter, 1981 and its entry into force in 1986, following receipt of sufficient instruments of ratification from AU member states.

As a human rights instrument, the charter is remarkable for the way it responds to African concerns, traditions, and conditions.[12] It is also remarkable for how it combines first-generation (civil and political) rights and second-generation (economic, social, and cultural) rights in a single document and makes both categories of rights justiciable.[13] The charter stands as one of the precious few international human rights instruments directly incorporating the concept of peoples' rights, solidarity rights, and collective rights.[14] For example, Articles 19 to 24 of the charter guarantee peoples' rights to equality, existence, the free disposal of wealth and natural resources, development, peace and security, and a generally satisfactory environment. All these human rights' categories are relevant to transitional justice praxis in Africa. For instance, the civil/political right to vote is critical to the enjoyment of political participation rights on the continent, as elsewhere, and to sustainable peace. The socio-economic right to food is as basic to creating the kinds of relatively just societies that tend to avoid, or return to, major conflict. And the enjoyment of the right to development is as much, or even more of, a necessity for enduring peace as these other rights.

c) THE PROTOCOL TO THE ACHPR ON THE RIGHTS OF WOMEN IN AFRICA

To address the perceived shortcomings of the ACHPR in relation to the protection of women in Africa, the OAU/AU adopted the Protocol to the ACHPR on the Rights of Women in Africa (the Maputo Protocol) on 11 July 2003, and it entered into force on 25 November 2005, after achieving the required minimum number of fifteen ratifications.[15] The Maputo Protocol was adopted to address three key issues: discrimination against women, traditional practices that are harmful to women, and violence against women.[16] The Maputo Protocol takes into account the specific concerns/realities of African women, and addresses these in a way the Convention on the Elimination of All Forms of Discrimination Against Women (CEDAW) fails to do. For example, it gives pride of place to the rights of widows and inheritance of property by women to a degree that CEDAW could not. To this extent, it contributes significantly to the normative framework that undergirds, or at least ought to undergird, transitional justice praxis in Africa.

d) OTHER RELEVANT TREATIES

Beyond the African charter system, there are other hard law instruments that can be linked to significant degrees with the goals of transitional justice (following upon conflicts) on the continent. These include:

i   the *African Charter on the Rights and Welfare of the Child*
     (the African Child Charter),[17] which seeks to protect children
     in Africa against abuse and torture[18] and armed conflicts.[19]
     It also deals with the refugee status of children in armed
     conflicts;[20]
ii   the AU *Convention for the Protection and Assistance of Inter-
     nally Displaced Persons in Africa* (the *"Kampala Convention"*)
     which has, as one of its objectives, the promotion and strength-
     ening of regional and national measures to prevent or mitigate,
     prohibit, and eliminate the root causes of internal displacement
     and provide for durable solutions;[21]
iii the *African Charter on Democracy, Elections and Governance*,
     which commits African states to the protection of demo-
     cratic values, human rights, and the rule of law, among other
     things;[22] and
iv   the *Protocol to the Establishment of the Peace and Security
     Council of the African Union*, adopted in July 2002 in Durban,
     South Africa, and entering into force in December 2003. The
     Protocol has, as its objectives, the promotion of peace, secu-
     rity, and stability in Africa; the anticipation and prevention
     of conflicts; the promotion of peacebuilding and post-conflict
     reconstruction; the coordination and harmonization of conti-
     nental efforts in the prevention and combatting of international
     terrorism; the development of a common defence policy for
     the AU; and the promotion and encouragement of democratic
     practices, good governance, and the rule of law, etcetera.[23]

   Clearly, these objectives are highly relevant to the transitional justice process in Africa.

The AU's Soft Law Instruments Relevant to Transitional Justice

Numerous soft law instruments form part of the normative framework that undergirds and partly constitutes African transitional justice architecture. These instruments include the Declaration on Shared
Values, the AUTJP, the Human Rights Strategy for Africa, *Agenda
2063*, the AU *Policy Framework for Post-Conflict Reconstruction and
Development (PCRD)*, and the *Report of the African Union: High-
Level Panel on Darfur* (also known as the Mbeki Report).

A) THE DECLARATION ON SHARED VALUES

The AU's shared values are a means of accelerating Africa's integration and agenda through principles embodied in various instruments, decisions, and declarations the AU has adopted.[24] These are the issues that the Declaration on Shared Values attends to. This declaration was adopted by the AU Heads of State and Government at the 16th Ordinary Session of the Assembly of the Union in Addis Ababa, Ethiopia, in 2011. Among other things, the declaration reaffirms the commitment of member states to hasten the ratification and domestication of shared values instruments and commits member states to efforts to reinforce a deeper understanding of these shared values along with their promotion and popularization among African peoples.[25] Among these shared values instruments are the hard law instruments relevant to transitional justice (discussed in the previous section) and the soft law instruments that similarly advance that objective (discussed in this section).

B) THE AUTJP

This policy was conceived as a continental-level guideline for AU member states to develop their own context-specific policies, strategies, and programs aimed at democratic and socio-economic transformation in Africa and the achievement of sustainable peace, justice, reconciliation, social cohesion, and healing on the continent.[26] As stated in Article 10 of the AUTJP document, the policy establishes the principles and approaches that should guide holistic and transformational transitional justice.[27] The policy is drawn from, among others, the AU Constitutive Act, *Agenda 2063*, the ACHPR and the AU shared values instruments. The policy offers guidelines, possible benchmarks and practical strategic proposals for the design, implementation, monitoring, and evaluation of African transitional justice processes. This policy forms an integral part of the transitional justice architecture in Africa.

C) THE HUMAN RIGHTS STRATEGY FOR AFRICA (HRSA)

The HRSA is a guiding framework for collective action by the AU, Regional Economic Communities (RECs), and member states aimed at strengthening the African human rights system. The strategy seeks to address the current challenges of the African human rights system in order to ensure the effective promotion and protection of human rights on the continent.[28] The HRSA reflects the commitment of AU member states to secure human rights protection. It responds to the challenges that are bedevilling human rights praxis on the continent (such as the slow pace of ratification, domestication, and implementation of human rights treaties and instruments; the similar delay in the implementation of the decisions of human rights bodies; and inadequate coordination and coherence among AU organs, institutions, and RECs in terms of policy initiation, development, and implementation) by pushing for a synergy of approach and action in the human rights universe of the AU system.[29] There is no need to dwell here on the deep link between the realization of human rights in Africa (the goal of this strategy) and the effectiveness of transitional justice praxis on the continent.

D) AGENDA 2063

The *Agenda 2063: The Africa We Want* framework document is inspired by reflections on fifty years of the African struggle for development, peace, dignity, and so on. As part of activities to mark the golden jubilee of the OAU/AU in May 2013, a solemn declaration covering seven aspirations for "the Africa we want" was reached and adopted in January 2015.[30] The document is Africa's blueprint for transforming itself into the global powerhouse of the future.[31] Of the seven aspirations of *Agenda 2063*, Aspiration 4, which deals with a peaceful and secure Africa, is the most relevant to the transitional justice project of Africa. There are three goals under this aspiration, as follows:

Goal 13 – Peace Security and Stability is Preserved;
Goal 14 – A Stable and Peaceful Africa; and
Goal 15 – A Fully Functional and Operational Africa Peace and Security Architecture (APSA) (*Agenda 2063*)[32]

We agree with the AU that these goals and the priority areas, targets, and key process actions / milestones, which have been developed under them, significantly advance a transitional justice paradigm that has been repurposed to suit the African context.[33]

E) THE AU'S PCRD

This policy document serves as a guide for the development of comprehensive policies and strategies that elaborate on measures that seek to consolidate peace, promote sustainable development, and pave the way for growth and regeneration in those countries in Africa emerging from conflicts.[34] The policy was adopted in Banjul in July 2006. It draws from the mandate and experiences of the OAU/AU in the area of transitional justice, including Article 5(2) of the Constitutive Act, the basis of which the Peace and Security Council was established.[35] As stated by Said Djinnit in the preface to the policy document: "the PCRD Policy is a comprehensive document that strives to effectively address the root causes of conflict and provide broad benchmarks and indicators of progress for activities undertaken to bring about sustainable peace and stability to countries emerging from conflicts."[36]

F) THE REPORT OF THE AFRICAN UNION: HIGH-LEVEL PANEL ON DARFUR (THE MBEKI REPORT)

This report has been included as a relevant policy document on transitional justice because of the experiential lessons on the ground in Darfur that it offers about the subject. The Mbeki Report outlines generic recommendations on integrated justice and reconciliation responses and highlights the utility of comprehensive national processes and principles for the establishment of hybrid courts in parallel with truth-telling and reconciliation processes.[37]

We draw two conclusions from the discussion in this section. First, although the need to redress gross abuses and violations of human rights in conflict situations greatly informs transitional justice praxis in Africa, the African transitional justice architecture (at least in terms of the legal instruments) extends beyond this orthodoxy. It includes other areas pertinent to the African condition, such as improving democratic rights, constitutionalism, and respect for the rule of law; enhancing access to socio-economic rights; and realizing the collective right to development. Second, the sheer breadth, depth, and intensity of the legal instruments that form part of Africa's transitional justice architecture point to the presence of a radiating effect from certain "constitutional" and other texts, in terms of the sorts of transitions that transitional justice praxis in Africa overtly, but also covertly, promotes.

MAPPING THE INSTITUTIONAL LANDSCAPE
OF TRANSITIONAL JUSTICE IN AFRICA

Another critical aspect of the African transitional justice architecture is the institutions and mechanisms that animate, frame, and drive it. Since at least the early 1990s, Africa has served as a vast testing ground for institutions and mechanisms seeking truth and justice and enabling reconciliation in fractured societies. While the results of these various accountability efforts have been uneven, Africa's experiences have contributed to the advancement of a plethora of domestic and international transitional justice initiatives.[38] The institutions that have driven this effort include those linked to the AU system, Africa's many RECs, and some national systems. Often, they overlap in their sphere of influence, creating challenges of effective coordination of processes.[39] Additionally, the mechanisms these institutions deploy range from judicial, such as international tribunals, hybrid courts, and domestic trials, to non-judicial, such as truth commissions, reparations, and traditional or community-based processes.[40] Here, we begin by examining the relevant institutions. Thereafter, we consider the mechanisms these institutions deployed in different conflict (and/or post-conflict) situations on the continent.

Transitional Justice Institutions

The principal institutional drivers of transitional justice praxis in Africa include the AU institutions, the various Regional Economic Communities (RECs) on the continent, certain national institutions in some African states, and non-state actors. An extensive analysis of these bodies and their relevant efforts is not possible here due to various constraints. We offer instead a broad outline of how these institutions have shaped the transitional justice landscape of Africa.

A) AU INSTITUTIONS
The implementation of the AU's transitional justice laws and policies would not be possible without the leadership provided by a number of organs and institutions of this body. These include the AU Commission; the APSA (which comprises the Peace and Security Council, the Panel of the Wise, Continental Early Warning System, African Standby Force, and the Peace Fund); the African Court on Human

and Peoples' Rights (AfCHPR); the African Committee of Experts on the Rights and Welfare of the Child; the African Peer Review Mechanism; the Economic and Social Council; the AU Board on Corruption; and the Pan-African Parliament.[41] These institutions also work in collaboration with other non-AU continental bodies, such as the African Development Bank and the African Capacity Building Foundation.[42] These organs and institutions of the AU serve as mobilizing forces for driving the transitional justice process on the continent, based on African shared values (relating to peace and security, justice or non-impunity, reconciliation, human and peoples' rights, and so on), as elaborated on in the pertinent AU hard and soft law instruments previously discussed.

B) REGIONAL ECONOMIC COMMUNITIES (RECS)

Regional mechanisms for conflict prevention, management, and resolution are central to the African transitional justice architecture. Given that some causes and impacts of conflicts on the continent are regional (e.g., West Africa and Eastern Africa), African governments have recognized the need to react when conflicts arise in neighbouring countries. To do so without individually interfering in the internal affairs of their neighbours, many have turned to existing regional organizations to intervene, ostensibly at least, in the collective pan-regional interest. For example, the Intergovernmental Authority on Development (IGAD) played a role in the mediation between Eritrea and Ethiopia;[43] the Southern African Development Community has played a role in peace negotiations in the Democratic Republic of Congo; and the Economic Community of West African States (ECOWAS) has been involved in several peacekeeping operations in Liberia and other West African states.[44] However, not all regions in Africa have suitable regional organizations or the capacity and legitimacy to positively engage in such transitional justice praxis.[45] When they do engage in transitional justice, regional actors have, correctly in our view, been urged to ensure harmonization between regional and continental instruments to enhance coordination.[46]

C) NATIONAL INSTITUTIONS

The primary responsibility for driving transitional justice processes has been acknowledged by the AUTJP to rest on member states. This is because they bear the main responsibility of removing the political and social impediments to the effective pursuit of transitional justice processes, guaranteeing the space for debate and advocacy on transitional justice, and mobilizing the support of all sections of society across political lines.[47] National institutions – situated in the legislature, administration, and judiciary – are key players in the transitional justice process and should ordinarily be the first point of reference where the right conditions have been met (including capacity, legitimacy, and so on). Article 117 of the AUTJP notes in this regard that "it is imperative that national and local actors take the lead in planning, implementing, monitoring, evaluating, and reporting on lessons learnt in all stages and phases of the implementation of the transitional justice policy. This will ensure national ownership and broad-based consultation and participation of key stakeholders. Thus collective leadership at national level is key to developing an inclusive national vision and to clarifying the division of labour, roles and responsibilities of each of the key stakeholders."[48]

National actors therefore have the responsibility to establish the institutions, promulgate the relevant legislation, develop strategies/programs/projects, and eliminate obstacles to the implementation of transitional justice processes. Where state institutions are too weak or incapacitated (as has happened in the aftermath of certain extended wars), there should be less hesitation in seeking regional, continental, and international support to implement transitional justice processes.

D) NON-STATE ACTORS
Members of civil society, including community-based organizations and the media, play an important role in campaigning for and facilitating the emergence of necessary public national dialogue on pursuing transitional justice processes. Equally so, faith-based and cultural processes have been pivotal means for members of affected communities to heal, reconcile, and harness local justice as part of the transitional justice process.[49] All in all, the processes of national dialogue, reconciliation, and healing should enable faith leaders, traditional leaders, and/or community leaders to not only play an active part at the national level but also pursue them at the local level.[50]

Transitional Justice Mechanisms

The range of transitional justice mechanisms that have been deployed in the African context includes criminal prosecutions (before international courts/tribunals, regional/sub-regional courts/

tribunals, and national courts); truth seeking; reparation (including work on memory, memorials, and memorialization); and local or community-based justice. These mechanisms have thus taken judicial and non-judicial forms.

A) INTERNATIONAL CRIMINAL PROSECUTIONS

Over the last two decades or so, the push for violators to face the possibility of international prosecution and punishment has increased significantly. Criminal prosecutions are now central to efforts to "close the impunity gap, restore the rule of law, and build a culture of human rights."[51] International courts (including international ad hoc tribunals, hybrid courts, and the International Criminal Court, or ICC) have become important transitional justice mechanisms for states unable or unwilling to fulfill their obligations to effectively address legacies of massive human rights violations. Examples of the utilization of international courts and tribunals in the African context include the UN International Criminal Tribunal for Rwanda, created in November 1994 to prosecute the masterminds of the Rwandan genocide and other serious violations of international humanitarian law.

Hybrid courts that combine domestic and international law and accommodate international and state officials to build the capacity of the local judiciary while securing accountability have also been utilized.[52] Examples include the Special Court for Sierra Leone and the Extraordinary African Chambers established in the Courts of Senegal in February 2013 to prosecute Hissène Habré. Doubts remain, however, as to how many hybrid courts actually contribute to enhancing the capacity of the local judicial system.[53] The ICC completes the cohort of international criminal prosecutions in the African context, with its case docket including state referrals (such as those from Uganda, Democratic Republic of the Congo, and the Central African Republic); UN Security Council referrals (such as the situation in the Darfur region of Sudan); and at least one *suo moto* prosecution by the Office of the Prosecutor (in the case of Kenya).[54]

B) CONTINENTAL-LEVEL AND REGIONAL HUMAN RIGHTS COURTS

Continental-level and sub-continental regional courts and tribunals also feature in the repertoire of judicial mechanisms for securing transitional justice in Africa. At the continental level, the AfCHPR complements international, regional, and national institutions seeking to hold states accountable for human rights violations on the continent.[55] The proposal to create an extended criminal jurisdiction for the AfCHPR to include crimes of genocide, war crimes, and crimes against humanity is momentous. The challenge remains as to how to ensure the continental judicial system corresponds to international norms and standards.[56] Furthermore, the protection of human rights, which has key knock-on effects for effective transitional justice praxis, features increasingly in the jurisprudence of many African REC courts (such as the ECOWAS Court and the East African Court of Justice). Murungi and Gallinetti suggest this development "can be regarded as a response to the regional agenda set out in the African Charter and the Abuja Treaty."[57] We agree that this is so, at least in part.

c) NATIONAL COURTS

Whether criminal courts or courts that apply human rights law, or both, national courts tend to form the bedrock of the judicial mechanisms that can be deployed in transitional justice praxis. National courts apply human rights law because of the requirement in almost all the constitutive texts of this court that local remedies be exhausted before the regional- or global-level human rights courts and quasi-judicial bodies are approached. Founded on the principle that national authorities should have an opportunity to remedy a breach within their own jurisdiction, this requirement is thus relevant to the relationship between the international/regional courts and the national courts.[58]

In this regard, Article 56(5) of the ACHPR establishes the rule for exhaustion of domestic remedies before the African Commission on Human and Peoples' Rights can consider communications sent to it. This is reinforced by Article 56(7) of the same charter, which provides that the African Commission may not admit for consideration cases that have been settled by the states involved in accordance with the principles of the UN, the charter of the OAU/AU, or the ACHPR.[59] Article 6 of the Protocol to the African Charter on the African Court of Human and Peoples' Rights also provides for the exhaustion of local remedies rule, by incorporating the provisions of Article 56 of the African Charter by reference. With regard to national courts that exercise criminal jurisdiction, their status as the bedrock of transitional justice praxis in most contexts is mainly because they can hold exponentially more perpetrators to account than international courts ever can – largely due to the exorbitant costs of international prosecutions.[60]

D) TRUTH SEEKING

Truth commissions, as a transitional justice mechanism, set out to address the root causes of conflict and offer recommendations for dealing with impunity. The first recognizable, if troubled, truth commission was established in Uganda in 1974 by President Idi Amin to investigate enforced disappearances under his own government.[61] Since then, truth commissions have become a means to investigate past human rights violations, uncover the repressive machinery of authoritarian regimes, and identify systemic socio-economic injustices.[62] South Africa's TRC and Nigeria's Human Rights Violations Investigation Commission, popularly referred to as the Oputa Panel, are examples of the deployment of truth commissions in the transitional justice context in Africa.[63]

E) REPARATION

Reparation focuses on the victims of human rights abuses committed in the context in which transitional justice praxis is being deployed. The right to reparation is well established under international law and in the AU's shared values instruments. It is found in several multilateral treaties, such as the International Covenant on Civil and Political Rights,[64] Convention Against Torture,[65] and Convention on the Elimination of All Forms of Racial Discrimination,[66] and is now accepted as a part of the emerging customary international law relating to specific areas, situations, and conduct.[67] Under UN principles, the right to remedy and reparation for human rights violations involves five key principles, namely: restitution (returning the victim to their situation before the crime was committed); compensation (payment for economically measurable damage); rehabilitation (more general medical or social assistance); satisfaction (a broad group of measures that includes access to justice and truth seeking); and guarantees of non-repetition.[68] In recent years, there has been an international trend toward a role for truth commissions in reparation policies: truth-seeking bodies in South Africa, Sierra Leone, and Liberia have all made recommendations on reparations with varying effects. Other states, such as Morocco and Malawi, have created dedicated institutions for reparations.[69]

F) LOCAL OR COMMUNITY-BASED JUSTICE
Local justice initiatives offer rich possibilities for transitional justice and, by their nature, tend to be close to victim groups. They
draw on traditional structures and local initiatives and thus may
avoid some of the pitfalls of international institutions (global or
regional) imposed from above.[70] But for the most part, they work
well when they are part of a holistic strategy to seek and publicize
the truth, restore broken relationships, and pursue justice for serious crimes.[71] Local justice initiatives have been utilized in peace
agreements in Uganda and Rwanda – in the context of the Gacaca
court system to address the problem of trying more than 120,000
people accused of genocide.[72]

In sum, the contours of the transitional justice architecture of
Africa reveal a robust (though imperfect) institutional framework
comprising multiple bodies at the continental, regional, national,
and local levels. It also shows a range of relevant mechanisms that
can and do, at times, apply judicial and non-judicial processes. This
reinforces the view that the African continent has, at least on the
formal level, opened itself fully to different approaches aimed at
seeking accountability against violations of human rights.[73]

STRENGTHS AND WEAKNESSES OF THE
AFRICAN HUMAN RIGHTS AND TRANSITIONAL
JUSTICE ARCHITECTURE

We suggest that despite the AU's formal embrace of progressive
transitional justice norms and policies and the presence on the
African continent of varied institutional frameworks and mechanisms for advancing that praxis, the effective implementation of
these norms/policies by AU member states has faced significant
challenges, which often obstruct the attainment of the goals of
transitional justice.[74] Numerous problems have arisen, such as the
relative institutional weakness of many of the bodies tasked with
fulfilling these goals and ineffective coordination of the multiple
institutional actors involved in transitional justice praxis on the
continent. Yet, the African human rights and transitional justice
architecture has many strengths, including the availability and
thickness of the instruments, institutions, and mechanisms for

advancing transitional justice and the textual robustness of many of the relevant instruments. What follows is a brief discussion of the strengths and weaknesses of this architecture.

Strengths

The first area of strength of Africa's human rights and transitional justice architecture is the textual robustness of many of the instruments produced to undergird, frame, and guide transitional justice praxis. The shared values instruments that have been promulgated and deployed to solidify the normative framework of transitional justice in Africa deserve special mention in this regard. These instruments uniquely take account of many of the realities of the African condition, such as the democratic rights enjoyment deficits, the urgent necessity for the implementation of socio-economic rights in the transitional justice context, and the imperative of the realization of the right to development on the continent. These instruments also seek to address such deficits. Consequently, the emergent AU socio-legal regime on transitional justice is particularly responsive, at least on the textual level, to the needs of African peoples.

The second area of strength is the availability of a range of institutional and non-institutional players involved in transitional justice praxis. At the continental level, a plethora of AU organs and institutions have been implemented to serve as active agents in advancing African transitional justice agendas. Regional institutions, national bodies, and non-state actors are equally involved in these processes. The result is a wide and variegated field of active agents in transitional justice architecture. Hence, there is no shortage of choice institutions to drive the agenda of transitional justice on the continent; no dearth of bodies that knowledgeable agents can leverage to achieve the continent's goals in the present regard.

The third area of strength is the extent of variety in types of mechanisms that have been utilized in transitional justice processes on the continent. Rather than a narrow focus on criminal prosecutions, other mechanisms (such as truth seeking, reparation, and local justice initiatives, which have been recognized as capable of being equally or even more effective) have been deployed in specific contexts where they have been deemed necessary. This has been demonstrated repeatedly in countries such as South Africa, Rwanda, Liberia, and Nigeria. In this sense, transitional justice in the African context differs significantly from the Africa-relevant praxis at the global geopolitical level, where a preference appears to have been shown for international criminal prosecutions of Africans by bodies such as the ICC.[75]

Weaknesses

One weakness in the African human rights and transitional justice architecture involves the slow pace of the ratification, domestication, and implementation of relevant instruments by African states, and similar tardiness in too many cases of their implementation of decisions from African human rights bodies. This problem impacts the ability of African people to truly benefit from the plethora of laws, institutions, and mechanisms that form part of the African human rights and transitional justice architecture.[76]

Second, as Wachira notes, collaboration and coordination among AU and RECs organs and institutions with the mandate to strengthen governance, human rights, and democracy have too frequently been ad hoc and unpredictable. At times, the results have been avoidable inefficiency, ineffectiveness, and duplication of efforts and resources.[77]

Third (and related to the second), in the absence of proper coordination of the various judicial institutions that undergird and drive the African human rights and transitional justice architecture; too much potential is created for varied (and perhaps even conflicting) interpretations of the substantive and procedural human rights norms that are key for the realization of transitional justice.[78] Given the multiplicity of RECs, and the courts that operate within them across the different sub-regions of the continent, this threat is heightened. The danger arises in the possibility that any interpretive benefit produced due to the work of one sub-regional body may not easily be enjoyed outside that sub-region. States in one sub-region may then be able to point to conflicting interpretations of the relevant human rights provisions in the other sub-region to justify and legitimize their resistance to the implementation of their sub-regional body's views and consequential decisions.

PROSPECTS FOR STRENGTHENING HUMAN RIGHTS AND TRANSITIONAL JUSTICE IN AFRICA

Although much can be said about what lies ahead for the African human rights and transitional justice architecture, in keeping with the outline nature of the above discussion, the comment here is equally succinct. The future promise of better coordination of human rights and transitional justice is evident in the establishment of the African Governance Architecture to provide an overall mechanism for the implementation and review of the AU's human rights strategy, especially through building on existing mandates and relationships among AU organs and institutions, RECs, and member states. Furthermore, the adoption of an HRSA and the imminent adoption of its successor text, the *African Human Rights Action Plan*, attest to considerable thought and effort toward enabling collective action by the relevant bodies and states aimed at strengthening the African human rights system. Given how integrated this human rights system is in the African human rights and transitional justice architecture, the former will likely positively affect the latter. The extent to which this architecture will positively impact transitional justice praxis on the continent and, optimally improve the everyday lives of Africans in the relevant states and locales will, ultimately, depend as much on the architecture's design, nature, and operation as on what Africans at all levels *do* with it, as a set of resources in their actual and figurative hands.

NOTES

1 George Wachira, "The African Union Transitional Justice Policy Framework and How it Fits into the African Governance Architecture (AGA): Promise and Prospects for the African Court of Justice and Human Rights," in *The African Court of Justice and Human and Peoples' Rights in Context: Development and Challenges*, ed. Charles C. Jalloh, Kamari M. Clarke, and Vincent O. Nmehielle (Cambridge: Cambridge University Press, 2019), 164.

2 Jean Chrysostome K. Kiyala, "Transitional Justice from an African Perspective," in *Child Soldiers and Restorative Justice: Participatory Action Research in the Eastern Democratic Republic of Congo* (Switzerland: Springer, 2019), 231.

3 International Center for Transitional Justice, "What Is Transitional Justice?," www.ictj.org/about/transitional-justice.

4   African Union (AU), *Transitional Justice Policy*, 2019, https://au.int/en/
    documents/20190425/transitional-justice-policy; "Editorial Note,"
    International Journal of Transitional Justice 7 (2013): 1–7.

5   AU, *Transitional Justice Policy*, 1; George Kararach, Hany Besada, and
    Timothy Shaw, "African Development, Political Economy and the Road to
    Agenda 2063," in *Development in Africa: Refocusing the Lens after the
    Millennium Development Goals*, ed. George Kararach, Hany Besada, and
    Timothy Shaw (Bristol: Policy Press, 2015), 365.

6   Here we borrow from Robert Alexy, who explains constitutional right
    norms in those terms. See Robert Alexy, *Theory of Constitutional Rights*,
    trans. Julian Rivers (Oxford: Oxford University Press, 2002), 352.

7   Alexy, *Theory of Constitutional Rights*, 352.

8   AU, *Transitional Justice Policy*, 2.

9   Kiyala, "Transitional Justice from an African Perspective," 231.

10 *Constitutive Act of the African Union*, 2000, https://au.int/sites/default/
    files/pages/34873-file-constitutiveact_en.pdf.

11 Victor O. Ayeni, "The African Human Rights Architecture: Reflections on
    the Instruments and Mechanisms within the African Human Rights
    System," *Beijing Law Review* 10, no. 2 (2019): 303; Frans Viljoen and
    Evarist Baimu, "Courts for Africa: Considering the Co-Existence of the
    African Court on Human and Peoples' Rights and the African Court of
    Justice," *Netherlands Quarterly of Human Rights* 22 (2004): 241.

12 Theo van Boven, "The Relations between Peoples' Rights and Human
    Rights in the African Charter," *Human Rights Law Journal* 7 (1986): 186.

13 Ayeni, "The African Human Rights Architecture," 304.

14 R.N. Kiwanuka, "The Meaning of Peoples' Rights in the African Charter
    on Human and Peoples' Rights," *American Journal of International Law*
    82, no 1 (1988); Obiora C. Okafor and Uchechukwu Ngwaba,
    "International Accountability in the Implementation of the Right to
    Development and the 'Wonderful Artificiality' of Law: An African
    Perspective," *Transnational Human Rights Review* 7 (2020): 40–74.

15 Ayeni, "The African Human Rights Architecture," 305.

16 C.A. Odinkalu, "Africa's Regional Human Rights System: Recent
    Development and Jurisprudence," *Human Rights Law Review* 2 (2002):
    99–106; Fareda Banda, "Blazing a Trail: The African Protocol on
    Women's Rights Comes into Force," *Journal of African Law* 50, no. 1
    (2006): 72–84; Frans Viljoen, "An Introduction to the Protocol to the
    African Charter on Human and Peoples' Rights on the Rights of Women
    in Africa," *Washington and Lee Journal of Civil Rights and Social Justice*
    16, no. 1 (2009).

17 Organization of African Unity (OAU), *African Charter on the Rights and Welfare of the Child* (African Child Charter), 11 July 1990, CAB/LEG/24.9/49 (1990), accessed 22 May 2020, www.refworld.org/docid/3ae6b38c18.html.

18 OAU, Article 16.

19 OAU, Article 22.

20 OAU, Article 23.

21 AU, *African Union Convention for the Protection and Assistance of Internally Displaced Persons in Africa* ("Kampala Convention"), Article 2(a), 23 October 2009, www.refworld.org/docid/4ae572d82.html.

22 AU, *African Charter on Democracy, Elections and Governance*, 30 January 2007. www.refworld.org/docid/493fe2332.html.

23 AU, *Protocol Relating to the Establishment of the Peace and Security Council of the African Union*, Articles 3(a) to (f), 9 July 2002, www.refworld.org/docid/3f4b1d374.html.

24 African Governance Architecture, "Shared Values," https://au.int/en/aga; Salim Latib, "African Shared Values in Governance for Integration: Progress and Prospects," in *Governance and the Postcolony*, ed. David Everatt (Johannesburg; Wits University Press, 2019), 43.

25 AU Assembly, *Declaration on the Theme of the Summit: Towards Greater Unity and Integration through Shared Values*, 30–1 January 2011, Assembly/AU/Decl.1(XVI), https://archives.au.int/handle/123456789/272.

26 AU, *Transitional Justice Policy*, 1.

27 AU, 2.

28 AU Commission, *Human Rights Strategy for Africa*, 7, https://au.int/sites/default/files/documents/30179-doc-hrsa-final-table_en3.pdf.

29 AU Commission, 7.

30 AU, "Overview," *Agenda 2063: The Africa We Want*, 2013, https://au.int/en/agenda2063/overview.

31 AU, *Agenda 2063*; Kararach et al., "African Development, Political Economy and the Road to Agenda 2063," 365.

32 AU, "Aspirations," *Agenda 2063*, 2013, https://au.int/en/agenda2063/aspirations.

33 AU, *Agenda 2063*, 71–3.

34 AU, *Policy on Post-Conflict Reconstruction and Development*, 2006, 1, www.peaceau.org/uploads/pcrd-policy-framwowork-eng.pdf; Gunter Bender, "Post Conflict Reconstruction in Africa: Lessons from Sierra Leone," *Insight on Africa* 3, no.1 (2011): 71.

35 AU, *Policy on Post-Conflict Reconstruction and Development*, 2.

36 AU, viii.

37 AU Panel of the Wise, *Peace, Justice, and Reconciliation in Africa: Opportunities and Challenges in the Fight against Impunity*, The African Union Series (New York: International Peace Institute, 2013), 29; AU, *African Union Convention*.

38 AU Panel of the Wise, "Peace, Justice, and Reconciliation in Africa," 27.

39 George Wachira, "Consolidating the African Governance Architecture," *Policy Briefing* 96 (2014): 1; New Partnership for Africa's Development (NEPAD), "African Post-Conflict Reconstruction Policy Framework," *Governance, Peace and Security Programme*, South Africa, 2005, https://gsdrc.org/document-library/african-post-conflict-reconstruction-policy-framework/.

40 AU Panel of the Wise, "Peace, Justice, and Reconciliation in Africa," 27.

41 AU, *Transitional Justice Policy*, 26.

42 AU, 26.

43 IGAD is an eight-country trade bloc in Africa. It includes governments from the Horn of Africa, Nile Valley, and African Great Lakes. It is headquartered in Djibouti City. See IGAD, accessed 27 May 2020, www.uneca.org/oria/pages/igad-intergovernmental-authority-development.

44 ECOWAS is a regional political and economic union of fifteen countries located in West Africa. It is headquartered in Abuja, Nigeria's capital. See ECOWAS, accessed 27 May 2020, https://www.ecowas.int.

45 L. Alexander and A. Higazi, "Regional Approaches to Conflict Prevention in Africa: European Support to African Processes," *In Brief* 4 (2003): 2.

46 AU, *Transitional Justice Policy*, 26.

47 AU, 25.

48 AU, 25.

49 AU, 26.

50 AU, 27.

51 AU Panel of the Wise, "Peace, Justice, and Reconciliation in Africa," 16.

52 AU Panel of the Wise, 19.

53 AU Panel of the Wise, 19; Charles C. Jalloh, "Special Court for Sierra Leone: Achieving Justice?" *Michigan Journal of International Law* 32, no. 3 (2011): 395–460.

54 Obiora C. Okafor and Uchechukwu Ngwaba, "The International Criminal Court as a 'Transitional Justice' Mechanism in Africa: Some Critical Reflections," *International Journal of Transitional Justice* 9, no. 1 (2015): 90–108.

55 AU, *Transitional Justice Policy Framework*, 19; Obiora C. Okafor, *The African Human Rights System, Activist Forces and International Institutions* (Cambridge: Cambridge University Press, 2007).

56 African Court on Human and Peoples' Rights, "Jurisdiction," https://en.
african-court.org/index.php/about-us/jurisdiction.

57 Lucyline N. Murungi and Jacqui Gallinetti, "The Role of Sub-regional
Courts in the African Human Rights System," *International Journal on
Human Rights* 7, no.13 (2010): 3. The Abuja Treaty establishes the
African Economic Community. It was adopted 3 June 1991 and entered
into force 12 May 1994, https://au.int/en/treaties/treaty-establishing-
african-economic-community.

58 Frans Viljoen, *International Human Rights Law in Africa* (Oxford:
Oxford University Press, 2007), 336; Murungi and Gallinetti, "The Role
of Sub-regional Courts," 126.

59 African (Banjul) Charter on Human and Peoples' Rights, Adopted 27 June
1981, OAU Doc. CAB/LEG/67/3 rev. 5, 21 I.L.M. 58 (1982), entered into
force 21 October 1986.

60 Jalloh, "Special Court for Sierra Leone: Achieving Justice?"

61 Carla Winston, "Truth Commissions as Tactical Concessions: The Curious
Case of Idi Amin," *International Journal of Human Rights* 25, no. 2
(2020): 251–73.

62 Robert I. Rotberg and Dennis F. Thompson, *Truth v. Justice: The Morality
of Truth Commissions* (Princeton: Princeton University Press, 2000);
Priscilla B. Hayner, *Unspeakable Truths: Transitional Justice and the
Challenge of Truth Commissions* (New York: Routledge, 2011); AU Panel
of the Wise, "Peace, Justice, and Reconciliation in Africa," 21.

63 H.O. Yusuf, "Human Rights Violations Investigation Commission, the
Oputa Panel (Nigeria)," in *Encyclopedia of Transitional Justice*, vol. 1, ed.
L. Stan and N. Nedelsky (Cambridge: Cambridge University Press, 2013),
161–5.

64 UN General Assembly, *International Covenant on Civil and Political
Rights*, 16 December 1966, UN, Treaty Series, vol. 999, Article 2(3)(a),
171, accessed 29 June 2020, www.refworld.org/docid/3ae6b3aa0.html.

65 UN General Assembly, *Convention Against Torture and Other Cruel,
Inhuman or Degrading Treatment or Punishment*, 10 December 1984,
UN, Treaty Series, vol. 1465, Article 14, 85, accessed 29 June 2020, www.
refworld.org/docid/3ae6b3a94.html.

66 UN General Assembly, *International Convention on the Elimination of All
Forms of Racial Discrimination*, 21 December 1965, UN, Treaty Series,
vol. 660, Article 6, 195, accessed 29 June 2020, www.refworld.org/
docid/3ae6b3940.html.

67 Christine Evans, *The Right to Reparation in International Law for
Victims of Armed Conflict* (New York: Cambridge University Press,

2012); Office of the United Nations High Commissioner for Human Rights, "Rule of Law Tools for Post-Conflict States: Reparations Programs," New York and Geneva: UN, 2008), 5–6.

68 See UN General Assembly Resolution 60/147, 16 December 2005, UN Doc. A/RES/60/147.

69 AU Panel of the Wise, "Peace, Justice, and Reconciliation in Africa," 23.

70 These pitfalls include lack of ownership and consultation with local stakeholders.

71 Augustine S.J. Park, "Community-based Restorative Transitional Justice in Sierra Leone," *Contemporary Justice Review* 13, no.1 (2010): 95–119; AU Panel of the Wise, "Peace, Justice, and Reconciliation in Africa," 25.

72 Hollie Nyseth Brehm, Christopher Uggen, and Jean-Damascène Gasanabo, "Genocide, Justice, and Rwanda's Gacaca Courts," *Journal of Contemporary Criminal Justice* 30, no. 3 (2014); AU Panel of the Wise, "Peace, Justice, and Reconciliation in Africa," 25.

73 Ayeni, "The African Human Rights Architecture," 306.

74 Wachira, "Consolidating the African Governance Architecture," 2.

75 Okafor and Ngwaba, "The International Criminal Court as a 'Transitional Justice' Mechanism in Africa: Some Critical Reflections."

76 AU Commission, *Human Rights Strategy for Africa*, 7.

77 Wachira, "Consolidating the African Governance Architecture," 1.

78 Murungi and Gallinetti, "The Role of Sub-regional Courts" 130.

4

Decolonization, Gender, and Transitional Justice in Post-Colonial Africa

Sylvia Bawa

Truth and Reconciliation Commissions (TRCs) have become important channels through which states reconcile histories of atrocities,
oppression, and subjugation.[1] Operating on human rights principles, these commissions emphasize amnesty and healing. There is
a recognition that without repairing the past through truth telling
and forgiveness, the collective healing and "closure" required to
move forward would be impossible. Reconciliation is expected to
forge national unity by caring for the emotional injuries inflicted
on portions of the population. Whether or not people are directly
affected by certain or all atrocities, it is believed that these traumatic
events negatively impact national harmony and progress. Reconciliation, to be gained from truth telling and amnesty, is necessary to
restore a state to what it was or ought to have been. In Africa, the
role of successful processes and outcomes of TRCs in forging new/
renewed national consciousness in a tumultuous post-independence
era cannot be overemphasized.[2] TRCs thus serve multiple purposes
at macro-, meso-, and micro-levels: state (re)building – achieved
through healing from individual and collective trauma; providing
social justice to individuals and groups through validation, recompense, and reparations; and finally, legitimizing regimes in Africa
who rely on the currency of human rights discourse to assert themselves on the world stage.[3]

Abena Asare argues that human rights have transformed the
acceptance of violence as a necessary part of war or civil strife
by providing the language of collective outrage.[4] Even though
TRCs' roles in forging national unity, however tenuous, cannot

be underestimated in nation building, truth commissions and the process thereof are contested, contradictory, and imperfect.[5] First, among other things, the mandates of national TRCs limit them to domestic events. This ignores broader historical and political events in the larger world that contribute(d) to atrocities. Second, their establishment depends on the political will of a ruling regime. Finally, because the underlying structures are not transformed, they seem like politically expedient exercises geared more toward appeasement than actual justice. For instance, the economic marginalization and systemic discrimination Black South Africans face (a continuing apartheid system) have been left largely unaddressed. Consequently, the long-term harm caused by the colonial apartheid system continues today, despite the apologies rendered and amnesties granted by the TRC process.[6]

In this chapter, using the example of Winifred Madikizela-Mandela (hereafter Winnie Mandela), I examine the role and place of gender in post-conflict and nation-building discourses, engendered particularly by national TRCs. I make two interconnected arguments. First, Winnie's particular case demonstrates the flaws of focusing on individuals in the TRCs. The focus on Winnie successfully diverted focus from holding the apartheid state accountable for its untold horrors. Thus, I position Winnie as a sympathetic figure whose victimhood was erased by the process and, more importantly, whose role in the successes of the freedom fighters is often downplayed. Interestingly, her gender is simultaneously erased and reified to justify the oppressive nature of the patriarchal state. Second, women continue to be sidelined in nation-building discourses. While TRCs are supposed to help give us a clean slate, they still reiterate the fact that the state is essentially a male affair and women's interests and gender justice remain elusive. Thus, while TRCs provide opportunities for a fresh start, they still largely ignore the meaningful inclusion of women in the process. In the chapter, I employ critical discourse analysis as a methodological tool. The sources of data and information that I analyze include scholarly literature, media reports, the final report of South Africa's TRC, and various biographical sketches on and about Winnie Mandela and Nelson Mandela.

This chapter begins by examining how national reconstruction discourses resurrect romanticized visions of the nation-state and how particular visions of *return* are embedded in a so-called decolonial process of reconciliation. In the second segment, I focus on how

South Africa's TRC, similar to others, assembles particular truths, bodies, and discourses. I suggest that the TRC's inability to move beyond a focus on the individual is a failing of the reconciliation process on several levels. In particular, its (TRC) treatment of Winnie Mandela poignantly illustrates gendered injustices in discourses of national reconstruction exercises. In the third and last segment, I deconstruct Winnie's simultaneous reification and vilification as mother of the nation. I suggest that such a treatment exemplifies women's concomitant indispensability and convenient marginalization in patriarchal nation-building projects.

DECOLONIZATION AND DISCOURSES OF NATION BUILDING AND NATION (RE)CONSTRUCTION IN AFRICA

While emphasizing self-governance and decolonization, Africa's immediate post-independence nation-building discourses largely retained the colonial infrastructure they inherited. Given the contingencies of the immediate post-independence era, one can argue there was no time to engage in the decolonization projects that would truly have transformed the continent. The focus on political survival, through consolidating the tenuous freedoms gained in that period, made it near impossible to imagine a different system, let alone one that was "African." Another practical issue with the decolonization movement was that African values had been so largely subsumed under a mostly Euro-Arabic system[7] that it would have been challenging to reclaim Africa in the pre-colonial period, let alone selectively reclaim progressive elements of indigenous governance systems. Not only were anti-colonial and independent leaders educated in Europe and steeped in the very ideological systems they were trying to dismantle, but they were also careful about not upending their own privileges to transform the system. Thus the "class/political suicide" that radical Pan-Africanists like Cabral (1979) imagined as necessary for transforming the underlying political and social structures did not occur. Perhaps the hope was that the real transformation work would naturally come about once freedom was consolidated. Six decades after independence, many African states have become *independent colonial states*. Mahmood Mamdani aptly describes the post-colonial African state as a decentralized despotism or an apartheid state.[8]

The colonial architecture of nation-states (and nation building) marginalizes women and other minority groups.[9] The patriarchal colonial state subjugated women by ranking them below their male counterparts.[10] While women's disenfranchisement did not begin with colonization, their disempowerment indeed became entrenched through colonial gender policies.[11] Consequently, although simultaneous and paradoxical, the indispensability and suppression of women in African political discourse are neither surprising nor unanticipated. Women have always been regarded as convenient *disposable indispensables* in the construction of nation-states. While their physical, cultural, and political labour is indispensable to the state's reproduction, they are marginalized in its politics.[12] Even though progressive radical leaders like Kwame Nkrumah of Ghana and Thomas Sankara of Burkina Faso extolled women's virtues and contributions to anti-colonial struggles, women's oppression and subjugation have not been taken seriously enough. Although central to national reproduction, women have been peripheral to state interests in post-colonial Africa. Consequently, even though women are disproportionately affected by war and political strife, post-conflict reconstruction – peacekeeping and restorative justice – focuses almost exclusively on conventional "war crimes," to the neglect of sexual violence that disproportionately impacts women.[13]

TRCs and special tribunals are a step further in national reconstruction following the conflict. While their principles, similar to human rights, are not foreign to African pre-colonial societies and cultures (and may, in fact, be considered de-colonial), they are predicated on a colonial court infrastructure that has traditionally excluded women as justice seekers. Several scholars have lamented the ill treatment of female witnesses at special tribunals and commissions, as well as the inability of such commissions and tribunals to fully grasp the nature and impact of the harm these women would have endured.[14] A question that arises here is how do national TRCs address gender injustice to reset the gender balance in the nation? This is especially important given the clout of decolonization, or indigeneity, that TRCs have in Africa.

Decolonization itself has become a politically charged buzzword. Its use or deployment is embedded in existing socio-economic and political processes. Consequently, its employment obscures hegemony and power dynamics and begs the question, in what ways does it expand spaces for progressive conversations about historically rooted phenomena? Applied to the question at hand, the TRC activities are framed as exercises of indigenization or decolonization. At its ideal, decolonization is an exercise in reclamation, reparation, and restoration. While truth commissions are anchored in modern judicial systems, they appear to take moral guidance from what is considered indigenous social justice principles of *Ubuntu* – reclaiming what was lost in the process of colonization: including dignity, identity, and being. TRCs are said to mirror indigenous models of restorative justice and therefore work well in the art of restoration: restoring an upset in the natural cosmological balance. The emphasis on restoration, collective responsibility, and transition is expressed in what has become the defining principle of African-ness and or African ontology. According to its famous proponent, Bishop Desmond Tutu:

> *Ubuntu* is very difficult to render into a Western language. It speaks of the very essence of being human. When you want to give high praise to someone, we say, "Yu u nobuntu"; "Hey, he or she has *Ubuntu*." This means they are generous, hospitable, friendly, caring and compassionate. They share what they have. It also means my humanity is caught up, is inextricably bound up, in theirs. We belong in a bundle of life. We say a person is a person through other people." It is not "I think therefore I am." It says rather: "I am human because I belong." I participate, I share. A person with *Ubuntu* is open and available to others, affirming of others, does not feel threatened that others are able and good; for he or she has a proper self-assurance that comes with knowing that he or she belongs in a greater whole and is diminished or oppressed, or treated as if they were less than who they are.[15]

While associated explicitly with central, east, and southern Africa, *Ubuntu* has become a concept with a global rallying power of defining and homogenizing indigenous African ontology. Its popularity has given it legibility that enables its users to transcend certain cultural boundaries. For some, it is a wholesome pre-colonial and decolonizing concept, meeting any native purity test possible.

Similarly, the popular concept of *Sankofa* taken from several Adinkra symbols in Akan cosmology makes legible, albeit it through simplification, a process of reflection, introspection, and reflexivity only known and practised as "go back for" or return to reclaim.[16] In this context, it is a return to reclaim past customs/practices. Similar to the concept of *Ubuntu*, *Sankofa* defies categorical definition, and its use is mediated by specific contexts. Its deployment, therefore, must also be cautious. Given the radically violent and disruptive impact of colonialism, it is important to acknowledge the flawed nature of reclamation projects, given the central role that power plays in what constitutes legitimate knowledge or reclamation. Yet, the reclamation and "*Sankofa*" language are hard to miss in the ways in which truth commissions are characterized.

For instance, reports from Sierra Leone and Nigeria poignantly illustrate this. First, from Sierra Leone:

> After years of brutal conflict in Sierra Leone, there existed a need to confront the past. The nation wanted to know what precipitated the wave of vengeance and mayhem that swept across the country. How was it that the people of Sierra Leone came to turn on each other with such ferocity? *Why did so many abandon traditions of community and peaceful co-existence? Why were long-held and cherished customs and taboos so wantonly discarded?* What needs to change? How will we affect the change?[17]

The Nigerian Truth Commission raises similar questions:

> *Where did we make the wrong turn?* Who was responsible for what? What opportunities did we miss and why? What are the major lessons to be learnt? What do we now need to do to put the past behind us and look to the future with renewed hope and patriotic zeal? What are the basic conditions for us to effect national catharsis?[18]

Obviously, there is consensus and collective outrage acknowledged here toward the inhumane and cruel atrocities of war. However, it is important to ask, how far back in time do references to *cherished customs and peaceful coexistence* go? And, is gender equality embedded in the end goal of restoring balance and harmony? In other words, whose "collective" humanity is being reclaimed? Whose "collective" humanity will be sacrificed in the process?

Anthony Kwame Appiah cautions that reclamation projects are fraught because of the intricately paradoxical nature of locating origins in a post-colonial cosmopolitan world.[19] For instance, while the operating philosophy of the Gacaca tribunals in Rwanda originates from indigenous restorative justice, they are not wholly indigenous/traditional conflict resolution mechanisms. Per the *Ubuntu* philosophy, the crimes of one individual upset the balance of the whole community. An individual does not exist in isolation because of the collective, and vice versa. This principle is often juxtaposed with the Euro-Western model of individualism. While a sharp and binary oppositional definition of the West vs. Africa in this context is difficult to sustain, asserting or recognizing philosophical and cultural differences plays a crucial role in anti-imperialist movements. The tactic of reifying cultural differences serves the interests of powerful groups on either side of colonialism and imperialism.[20] The re-visioning, or invention, of so-called pre-colonial traditions and cultures enabled elites to assert or reassert their own power in order to strategically gain control over people and resources in the wake of departing foreign powers.

Given the new hegemonic contexts (predicated on past colonial history) within which Africans must articulate themselves, a certain positively reinforcing (re)visioning is important in reclaiming our humanity from its malignity in traumatic histories of enslavement and colonization. In this regard, historians draw our attention to a more egalitarian pre-colonial era, where gender was not a central organizing principle.[21] This begs the question as to how TRCs are working to restore gender balance in post-colonial societies. Does reconciliation include purging our systems of colonial gender hierarchies that often result in injustices for women?

In the following segment, I turn to the example of South Africa's Truth Commission, and in particular, the case of Winnie Mandela, to illustrate (1) the failings of truth commissions to attain social justice for oppressed groups, and (2) the gendered discourses that lead to the disposable indispensability of women in Africa's nation-building discourses.

Assembling the "Truth": The State's Arena of Performative Wrestling

People - Lawyers, Commissioners. Witnesses, petitioners, Survivors. Things - A box (or more of tissues/handkerchiefs), Standing Fans, Banners, Inscriptions, Insignia, Cameras. Microphones. Pens and paper. Recorders.

Emotion - Tensed Air. Emotion-Filled Air. Eyes. Lots of Eyes. Attention.
Non-Human Others - Imaginary other beings –supreme being watching over the proceedings, the ghosts of victims or perpetrators summoned by the echoes of their names by grieving relatives, b) posterity –summoned to travel to this past to see the doing of justice, c) the balance of the universe, awaiting restoration for rights about to be wronged.

Emotion – real or anticipatory – is the brick which undergirds the arena/infrastructure of truth and reconciliation theatres. Expectations of particular performances of truth seeking and truth telling by victim and perpetrator are based on a common-sense understanding of underlying moral norms in any given society. For purposes of analytical clarity in this segment, I abstract and reconstruct categories of victim and perpetrator. The two broad categories, victim and perpetrator, are understood as homogenous, stable, and straightforward. The complexities these categories inhabit are not easily unmasked in the arena of these tribunals. Reactions to these two constructed personas follow naturally: sympathy and empathy for a truth seeker; contempt, skepticism, and judgment for the perpetrator. The perpetrator at this time can either transform to remorseful sinner for whom amnesty is possible, or remain, simply, the unrepentant sinner. The truth seeker is expected to proceed from a place of moral superiority and hurt (a simple victim) and the truth teller from that of remorse and contemplation (a simple perpetrator).

Often TRCs, de facto, replicate some aspects of the traditional court, where individual participants are constructed as mere individual actors whose actions can be divorced from the weight and circulating powers of the state. Even though TRCs understand the complexity of the systemic issues at stake, in the end, the systems remain largely unchanged. More importantly, TRCs fail woefully to address group-based violence en masse. The individuals that appear before truth commissions are rarely treated as embodiments of groups with varying degrees of power. The complicated roles individuals play as witnesses and petitioners in hearings are also rarely captured. For instance, in the South African case, the focus on individual suffering and truth telling revealed the horrors of the apartheid system but did not entirely transcend the bodies of the particular individuals.[22]

What would it mean to imagine different configurations of these categories? In other words, what distinguishes TRCs from traditional court infrastructure? The mechanisms of adjudicating instances of wrongdoing are quite similar to conventional courts. Subsequently, TRCs are endowed with power and act within particular power structures that enable certain truths and constrain others. TRCs are not mass movements. They are sanctioned by the state, which has the power to sanction violence and is often complicit in the atrocities being adjudicated. In other words, TRCs are also about power and powerlessness.

The case of Winnie Mandela stands out as an example. Winnie Mandela's arrival to testify at the TRC was greeted by large crowds (friend and foe alike), cameras, and press. Her testimony at the commission was as anticipated as her now muddied reputation. Those sympathetic to her hoped to be appeased somehow by her testimony. Those who opposed her probably hoped that she would at least confess to the crimes she had been accused of to give some peace to their departed loved ones and their surviving relatives. Winnie appeared before the commission as a perpetrator of violence. She is mentioned in the commission's records as a victim, even though her appearance at the commission was more to answer for her crimes than provide testimony of her torture. As victim and perpetrator, Winnie immediately collapses the binary of truth seeker and truth teller. This is only one of many ways in which she complicates the focus on individuals in TRCs.

Winnie Mandela also belongs to a large powerless and oppressed group of Black South Africans. Paradoxically, she is lumped together with perpetrators of atrocities in the apartheid era (i.e., the state, by and large). She is thus at once powerful and powerless, victim and oppressor. She is part of the system that oppresses her compatriots. This example offers an opportunity to deconstruct these ideal types through intersectional thinking and examine how power imbricates and circulates in these processes. In other words, the perpetrating authority during the apartheid era in South Africa managed to reduce the burden on itself as morally repugnant by distorting the image of Winnie, the victim, as deserving of the oppression the state meted out to her. In some ways, the spotlight on her wrongdoings (however that is determined and weighed) removed the focus from the apartheid regime. Given the kind of negative publicity she received following her appearance, her wrongdoing seemed to overshadow the atrocities of the apartheid regime.

In his opening statement before Winnie's much-anticipated trial, Desmond Tutu iterated that the commission was primarily concerned about victims and survivors. Staggeringly, this statement, under the circumstances, would appear to cast Winnie Mandela as a perpetrator and not as a victim. Yet, as a complicated victim, she embodied the complex categories victim (of tremendous police brutality), freedom fighter, and member of the Black and collectively oppressed majority. In short, she was a victim of the system who was socialized into political violence – the very habitus of that system. Yet, in the charged context of her testimony, her status as victim and survivor was significantly downplayed. Similarly, the final report of the TRC states:

> What is, of course, representative of these stories is that they are about *ordinary men and women* whose lives were irrevocably changed by the violations they suffered during the period of *political conflict.* Some of the arguments politicians have raised in response to calls to implement the recommendations of the Commission's RRC have caused concern. *They make the point that the majority of victims were political activists who, in one way or another, made a conscious decision to engage in a political struggle against apartheid.* The argument is often expressed thus: we were not in the struggle for money. *While the Commission understands the grounds upon which this statement is made, in terms of international human rights law on reparations and rehabilitation, even political activists who decided to become involved in the struggle against apartheid should be compensated if they became casualties of the conflict.*[23]

The characterization of the victims here, not as a collective (of Black and majority South Africans) but as politically active individuals – as though they chose to fight for their humanity – who made *a conscious decision* (as opposed to being repressed) points to a significant flaw of this TRC. It is the very definition of an individual habitus in a situation where Bishop Tutu invoked an *Ubuntu* consciousness. Similarly, and shockingly, the joint Nobel Peace Prize for Nelson Mandela (a symbol of the struggle for human dignity) and Frederik W. de Klerk (the symbol of the oppressive apartheid system) solidifies skepticism with which this particular reconciliatory effort is viewed. The rhetoric of Kumbaya emphasized by "forgive and move forward" sharply contrasts with the treatment of Winnie

Mandela and the average Black South African. If Frederick de Klerk, who presided over such a brutal regime, could be given a Nobel prize, how is a freedom fighter like Winnie vilified for her actions? In this sense, the TRC failed woefully to reconcile the nation by its inability to address systemic and historical human rights abuses. Calling victims "ordinary men and women," while true, fails to recognize them as members of the oppressed and repressed group who suffered wide-ranging systemic subjugation.

RECONCILING THE PERSONAL-PUBLIC POLITICS OF WINNIE AS MOTHER OF THE NATION

> I am not sorry. I will never be sorry [...] I would do everything I did again if I had to. Everything. – Winnie Mandela

Known popularly as Mama or Maa Winnie, Winnie's iconic status as mother of the nation began innocuously, perhaps, as a biological mother to daughters of the most prominent figure of the liberation struggle, also known as Tata (father) Mandela. However, it was during the period following her return to Soweto that she became *the Mother* of the nation. The Soweto student uprising of 1976 solidified this image. Ironically, her work and involvement with youth, in this case the Mandela United Football Club, also erased that image and replaced it with its insidious other. It is intriguing that Winnie is read in tragic terms for her militancy and praised for conforming to conservative mothering ideals. Her agency, in rejecting the latter, coming out from under the shadow of male freedom fighters, is important to understand how gender informs nation-building discourses. How was Winnie Mandela constructed as wife and mother of the nation? Public and media discourses of her life often highlight her relationship to Nelson Mandela. For instance, in an Al Jazeera article called "Who Was Winnie Mandela?," the first three paragraphs describe her by her status as a wife to Nelson Mandela.

> Winnie Madikizela-Mandela, the ex-wife of South Africa's former President Nelson Mandela, has died at the age of 81.
>   The anti-apartheid campaigner and second wife of the late Mandela, passed away after a long illness, her personal assistant confirmed on Monday.

She was married to Nelson Mandela, the Nobel Peace Prize winner and icon of South Africa's anti-apartheid struggle, for 38 years, with Mandela spending 27 of those behind bars.[24]

While Winnie Mandela, arguably, did more work and endured more harassment and torture from the apartheid regime and became the face of the revolution, she still only occupies a secondary role. She is often portrayed as a wife and a mother. Nelson Mandela, however, is hardly described as husband to Winnie Mandela. In her own words, Winnie rejects this peripheralization of her work and identity:

I had noticed even before I left Johannesburg that the name Winnie was beginning to be forgotten even by my family. Everything I said was *Mandela's wife. I became a nobody.* I am now losing myself and being absorbed into this name, Yea, I'm married, but I am still Winnie. That scared me. And the reason why *I fought as hard* as I did in Brandfort was that I *wanted it known that it was Winnie Mandela and not Mandela's wife* and that it was a woman and that I would take on the enemy as much as they oppressed me. *I decided I would fight them to the last drop of my blood and I would show them that women are going to bring about change in S. Africa and we did.*[25]

Winnie Mandela's resistance to losing her identity to wifehood is not surprising given that she is also an avowed feminist who, in fact, went to jail for participating in the women's liberation movement in South Africa in 1958. This was long before she gained prominence as an African National Congress (ANC) political activist. In resisting the rather docile and subservient role of wifehood and opting instead to embrace that of motherhood, Winnie Mandela was reclaiming African indigenous identity ethos. The identity of mother is an honorific that is, in fact, not tied to biological mothering. Rather, it symbolizes a duty to protect, care, and ensure continuity.[26] Winnie Mandela defined these roles in her own terms. She not only demonstrated her agency, but she also carefully reclaimed her identity and curated her image as a fighter, one who did not merely react but in some cases created the conditions of her fame in order to keep the revolutionary light burning.

As previously described, Winnie also attempted to reinstate the role of women in the liberation fight. She did this in part by moving women from the periphery to the centre stage, drawing attention to the fact that they were successful in the struggle for social justice and change.[27] Furthermore, the domestic role ascribed to women in marriage and in discourses of nationhood is usually performed to some extent by women or rejected in its entirety. Case in point, as Winnie articulated: "We [me and Nelson] never lived together. I was the most unmarried married woman."[28] For defying the assigned place for women, Winnie was vilified. For instance, Shireen Hassim argues that instead of understanding the marriage between Winnie and Nelson as unconventional, given the commitment of both leaders to the liberation movement:

> Nelson Mandela's biographers rarely understand the
> marriage in these terms. For example, Anthony Sampson,
> who devotes a considerable part of his biography of Nelson
> to discussing Winnie, mostly in sympathetic terms, nevertheless
> casts her in the role of a bad wife. He describes Madikizela-
> Mandela as a "passionate girl, with her own demands."
> She was unlike Albertina Sisulu, the epitome of a good wife:
> "Walter still had Albertina as his 'backbone,' subsidising his
> meagre pay and sharing all his political commitment: 'I could
> rely on her, and there was no complaining ... she had mastered
> the situation in an amazing way, and that gave me wonderful
> courage.'" This distinction that Sampson draws reveals a stan-
> dard line in biographies of Nelson Mandela: that Winnie was
> either too young and naïve to match her husband, or a disap-
> pointment to his stature.[29]

While it is easy to imagine that Winnie had the typical upbringing as a woman and as one whose life only entered into the public stage after meeting Mandela, Winnie herself discounts this distorted simplification of her life. Indeed, per conventional discourses, she was raised as anything but a woman. As Winnie intimated, she (together with those comrades left on the outside) endured the wrath of the apartheid government while they fought in the trenches. The torture she endured was inhumane and life-changing. She further indicated:

> The leadership of Robben Island was the cream of our society
> and they were not subjected to the violence we were subjected
> to. [...] You are interrogated for 7 days and 7 nights without any

sleep. God provided a mechanism I had never thought of at the time. I reached a point, a threshold where the body could not take the pain anymore and then I would faint. These were the most beautiful moments. The body rested, and when they threw a bucket of water to wake me up, it didn't matter that I was soaking wet. I got up. I was so refreshed, and I started fighting all over again.[30]

This recounting describes her relentless fight for justice while also attending to how collective resilience shapes perseverance in the pursuit of structural change. In this way, Winnie would demonstrate that she could exhaust any means possible to win the war, including the infamous endorsement of violent lynching that came to be known as "necklacing."

Even so, Winnie defies categorization at any particular time. African feminists have theorized the importance of understanding the multiple identity indices of women, rejecting the temptation to reduce these to simple and stable identities.[31] Thus, like many women on the continent, and especially in post-conflict societies, Winnie exists in the messy other middles of binary gender categorizations. The complementarity and reinforcing nature of these roles is exemplified in her reflection on the Soweto student massacre:

If you were picking up the bodies of children on *June the 16th, 1976*, I can't pretend that I suddenly woke up the following day, prayed to God, and I was this angel, I forgave. *It was a battle. It is a process. It is still a process.*[32]

Here, Winnie was speaking about the famous Soweto student uprising and the subsequent massacre of schoolchildren by the apartheid state. In the statement, Winnie embodies the suffering of a parent – a mother – who is changed by the unbearable pain of burying their children. It is also, clearly, yet another moment that mobilizes her into more militant action.

In the following section, I return to the gendered nature of state-building infrastructure, where marginalization and social injustice mark the lives of vulnerable groups whose bodies, labours, and identities are exploited and strategically deployed to hold tenuous structures of states together.

FATHERS AND MOTHERS OF THE NATION: DISRUPTIONS IN GENDERED NATIONALITIES

> When the commission treats me like a leper and its chairperson hugs our former oppressors, then I worry about what type of reconciliation we are fostering. – Winnie Mandela

Here, I juxtapose two gendered images to help unpack how the reconciliation process in South Africa reinforced gendered nationalist discourses. The juxtaposition illustrates ways in which gender organizes nationalist understandings of heroes, victims, villains, scapegoats and rewards, punishments and abandonments. I argue that women's place in the national imaginary continues to be simultaneously indispensable and disposable. The two gendered images are as follows:

1 "The Nobel Peace Prize 1993 was awarded jointly to Nelson Mandela and Frederik Willem de Klerk 'for their work for the peaceful termination of the apartheid regime and for laying the foundations for a new democratic South Africa.'"[33]

2 "The mother of Stompie Seipei has visited the house of struggle [of] stalwart Winnie Madikizela-Mandela [in 2018] to pay her respects to the Mother of the Nation. Stompie was found dead near Madikizela-Mandela's house in 1989. Many blamed her for the 14-year old's death [...] When asked about the death of her son, Seipei said South Africans should not spread rumours about events that did not take place."[34]

In the first case, two men – Nelson Mandela and Frederik W. de Klerk – representing the two sides of the apartheid system jointly received a Nobel prize. Mandela represents Black South Africans who have been brutally oppressed by the system. De Klerk represents the very apartheid system that subjugated Black people and imprisoned leaders of the ANC. They each hold varying degrees of power and clout. The two men, unlikely allies as they are, are praised for their peace work in South Africa. Mandela is easily classified as both hero and victim. De Klerk, similarly as oppressor and villain. Why the Norwegian Nobel Committee decided to value their "contributions" in this manner is understandable within the context of global power inequality, where powerful actors protect their own.

This controversial joint peace award raises several questions regarding amnesty and reconciliation. If the starting point here is that the two sides of the conflict make peace in such a manner, then what happens to the messy middles of those two sides? Standing in that gap, the cost and bridge of peace, are the bodies of the disposable powerless others.

In the second case, two Black women – Winnie Mandela and Joyce Seipei – defined by the struggle for freedom in South Africa, highlight the failures of a reconciliation process that was considered successful by and large. The gendered malignment of Winnie Mandela (as a freedom fighter) and elevation of Joyce Seipei as a victim of Winnie's failings speak to the intersections of gender, race, and class. These two women have been constructed as two sides within the Black South African side of apartheid. Once indisputably considered mother of the nation, Winnie became vilified as a murderer or, as one news outlet described her, "mugger of the nation."[35] That the notion of motherhood, which elevated her, would also doom her is a paradox familiar to many oppressed groups, especially Black women.

Mama Winnie and Mama Joyce are brought together through a child, Stompie Seipei, and injustice, for they are both victims of injustice. One of them has always been considered a threat to the state and constantly reminded of her place – in the peripheries of the public sphere – while the other occupies the domestic stage assigned to women. Winnie occupied a public place, a place reserved for men. In juxtaposition, a previously unknown woman, brought into national prominence by the TRC's proceedings, became the indisputable face of a grieving mother of the nation. Joyce Seipei, who showed up to the hearings with her grandchild, is a more sympathetic figure: she is the Black mother embodying the pain of the nation. She is unblemished in terms of the crimes of the state, all of which somehow suddenly fall on the shoulders of Winnie Mandela. Madam Seipei is simply a woman and mother who has endured unimaginable pain from losing her child.

CONCLUSION

In conclusion, it is important to return to the question of social justice for oppressed and marginalized groups. How does the TRC process account for recognition and redistribution as two pillars of social justice?[36] There is no doubt that the attempts at genocide and systemic erasure of the Black population in South Africa have had generational ripple effects for Black people as a group. Providing individual reparations is insufficient to atone for such horrendous crimes. While this chapter is not a comprehensive overview of the South African TRC, it nonetheless poses questions about what *Ubuntu* means in the context of efforts at reconciling a nation through a skewed focus on individual harms, crimes, and reparations. How was *Ubuntu*, a discourse of relational collectivism, employed to render amnesty and reconciliation of and to individuals while neglecting equitable restoration of the collective? By focusing on Winnie Mandela, the chapter highlights the flaws of reconciliation that did little to redress the oppression and marginalization of women in nation-building discourses. She personifies the intersecting, gendered, and complex historical and systemic oppression of Black Africans in colonial and post-colonial nation-building discourses.

Winnie Mandela became an anomaly in South Africa the moment she ventured into the public sphere as a woman and a freedom fighter. As a woman, her high-level involvement in freedom fighting was unsettling. She refused, in her actions, to be domesticated into the background, deemed the place for women. Instead, she crossed the bifurcated lines of nation building and nationalism. On the one hand, she crossed the lines by venturing out of the subservient position Blacks were relegated to. She resisted on account of being a Black body beyond the "homelands" and townships. Second, she resisted a Black nationalist placement as a wife of the figurehead of the liberation movement and mother. She intentionally courted the "public domain."

In this way, Winnie Mandela signalled a need to decolonize gender politics within post-colonial and post-independent African states. She refused the compromise built on the labour and blood of women, whose biological reproductive labour the state relies on for continuity. She highlights a significant point about recognizing women's desire to define their citizenship for themselves, beyond the parochial domestic realm. Indeed, if Winnie Mandela's vilification and marginalization were amplified by the TRC, then her death raised more questions about how the TRC "dehistoricized and decontextualized apartheid through its focus on individuals."[37]

NOTES

1 Bonny Ibhawoh, "Beyond Retribution: Truth and Reconciliation in South Africa as Universal Paradigm for Restorative Transitional Justice," *Covenant University Journal of Politics and International Affairs* 2, no. 2 (2016); James L. Gibson, "The Contributions of Truth to Reconciliation: Lessons from South Africa," *Journal of Conflict Resolution* 50, no. 3 (2006): 409–32; Abena Asare, "The Ghanaian National Reconciliation Commission: Reparation in a Global Age," *The Global South* 2, no. 2 (2008): 31–53; Paul van Zyl, "Dilemmas of Transitional Justice: The Case of South Africa's Truth and Reconciliation Commission," *Journal of International Affairs* (1999): 647–67.

2 Ibhawoh, "Beyond Retribution"; Gibson, "The Contributions of Truth to Reconciliation"; Asare, "The Ghanaian National Reconciliation Commission"; Van Zyl, "Dilemmas of Transitional Justice."

3 Bonny Ibhawoh, "Human Rights and the Politics of Regime Legitimation in Africa," *Expanding Perspectives on Human Rights in Africa* 21 (2019): 21.

4 Asare, "The Ghanaian National Reconciliation Commission."

5 See Mahmood Mamdani, "Amnesty or Impunity? A Preliminary Critique of the Report of the Truth and Reconciliation Commission of South Africa (TRC)," *Diacritics* 32, no. 3/4 (2002): 33–59.

6 Mamdani, "Amnesty or Impunity?"

7 See Ali A. Mazrui, "The Reincarnation of the African State: A Triple Heritage in Transition from Precolonial Times," *Nouvelle série* 127/128 (1983): 114–27.

8 Mahmood Mamdani, *Citizen and Subject: Contemporary Africa and the Legacy of late Colonialism* (Princeton: Princeton University Press, 1996).

9 Nira Yuval-Davies, *Woman – Nation – State* (New York: Palgrave Macmillan, 1989).

10 Oyeronke Oyěwùmí, *The Invention of Women: Making an African Sense of Western Gender Discourses* (Minneapolis, MN: University of Minnesota Press, 1997).

11 Oyěwùmí, *The Invention of Women*.

12 Yuval-Davies, *Woman – Nation – State*.

13 Jonneke Koomen, "'Without These Women, the Tribunal Cannot Do Anything': The Politics of Witness Testimony on Sexual Violence at the International Criminal Tribunal for Rwanda," *Signs: Journal of Women in Culture and Society* 38, no. 2 (2013): 253–77.

14 Koomen, "'Without These Women, the Tribunal Cannot Do Anything'"; Helen Scanlon and Kelli Muddell, "Gender and Transitional Justice in

Africa: Progress and Prospects," *African Journal on Conflict Resolution* 9, no. 2 (2009).

15 Tutu quoted in Tim Murithi, "African Approaches to Building Peace and Social Solidarity," Accord, 25 September 2006, www.accord.org.za/ajcr-issues/african-approaches-to-building-peace-and-social-solidarity/.

16 This is a popular Akan folkloric adage usually represented by a symbol of a bird looking and reaching around its tail.

17 Sierra Leone TRC report (https://www.sierraleonetrc.org/), my emphasis.

18 Nigeria, Truth Commission: Human Rights Violations Investigation Commission (2002), 3.

19 Anthony Kwame Appiah, *In My Father's House: Africa in the Philosophy of Culture* (Oxford: Oxford University Press, 1992).

20 Gayatri Chakravorty Spivak, *In Other Worlds: Essays in Cultural Politics* (New York: Routledge, 1987).

21 Oyěwùmí, *The Invention of Women.*

22 Mamdani, "Amnesty or Impunity?"

23 South Africa's TRC Final Report, 135, (https://www.sierraleonetrc.org/), my emphasis.

24 "Who Was South Africa's Winnie Mandela?" Racism News | Al Jazeera (website), 3 April 2018, www.aljazeera.com/news/2018/04/south-africa-winnie-mandela-180402161736297.html.

25 Shireen Hassim, "Not just Nelson's Wife: Winnie Madikizela-Mandela, Violence and Radicalism in South Africa," *Journal of Southern African Studies* 44, no. 5 (2018): 898. My emphasis.

26 Oyěwùmí, *The Invention of Women.*

27 See Shireen Hassim, "The Impossible Contract: The Political and Private Marriage of Nelson and Winnie Mandela," *Journal of Southern African Studies* 45, no. 6 (2019): 1151–71; Sisonke Msimang, *The Resurrection of Winnie Mandela* (Johannesburg: Jonathan Ball Publishers, 2018).

28 *Winnie,* directed by Pascale Lamche (2017; film), 28:15.

29 Hassim, "The Impossible Contract," 1159.

30 *In Her Own Words: Winnie Madikizela-Mandela* (W.M.M.), An Ichikowitz Family Foundation Initiative. The African Oral History Archive, n.d., www.youtube.com/watch?v=kmNZK8D1EgQ.

31 See, Obioma Nnaemeka, "Nego-feminism: Theorizing, Practicing, and Pruning Africa's Way," *Signs: Journal of Women in Culture and Society* 29, no. 2 (2004): 357–85; Gertrude Mianda, "Féminisme africain: divergences ou convergences des discours?," *Présence africaine* 155 (1997): 87–99; Filomina Chioma Steady, "African Feminism: A Worldwide Perspective," in *Women in Africa and the African Diaspora,*

ed. Rosalyn Terborg-Penn, Sharon Harley, and Andrea Benton Rushing
(Washington, DC: Howard University Press, 1987), 3–24.

32 W.M.M., n.d., https://www.youtube.com/watch?v=kmNZK8D1EgQ.

33 "The Nobel Peace Prize," NobelPrize.org, 1993.

34 News 24, "Stompie Seipei's mother" YouTube, 10 April 2018, www.
news24.com/news24/southafrica/news/stompie-seipeis-mother-visits-
house-of-winnie-madikizela-mandela-20180410; other media outlets
reported on madam Seipei's attendance of Winnie's funeral. See SABC
News, "Stompie's Mother Arrives"; "Stompie's Mother Signs
Condolence."

35 Peter Hawthorne, "South Africa: Mugger of a Nation?" *Time*,
8 December 1997, https://content.time.com/time/subscriber/
article/0,33009,987496,00.html.

36 Nancy Fraser, "From Redistribution to Recognition? Dilemmas of Justice
in a "Post-socialist' Age," *New Left Review* (1995): 68; Iris M. Young,
Justice and the Politics of Difference (Princeton: Princeton University
Press, 2011).

37 Mamdani, "Amnesty or Impunity?" 57.

SECTION TWO

Methods and Processes

Whites and the South African Truth and Reconciliation Commission

Roger Southall

White settlers in Africa had consistently been fearful of Black major-ity rule. Its arrival in Algeria, Kenya, and Rhodesia heralded the mass departure of whites. In British Africa, especially, whites who did not return "home" to Britain looked for new pastures, the majority of them leaving for the former dominions of Canada, Australia, and New Zealand. However, many – especially white Rhodesians fleeing liberation war – opted to move to South Africa, where the apartheid regime gave them a hearty welcome and where, it seemed to many, the then government was strong enough to resist the tide of decolo-nization. Yet by the mid-1980s, it was becoming increasingly clear that "white South Africa" was increasingly vulnerable, and unlike in Africa's other settler colonies, the large majority of whites had thought of themselves as permanent and had no place else to run.

Surveys conducted at this time indicate that while whites remained strongly opposed to Black majority rule, their fears were reinforced by government propaganda and perceptions of the con-sequences of Black rule in other parts of Africa. In 1987, the Human Sciences Research Council reported that 75% of whites expected their physical safety would be threatened under Black rule, 81% expected their living standards would decline, 86% expected that whites would be discriminated against, 80% that law and order would not be maintained, and a similar 80% that property would no longer be safe. Despite these stridently negative feelings, the same survey reported that 63% of white respondents thought the arrival of Black majority rule was inevitable. This supports a poll conducted for the London *Times* in 1986 that found 72% of whites believed apartheid would be gone within ten years.[1] Nor should we discount indications that there were growing doubts among whites not only about the practicality but also the justice of apartheid. The fact that white politics was becoming more fluid within both Afrikaner and English-speaking communities meant that electoral support for established parties had to be earned, rather than simply being a result of ethnic inheritance and static party divisions based on language.

Mounting doubts about the durability of the regime, especially but far from exclusively among English-speaking whites, had provided a platform for F.W. de Klerk to enter negotiations with the African National Congress (ANC). Similarly, the accompanying fears about the consequences of Black majority rule ensured that whites would extend the gospel of reconciliation – as preached most notably by Nelson Mandela – a warm, if still highly cautious, welcome. Relatively few whites proceeded to vote for the ANC in the first democratic election, but there was no doubting the hero worship accorded Mandela as president.[2] Surprise that the ANC was not vengeful was accompanied by a massive sense of relief. After years of being condemned as outcasts by the outside world, whites were now enabled to bask in the feel-good aura of rainbowism. In 1994, South Africa was a land of hope, for white as well as Black. Even so, there were signs aplenty that whites' responsibility for apartheid could not simply be ignored and wished away. There was no alternative, even amid the warm glow of rainbowism, but for whites to confront the past. In turn, this raised two issues.

The immediate forum for exploring these issues was provided by the Truth and Reconciliation Commission (TRC). Established as an integral component of the transition, this commission sat between December 1995 and October 1988, before handing over the first five volumes of its findings to the new government. (Another two volumes followed later.) Today, even while it has been subjected to extensive criticism, the TRC is widely acclaimed as having made a major contribution not only to the holding of similar bodies internationally but also as having eased South Africa's transition to democracy.[3] No attempt is made here to review what amounts to a vast literature. Instead, what follows is an outline of how the white minority, most especially those connected to the pre-1994 regime, responded to the opportunity to engage with the TRC and accept responsibility for abuses against human rights committed under apartheid.[4]

THE TRC

Transitions to democracy take place in a wide variety of circumstances, ranging from the total defeat of one party to conflict by another (as occurred in Germany in 1945) to situations where parties to conflict conclude that the costs of continuing the conflict outweigh the benefits (as in South Africa by the early 1990s). An extensive literature on democratic transitions is constructed around the dynamics of such processes, its "realistic" thrust being that successful transitions are required to be pragmatic as much as idealistic and to engage in the search for viable "second-best" solutions, which reflect the particularities of power differentials in local conditions.[5] Building upon this foundation, the idea of transitional justice proposes that transitions to democracy are likely to be successful only to the extent that they incorporate significant efforts to actively reconcile previously conflicting parties.

The fundamental proposition of transitional justice theory is that societies which have experienced deliberately inflicted traumas, such as genocide or extreme assaults on human rights, need to "confront their past" if a successful transition from authoritarian rule to democracy or from violent conflict to peace is to be achieved.[6] The brutality of humans toward each other is as old as history, yet serious attempts to address human rights violations as a foundation for the construction of democracy date back only to the Allies' defeat of Nazi Germany and Imperial Japan following the Second World War. These efforts were seriously compromised by the changing political priorities of the victors in the immediate aftermath of the war and had contradictory outcomes.[7] Nonetheless, the lessons learned from those tumultuous years were extensively drawn upon during the 1980s and 1990s, a period when a series of countries in Latin America and Southern Europe were undergoing transitions away from authoritarian (often military) rule, and countries in Eastern Europe from communist rule.

Broadly speaking, reconciliation and reconstruction were prioritized over the will for revenge and the attendant danger of transitions from authoritarianism sparking a civil war. In establishing the TRC,

South Africa was to join this pack, its example subsequently to be followed by a significant number of other countries in Africa. The TRC was a response to the particularities of South Africa's negotiated transition and the insights those South Africans who were pressing for accountability drew from other nations' experiments with "dealing with the past."

There had been strong resistance to accountability by the National Party (NP) government. Indeed, it had made vigorous efforts to secure the right to grant amnesty for human rights offences to members of the security forces and others whom it wanted to protect.[8] However, these did not withstand the negotiation process, which, after numerous interruptions and tough bargaining, culminated in the drawing up and ratification of the Interim Constitution on 18 November 1993. This specified that it would be left for a democratically elected government to decide about how amnesty might be granted. The specific proposal for a truth commission was put forward by Dullah Omar, the minister of justice, and was subsequently translated into law by the Promotion of National Unity and Reconciliation Act in July 1995.[9]

The TRC formally convened in December 1995. Its seventeen full-time commissioners, headed by Archbishop Emeritus Desmond Tutu, were required to be "fit and proper persons who are impartial and do not have a high political profile" and came from a wide range of professions and occupations. They were allocated to the three committees (for Reparations and Rehabilitation or RRC, Amnesty, and Human Rights Violations) stipulated by the enabling legislation. Supported by a substantial backroom staff and a research department headed by Charles Villa-Vicencio, the TRC established itself across regional centres in Johannesburg, Durban, and East London.

The commission was charged with: (i) establishing "as complete a picture as possible of the causes, nature and extent of the gross violations of human rights committed between 1 March 1960 and 10 May 1994"; (ii) "facilitating the grant of amnesty to persons who made full disclosure of all the relevant facts relating to acts associated with a political objective" and who complied with other requirements laid down in the Act; (iii) "establishing and making known the fate of victims and whereabouts of victims" by giving them the opportunity to relate the accounts of the violations they had suffered, and by making recommendations for reparations for victims; and (iv) compiling a report of its activities and findings and providing "recommendations of measures to prevent the future violation of human rights."[10]

The TRC was to engage in a strategy of maximum publicity. This was a break with previous truth commissions, which had conducted private investigations and only then produced reports for public consumption. Its operations were, therefore, characterized by transparency, open to all to attend its proceedings, and the TRC sought to encourage extensive citizen participation through extraordinarily widespread coverage in the media (television and radio as well as newspapers).[11]

Victims were invited to provide testimony of the violations of their human rights. Of the 22,000 victims who provided statements, some 2,000 offered their testimonies to the Human Rights Committee's numerous public hearings. These were held around the country and conducted in the full glare of the media. It was a phase when, according to one account, "a religious and therapeutic sense of reconciliation" through "truth-telling" prevailed.[12] Statements were subjected to careful verification and corroboration, and if specific alleged perpetrators were named, they had a right to be informed, were given an opportunity to respond, and might be invited to apply for amnesty.

As the public hearings drew to a close, the Amnesty Committee's proceedings became central, with a corresponding shift from storytelling to fact-finding and legal concerns with due process. Individual perpetrators (not parties, public bodies, or organizations) were required to submit applications for amnesty and had to demonstrate that their violations were politically motivated, and they had fully disclosed their nature and extent. The committee received some 7,000 applications, of which 1,793 were heard in public hearings.[13]

Third, the RRC undertook the complex task of elucidating the concept of reparation and turning it into some form of reality. Considerable attention was paid to the notion of symbolic reparations (in the form of memorials), programs devised to promote healing, and thought given to the potential for reparations at the community level. However, the major burden of the committee's work revolved around the issue of financial reparation. Ultimately, it decided that all those recognized as victims by the commission could apply for financial help, although in recognition of competing calls upon state funds, the amounts of recompense it recommended were extremely modest.[14]

The final stage of the TRC's work was the writing of its final report. Its first five volumes were handed over to the government in October 1998. However, these were met with a blistering response from the ANC, which sought a court interdict preventing publication of any part of the final report that implicated the ANC in human rights abuses until the TRC had considered a submission from the party. The court rejected the ANC's bid, but this did not prevent President Thabo Mbeki from attacking the commission for its stance of "equivalence" in its evaluation of the conduct of the different parties, arguing that actions taken by the liberation movement, which had resulted in the loss of human life or violations of human rights, could not be fairly compared to the worse violations conducted by an immoral and illegitimate regime. This fractious finale to the TRC's work had deleterious consequences, most notably for those who should have been primary beneficiaries of the TRC's recommendations.[15] Payment of reparations was delayed for some five years, and then the amount paid – a once-off payment of R30,000 – was much less than the recommended amount.[16] This prefaced a much wider failure by the ANC government to effect reparations to victims of apartheid.[17]

It is a tribute to the wider significance of the South African TRC that it has attracted extensive criticism, scholars attesting widely to the limitations in its terms of reference (which by-passed how apartheid was rooted in the long past),[18] flaws in and biases of its processes,[19] and its inability to ensure the payments of reparations,[20] as well as querying whether it actually contributed positively to "nation building," especially given the limited enthusiasm of the post-1994 government for prosecuting perpetrators who had not applied for amnesty.[21] Despite these and other controversies, as the introductory chapter to this volume suggests, the TRC remains highly regarded as offering a benchmark as to how other such commissions in other countries are judged. In this vein, over a decade after its work had been concluded (bar continuing exhumations), John Daniel, a political scientist and former researcher at the TRC, offered a broadly positive assessment of the commission's achievements, which provides a useful framework for discussing the specific issue at hand here.

First, argued Daniel, although the TRC was unable to uncover the entire "truth" about apartheid, "much truth was established"; second, by rendering the granting of amnesty conditional on full disclosure, it made a major contribution to the theory and practice of transitional justice; third, its exposures of state brutality and criminality neutralized a potential right-wing threat to democracy; fourth, it further contributed by "mainstreaming a reconciliation narrative as an instrument of nation-building."[22] Daniel's judgments provide a useful framework for evaluating the extent to which whites embraced the TRC and what effect it may have had on them.

AMNESTY AND THE DEMOBILIZATION
OF THE RIGHT WING

The grant of amnesty to perpetrators of human rights offences had been deemed necessary to secure the success of transitions to democracy across a swathe of countries in Latin America and Eastern Europe. Likewise, there were influential figures in South Africa, amongst whom Archbishop Desmond Tutu was the most prominent, who had contended that the offer of amnesty would be a necessary ingredient of the democratic transition. This flew in the face of considerable opposition from many who opposed such a crucial concession to the apartheid government. However, the genius of the Promotion of National Unity and Reconciliation Act was its countering opposition from both left and right by rendering any grant of amnesty conditional on applicants making full disclosure of their criminal actions.[23]

It was those whites who had actively committed politically motivated crimes or delicts (civil wrongs) on behalf of the apartheid state who were invited to apply for amnesty subject to the conditions prescribed by the TRC. The amnesty process did not require perpetrators to show remorse for their past actions, to apologize, or to take responsibility for their criminal deeds. All that was required was that they offer full disclosure of their crimes and prove that they were politically motivated (which in practice meant that they had been authorized by a political authority or movement). The logical consequence was that perpetrators of human rights offences who did offer full disclosure were enabled to walk free without taking any responsibility for the suffering they had caused. Furthermore, the grant of amnesty removed the risk that the perpetrator could be the subject of civil claims. Further still, it did not exclude those who were amnestied from occupying public office (lustration), nor did it impose any obligation upon them to make any compensatory contribution to society.

These conditions came as a disappointment to many who felt that remorse or apology was fundamental to the process of reconciliation.[24] The standard response to such criticism, one which Archbishop Tutu employed, was that however distasteful, amnesty was a price worth paying if it served to secure the necessary political compromises to bring about peace.[25] Yet, Tutu was hopeful that the conditional amnesty on offer would lower the costs of amnesty as it had been implemented in other countries. It would not be blanket amnesty offered for undisclosed crimes, nor would it be amnesty granted by criminalized governments to themselves. Instead, it would be granted only by individual application, subject to legislative criteria, and administered impartially by a quasi-judicial committee headed by judges in a process that would offer a voice to victims. "It was thus a process which seemed to promise not secrecy, impunity, and frustration for victims – typical of so many amnesties – but disclosure and at least some form of accountability and redress." Although it was clearly desirable that disclosure be accompanied by remorse, this was too idealistic a condition to impose, and as Villa-Vicencio has observed, might well have inhibited some of the "more resolute and proud perpetrators" from making disclosures.[26]

The major problem for the TRC was that relatively few of those who had committed crimes on behalf of apartheid came forward. In total, there were just 7,000 applications for amnesty. This compared with some 22,000 victims' statements complaining about human rights violations, while in many cases perpetrators asked for amnesty for crimes about which no complaint had been made. Furthermore, 65% of those who applied for amnesty were already in custody at the time of their application, and of the rest, some had already completed a sentence. As Catherine Jenkins remarks, this meant that in practice, the Amnesty Committee served as a de facto parole board for thousands of prisoners who had already served part or all of their sentences for acts which they claimed had been committed for political reasons (although a large number of these claims were dismissed as lacking merit).[27]

The majority of applications for amnesty were made by members of the liberation movements rather than by members of the apartheid-era security apparatus. Only 293 amnesty applications were received from serving or former members of the security services, 256 from serving or former members of the police, and just 31 from members or former members of the South African Defence Force. As Jenkins further remarks, if these figures were taken at face value, it would seem that the crimes of the apartheid era were committed predominantly by the liberation movements, a conclusion which would be "absurd." In any case, some applications were for quite minor offences, such as illegal possession of a firearm.

Even more problematic was that the overwhelming majority of amnesty applications for crimes committed on behalf of apartheid were mostly made by "foot soldiers" of the apartheid regime rather than by those directing them. While those who applied from the security forces did include police commissioners and generals, most of the latter who could and should have applied chose not to. Politicians were not any more forthcoming. Only two apartheid-era cabinet ministers, Adriaan Vlok, a former minister of police, and Piet Koornhof, most recently minister of co-operation and development (formerly known as Bantu affairs), made applications for amnesty. In contrast, former president P.W. Botha proved resolute in his defiance of the TRC, declining to appear before it or answer written questions. Ultimately, he was dragged to court and found guilty of contravening sections of the Promotion of National Unity and Reconciliation Act, only for him to win an appeal on a technicality, at which point, the TRC gave up.

Former president de Klerk was more co-operative and appeared before the TRC in August 1996. However, he was insistent that within his "knowledge and experience," the government of which he had been a part had never authorized "assassination, murder, torture, rape, assault of the like," and that he personally had never authorized or ordered any such action. Later, when given notice of findings made by the TRC against him, he resorted to court action to prevent their publication. Under legal advice, the commission opted to redact its findings from its final report (which had already been printed). Subsequently, it reached an agreement with de Klerk to make a revised finding, published in volume 6 of the report – one of the two volumes which made up the "codicil" presented to President Mbeki in March 2003.[28]

The implication of the amnesty process was that those who had not applied or applicants who had been denied amnesty by the commission would be liable to prosecution. However, in practice, there was very limited action taken in this regard. The reasons for this have been well rehearsed. Despite concern that a failure to launch

prosecutions risked undermining the purpose and reputation of the
TRC, the authorities soon found themselves confronting numerous
dilemmas and difficulties.

A first was that although the required evidence to prosecute foot
soldiers would be more easily available (because victims could often
name or recognize those who had abused them), it would be much
more difficult to pursue those who had been politically responsible for
setting policies, giving orders, or tacitly encouraging actions by subordinates that led to human rights offences. However more practical the
process, this would be a less than satisfactory outcome. An alternative
would have been to take a few high-profile, symbolic cases to trial.
Apart from the problem of which particular individuals should be
pursued and which left alone, there was always the danger that resulting court cases might become pilloried as politically driven.

Furthermore, the prosecution authorities were confronted by the
dilemma of impartiality. If they prosecuted high-ranking members
of the security establishment, would this provoke a furious counter-
reaction from lawyers representing the latter, triggering the bringing
of civil claims against the ANC leadership and operatives? Beyond
that, there was the sheer difficulty of accumulating the weight of
evidence required to secure convictions, especially in the cases of
the highest-ranking members of the apartheid security establishment
and politicians, many of whom had gone to remarkable lengths to
cover their tracks to ensure "plausible deniability." In any case,
there was also the matter of finance, as prosecutions were likely to
be exorbitantly costly, and it might be claimed that such expenditure
would come at the cost of social needs.

The most high-profile prosecution of a perpetrator was that of
Eugene de Kock, a colonel in the police and commander of the notorious Vlakplaas counter-insurgency group, which had functioned as
a paramilitary squad, executing anti-apartheid activists or torturing
them. When de Kock appeared before the TRC, he not only revealed
his involvement in ANC deaths but also testified to the involvement
of political leaders, inclusive of then president de Klerk. Although
he was granted amnesty for some fifty offences, he was denied it for
his involvement in murders of victims who had had no links to the
liberation movements. He was subsequently tried for these and was
sentenced to 212 years in prison in 1996.[29]

The denial of amnesty to de Kock, and his subsequent conviction, is likely to have discouraged other low- and middle-ranking

members of the apartheid security services from appearing before the TRC. Even were they to admit to heinous wrongdoing, there was always risk that they would be denied amnesty and their superiors would be happy to hang them out to dry. In the end, there were very few successful prosecutions.

The difficulties of pursuing high-profile prosecutions were brought home by two spectacular failures to secure convictions. The first was in the case of former defence minister Magnus Malan and nineteen co-accused. They had pleaded not guilty to charges of murder and attempted murder relating to the massacre of thirteen people in KwaMakhutha township south of Durban in 1987. All were to be acquitted. The second case was that of Wouter Basson, the head of the apartheid state's chemical biological warfare program. He had appeared before the TRC, which had recommended that he should be put on trial. He was subsequently to face 67 charges, including 229 murders, but after a trial of some thirty months, he was also acquitted. When the state sought to have the judgment overturned in the Supreme Court, and this failed, it appealed to the Constitutional Court, which found it in its favour, but subsequently the National Prosecuting Authority opted not to pursue the case further.

In both of these cases, the failure to secure convictions was ascribed to unsympathetic judges, hold-overs from the apartheid era, one of whom (in the Basson case) refused to grant key state witnesses immunity from prosecution, thus dissuading them from co-operating with the prosecuting authorities. These failures to secure convictions appear to have reinforced a general reluctance of the democratic government to prosecute perpetrators. Instead, there are suggestions that behind the scenes there was dealing between the ANC leadership and the former security establishment to implement a de facto general amnesty, although it has continued to be denied to a number of convicted prisoners, notably those associated with the far right.[30] Further prosecutions have tended to come as a result of determined private initiatives to secure justice.[31]

Even though few perpetrators faced prosecution, applications for amnesty did not come without cost. The requirement of full disclosure meant that applicants could not obtain amnesty if they refused to acknowledge an illegal act to the commission, and the publicity surrounding the amnesty hearings might amount to a "public shaming." Full disclosure required applicants to provide chapter and verse of their involvement in horrific deeds in often appalling detail amid the full glare of publicity. Revelations of brutal wrongdoing by ordinary state functionaries, who might be regarded as decent and hard-working individuals within their families and immediate communities, could make considerable psychological demands on individual perpetrators. Asked why he himself had not applied for amnesty, one state witness in the trial of Wouter Basson responded that the process would have been too humiliating. Jenkins, therefore, argues that even if the device of conditional amnesty was unable to exact legal accountability, it was capable of achieving moral and social accountability. Even so, she acknowledges that in practice, the work of the Amnesty Committee was beset by limitations.

Members of the apartheid state's security forces were generally reluctant to apply for amnesty, assessing the risk of applying against the likelihood of their being prosecuted. Indeed, the risks of their prosecution had been much reduced by the systematic destruction by the former government and its agents of mountains of records relating to the police, defence force, and national intelligence agencies, all of which hugely impeded the capacity of the TRC to reconstruct the past and hold individuals to account.[32] Indeed, this continued after 1994, in defiance of the new government's instructions. Aware that their tracks had been obliterated, most agents of the former regime opted to keep their heads down, although some individuals managed to avoid the risk of prosecution by turning state witness in the trials of others, thus guaranteeing themselves indemnity from the risk of prosecution. Yet, others appear to have calculated that the advantages of securing amnesty from prosecution might be outweighed by the risk of applicants launching civil claims against them, with all the financial cost this might incur.

Jenkins defends the Amnesty Committee against the charge that it was "perpetrator friendly," arguing that its legal limitations had been imposed by politicians. Furthermore, the committee had to operate within a difficult political context, it lacked adequate investigatory resources, and in many ways had to learn as it proceeded. Jenkins also reminds us that the TRC was pioneering a new way of dealing with past human rights abuses while having to respond to the constraints and demands of negotiated peacemaking.[33] Additionally, the committee's mission and processes faced concerted resistance from members of the former government, their security forces, and the white right.

That less than 600 members of the former security establishment applied for amnesty testifies to the extent of this hostility to the TRC.

Yet as Daniel observes, the proceedings of the TRC brought forth an "avalanche of revelations – mainly from the lips of apartheid operatives seeking amnesty" – about killings and other atrocities committed by the former regime.[34] These proved devastating to the morale and reputation of the NP and former security services, many of whom retreated into dark corners and sought to hide from public view. According to Madeleine Fullard and Nicky Rousseau, the exposure of shocking deeds and brutally callous behaviour by perpetrators "extinguished the possibility of ongoing denial" and decimated "the moral underpinning of the NP and right-wing." It thereby served to de-legitimize the entire apartheid project and destroy the façade of legalism to which the apartheid state had clung.[35] It extinguished any remaining possibility of a right-wing coup. Although it left some peculiarly unpleasant individuals at large, the overwhelming majority subsequently kept their heads firmly down and out of the limelight.

For all its flaws and imperfections, therefore, the TRC ensured that thereafter, few members of the former establishment were prepared to proclaim their support for the politics of the past. The attempt by the NP after 1994 to rebrand itself as the New National Party failed miserably to provide the ground for its political survival, and within a few years, it was dead, its membership absorbed into the ranks of other political parties. Few members of the apartheid establishment now wanted to admit their support for the politics of the past, and so many whites now chose to deny that they might have voted for the NP that it became a matter of wonder how the NP had managed to win any elections at all! Yet to what extent did this imply that whites as a whole bought the project of reconciliation and state building?

WHITES AND RECONCILIATION

The TRC Act was guided by the notion of "restorative justice" as its foundation for both its truth-seeking and reconciliation processes. According to Villa-Vicencio, this justice sought to reincorporate the perpetrator into society while restoring the dignity and well-being of the victim. He also accepts that this was a statement of the ideal, and he goes on to concede that the commission's realizable goals were "simple coexistence, a reduction in revenge killing, and the creation of a climate where former enemies can sit down together and negotiate (sometimes in anger) the creation of a better society for all." Yet, as Martha Minow has observed, truth commissions aspire to do more than that, for they also seek to encourage reflection on the past by "bystanders," those who were not directly perpetrators or victims but who had been indirectly affected by violence and trauma or who, by inaction, had been complicit in it. From this perspective, the object of the commission was not merely to heal victims but to "reconcile opposing groups" in a context where they were "poised to reclaim or restart a nation under terms conducive to democracy."

The TRC was to come under strong attack from critics on the grounds that it had focused too narrowly upon individual victims and individual perpetrators to the unwarranted exclusion of examination of some of the worst injustices of apartheid, such as the implementation of the pass laws, land seizures, and forced removals as gross violations of human rights.[36] While acknowledging the moral force of such critiques, John Daniel responded that the TRC was bound by its terms of reference, as laid down by its founding Act.[37] Supporting Daniel's interpretation, André du Toit, a University of Cape Town professor of political studies who had been deeply, albeit indirectly, involved with the commission, argued that the focus on individual gross human rights violations had enabled the TRC to highlight the extent and brutality of these political atrocities and to establish a baseline of historical truth in public consciousness which will not be easily eradicated or denied. This conclusion is shared by others. Reflecting on her experiences as one of the TRC's commissioners, Mary Burton has similarly argued that the public admissions of crimes by applicants, notably white policemen and soldiers, contributed to encouraging the white sector of South African society to begin addressing the truth of their involvement in maintaining the violence of the apartheid system.[38] At a less exalted, intensely personal level, Villa-Vicencio cites an eighty-year-old Afrikaner lady, who had been loyal to the NP all her life, as responding to the confessions of deliberate suffering inflicted on victims by commenting, "I did not know that my people could have done such terrible things."[39]

The extent to which whites as a collective were complicit in apartheid will remain a matter for debate by historians, philosophers, theologians, and others for the foreseeable future.[40] It is a debate which is unlikely to be easily resolved. More likely, there

can be agreement around the suggestion that, in Minow's termi-
nology, the majority of whites – those "ordinary whites" who
were not deeply embroiled in the apartheid state machinery – were
"bystanders." They "stood by" while crimes were committed in
their name. By implication, some might have justified them perhaps as regrettable but necessary. Some might have averted their
eyes, choosing not to acknowledge them. Some will have been gen-
uinely ignorant or have pleaded ignorance, claiming that they did
not know they were happening. Whatever their position, it would
seem that, despite what critics thought to be the unjustifiably narrow focus of the TRC's terms of reference, exposure of the extent
and brutal nature of gross human rights violations by the apartheid state and its henchmen minimized (if it did not eliminate) the
grounds for denial. This, in turn, poses the question of the effect
the TRC may have had in convincing whites of the rightness or wisdom of engaging in reconciliation.

In retrospect, the immediate impact of the TRC's revelations seem
to have been more ambiguous than Burton's broad conclusion suggests. That the TRC massively narrowed the scope for denial is not
in doubt, yet the extent and nature of its impact on whites remains
difficult to assess. What we do know is.that there was a considerable
disappointment on the part of the commission itself to the white
response to its work. Indeed, in its final report, it argued that "the
white community often seemed either indifferent or plainly hostile"
to its work and that "with rare individual exceptions, the response
of the former state, its leaders, institutions, and the predominant
organs of civil society of that era was to hedge and obfuscate," with
few individuals grasping "the olive branch of full disclosure." To be
sure, a Register of Reconciliation created by the TRC for people to
write their reactions even if they were not victims or applicants for
amnesty received a flood of comments, many from people admitting
that they should have done more to resist apartheid. As bystanders,
they were responding positively to the opportunity for reconciliation.
Presumably, many of these respondents were whites. Nonetheless,
there were too few signings for Archbishop Tutu's liking, and six
months before the register was due to be closed, he made a heartfelt
plea for more participation and signing by whites.[41]

If it was not due to their outright hostility, failure by white individuals to sign the register or otherwise engage openly and actively
in reconciliation probably followed from a mix of motives and

opportunities. Many may have been willing but unable to sign given travel and distances involved;[42] some may have been too embarrassed; some, given the social apartness which apartheid engendered between the races, may have felt too awkward to cross-cultural boundaries and/or geographical spaces separating white from Black communities. Nonetheless, the poor response by whites seemed to indicate a widespread reluctance to take responsibility for the past.

This was confirmed by the failure of collectivities dominated by whites to admit their complicity with apartheid. Complicity was not the same as the commitment of a legal wrong associated with a political objective. Accordingly, it was always unlikely that individual professionals would have had any reason to apply for amnesty, and very few did. A few individual judges sought amnesty for their personal acts performed in the apartheid courts. A few even signed a document acknowledging that the judiciary as an institution had enforced apartheid and had failed to protect people from torture. Overall, however, there was an almost total failure by professional bodies (such as those of lawyers, doctors, and journalists), business, and bodies such as the leading universities to acknowledge the extent to which they had actively benefited from apartheid, even though they were rhetorically eager to subscribe to visions of reconciliation. It is, therefore, difficult to disagree with Katherine Mack's judgment that, in essence, "the liberal individualism that underlay the TRC's rhetoric of accountability" effectively let collectivities off the hook.[43] The TRC's powers and processes were not designed to require collective reflection, far less to elicit collective apologies.

Assessing the success or otherwise of the commission in advancing the cause of reconciliation goes far beyond the extent to which it received buy-in from whites as a whole. Numerous commentaries prioritize the extent to which it facilitated the process of healing, of getting over the trauma of apartheid, by victims and their families. Nonetheless, the response of whites to the TRC, the extent to which it was positive or negative, remains an important criterion of its achievement in the building of a democratic state.

A valuable overview of how whites were dealing with the past, compiled by Gunnar Theissen on behalf of the Centre for the Study of Violence and Reconciliation, was published in 1997 after the TRC had been established but before it had finalized its report and made its recommendations.[44] Basing itself upon a mix of its own survey findings with those of other previous surveys, it provided unambiguous evidence that support for apartheid among whites of all backgrounds had been strong. Not only had the NP enjoyed majority support among whites in all elections since 1958, but also large majorities had supported "fundamental structures" of apartheid such as separate voters' rolls (79%), the homeland policy (76%), group areas (89%), the Immorality Act (61%) and the Mixed Marriages Act (61%). Likewise, during the 1970s and 1980s, there had been overwhelming support among whites for the NP government's actions against "terrorism" (89% supported the SADF's attacks on the suburbs of Maputo in 1983), and 85% backed stronger action against the ANC in 1988. Although there was unease, especially among English-speaking South Africans with human rights violations, there was still a comfortable majority (57%) for detention without trial for suspected violators of security laws as late as 1989.

Given these findings, it was not surprising that when surveyed in 1995, 58% of whites were unhappy with the new democratic political system, and white support for policies which would promote socio-economic justice (opening white schools to Black people, preferential employment for Black individuals in the public service, and redistribution of land for Black communities) was consistently less than 50%. Similarly, support for the TRC among whites was decidedly mixed. In 1992, 60% of all South Africans backed the idea of a commission to investigate crimes committed under the previous government, but only 39% of whites. Likewise, whereas in 1995, 72% of Black South Africans felt that the TRC would uncover what really happened with regard to human rights violations, the prevailing view toward the commission among whites (63%) was one of mistrust. Additionally, support for amnesty for human rights violators among whites (56%) was higher than their support for the investigation of politically motivated human rights investigations.[45] Subsequently, after the TRC had submitted its report in 1998, 39% of whites felt that the TRC had failed in its mission to expose the truth about past human rights abuses in contrast to just 5% of Black South Africans.[46]

These and a host of other findings raised considerable doubts about whether whites were prepared to take responsibility for and make amends for the injustices inflicted upon Black South Africans in the past. Nonetheless, Theissen was at pains to stress that "the transition to a new democratic order" was likely to be a lengthy process and that "a glib condemnation of white South Africans should be avoided." It was unrealistic to imagine that the death of apartheid would be accompanied by the instantaneous creation of a democratic political culture – among Black as well as white South Africans. It had taken some twenty years for a democratic political culture, sustained by an "economic miracle," to take root in postwar West Germany, and only then because of the demand of a generation of Germans born after the war for greater accountability regarding the country's dark past. Theissen, therefore, rested his hopes for a new democratic culture among whites upon "a nascent new political generation of white South Africans who are significantly more critical of apartheid and more accepting of the new democracy than the older generation."[47] As in West Germany, the younger generation was less burdened by feelings of guilt and more easily able to distance themselves from apartheid and its values. "In the long run," therefore, it seemed likely that "the political culture of white South Africans (would) become more democratic and non-racial as more members of the 'rainbow generation' start(ed) to occupy positions in society."[48]

Space is too short to discuss in detail the extent to which Theissen's optimism was justified. However, it is worth noting that recently conducted research using nationally conducted focus groups, supported by reference to regular surveys conducted by the Institute for Reconciliation and Justice, indicates that, in general, his prediction about the whites becoming more democratic and accepting of non-racialism has been borne out by reality, albeit with considerable qualifications. Whites now accept the premises of democracy (if only because they see no other realistic alternative); and they accept the moral wrongfulness of apartheid and accept that apartheid was a crime against humanity. What they continue to wrestle with is the issue of complicity and acceptance of guilt, indicating a pronounced tendency to shuffle the blame for atrocities on to the political leaders and security forces.[49] This indicates the continuing challenge of reconciling the white minority to the broader South African nation.

NOTES

This chapter draws heavily on the chapter titled, "Securing the Transition? Whites and the TRC," in my book *Whites and Democracy in South Africa* (Woodbridge, Suffolk: James Currey; Stellenbosch: African Sun Media, 2022).

1 Cited in Robert Schrire, *Adapt or Die: The End of White Politics in South Africa* (Ford Foundation-Foreign Policy Association, 1991), 27–8.

2 On the construction of Mandela as an icon of the new South Africa, see Tom Lodge, *Mandela: A Critical Life* (Oxford: Oxford University Press, 2006).

3 See the introduction to this volume: Bonny Ibhawoh, Sylvia Bawa, and Jasper Abembia Ayelazuno, "Truth Commissions and the Politics of State Building."

4 See also Roger Southall, "'Looking Back': Whites and the TRC Today," in *Whites and Democracy in South Africa* (Woodbridge, Suffolk: James Currey; Stellenbosch: African Sun Media, 2022), for how whites view the TRC as a process some two decades after it presented its findings.

5 See, for instance, Guillermo O'Donnell, Philippe Schmitter, and Laurence Whitehead, *Transitions from Authoritarian Rule: Comparative Perspectives* (Baltimore: Johns Hopkins University Press, 1986); Gerardo Munck, "Democratic Transitions in Comparative Perspective," *Comparative Politics* 26, no. 3 (1994): 355–75; Kathryn Stoner and Michael McFaul, eds, *Transitions to Democracy: A Comparative Perspective* (Baltimore: Johns Hopkins University Press, 2013).

6 See *inter alia* Cheryl Lawther, Luke Moffett, and Dov Jacobs, eds, *Research Handbook on Transitional Justice* (Cheltenham, UK: Edward Elgar Publishing, 2017).

7 Ian Buruma, *The Wages of Guilt: Memories of War in Germany and Japan* (New York: Farrar Straus Giroux, 1994); Mark Mazower, *Dark Continent: Europe's Twentieth Century* (London: Penguin, 1998), 232–40.

8 Notably by passage of the Indemnity Act of 1990 and the Further Indemnity Act in 1992.

9 How the specific amnesty provisions were arrived at remains highly contested, although there was a commitment to amnesty in the post-amble to the interim constitution of 1993. Subsequently, demands for accountability and truth telling emerged within civil society and the churches, with the seminal proposal for a TRC, which would combine amnesty with truth telling, being made by Alex Boraine (Interview, Professor André du Toit, 14 May 2019).

10 Promotion of National Unity and Reconciliation Act, Act 34 of 1995. www.gov.za/documents/promotion-national-unity-and-reconciliation-act.

11 Katherine Mack, *From Apartheid to Democracy: Deliberating Truth and Reconciliation in South Africa* (University Park: Pennsylvania State University Press, 2014), 19.

12 André du Toit, "The Moral Foundations of the South African TRC," in *Truth v. Justice: The Morality of Truth Foundations*, ed. Robert Rotberg and Dennis Thompson (Princeton: Princeton University Press, 2000), 122–40 (citation from p. 131).

13 Mack, *From Apartheid to Democracy*, 20–1.

14 Mary Burton, *The Truth and Reconciliation Commission* (Auckland Park: Jacana Media, 2014), 82–94.

15 John Daniel, "The Truth and Reconciliation Committee Process: A Retrospective," in *Law, Nation-Building & Transformation: The South African Experience in Perspective*, ed. Catherine Jenkins and Max du Plessis (Cambridge: Intersentia, 2014), 65–90.

16 The committee had recommended victims receive six annual payments between R17 029 and R23 023 (calculated according to a set of criteria such as family size and need).

17 In an authoritative review of the reparations issue, Catherine Jenkins has queried whether the ANC government's failure to effect reparations has rendered the TRC's many accomplishments "a hollow victory." See her "After the Dry White Season: The Dilemmas of Reparation and Reconstruction in South Africa," *South African Journal of Human Rights* 16, no. 3 (2017): 415–85.

18 For instance, Mahmood Mamdani, "When Does Reconciliation Turn into a Denial of Justice," *Sam Nolutshungu Memorial Series: Human Sciences Research Council* 1 (1998); Mamdani, "The Truth According to the TRC," in *The Politics of Memory: Truth, Healing and Social Justice*, ed. I. Amadiume and A. An-Naim (London: Zed Books, 2000), 176–83.

19 See Sylvia Bawa, "Decolonization, Gender, and Transitional Justice in Post-Colonial Africa," in this volume; and Fiona Ross, *Bearing Witness: Women and the Truth and Reconciliation Commission in South Africa* (London: Pluto Press, 2003).

20 Brandon Hamber, "Repairing the Irreparable: Dealing with Double-Binds of Making Reparations for Crimes of the Past," *Ethnicity and Health* 5, no. 3&4 (2000): 215–26.

21 Brandon Hamber, "'Ere Their Story Die': Truth, Justice and Reconciliation in South Africa," *Race and Class* 44, no. 1 (2002): 61–79.

22 Daniel, "The Truth and Reconciliation Committee Process: A Retrospective," 89.

23 Catherine Jenkins, "'They Have Built a Legal System without Punishment': Reflections on the Use of Amnesty in the South African Transition," *Transformation* 64 (2007): 27–65.

24 Charles Villa-Vicencio, "Restorative Justice in Social Contest: The South
    African Truth and Reconciliation Commission," in *Burying the Past:
    Making Peace and Doing Justice after Civil Conflict*, ed. Nigel Biggar
    (Washington, DC: Georgetown University Press, 2003), 235–50.

25 Tutu contended that the offer of amnesty in 1993 "was a crucial ingredi-
    ent of the compromise which reversed the country's inevitable descent into
    a bloodbath" (*Sunday Times*, 4 December 1996).

26 Villa-Vicencio, "Restorative Justice," 238.

27 Jenkins, "'They Have Built a Legal System without Punishment,'" 48.

28 Burton, *The Truth and Reconciliation Commission*, 120–2; 129–30. It is
    of interest that a former NP MP who I spoke to about this issue indicated
    that de Klerk's claim to ignorance lacked credibility and that it would
    have been impossible for him not to have been aware of the atrocities will-
    fully committed by the security forces.

29 He was later released on parole in 2015.

30 Madeleine Fullard and Nicky Rousseau, "An Imperfect Past: The Truth
    and Reconciliation Commission in Transition," in *State of the Nation:
    South Africa 2003–2004*, ed. John Daniel, Adam Habib, and Roger
    Southall (Cape Town: HSRC Press, 2003), 78–104. Janusz Waluś and
    Clive Derby-Lewis, convicted for the 1992 murder of the South African
    Communist Party's (SACP) Chris Hani (which nearly derailed the negotia-
    tion process), remain in jail to this day, as do over twenty operatives of
    the PAC-aligned Azanian People's Liberation Army.

31 According to the police, Ahmed Timol, an SACP activist, allegedly
    jumped from a tenth-floor police building in 1971, but his family had
    evidence that he was pushed. Stung by lack of official action, they pursued
    court action to compel the state to charge Joao Rodrigues, a former
    Security Branch operative, with his murder. Their campaign attracted the
    support of six TRC commissioners, including Tutu. In February 2013, the
    National Prosecuting Authority, which by now was opposing Rodrigues's
    application to the court for a permanent stay of prosecution, admitted
    that there had been political intervention in truth commission related cases
    in 2003, which led to a moratorium on all investigations. Ra'eesa Pather,
    "TRC Commissioners Demand Justice," *Mail & Guardian*, 13–21 March
    2019.

32 Martin Meredith, *Coming to Terms: South Africa's Search for Truth* (New
    York, Public Affairs: Perseus Books, 1999), 287–8.

33 Jenkins, "'They Have Built a Legal System without Punishment,'" 59.

34 Daniel, "The Truth and Reconciliation Commission Process," 85.

35 Fullard and Rousseau, "An Imperfect Past," 82.

36 Notably by Mahmoud Mamdani, "Amnesty or Impunity? A Preliminary
    Critique of the Report of the Truth and Reconciliation Commission,"
    Diacritics 32, no. 3/4 (2002): 32–59.
37 Daniel, "The Truth and Reconciliation Process," 70–6.
38 Burton, *The Truth and Reconciliation Commission.*
39 Villa-Vicencio, "Restorative Justice," 243.
40 For details on how white participants in my focus groups wrestled with
    the issue of complicity, see chapter 4 in my book *Whites and Democracy
    in South Africa.*
41 Martha Minow, *Between Vengeance and Forgiveness: Facing History after
    Genocide and Mass Violence* (Boston: Beacon Press, 1998), 75.
42 And of course, the lack at that time of the possibility of signing through
    the internet.
43 Mack, *From Apartheid to Democracy*, 74.
44 Gunnar Theissen, "Between Acknowledgement and Ignorance: How
    White South Africans have Dealt with the Apartheid Past," Johannesburg,
    Centre for the Study of Violence and Reconciliation and Department of
    Political Science, Free University of Berlin.
45 The need for economy forbids a more extensive replay of Theissen's find-
    ings, but it should be noted that, generally, he found that acceptance of
    the TRC was higher among female and English-speaking respondents, and
    there were marked differences of opinion between young white South
    Africans and the older generation. Furthermore, metropolitan whites were
    more open to the TRC than those inhabiting small towns or living in the
    countryside, while support for the TRC increased with higher educational
    qualifications.
46 Gunnar Theissen, "Object of Trust and Hatred: Public Attitudes toward
    the TRC," in *Truth and Reconciliation in South Africa: Did the* TRC
    Deliver?, ed. Audrey Chapman and Hugo van der Merwe (Philadelphia:
    University of Pennsylvania Press), 207.
47 Ibid., 75.
48 Ibid., 77.
49 Southall, *Whites and Democracy in South Africa*, 75–100.

6

Truth, Reconciliation, and Peace:
Building a National Infrastructure for
Peace in Sierra Leone

Teddy Foday-Musa

In the wake of the eleven-year civil war that became notorious to the international community for carrying out sexual violence against women and teenage girls, mutilation, and targeting innocent civilians, a Truth and Reconciliation Commission (TRC) was set up in Sierra Leone. The TRC began its public hearings in April 2003. Throughout the world, truth commissions have been created with the assumption that getting people to understand the narratives of the past will enhance reconciliation and contribute to social cohesion. The truth and reconciliation process is clearly based on the premise that knowledge of the past will lead to forgiveness, tolerance, and reconciliation – a widely shared perception by Rosalind Shaw, who noted that "increasingly, truth commissions are regarded as a standard part of conflict resolution 'first aid kits.'"[1]

Sierra Leone's TRC provides crucial frameworks for debates about violence, repression, and peacebuilding. The Truth and Reconciliation Commission of Sierra Leone Act (2000) noted that one of the key causes of the brutal civil war in Sierra Leone was the lack of "a culture of tolerance and inclusion in political discourse." The report recommended that structures be put in place to ensure political tolerance and promote peace and national cohesion as part of the strategy for postwar reconstruction in Sierra Leone. As argued throughout this chapter, until peace in Sierra Leone is institutionalized by establishing an infrastructure for peace, the implementation of the TRC report will not materialize to its fullest. This argument considers how local peacebuilding initiatives can be implemented through established state institutions with formal recognition.

This chapter makes a case for a permanent infrastructure for peace in Sierra Leone, one that will work relentlessly to implement the recommendations of the TRC report and resolve conflict internally and with local skills, institutions, and resources, thereby seeking a truly Sierra Leonean solution for Sierra Leonean problems as a first resort and reducing the constant dependency on outsiders to resolve local conflicts. Sierra Leoneans need a platform that will seek a local approach to peacebuilding and conflict management. An infrastructure for peace will create some form of predictability in line with early warning mechanisms to help prevent the recurrence of conflict and foster peace and national cohesion, critical to rebuilding the Sierra Leonean state. This puts into perspective the relationship between peace infrastructure and state building. It illustrates the process of liberal peacebuilding and local ownership in a postwar reconstruction trajectory.

The Sierra Leone government has increasingly focused on measures to enhance peace and unity by proposing to establish an independent infrastructure for peace, now formally known as the Independent Commission for Peace and National Cohesion, commonly referred to as the Peace and National Cohesion Commission. This locally driven initiative is in tandem with the peacebuilding "ownership" advocacy by the international community. This advocacy has been enforced by a growing consensus, both within and outside the UN system, on the significance of national ownership to sustain post-conflict peacebuilding efforts at the national level. Former UN Secretary-General Annan, who supported the local peacebuilding initiative, clearly articulated as much: "Essentially, the aim should be the creation of a sustainable national infrastructure for peace that allows societies and their governments to resolve conflicts internally and with their own skills, institutions and resources."[2]

The delay in establishing a national infrastructure for peace in Sierra Leone threatens the country's peacebuilding and state-rebuilding processes. This threat undermines the country's potential for national cohesion and continues to test the resilience of these processes. Of particular concern is the hate-driven politics that exist between the two main political parties – the opposition All Peoples' Congress (APC) and the ruling Sierra Leone People's Party (SLPP).

Even after the 2018 elections, political interaction between the two parties is expressed in the form of tension and threats to the country's peace and security. Current challenges include how to address such mutual mistrust, suspicion, anger, and animosity that are spilling into significant national issues of development such as the fight against corruption and attracting foreign investment to the country.

This chapter provides new perspectives on how the Sierra Leonean state can take full ownership of its peacebuilding process. The 2019 "Bintumani-III" conference stimulated national dialogue on issues of peace and national cohesion and proffered ways to address them. Hundreds of Sierra Leoneans, representing various facets of society, took part in the three-day conference and overwhelmingly endorsed the establishment of an independent peace infrastructure. Above all, they laid a strong foundation for development and good governance in the country as recommended by the TRC. Civil society groups, persons with disabilities, women, youth, children, the interreligious council, and paramount chiefs presented position papers identifying key issues relevant to national cohesion, peace, and security. Additionally, it generated consensus on the nature and character of the proposed Independent Commission for Peace and National Cohesion, considering Sierra Leonean political history and current realities.

The theoretical approach underpinning this chapter is interpretivism. Andy Summer and Michael Tribe noted that this approach "underscores the value of interaction between the researcher and those researched."[3] Semi-structured interviews and focus group discussions were conducted during the nationwide district and regional consultations across the country from February to March 2019. Interviews were conducted with participants from 23 to 25 May 2019 during the three-day Bintumani-III National Dialogue Forum in Freetown. Interviewees were randomly selected based on their knowledge of specific historical events about peace and reconciliation in Sierra Leone. This chapter also draws from comparative studies and existing practical experiences in setting up infrastructures for peace in different countries, focusing on Ghana, Kenya, and Rwanda. These studies, reports of lessons learned, and models of best practices enriched the assessment of patterns and trends of benefits and challenges derived from national peace infrastructures.

The chapter is divided into four sections. This first section introduces the topic. The next section provides a brief background of the country profile, in which the pre-war status quo and the civil war are discussed. The third section discusses the postwar reconstruction and peacebuilding process, with particular emphasis on activities related to the hearings and processes of the TRC and its activities to promote a culture of tolerance and social inclusion. The fourth section focuses on the current status of the country's national agenda to consolidate peace and promote national cohesion, putting into perspective the 2019 Bintumani-III conference and the debate about the establishment of the Peace and National Cohesion Commission. The conclusion provides a new perspective on how Sierra Leone can take full ownership of its peacebuilding process at the national level.

SIERRA LEONE: POLITICS AND CONFLICT

The building of the post-colonial Sierra Leonean state faced significant challenges of governance. Shortly after independence from Britain in 1961, the foundation of the country was weakened, characterized by inequitable distribution of state resources and power, creating socio-economic and political imbalance. The tenure of President Siaka Stevens, who ruled the country from 1967 to 1985, was the most extreme in misappropriating the nation's economy for his political gains. Additionally, Stevens did not create the platform to enable society to have a voice in running the state – a widely shared perception by several scholars. As noted by Clotilde Asangna, "the transformation of Sierra Leone from multiparty politics to a single-party state – under Stevens's administration – tremendously reduced civilian participation in politics. Civilian participation in the political process usually enables society to have a voice in the affairs of the state."[4]

During Stevens's reign, political governance in the country after independence degenerated from a "*patrimonial structure*" to a "*patron-client*" system in which state functionaries were appointed based on his politically motivated self-interest and were responsible only to him and not accountable to the state. Stevens governed Sierra Leone through a corrupt personalized system with disregard for fair resource distribution. He also politicized the security sector with a partisan recruitment scheme for the military and police. Stevens's government lavishly spent income generated from natural resources, mainly diamonds, on their personal and partisan interest, rather than on promoting socio-economic growth for the citizenry. The country's diamond boom, which had the potential to serve as the breadbasket of Sierra Leone, was mismanaged and saddled with corruption. J. Sorie Conteh opined that the diamond boom became a curse on the nation. He added that the economic benefits of diamonds, which were meant to free people from the clutches of poverty, instead enslaved them in the clutches of greed.[5]

The patron-client structure of Stevens's government did not promote the rule of law, transparency, and sustainable economic growth. Instead, corruption flourished, and the distribution of national wealth was based on political patronage. In 1985, Stevens hand-picked Joseph Saidu Momoh as his successor. Things went from bad to worse under Momoh, and he is on record as publicly pronouncing that he "failed the nation" as a president. David Harris noted that President Momoh went as far as to declare that "education was a privilege and not a right."[6] Sierra Leoneans became disgruntled, directing their grievances for Stevens at Momoh. These grievances increased within the populace, resulting in the eleven-year civil war by the Revolutionary United Front (RUF). The undemocratic and dictatorial leadership style by Stevens and Momoh, including the corrupt nature of the APC government, were the key reasons advanced by Foday Sankoh and his RUF for invading Sierra Leone in 1991. Sankoh remarked: "We are fighting for a new Sierra Leone. A new Sierra Leone of freedom, justice and equal opportunity for all. We are fighting for democracy, and by democracy, we mean equal opportunity and access to power to create wealth through free trade, commerce, agriculture, industry, science and technology."[7]

Paul Richards argue that "wars are never static; they evolve taking on many forms and parameters."[8] In Sierra Leone's narrative, as the war progressed, the RUF reneged on its initial promise of fighting for democracy and creating equal opportunity. Instead, it started abducting youth and using torture and intimidation as a weapon of war. Richards further noted: "The RUF, though exercising strict discipline in their bush camps, was grossly unruly during attacks, wreaking the worst havoc probably under the influence of drugs. As such, the war quickly became about waging terror on the innocent."[9] The involuntary conscription of child soldiers by the RUF and the brutal killing of innocent citizens were the most highlighted features of the civil war perpetuated by Sankoh and his rebels. One of the child soldiers, Kamara, who was with the RUF, attested to the brutality: "Before I was captured, the rebels shot both my parents in front of me, grabbed me by the throat, tied both of my hands, cut parts of my body with a blade and placed cocaine in it. I had no option but to join them because I no longer had parents."[10]

The end of the civil war in 2002 gave Sierra Leoneans a renewed hope for peace and stability. The international community has often portrayed the country's transition from conflict to peace and development as a success story. Significant efforts and resources have been invested in reforming governance institutions to promote democracy and enhance the peacebuilding process. As part of the postwar reconstruction process, the government of ex-president Tejan Kabbah prioritized the establishment of key institutions, which included the Office of National Security, the Central Intelligence and Security Unit, the National Social Security and Insurance Trust, Human Rights Commission of Sierra Leone, and the Anti-Corruption Commission. The two post-conflict governments of Sierra Leone – Sierra Leone Peoples' Party, from 1996 to 2007, and the All Peoples' Congress, from 2007 to 2018, showed a desire to reclaim and sustain peace. Sierra Leoneans also demonstrated their quest for peace by conducting four democratic elections with a peaceful transfer of power from the incumbent to the opposition.[11] The civil war ended with the recommendation to establish a TRC in Sierra Leone.

SIERRA LEONE'S TRUTH & RECONCILIATION COMMISSION (TRC)

The official pronouncement of the end of the Sierra Leone Civil War came on 18 January 2002. An end of war peace ceremony was attended by representatives of the RUF, President Kabbah – on behalf of the government of Sierra Leone – and dignitaries of the international community. The war ended with commitment from both the international community and the government of Sierra Leone to promote reconciliation and support the Disarmament, Demobilization and Reintegration process, alongside resettling Internally Displaced Persons.

In July 2002, a TRC was inaugurated in Sierra Leone, coordinated by the Office of the UN High Commissioner for Human Rights, and assisted by the International Center for Transitional Justice in New York. The establishment of the TRC in Sierra Leone is best understood as an attempt to enhance healing and reconciliation through the therapeutic efficacy of truth telling. The Truth and Reconciliation Act of 2000 was the primary legal document by which the TRC manifested the five goals of its mandate, among which was "to create an impartial historical record of violations and abuse, ... to address impunity, to respond to the needs of the victims, to promote healing and reconciliation and to prevent a repetition of the violations and abuses suffered."[12]

Despite pressure from some local civil society organizations (CSOs) and human rights activists for a TRC, there was little popular support for the establishment of a TRC in Sierra Leone, since most people preferred a "forgive and forget" approach – a Sierra Leonean cultural practice of healing and reconciliation. In explaining local popular responses to the TRC hearings, RUF-captured teenage survivor Joseph Larkoh, who is now an adult and one of those interviewed as part of the study underpinning this chapter, noted: "We were not interested in what happened and didn't happen. What we needed was to forgive and forget rather than to talk about what happened."[13]

In Sierra Leone, the imperative to recall violent incidences during the TRC hearings was at odds with local approaches to healing and reintegration, which are based on the social forgetting of violence. It is widely argued that before a TRC is initiated in a particular country, it is important to investigate whether local strategies of recovery and reintegration are established in the host country. Additionally, it is important to note that TRC establishment should have widespread support with a majority of the citizens, including survivors. In Sierra Leone, citizens in urban and rural communities held different views about the operations of the TRC, and in most communities people collectively eschewed TRC activities such as statement-making and attending hearing sessions. For them, the attempt to link the Special Court of Sierra Leone (SCSL) trial of those responsible for war crimes concurrent with the TRC hearings undermined the country's postwar peacebuilding agenda. The SCSL was also viewed as a challenge in establishing a peace infrastructure as the Lomé Peace Agreement (1999) recommended. Nevertheless, the activities of the TRC were implemented as planned.

TRC'S PROCESSES AND EVENTS

Like others, Sierra Leone's TRC was based on verbal truth telling of personal memories of violence, torture, and abuse as a pathway to reconciliation and peaceful coexistence. The hope was that this would serve as a new beginning and a promising start for the country's reconciliation process. The head of the commission, Bishop Joseph Humper, assured Sierra Leoneans that the TRC would help rebuild the nation. He was upbeat when he noted that "Sierra Leone, yes Sierra Leone, can rise again."[14] The TRC started to collect statements in 2002 and held public hearings in the form of workshops in Freetown and the twelve administrative districts from April to August 2003.

Across the country, sensitization materials like posters, banners, and leaflets presented messages announcing the TRC's hearing workshops. Skits and jingles were also prepared for radio and television programs in Sierra Leone's lingua franca (Krio) as illustrated in table 6.1.

These messages were often reinforced by individual speakers in their remarks at the opening ceremonies of each hearing workshop. Banners displayed in the TRC hearing workshops had such printed messages as: *"truth hurts"* but *"war hurts more," "truth today and peaceful Sierra Leone tomorrow."* During the hearings, individuals were often guided in their testimonies to recount certain things they did to vent their anger publicly, which according to the TRC officials, would bring about healing and would also be suitable for the reconciliation process. Testimonies at the TRC public hearings resonated with most Sierra Leoneans and served as an explicit reminder of nation building with commitment to reconciliation and peace, yet there were challenges.

Challenges in TRCs

Truth commissions worldwide are faced with two main challenges: fear of retaliation by perpetrators and fear of government reprisals, which generally hinder the reconciliation process. In addition to these two challenges, the international community did not address a crucial scenario around the establishment of the TRC in Sierra Leone. First, before the TRC was established, most people in Sierra Leone preferred a "forgive and forget" approach of *social forgetting* derived from local strategies of social recovery and reintegration. There was an established local pattern of healing and reconciliation, as expressed by Shaw, who noted: "In northern Sierra Leone, social forgetting is a cornerstone of established processes of reintegration and healing for child and adult ex-combatants. Speaking

Table 6.1 | Sierra Leone TRC sensitization messages

KRIO (LINGUA FRANCA)	ENGLISH INTERPRETATION
Kam Blo Maind Mek Pis Sidom Nar Salone	Come Speak your Mind for Peace to Prevail in Sierra Leone
Memba wetin Don Bi	Remember what has happened
Mek we Tok Tru en Joyn Han as Wan Pipul	Let's tell the Truth and Join Hands Together as One People
TRC for wan Salone	TRC for one Sierra Leone
Blo Maind to TRC en Ge u Sef Pis	Speak your mind to the TRC and get inner peace

of the war in public often undermines these processes, and many believe it encourages violence."[15] Therefore, the TRC's public motivation for recounting violence was against Sierra Leonean cultural healing methods. This did not encourage participation in the hearing sessions. In essence, there was a trade-off between peace and justice in a post-conflict reconciliation setting in alignment with cultural values.

Second, the widespread perception of Sierra Leoneans that the TRC could be a covert conduit for the SCSL was another challenge the TRC encountered. The SCSL was a tribunal established to prosecute those who bore the greatest responsibility for war crimes and crimes against humanity. The TRC's operations coincided with the SCSL's indictments, resulting in widespread speculation from ex-combatants that taking part in the TRC would facilitate their arrest by the SCSL. Consequently, ex-combatants were fearful of the TRC, believing that information they gave would find its way to the SCSL, and they would be implicated. For this reason, most of the ex-combatants refused to co-operate with the TRC hearings.

A third prevalent challenge was the lack of protection for those who testified before the TRC; many Sierra Leoneans feared retaliation by ex-combatants and their relatives. Amid these challenges, the TRC proceedings were carried out and impacted the country's peacebuilding landscape with broad-ranging outcomes and legacies.

Outcomes, Impacts, and Legacies

Part of the TRC's work involved the creation of a database of captured details of the violations, victims, and perpetrators described in the more than 7,000 statements received by the commission. The most obvious outcomes of this effort are the TRC's lists of victims and the statistical compilation attached to the report. These data have frequently served researchers looking at the extent to which some violations were targeted against women and children. Additionally, the data proved to be a valuable tool for assisting qualitative research work.

Another key legacy of the TRC that brings hope and aspirations to Sierra Leoneans is the TRC Report Recommendations. Among these it is recommended that the country promotes a postwar peacebuilding agenda geared toward establishing an infrastructure for peace to enhance national cohesion. The 2019 Bintumani-III conference, in fulfillment of that recommendation, brought together Sierra Leoneans in an inclusive process to discuss how to establish just such an infrastructure

Peace Infrastructure

Peace infrastructure, as a concept and methodology, emphasizes the transfer of ownership of peacebuilding from the international community to state and non-state actors at the national level. The earlier notion of peace infrastructure attempted to provide a practical proposition for achieving a functional level of peace. The work of John Paul Lederach has been generally influential. Lederach proposed the idea of an infrastructure for peace as "a core ingredient of a comprehensive approach to peacebuilding in *Building Peace: Sustainable Reconciliation in Divided Societies.*"[16] Since then, attempts have been made by various institutions and other scholars to define the concept of peace infrastructure. The United Nations Development Programme (UNDP), for instance, defines peace infrastructures as "a network of interdependent systems, resources, values and skills held by the government, civil society and consultation; prevent conflict and enable peaceful mediation when violence occurs in a society."[17] This definition added an "institutional-support" value to the concept of peace infrastructures. Today, the UNDP has facilitated the creation of peace infrastructures in more than thirty conflict-affected or post-conflict countries.

A body of literature in academia also seeks to define the concept of peace infrastructures. Most of these definitions rely on structuralism, projecting the idea of a physical structure and a degree of organization. For instance, Jeannine Suurmond and Prakash Mani Sharma defined peace infrastructure as "the structures, resources, and processes through which peace services are delivered at any level of a society." They make a useful distinction between formal and informal peace infrastructures: "Formal infrastructures for peace have a physical structure, a degree of organization, stability, mandate, resources, training and are recognized as such by their beneficiaries, or 'users.' Examples include community mediation committees, local peace committees, peace radio stations, peace agreement monitoring mechanisms, religious institutions, and zones of peace. By contrast, informal infrastructures for peace are those that emerge on an ad hoc basis, do traditional disputes resolution mechanisms. Together they make up the Infrastructure for Peace of a society."[18] Sharing her understanding of peace infrastructure, Ulrike Hopp-Nishanka noted: "Peace infrastructure [is] a concept that helps us understand the domestic, internal efforts in a conflict or fragile context to create or build on existing mechanisms and organizations that engage in reducing violence and problem-solving. The focus is less on the role of external assistance to support these peace infrastructures, although insights on capacity building and other means of (external) support are offered 'between the lines.'"[19]

Clearly, these definitions represent different theoretical approaches. On the one hand, the UNDP and Hopp-Nishanka argue in support of institutionalization of the peace process, advocating for more formal and distinct approaches. In this vein, Hopp-Nishanka emphasizes "ownership," underpinning domestic contribution. On the other hand, Suurmond and Sharma adopt the language of process and not events in a free-market-oriented economy. Their approach enhanced the concept of informal peace infrastructures.

A ROAD MAP TO PEACE
AND NATIONAL COHESION

The 1999 Lomé Peace Agreement, signed between the government
of Sierra Leone and the RUF, recommended that the country insti-
tutionalize the consolidation of peace.[20] The parties agreed to abide
by the agreement and take appropriate steps to implement the provisions for establishing the Commission for the Consolidation of
Peace. Article 6 of the agreement stated:

> A Commission for the Consolidation of Peace (hereinafter
> termed the CCP) shall be established within two weeks of the
> signing of the present Agreement to implement a post-conflict
> program that ensures reconciliation and the welfare of all parties
> to the conflict, especially the victims of war. The CCP shall have
> the overall goal and responsibility for supervising and monitor-
> ing the implementation of and compliance with the provisions
> of the present Agreement relative to the promotion of national
> reconciliation and the consolidation of peace.

Although the 2018 elections, which ushered in a new government headed by President Julius Maada Bio, were generally
conducted in a peaceful manner, there was some scale of political
violence. That aside, the election results showed a clear pattern
of ethnic and regional allegiance. As well, the media and public
engagement were politicized, and social media became a platform
for disseminating misinformation and hate speeches. In the immediate aftermath of the elections, further incidents of violence were
reported in some regions of the country. These actions were reason
for concern because of their potential threat to national cohesion
and peaceful coexistence across communities in the country. It is
widely believed that during the period of electioneering, ethnic and
regional tensions fuelled disunity among Sierra Leoneans.

In explaining popular local responses to decades of disunity, which
undermine national cohesion, Andrew Lavalie, a civil society activist noted: "Unfortunately, ethnicity plays a salient role in national
politics both as a source for political organization and a basis for
support."[21] Against this backdrop, shortly after the 2018 elections,
the government identified the strengthening of national cohesion as

one of its top priority areas. Consequently, President Bio announced the creation of an Independent Commission for Peace and National Cohesion to be established by an Act of Parliament.[22]

Establishing infrastructures for peace has become a global campaign by local CSOs, intergovernmental agencies, committed citizens, and government officials. In Sierra Leone, the idea to establish an infrastructure for peace first surfaced during the signing of the Lomé Peace Agreement between the government of Sierra Leone and the RUF in 1999. Since then, a series of campaigns by local CSOs have made notable progress. Some of those campaigns included the in-country consultations that the campaigners held with various stakeholders. The outcomes were shared with embassies, foreign missions, and relevant government ministries.

The move was aimed at calling on the government of Sierra Leone to consider the creation of a Commission for Peacebuilding and National Reconciliation. Advocacy and information sharing sessions were also organized in 2013 for the Sierra Leone House of Parliament through the Parliamentary Committee on Human Rights, which resulted in establishing a parliamentary CSO working group on infrastructure for peace. Many Sierra Leoneans hoped that such an infrastructure would serve to uphold the rights of citizens, enhance political freedoms, and diminish divisive tendencies that undermine peaceful coexistence between the different ethnic groups.

The Green Paper

As a demonstration of political will to ensure national cohesiveness, the government of Sierra Leone produced a Green Paper, a consultative document to be used by citizens, political parties, religious groups, civil society leaders, and other stakeholders, as a guide in seeking their views and opinions for the establishment of the Commission of Peace and National Cohesion. In explaining the rationale and content of the Green Paper, the local consultant Hawa Samai stated that it is not in itself a documented government policy but a consultative document designed to raise issues and questions that need to be answered for government to formulate policies geared toward the establishment of the Peace and National Cohesion Commission. In her first engagement with the public on radio land, Samai categorically noted that "the Green paper document aims to provide a framework for focused policy discussions and to foster the interaction between stakeholders and the Government, reinforcing the culture of consultation and dialogue."[23]

The Green Paper makes a case for a permanent Independent Commission for Peace and National Cohesion to help prevent the recurrence of conflict and foster peace and national cohesion. It puts forward options designed to stimulate a response from the public and interested parties. It examines pertinent national issues and suggests a structure, composition, mandate, and possible funding sources of the commission for further public deliberations. It looks at other commissions within and outside Sierra Leone and proffers suggestions that the proposed commission may benefit from. The Green Paper puts into perspective the role of traditional leaders, the influential role women have played in the peace process in Sierra Leone, and the crucial role of youth and CSOs. Expressing the government's commitment to nurturing the culture of consultation in the process of establishing an independent infrastructure for peace, one government official stated: "It is essential for all relevant parties to any public interest reforms to be consulted throughout the process as this will ensure that all views are taken on board, and an attempt is made to reach consensus."[24]

District Consultations – Nationwide

The nationwide consultations were conducted in the form of town hall meetings and focus group discussions in all sixteen administrative districts across the country. Mohamed Koroma, a resource person from African Peer Review Mechanism (APRM) and a member of the strategic planning team, noted that the key objective of the consultations is to provide a framework for a National Dialogue Forum for the consolidation of peace and national cohesion, reinforcing the culture of consultation and dialogue. "These consultations sought the voices, views and opinions of the citizenry on key thematic areas for inclusion in the design of the agenda for the National Dialogue Forum – Bintumani-III, and enhance[d] frank discussions on the proposed establishment of the Peace and National Cohesion Commission in Sierra Leone."[25]

The field component of this consultation was undertaken on 23 March 2019. The technical team was comprised of experts and resource persons from government agencies and academic institutions

from within and outside Sierra Leone, including the Ministry of
Political and Public Affairs, the APRM, the Department of Peace and
Conflict Studies Fourah Bay College, and the National Commission
for Democracy. Participants at the town hall meetings were drawn
from a cross-section of key stakeholders in each district. A sample
size of fifty stakeholders per district was engaged in the process across
the sixteen political administrative districts of Sierra Leone. The discussions were in key local languages to help participants understand
and contribute to the sessions. Participants thoroughly discussed the
thematic areas, made plenary presentations on findings, and posed
recommendations for government action. The findings brought to the
forefront key issues threatening the national unity and cohesion of the
country. The responses have aided in identifying the main sources of
violence in local communities and offered perspective on enhancing
national unity and social cohesion.

Participants raised concerns about bad governance, corruption,
negative messages in the form of hate speeches from political leaders and political party supporters. Regarding the main sources of
violence in communities and households, participants highlighted
issues of political affiliation, ethnicity, regionalism, and lack of political tolerance during the country's electioneering period. To attain
sustainable national unity, participants recommended that Sierra
Leoneans and governments demonstrate respect for diverse cultures,
traditions, laws, and values as enshrined in the national constitution.

The consultations shed light on citizens' perspectives with regard
to the functions and impacts of political parties on society. Many
have formed the opinion that there is a strong correlation between
political parties and election-related violence. To combat this violence, participants expressed the desire for state security institutions
to remain neutral when carrying out their assigned duties during
the electioneering process. In addition, they noted there should be a
reduction of street rallies, and campaign messages should not incite
hatred, ethnicity, and regionalism but rather focus on promoting
national cohesion.

The consultations also enabled participants to answer crucial
questions relating to the size and composition of the proposed
Peace and National Cohesion Commission. The roles of CSOs,
women, and media houses, as well as the mandate, structure, size,
and composition of the commission were discussed. Regarding
the perspectives on the mandate and structure of the commission,

participants suggested cascading the commission from national, regional, and district levels to chiefdom level. They recommended creation of departments that should address issues relating to persons with disabilities, youth, gender, alternative dispute resolution, peace and civic education, public relations, research, and outreach. Participants also stressed that the appointment of commissioners should not be based solely on political affiliations, and employees should be formally educated on peace and conflict issues in Sierra Leone. They called for gender balance in terms of government appointments and staffing, emphasizing that commissioners must be law-abiding persons of integrity, and appointees ought to be individuals committed to peace with requisite knowledge of conflict prevention and management.

The 2019 National Dialogue Forum – Bintumani-III

At a well-attended opening ceremony of the 2019 Bintumani-III conference, Professor David Francis, the government chief minister, made the following remarks: "'Bintimani-1 and II' held in 1995/96, respectively, laid the foundation pillars for stable and democratic governance. 'Bintumani-III' was about consolidating and solidifying those foundation pillars to enhance peace and national cohesion. The 2019 Bintumani-III conference is a Presidential initiative to promote peace and national cohesion. The stated purpose of the Conference is to bring Sierra Leoneans together in an inclusive process to discuss how to build an infrastructure for Peace in the form of an Independent Commission for Peace and National Cohesion as announced by the President."[26]

According to President Bio, Bintumani-III provided a unique opportunity to build the local capacity for dialogue, because in his view, for far too long, Sierra Leone has been relying on external actors and the international community to help resolve and manage violent conflicts. This view was widely shared among conference participants interviewed for this study. Dr Alpha Khan, a former minister in the APC government under President Ernest Bai Koroma opined, "Our problems are not insurmountable, but we must solve them ourselves. Tomorrow I will be moderating an important session at the Bintumani-III conference. I would like some of our comrades to attend. We can put our issues across. To jaw-jaw is better than to war-war. Dialogue leads to resolutions.

Our party still has the opportunity to correct our past mistakes. So for tomorrow's session, I am the chair and so time is available for healing and reconciliation."[27]

Hundreds of Sierra Leoneans representing various facets of society took part in the three-day National Dialogue Forum on Democratic Consolidation for Peace and National Cohesion in May 2019. There were open discussions and recommendations by Sierra Leoneans along with the experience sharing from Kenya, Ghana, and Uganda. Participants made reference to the numerous inter-ethnic marriages and interfaith relations across the country as indicative of social cohesion. However, there was consensus in many presentations that the country remains socially and politically fractured and there is a need to enhance national cohesion.

The constitution also came under review. Many Sierra Leoneans believe the 1991 constitution has several flaws, which governments and past political leaders have exploited over the years. Review was recommended for areas in the constitution related to women, land rights, and executive powers. There was also the case of the TRC, which made several recommendations, including the establishment of a Peace and Reconciliation Commission. Sierra Leoneans expressed their frustration at past governments that failed to implement the TRC recommendations. It was also noted that the religious bodies failed to use their platforms to publicize the recommendations of the TRC.

The independence of critical state institutions like the police and the judiciary was also questioned. Many citizens are of the opinion that the judiciary and the Sierra Leone police have been used more to support ruling parties and the government of the day than to serve the people. It was asserted at the conference that successive governments had used the courts to oppress their political opponents, and justice for the poor was almost impossible and unachievable. Conference participants also noted that the Independent Commission for Peace and National Cohesion and its commissioners should have high integrity, credibility, and be above politics. They called for the commission to be inclusive and have the responsibility and resources to manage conflict and promote national cohesion.

Concluding the Bintumani-III conference, many participants declared the event a success, as they believed it effectively responded to the needs of the vast majority of Sierra Leoneans by stimulating national dialogue on critical national issues affecting the state and proffering solutions. Government officials reassured participants that the proposed peace commission could be a "people centred commission," and the government would facilitate its establishment, support its operations, and ensure it made a meaningful impact.[28] The conference communiqué called for establishing an independent, inclusive, decentralized commission for peace to be staffed by competent, apolitical, and patriotic Sierra Leoneans with reputable integrity and knowledge in peacebuilding and conflict management. Participants at the conference insisted the commission should be representative and inclusive; independent with the requisite capacity to respond to the multifaceted challenges of peacebuilding in the country; have solid institutional outlets at various levels, including chiefdoms, district, and national levels; and have gender balance and a youthful outlook.

CONCLUSION

While Sierra Leone has demonstrated commitment to peace and democracy by conducting four peaceful elections in 2002, 2007, 2012, and 2018, the country continues to confront political division and other issues that undermine national unity and social cohesion. As this chapter has shown, the consolidation of peace and national unity remains a key challenge. There is widespread recognition of the potential for a relapse into violence if the political tension and conflictual divisions in society are not addressed. This threat has been aggravated by the negative use of social media as a platform for disseminating hate speeches and messages that promote violence. Compounding the threat is the hatred-driven politics that exist between the two main political parties in the country – SLPP and the APC. The political tension between these parties is fodder for future violent conflict. There is a need for a new perspective on how Sierra Leone can take full ownership of its peacebuilding process at both local and national levels. Establishing an infrastructure for peace is a vital foundational step in this direction. Although the Independent Commission for Peace and National Cohesion is a welcome initiative in the quest for national cohesion, the commission can only thrive if it is inclusive and devoid of political interference.

NOTES

1 Rosalind Shaw, *Rethinking Truth and Reconciliation Commissions: Lessons from Sierra Leone* (Washington DC: United States Institute of Peace, 2005), 1.

2 See Kofi Annan, *Prevention of Armed Conflict* (New York: UN, 2006).

3 Andy Summer and Michael Tribe, *International Development Studies: Theories and Methods in Research and Practice* (London: Sage, 2008), 59–63.

4 Clotilde Asangna, "An Examination of the Sierra Leone War," *African Journal of Political Science and International Relations* 11, no. 5 (2017): 103–11.

5 J. Sorie Conteh, *The Diamonds* (New York: Lekon Dimensions Publishing, 2001).

6 David Harris, *Sierra Leone: A Political History* (Oxford: Oxford University Press, 2014), 76.

7 See "Footpaths to Democracy: Toward a New Sierra Leone," http://fas.org/irp/world/para/docs/footpaths.htm.

8 Paul Richards, "The Political Economy of Internal Conflict in Sierra Leone" Conflict Research Unit working paper 21 (The Hague: Netherlands Institute of International Relations "Clingendael," 2003), 22.

9 Richards, "The Political Economy," 27.

10 Foday Kamara was captured by the RUF as a teenager. He recounted his first encounter with the RUF during one of the TRC hearings.

11 Mohamed Ibn Chambas is the Special Representative of the Secretary-General for West Africa and the Sahel Freetown. He made these comments at the opening of the 2019 Bintumani-III National Dialogue Forum for Peace and National Cohesion held in Freetown, 2–25 May 2019.

12 See Government of Sierra Leone, *Truth and Reconciliation Act 2000* (Freetown: Government Printing Department, 2001), 15.

13 Joseph Larkoh, interview with author, Freetown, 2 May 2019.

14 Bishop Joseph Humper was the chair for Sierra Leone's TRC. He made this declaration at the closing ceremony of the TRC hearing at Makeni in May 2003.

15 Shaw, *Rethinking Truth and Reconciliation Commissions*.

16 John Paul Lederach, "The Origin and Evolution of Infrastructures for Peace: A Personal Reflection," *Journal of Peacebuilding & Development* 7, no. 3 (2012): 8.

17 UNDP, "UNDP Bureau of Crisis Prevention and Recovery, Issue Brief: Infrastructure for Peace," 2013, www.undp.org/publications/issue-brief-infrastructure-peace.

18 Jeannine Suurmond and Prakash Mani Sharma, *Serving People's Need for Peace: Infrastructure for Peace, the Peace Sector, and the Case of Nepal* (Berlin: Berghof Foundation, 2013), 10.

19 Ulrike Hopp-Nishanka, "Giving Peace an Address? Reflecting on the Potential and Challenges of Creating Peace Infrastructures," in *Peace Infrastructures: Assessing Concepts and Practice*, ed. Barbara Unger, Stina Lundström, Katrin Planta, and Beatrix Austin (Berlin: Berghof Foundation. 2013), 2.

20 Government of Sierra Leone, *Lomé Peace Agreement* (1999) (Freetown: Government Printing, 2000), Article 6.

21 Andrew Lavalie, interview with the author, Freetown, 7 June 2019.

22 In his address on 10 May 2018, at the state opening of the first session of the fifth parliament of the second republic, the president of Sierra Leone, His Excellency Julius Maada Bio announced the creation of an Independent Commission for Peace and National Cohesion by an Act of Parliament.

23 Hawa Samai, interview with author, Freetown, 9 February 2019.

24 Foday Amara Kallon is the deputy minister of Political and Public Affairs in the Bio-led administration. He was a member of the Infrastructure Planning Technical Team (PTT) representing the government. He made this statement at one of the PTT meetings in Freetown.

25 Mohamed Koroma, interview with author, Freetown, 4 February 2019.

26 David Francis is the government's chief minister. He made these comments at the opening of the Bintumani-III conference. He expressed his gratitude to serve as chair of the National Conference on Peace and National Cohesion.

27 Hon. Dr Alpha Kanu, interview with author, Freetown, 23 May 2019.

28 Dr Mohamed Juldeh Jalloh, the country's vice-president, made these comments after receiving the communiqué on the final day of Bintumani-III, containing highlights of the deliberations during the three-day conference.

7

Truth, Justice, and National Reconciliation: The Dilemmas of Transitional Justice in Burkina Faso

Aboubacar Dakuyo

After the fall of President Blaise Compaoré's regime following the popular uprising of 30 and 31 October 2014 in Burkina Faso, leaders of civil society, the military, and political parties of the former opposition initiated a "political transition"[1] to deal with the crimes of the past, reconcile the divided population, and consolidate a democratic rule of law state.[2] This process falls within the framework of "transitional justice," which can be defined as "the full range of processes and mechanisms associated with a society's attempts to come to terms with a legacy of large-scale past abuses, in order to ensure accountability, serve justice and achieve reconciliation."[3]

At the time of its conceptualization in the early nineties, transitional justice endeavoured to lead countries transitioning from violent conflicts or dictatorship to a peaceful, democratic, and rule of law state.[4] The tools it generally mobilized to respond to these complex challenges have been organized around four measures: the right to the truth about the crimes committed, the right to justice, the right to reparation, and the right to guarantees of non-repetition.[5] According to the former UN Secretary-General's report, "The Rule of Law and Transitional Justice in Conflict and Post-Conflict Societies": "Where transitional justice is required, strategies must be holistic, incorporating integrated attention to individual prosecutions, reparations, truth-seeking, institutional reform, vetting and dismissals, or an appropriately conceived combination thereof."[6]

In addition, from its initial emergence as a separate field of theory and practice, transitional justice has become an integral part of the broader framework of peacebuilding processes,[7] which the

United Nations (UN) defines as a set of mechanisms that are "aimed at preventing the outbreak, the recurrence or continuation of armed conflict and therefore encompasses a wide range of political, developmental, humanitarian and human rights programmes."[8] In this context, it is worth noting that like some countries of the Arab Spring such as Tunisia or Egypt, Burkina Faso is experiencing a transitional justice process that is not strictly speaking a democratic transition, as this has taken place since the adoption of the 1991 constitution that ended the country's successive military regimes.[9] The transitional justice process is characterized by a "revolutionary" dynamic. The main objective is to break completely with the twenty-seven years of the Compaoré regime to affect a substantial social and political transformation and consolidate the building of a democratic state in the country.

However, when one examines the last three decades of transitional justice practice, it appears to have, at best, a mixed record, if not a disappointing one. Its results include non-democratic transition situations, transitions from violent conflict to peace, contexts in which there is no political transition, and situations that could be described as "transitional injustice." Nevertheless, transitional justice remains committed to the idea of leading post-conflict societies to democracy rather than any other form of political regime.[10] In this regard, the goal of this chapter is to analyze the relationship between transitional justice mechanisms and democratic state building under the Roch Marc Christian Kaboré regime in Burkina Faso. It examines on the one hand the work of the Commission for National Reconciliation and Reforms (CNRR) and, more specifically, the work of its Sub-Commission on Truth, Justice, and National Reconciliation, and of the High Council for Reconciliation and National Unity (HCRNU) and, on the other hand, the criminal cases opened before the justice system.

This study seeks to answer the following question: What determines the positive impact or failure of these mechanisms on democratic consolidation? To answer the question, this study conceptualizes on the one hand the causal relationship between transitional justice and democratic consolidation and on the other hand transitional justice as inherently a "political field." The study's findings then affirms that it is the power relations emanating from political and social actors that determine the success or failure of the impact of transitional justice on democratic consolidation.

In the first part of the chapter, I elaborate on the theoretical frame-works conceptualizing the causal relationship between transitional justice and democracy and transitional justice as a "political field." In the second part, I show the historical background of transitional justice in Burkina Faso. I examine some of the major crimes that have been committed by the Compaoré regime and the state of non-effective transitional justice that the regime had implemented from its advent to the popular uprising of October 2014. In the third part, I analyze the post-insurrectional context where transitional justice is confronted with tensions between supporters of the former regime who want to safeguard their interests and "revolutionary" forces who favour a complete break with the precedent political order. Here, I highlight the dilemmas of the transitional justice process with regard to its competing objectives of the duty of truth and justice over past crimes and, at the same time, the need for national reconciliation in a context characterized by terrorist groups and political-military forces allied to the former regime who oppose these measures.

TRANSITIONAL JUSTICE AND DEMOCRACY

This section explores the causal relationship between transitional justice and democracy. As stated earlier, transitional justice has historically been associated with the aim of facilitating the transition of countries emerging from violent conflict or dictatorship to democratic regimes. Today, even if we note that several past experiences of transitional justice did not lead to the building of democratic states, it remains the case that such a political regime generally remains the intended or rather the most desired goal.[11] Therefore, in order to better understand the impact of transitional justice on the building of a democratic state in Burkina Faso, it is necessary to first understand what is meant by "democracy." In this context, democracy is a polysemic concept with a plurality of meanings that have no agreement on the factors that make some states more successful democracies, while others struggle in the process.[12] Thus, among the various possible understandings of democracy,[13] the concept can be defined minimally as "a political regime characterized by universal adult suffrage, the holding of periodic, free, competitive and fair elections, the existence of several political parties and several sources of information."[14]

As for what could be described as "democracy of intermediate quality," Terry Lynn Karl considers that it refers to "a set of institutions that permits the entire adult population to act as citizens by choosing their leading decision-makers in competitive, fair, and regularly scheduled elections which are held in the context of the rule of law, guarantees for political freedom, and limited military prerogatives."[15] Moreover, on the basis of the criteria of procedure, content, and outcome, Leonardo Morlino describes what we might call "quality democracy" or "good democracy," such as the democracy by which a "stable institutional structure ensures the freedom and equality of citizens through the legitimate and correct functioning of its institutions and mechanisms."[16]

Whether it is "democracy of intermediate quality" or "democracy of quality," respect for the rule of law is at the heart of these political regimes.[17] "Rule of law" can be broadly defined as a governance principle that holds individuals and institutions accountable for the observance of laws that are publicly promulgated in ways consistent with international human rights norms and standards.[18] To measure the impact of criminal justice on democracy, I use the frameworks of (de)legitimization, reform, and empowerment of state institutions.[19]

Because of the equality the rejection of impunity for crimes expresses between the sovereign and the citizens, it is one of the main attributes of the democratic state.[20] By prosecuting, for example, those most responsible for international crimes, such as the architect of the Tutsi extermination plan, Théoneste Bagosora, and the prime minister of the Rwandan interim government of 1994, Jean Kambanda, by the International Criminal Tribunal for Rwanda and the former Liberian president Charles Taylor by the Special Court for Sierra Leone; or the former president Hissène Habré by the Extraordinary African Chambers in Senegalese Courts, international criminal justice has managed to put behind the dock people who were once considered all-powerful and untouchable. Thus, criminal trials contribute doubly to the project of democratization of states emerging from violent conflicts: they remove from political life criminals who violate the most fundamental rights of their fellow citizens by putting them in jail, and therefore send a clear message to their subordinates to think more carefully in the future before obeying orders that are unquestionably immoral.[21]

In the past, international or hybrid criminal justice has served to delegitimize some leaders of previous violent regimes and to legitimize others in order to facilitate the emergence of a new democratic regime.[22] Delegitimization can also be accomplished by "naming and shaming" political and economic predators through the criminal trial process.[23] The capacity of criminal justice to legitimize and delegitimize can promote alternation of state leaders and therefore allow political stability in post-conflict societies.[24] Criminal prosecutions can also contribute to building a democratic state through the institutional, constitutional, and legislative reforms they can foster in a country. For example, they can expose some of the root causes of violence and then make it essential to dismantle some abusive groups and institutions; create human rights monitoring structures; reform the military, police, and security services, and guarantee the independence of the judiciary.[25]

Finally, criminal prosecutions can contribute to building a democratic state through the empowerment they can infer to some state institutions. They may, for example, not only highlight the historical exclusion or marginalization of particular ethnic, political, or religious groups or minorities to allow them to receive support from state institutions for their full participation in democratic life but also identify unequal power relations within certain institutions and make necessary reforms to the rule of law.[26] Having presented the potential contributions of criminal prosecution to the building of a democratic state, it should be noted that such contributions will be insufficient if they are not combined with other measures of transitional justice in a more holistic approach.[27] For this reason, I turn now to the contributions of Truth and Reconciliation Commissions (TRCs).

TRCS AND THE BUILDING OF DEMOCRATIC STATES

Through their functions, TRCs can contribute to the building of democratic states in post-conflict societies in a variety of ways. First, they can be defined as "bodies set up to investigate a past history of violations of human rights in a particular country – which can include violations by the military or other government forces or by armed opposition forces."[28] By revealing the historical truth, contributing to the healing and reconciliation of populations, educating societies on the causes of violence, and instigating institutional and normative reforms, TRCs, in general, participate in the emergence of democracy in post-conflict societies.[29] The main argument of this contribution is that a "quality democracy" cannot be based on a lie about the wrongs of the past.[30] Martha Minow notes that truth commissions restore victims' dignity and hold people accountable for their failure to prevent violence.[31] The wrongs must be revealed to heal the victims, trigger accountability of criminals, and set out reparations measures for the victims to generate civic trust and the people's commitment to state institutions.

In this regard, Paul Gready and Simon Robins draw attention to truth commissions as potential vehicles of social transformation only when they are not instrumental, that is, designed as fora in which victims are used as mere actors who perform their role without an opportunity to change the power relations in force or speak about the choice of devices and how they should be implemented to meet their needs.[32] To achieve this social transformation, the process of "deliberative democracy" is the best way to link the work of TRCs to democratic consolidation. Deliberative democracy can be defined as the right of citizens to participate in decision-making processes by challenging government actions taken on their behalf and proposing others that truly meet their needs.[33] This was done, for example, by the truth commissions of Peru (2001–2003) and South Africa (1995–2002). Peru's Truth Commission, conceived as a body of deliberative democracy, organized its hearings and public interviews following a democratic process that gave voice to the population at large and especially to marginalized communities of the past.[34] Similarly, the South African TRC, also using a public deliberation process, has promoted the revelation of scientific and subjective truths that led to the catharsis of the victims of apartheid, those responsible for the policy of repression, and those who have benefited from it.[35] The scientific or legal truth was corroborated by evidence obtained through an impartial and objective procedure; the subjective or narrative truth was the common narrative of the subjective opinions of individuals.[36]

In these contexts, by allowing victims to participate and express their sufferings and receiving the confessions of the perpetrators of violence, both privately and in public, the truth commissions helped generate a civic trust in the institutions that contributes to strengthening the democratic process. However, caution should be exercised regarding the role of truth as an instrument of social transformation, and therefore as an agent of democratization. Truth can have only a minor or even negligible impact in a country if rulers have autocratic ambitions or envision predatory projects.[37] Therefore, Jack Snyder and Leslie Vinjamuri point out that TRCs can only consolidate democracy when they operate in contexts where post-conflict rulers are supporters of democracy and where state institutions are already fairly strong. They assert that when this is not the case, TRCs can increase social tensions.[38]

TRCs can also contribute to building a democratic state through the material and symbolic reparations measures they implement. As these measures are at the heart of peacebuilding processes, they express to the victims a government's commitment to political and social transformation.[39] They also recognize victims' suffering that represents a form of justice.[40] Moreover, if TRCs are well conducted in accordance with the *Basic Principles and Guidelines on the Right to a Remedy and Reparation for Victims of Gross Violations of International Human Rights Law and Serious Violations of International Humanitarian Law*, in the form of restitution, compensation, rehabilitation, satisfaction, and guarantees of non-repetition,[41] reparations give a sense of justice that can indirectly have a strong impact on democracy through the trust they create between victims and state institutions.[42] After highlighting the existence of a causal relationship between transitional justice and democratic consolidation, there is still a missing piece to understand why some societies in transition succeed in building or consolidating democracy while others fail. This is where the relevance of conceptualizing transitional justice as inherently a "political field" comes into play.

TRANSITIONAL JUSTICE AS A "POLITICAL FIELD"

In the post–Cold War transitions in Latin America, which bear some relevance to African contexts, transitional justice mostly takes place against a backdrop of political compromise due to the destabilizing nature of criminal prosecutions. In the contexts of transitions in Argentina in 1984 and Chile in 1990, for example, truth commissions have been adopted as alternatives to criminal prosecutions in the face of tensions with the military.[43] In Ruti Teitel's genealogical studies on transitional justice, she highlights that law and politics appear closely intertwined in all periods of evolution of this practice.[44] Transitional justice thus presents itself "as an inherently political process [where it's decided] how a society should be organized and how norms and perceptions will be translated into legally binding institutions."[45] Before analyzing how this operates in the transitional justice process of Burkina Faso, it is first necessary to describe briefly the historical background of transitional justice in the country.

TRANSITIONAL JUSTICE IN BURKINA FASO

Blaise Compaoré came to power on 15 October 1987, following a *coup d'état* in which the president of the National Council of the Revolution, Captain Thomas Sankara was murdered along with thirteen of his close collaborators and bodyguards on the premises of the Conseil de l'Entente. Due to his regime's policy based on social justice, probity, the moralization of the public domain, the fight against corruption, the policy of health and education for all, and access for all to drinking water, local clothing, and food,[46] Sankara's assassination was considered "the murdered hope" of a whole people, if not of an entire generation.[47] Because of his approach to governance, which focused on the poor and marginalized, his virtues of integrity, his anti-imperialist and anti-capitalist stance, the "father of the Burkinabe revolution" was regarded by many Africans in general, and Burkinabe in particular, as a symbol of a rediscovered identity, a hero of the liberation from the colonial yoke. His murder on 15 October 1987, at the advent of the Popular Front led by Blaise Compaoré, was seen by many of his admirers as a vile and unforgivable act.

To strengthen his regime, Compaoré repressed voices of protest.[48] Those who posed threats to his power were persecuted, and several were killed. The crime that perhaps most seriously shook the Compaoré regime was the murder of Norbert Zongo, an investigative journalist of the weekly *L'Indépendant* on 13 December 1998, along with two companions. These murders, which later became known as the "Norbert Zongo affair," led the country in the turmoil of the most important socio-political crisis of the Compaoré regime.[49] However, there has been no justice in this case to assign responsibility and punish the perpetrators.[50] In order to appease the protests arising from the murder of Norbert Zongo, the president created by decree on 18 December 1998 a Commission d'enquête indépendante (CEI) to clarify the circumstances of the journalist's death. The commission submitted its report to the government on

7 May 1999, in which it clearly states that "Norbert Zongo was murdered for political reasons because he practiced engaged investigative journalism." Six suspects of the crimes were identified as members of the Presidential Security Regiment, the praetorian guard of the head of state. In response to the CEI report, the regime promised legal action to prosecute the perpetrators of the crimes. An investigating judge was assigned to the crimes, but the proceedings ended three years later with no trial.

As a political strategy, the government established a "College of the Wise" whose mandate is to shed light on all unpunished crimes and all homicide cases resulting or alleged to result from political violence for the period from 1960 and make recommendations that can promote national reconciliation and social peace.[51] Within a short period of forty-five days, the college tabled its report on 30 July 1999. For the period between 1960 and 1999, it listed ninety-one cases of "blood crimes," eighty-one cases of economic crimes, and forty-nine other cases of crimes involving kidnappings, torture, and broken careers.[52] In response to these crimes, the college recommended the creation of a Truth and Justice Commission for National Reconciliation whose mission would be to establish the truth about the crimes, ensure the right to reparation, and lead the country toward national reconciliation.

Following this, the government established by decree of 11 November 1999 a Commission for National Reconciliation (CNR).[53] The commission issued its report on 22 February 2000 and concluded that there was shared responsibility between the military that held the coups in Burkina Faso and the civilians who were their sponsors.[54] In response, the political authorities set up by decree of 11 April 2000, a commission to implement the recommendations of the CNR. After twelve months of work, the commission issued a report listing the crimes committed in Burkina Faso from 1960 to 2000. The blood crimes record stands at 102 cases that resulted in the loss of life.[55] The commission clarifies the situation of missing persons, the location and identification of the graves of deceased persons, and establishes contacts with the families of all missing persons. The commission investigated ten famous cases of missing persons, including those of Professor Guillaume Sessouma and the seventh-year medical student Boukary Dabo, who were killed in 1989 and 1990, respectively.

It is against the backdrop of this past, characterized by numerous blood and economic crimes without successful trials, that the

Compaoré regime was overthrown in 2014. This was a result of the popular uprising of 30 and 31 October 2014 against the president's plan to once again amend Article 37 of the constitution to be able to stand for re-election in the elections scheduled for 2015. According to the report of the national anti-corruption network, Le Réseau national de lute anti-corruption (REN-LAC) of 2014, the popular uprising was not only a refusal of Compaoré's attempt to amend Article 37 of the constitution that would allow him to stay in power, but it also reflected much more the rejection of a system of governance that was built on impunity to crimes, nepotism, corruption, organized plundering of public resources, and fraudulent sale of mining resources.[56]

Following the collapse of Compaoré's regime, the national charter of transition, adopted under the leadership of actors of civil society and political parties of the former opposition, established under the governance of the prime minister (see Article 17 of the charter) the CNRR.[57] The objective of the CNRR was to set out the foundations of a truly democratic, just, free, and inclusive society in Burkina Faso. The CNRR submitted its report, *Les voies du renouveau*, to the prime minister on 13 September 2015,[58] with the following recommendations: strong actions for political and institutional renewal; modernization of the electoral system; effective media and information management; challenges of governance of the public finances and the economy; rehabilitation of health and education; environmental peril and the land tenure; need of truth and justice; and the imperative of national reconciliation. In addition, it recommended the establishment of a High Council for National Reconciliation and Unity (HCNRU) (also known as Haut conseil pour la réconciliation et l'unité nationale) and, later, a monitoring and evaluation body for the implementation of reforms and national reconciliation.

By decree of 6 November 2015, deputies of the transitional parliament, the Conseil national de la transition (CNT), adopted the act on the allocation, composition, organization, and functioning of the HCNRU.[59] The HCNRU had a five-year mandate aimed at fostering reconciliation and national unity, social cohesion, and guaranteeing peace and stability for sustainable development. It was also responsible for implementing the recommendations of the Sub-Commission on Truth, Justice, and National Reconciliation of the CNRR and for seeking and determining responsibility for political crimes and other serious human rights violations committed in Burkina Faso from

1960 to 2015. To accomplish this, it was expected to process 5,065 files already registered as well as those in the process of registration and produce an annual report. It is in this context that I now evaluate the impact of transitional justice measures on democratic consolidation in the country.

TRANSITIONAL JUSTICE MEASURES AND THE BUILDING OF A DEMOCRATIC STATE

The CNRR was created with a multifaceted mission to, in part, "create conditions and frameworks conducive to the manifestation of truth, justice, forgiveness and national reconciliation" in Burkina Faso.[60] But because of the short five-month mandate the CNRR had to carry out its mission and fear of the military forces allied to the fallen regime, it was unable to reveal the truth about the unexplained crimes committed during the Compaoré regime and those of the two-day insurrection.[61] Therefore, following the recommendations of the CNRR, the HCNRU was created with the mission to continue the work of the Sub-Commission on Truth, Justice, and National Reconciliation of the CNRR, to "situate responsibilities," that is, to reveal the truth about the authors of political crimes and other serious human rights violations perpetrated in Burkina Faso since its independence. However, in observing the work of the HCNRU, it appeared it has limited itself to only listening to victims of the crimes and has focused on seeking national reconciliation and not the revelation of the truth. The truth about a violent past is constituted by diverse perceptions,[62] and the process of creating a shared narrative, while potentially a source of tension in post-conflict societies, is often necessary for victims to move on. As several transitional justice scholars have noted, only when well managed can truth be a source of healing and reconciliation for a nation.[63]

In the current context of Burkina Faso, it is evident the country is in serious need of healing and reconciliation to move forward. Therefore, it was essential that the HCNRU sees its mission as contributing to the establishment of a democratic state in the country by building a new post-insurgency society based on truth and accountability. Its activities should have aimed at involving the entire population through the process of deliberative democracy. As Christian Nadeau has argued, a deliberative democracy takes place through exchanges of opinions between parties based on the norms of transparency and reciprocity. He adds that although this procedure may generate new crises, it is necessary to ensure the stability of the institutions.[64]

When the HCNRU started its work, instead of limiting itself to information and awareness-raising sessions in a few regions of the country, it should have organized real fora of deliberative democracy, giving the opportunity not only to the direct victims of political and economic crimes but also to the general population to express their views and expectations on the past discord and make suggestions for the future. This process aligns with the historicist perspective of truth commissions, which is that they constitute fora for the discovery of historical truth that can be a reference point to educate a society about the wrongs of the past and build a better community for the future.[65]

Such a process has strong potential to lead to a collective catharsis of the populations as a whole that would lay the foundation for real national reconciliation, essential to the building of a democratic state. The commission president himself acknowledged the ignorance of the population about the commission's work, when submitting his first annual report to the president of Burkina Faso in 2019.[66] The lack of public deliberation on the truth in the transitional justice process under the Kaboré régime can be explained by power relations in favour of the regime, which controlled the management of the process. The twenty-one members of the HCNRU were chosen by the president of the state, the prime minister, and the president of the National Assembly, which implies the commission was under government control and in line with its political agenda. The further implication is that the commission's work took into consideration the socio-political and security context of the country, which is marked by the presence of terrorist groups and political-military forces allied with the former regime, who represent a serious threat to an effective transitional process.

Following the failed coup during the political transition organized by these same political-military forces, analysts and some leaders of the Kaboré regime have explained the recurrent terrorist attacks in the country as acts of revenge for the fall of the Compaoré regime.[67] In this context, one can understand the circumspection of the Kaboré regime to encourage the revelation of the truth of the past crimes. This caution could explain why the HCNRU's first report, submitted in 2019, has not been made public.

TAKING MEASURES TO PROVIDE JUSTICE

Driven by the wind of the post-insurrectional "revolution," the transitional government opened for trial several criminal cases, such as the murder of Thomas Sankara, Boukary Dabo, and Norbert Zongo. In the last case, an international arrest warrant was issued against François Compaoré, the younger brother of Blaise Compaoré, in exile in France, due to allegations that he is the main sponsor of the death of the journalist and his companions. As for the former president Compaoré, he was accused of "acts of high treason and an attack on the Constitution," while ministers of his last government were prosecuted for "acts of voluntary assault, complicity in assault, assassinations and complicity in assassinations."

With the opening of these cases, the criminal justice process has shown some effectiveness. This judicial progress can be explained by the "revolutionary" transitional context where civil society, political opposition, and a majority of the population have pressured the government to break from past approaches to governance by holding accountable those responsible for crimes.[68] Under the Kaboré regime, however, the criminal justice process has been slow in terms of accountability for past crimes. Progress on criminal justice began only in 2019, a year before the end of the president's first term, with the conviction of the perpetrators of the failed coup of 2015, whose leader, General Gilbert Diendere, was sentenced to twenty years' imprisonment, and the trial for the assassination of Thomas Sankara, at the end of which Blaise Compaoré (tried *in absentia*) and Gilbert Diendere, Blaise's right-hand man at the time of the events, were both sentenced to life imprisonment in April 2022.

The trial of those responsible for the failed coup and of Blaise Compaoré *in absentia* has had several positive consequences for the consolidation of democracy in Burkina Faso. First, it has upheld the rule of law, reminding the population that there are rules governing the state's institutions and that those who commit crimes or threaten state security will be prosecuted and punished no matter how high-ranking they are in the military or in public service. In addition, through its power of delegitimization, the trials have made it possible to put disruptive high-ranking military officers behind bars, thereby preventing them from impeding the smooth running of democratic governance. Given its claims to being democratic and republican, the Kaboré regime was obliged to punish the perpetrators of this flagrant breach of state security. In addition, civil society and opposition political parties pressured the government to bring to justice those responsible for the coup.

Much remains to be done in terms of justice reforms and holding violators accountable for their crimes and human rights abuses. For example, the Kaboré regime appeared not to have made it a priority to seek the extradition of Blaise Compaoré, exiled in Côte d'Ivoire, to Burkina Faso, to answer in person for the crimes committed during his presidency, such as the assassination of Sankara. In addition, several high-profile corruption cases have not been addressed, which calls into question the Kaboré regime's commitment to transparent governance. One such case was the "fine coal case" relating to the fraudulent export of gold from Burkina Faso and involving the minister of mines and quarries while he was in office.

The slowness of the justice system in this and other cases can be explained in terms of several dilemmas the government faced. The regime has appeared lenient toward those in its own party accused of plundering public wealth, and cautious toward former leaders of the Compaoré regime, fearing they might overthrow it in a coup. This last fear transpired: the president was overthrown on 24 January 2022 by a group of military officers blaming him for his failure to effectively combat terrorism in the country and recover several parts of the territory from under the control of terrorist groups. Despite the progress in justice with the judgment of some major cases, the coup d'état has seriously compromised the idea of consolidating the democratic rule of law state. The construction of such a state requires in-depth work to ensure that all political and military actors abide by the rule of law and in particular the constitutional rules for the devolution of power. In this context of the weaknesses in the justice system and the rule of law, it should be noted that national reconciliation remains a quest to achieve.

THE QUEST FOR NATIONAL RECONCILIATION

Reconciliation is important for all post-conflict and post-authoritarian ruled societies. Indeed, without it, none of these societies can endure. In the context of South Africa, for example, James L. Gibson points out that no one seems to know what "reconciliation" truly means, while everyone is convinced it has failed or at least not met expectations.[69] In Burkina Faso, among political leaders, academics, or civil society activists, there are generally two understandings of "reconciliation." For some, it means forgiving the wounds, the grudges of the past, in order to turn the page, and for others, it must necessarily involve truth, justice, and reparation.[70] Reconciliation is an elusive and complex concept whose exact meaning is far from certain among transitional justice scholars.[71] This is fully apparent in Burkina Faso, where the HCNRU, the ruling party, the opposition, and civil society organizations are all calling for national reconciliation, but no one seems to know how to achieve it, and there is a lack of agreement about what it really means.

From a heuristic perspective, it is worth highlighting some differing understandings of the concept developed by various authors. David Croker, for example, believes there are at least three meanings to the notion of reconciliation, ranging from the narrow (thin) to the broad (thick) conception. He argues that at the minimum level, reconciliation can refer to "mere coexistence" in the sense that former enemies comply with the law and stop killing each other. The second meaning is that old enemies go beyond mere coexistence to respect each other as citizens. He calls this form of reconciliation "democratic reciprocity." The third broad meaning he associates with the notion of forgiveness and mercy instead of justice, of common vision and healing, or even harmony. He links this form of reconciliation to Desmond Tutu's conceptualized notion of *Ubuntu*, which he criticizes as too idealistic.[72] In Burkina Faso, because of the terrorist attacks and the continuing political tensions in the country that led to the overthrow of president Kaboré, it can be said that reconciliation, according to Crocker's three meanings, is not yet a reality. How to achieve it then?

For Elin Skaar, reconciliation could be viewed as a goal, process, or both.[73] She refers to Susan Dwyer, who considers that "reconciliation is fundamentally a process whose aim is to lessen the sting of tension: to make sense of injuries, new beliefs, and attitudes in the overall narrative context of a personal or national life."[74] Reconciliation, therefore, presents itself as a procedure aimed at establishing harmony between parties through a transformation of their conflicting relations. Jonathan Sisson defines this goal's conceptual framework as based on the right to truth, the right to justice, the right to reparation measures, and the implementation of guarantees of non-repetition.[75]

In the context of Burkina Faso, evidence suggests that for authentic reconciliation, truth, justice, reparation, and guarantees of non-repetition of the crimes of the past are all necessary. But as we have seen, the HCNRU and the Kaboré regime as a whole have fallen short of this goal. By simply listening to the victims and compensating them, and by making some trips to regions of the country to discuss with the customary and "traditional" author-ities, the commission's activities have only superficially relieved the wounds of society; it has not engaged in the deep healing to ensure that the violence of the past does not recur in the future. Consequently, this "superficial reconciliation" does not appear to have led to a real unity of the country. Only a "genuine reconcilia-tion" – one that mobilizes all social strata and leads civil, political, and military actors to prioritize the nation's best interests by recog-nizing the rule of law and accepting the revelation of truth, justice, and reparation, with the effective participation of the victims – can foster the stability of state institutions and, in so doing, contribute to the consolidation of democracy in the country.

While no transitional justice experience is perfect, in itself, Burkina Faso could draw on the South African experience of truth, amnesty, and reparation, and Rwanda's punitive justice to implement an effec-tive reconciliation process that will enable the country to lay a solid foundation for a stable and democratic rule of law state. The efforts of the Kaboré regime at instituting the rule of law and promoting national reconciliation have been constrained by the challenges of the terrorist threat to national security and by political-military forces linked to the former regime. While such considerations are legitimate, they have dangerously compromised the aspiration for change in general and the democratic consolidation in particular, so much desired by the people of Burkina Faso through the popular uprising of October 2014.

CONCLUSION

The transitional justice process in Burkina Faso has recorded some achievements. Despite the security challenges faced by the transi-tional government, it has successfully opened many court cases, adopted the CNRR to shed light on past crimes, proposed measures to contribute to justice and national reconciliation, and recommended constitutional and institutional reforms. In addition, the transitional government established the HCNRU as part of the transition process aimed at continuing the work of the CNRR's Sub-Commission on

Truth, Justice, and National Reconciliation to establish responsibilities for the crimes, repair the harm suffered by the victims of the past regime and the popular uprising, and reconcile the people of Burkina Faso. However, under the Kaboré regime, although there have been some trials such as the 2015 *coup d'état* and Thomas Sankara cases that ended with convictions, the measures adopted by transitional justice seemed globally inadequate for the sustained social reconstruction and national reconciliation needed to build a democratic Burkinabe state.

The process appeared to be caught between major dilemmas: on the one hand the demand for truth, justice, and reparation over the crimes of the past, and on the other hand the socio-political and security context of the country marked by recurrent terrorist attacks and the political-military forces allied to the former regime that oppose these measures. In response to these dilemmas, the Kaboré regime appeared to have chosen caution in the search for truth and justice. In doing so, not only were these measures lacking effectiveness, but they also undermined the potential for national reconciliation to serve as the foundation for building a democratic state in the country. The fact that the Kaboré regime was overthrown by a *coup d'état* on 24 January 2022 and that some months later the country experienced another *coup d'état* on 30 and 31 September 2022, can be seen as a sign that the transitional justice process implemented under the regime did not have enough positive impact on the building of a Burkinabe democratic state.

NOTES

1 The "political transition" began with the installation of the transitional government in November 2014 and ended with the installation of an elected government in December 2015.

2 Commission de la réconciliation nationale et des réformes, *Rapport général: Les voies du renouveau*, 2015.

3 UN Secretary-General, "The Rule of Law and Transitional Justice in Conflict and Post-Conflict Societies," (2004): 4.

4 Aboubacar Dakuyo, "Insurrection populaire et justice transitionnelle au Burkina Faso: entre dynamique 'révolutionnaire' et réalisme politique," *Politique et Sociétés* 38, no. 2 (2019): 32; Dustin N. Sharp, "Addressing Dilemmas of the Global and the Local in Transitional Justice," *Emory International Law Review* 29 (2014): 78; Rosemary Nagy, "Transitional

Justice as Global Project: Critical Reflections," in *Law in Transition: Human Rights, Development and Transitional Justice*, ed. Ruth Buchanan and Peer Zumbansen (Oxford: Hart Publishing, 2014), 218; Paige Arthur, "How 'Transitions' Reshaped Human Rights: A Conceptual History of Transitional Justice," *Human Rights Quarterly* 31, no. 2 (2009): 325–6; Ruti Teitel, *Transitional Justice* (Oxford: Oxford University Press, 2000), 7.

5 Louis Joinet, *Rapport au Conseil économique et social des Nations Unies sur la Question de l'impunité des auteurs des violations des droits de l'homme (civils et politiques)*, Rapport final révisé, E/CN.4/Sub.2/1997/20/ Rev.1.; Diane Orentlicher, *Rapport de l'experte indépendante chargée de mettre à jour l'Ensemble des principes pour la lutte contre l'impunité*, E / CN.4/2005/102/Add.1.

6 UN Secretary-General, "The Rule of Law and Transitional Justice," 9.

7 Chandra Sriram et al., eds, *Transitional Justice and Peacebuilding on the Ground: Victims and Ex-Combatants*, 1st ed. (Oxon: Routledge, 2013); Wendy Lambourne, "Transformative Justice, Reconciliation and Peacebuilding," in *Transitional Justice Theories*, ed. Susanne Buckley-Zistel et al. (Oxon: Routledge, 2009): 28–39; Lisa J. Laplante, "Transitional Justice and Peace Building: Diagnosing and Addressing the Socioeconomic Roots of Violence through a Human Rights Framework," *International Journal of Transitional Justice* 2, no. 3 (2008): 331–55.

8 UN Security Council. "Statement by the President of the Security Council," S/PRST/2001/5, 2001, 1.

9 The military regimes that have succeeded one another in Burkina Faso are that of General Sangoulé Lamizana (1966–1980), Colonel Saye Zerbo (1980–1982), Doctor-Commander Jean-Baptiste Ouédraogo (1982–1983), Captain Thomas Sankara (1983–1987) and, finally, Captain Blaise Compaoré (1987–2014). With the exception of the Lamizana regime, the others are all the result of a *coup d'état*. See Roger Kaboré, *Histoire politique du Burkina Faso 1919–2000* (Paris: L'Harmattan, 2002), 77–222.

10 Valérie Arnould, "Transitional Justice and Democracy in Uganda: Between Impetus and Instrumentalization," *Journal of Eastern African Studies* 9, no. 3 (2015): 355.

11 Nour Benghellab, "Des mythes aux réalités de la justice transitionnelle: catharsis thérapeutique, (re)constructions nationales et légitimation politique," *Champ pénal/Penal field* 13 (2016): 11; Noémie Turgls, "La justice transitionnelle, un concept discuté," *Les Cahiers de la Justice*, no. 3 (2015): 333; Christian Nadeau, "Conflits de reconnaissance et justice transitionnelle," *Politique et Sociétés* 28, no. 3 (2009): 191.

12 Arnould, "Transitional Justice and Democracy in Uganda," 355.

13 See, for example, Gerardo L. Munck, "What is Democracy? A Reconceptualization of the Quality of Democracy," *Democratization* 23, no. 1 (2014): 1–26; Robert A. Dahl, *Polyarchy: Participation and Opposition* (New Haven: Yale University Press, 1971); Dankwart A. Rustow, "Transitions to Democracy: Toward a Dynamic Model," *Comparative Politics* 2, no. 3 (1970): 337–63; Seymour M. Lipset, *Political Man: The Social Basis of Politics* (New York: Anchor Books, 1963).

14 Leonardo Morlino, "Légitimité et qualité de démocratie," *Revue internationale des sciences sociales*, no.196 (2010): 42.

15 Terry Lynn Karl, "Dilemmas of Democratization in Latin America," *Comparative Politics* 23, no.1 (1990): 2.

16 Morlino, "Légitimité et qualité de démocratie," 43.

17 Arnould, "Transitional Justice and Democracy in Uganda," 357.

18 Olivier Beauvallet, "La lutte contre l'impunité: concept et enjeux modernes de la promesse démocratique," *Les Cahiers de la Justice*, no. 1 (2017): 27.

19 Arnould, "Transitional Justice and Democracy in Uganda," 357.

20 Beauvallet, "La lutte contre l'impunité," 16.

21 Cécile Aptel, "Justice pénale internationale: entre raison d'État et État de droit," *Revue internationale et stratégique*, no.67 (2007): 75–6.

22 Anja Mihr, ed. *Transitional Justice: Between Criminal Justice, Atonement and Democracy* (Utrecht: Universiteit Utrecht, SIM Special 37, 2012), 17.

23 Arnould, "Transitional Justice and Democracy in Uganda," 358.

24 Beauvallet, "La lutte contre l'impunité," 19.

25 Valérie Arnould and Chandra Sriram, "Pathways of Impact: How Transitional Justice Affects Democratic Institution-Building," Impact of Transitional Justice Measures on Democratic Institutions-Building Policy Paper 1-10, 2014.

26 Arnould, "Transitional Justice and Democracy in Uganda," 359.

27 Matthew Mullen, "Reassessing the Focus of Transitional Justice: The Need to Move Structural and Cultural Violence to the Centre," *Cambridge Review of International Affairs* 28, no. 3 (2015): 468.

28 Priscilla B. Hayner, "Fifteen Truth Commissions – 1974 to 1994: A Comparative Study," *Human Rights Quarterly* 16, no. 4 (1994): 600.

29 David Mendeloff, "Truth- Seeking, Truth-Telling, and Postconflict Peacebuilding: Curb the Enthusiasm?" *International Studies Review* 6, no. 3 (2004): 355–80.

30 Elin Skaar, Camila Gianella Malca, and Trine Eide, "Towards a Framework for Impact Assessment," in *After Violence, Transitional Justice, Peace, and Democracy* (Oxon: Routledge, 2015), 9.

31 Martha Minow, "The Hope for Healing: What Can Truth Commissions Do?" in Rotberg and Thompson, *Truth v. Justice*, 239.

32 Paul Gready and Simon Robins, "From Transitional Justice to Transformative Justice: A New Agenda in Practice," *The International Journal for Transitional Justice* 8, no. 3 (2014): 357.

33 Amy Gutmann and Dennis Thompson, "The Moral Foundations of Truth Commissions," in Rotberg and Thompson, *Truth v. Justice*, 35–6.

34 Sandrine Lefranc, "Les commissions de vérité: une alternative au droit?" *Droit et Cultures* 56 (2008).

35 Sandra Young, "Narrative and Healing in the Hearings of the South African Truth and Reconciliation Commission," *Biography* 27, no. 1 (2004): 153–7.

36 Truth and Reconciliation Commission, *Truth and Reconciliation Commission of South Africa Report*, vol. 1, chapter 5 (1998): 29–45.

37 Skaar, Gianella Malca, and Eide, "Towards a Framework for Impact Assessment," 9.

38 Jack Snyder and Leslie Vinjamuri, "Trials and Errors: Principle and Pragmatism in Strategies of International Justice," *International Security* 28, no. 3 (2003): 20.

39 Jemima García-Godos and Chandra Sriram, "Introduction," in *Transitional Justice and Peacebuilding on the Ground: Victims and Ex-combatants*, ed. Sriram et al. (Abingdon: Routledge, 2013), 11.

40 Nancy Fraser, *Justice Interruptus: Critical Reflections on the "Postsocialist" Condition* (New York: Routledge, 1997), 11–39.

41 UN General Assembly. *Basic Principles and Guidelines on the Right to a Remedy and Reparation for Victims of Gross Violations of International Human Rights Law and Serious Violations of International Humanitarian Law*, Adopted and proclaimed by General Assembly resolution 60/147, 2005.

42 Skaar, Gianella Malca, and Eide, "Towards a Framework for Impact Assessment," 11.

43 Bronwyn A. Leebaw, "The Irreconcilable Goals of Transitional Justice," *Human Rights Quarterly* 30, no. 1 (2008): 99.

44 Ruti Teitel, "Transitional Justice Genealogy," *Harvard Human Rights Journal* 16 (2003).

45 Sandra Rubli, "(Re)making the Social World: The Politics of Transitional Justice in Burundi," *Africa Spectrum* 48, no. 1 (2013): 9.

46 Sennen Andriamirado, *Il s'appelait Sankara: Chronique d'une mort violente* (Paris: Jeune Afrique Livres, 1989), 164–5.

47 Valère D. Somé, *Thomas Sankara: l'espoir assassiné* (Paris: L'Harmattan, 1990).

48 Robin Luckham, "The Military, Militarization and Democratization in Africa: A Survey of Literature and Issues," *African Studies Review* 37, no. 2 (1994); Céline Thiriot, "La place des militaires dans les régimes post-transition d'Afrique subsaharienne: la difficile resectorisation," *Revue Internationale de Politique Comparée* 15, no.1 (2008).

49 Augustin Loada, "Réflexions sur la société civile en Afrique: le Burkina de l'après-Zongo," *Politique africaine*, no 76 (1999); Kaboré, *Histoire politique du Burkina Faso 1919–2000*, 289.

50 For more details, see S. Ouédraogo, *Collectif des organisations démocratiques de masse et de partis politiques contre l'impunité*. Cahiers du CRISES, 200.

51 Collège des sages, Décret de création no. 99-158/PRES du 1er juin 1999 *portant création, composition et missions d'un Collège des sages*.

52 *Rapport du Collège des sages*, 1999.

53 Commission nationale de la réconciliation, Décret de création no. 99-390/PRES/PM du 11 novembre 1999.

54 *Rapport de la Commission de la réconciliation nationale*, 2000.

55 *Rapport général sur la mise en œuvre des recommandations de la Commission de réconciliation nationale*, 2001.

56 REN-LAC, 2004. *Rapport de 2014 sur l'état de la corruption au Burkina Faso*, 66–7.

57 Commission de la réconciliation nationale et des réformes, Décret no 2014-026/PRES-TRANS du 4 décembre 2014 *portant création de la Commission de la Réconciliation Nationale et des réformes*.

58 *Rapport de la Commission de la réconciliation nationale et des réformes*, 2015.

59 Loi No. 074-2015/CNT du 6 November 2015.

60 Décret no 2015-175/PRES-TRANS du 13 février 2015 promulguant la Loi no 003-2015/CNT du 23 janvier 2015 *portant attributions, composition, organisation et fonctionnement de la Commission de la réconciliation nationale et des réformes, Journal officiel*, no. 29 (16 July 2015): Article 3.

61 Dakuyo, "Insurrection populaire et justice transitionnelle au Burkina Faso," 38.

62 Robert I. Rotberg, "Truth Commissions and the Provision of Truth, Justice, and Reconciliation," in Rotberg and Thompson, *Truth v. Justice*, 6.

63 Erin Daly, "Transformative Justice: Charting a Path to Reconciliation," *International Legal Perspectives* 12, no. 1–2 (2001): 128; Minow, "The Hope for Healing," 240–55.

64 Christian Nadeau, "Quelle justice après la guerre? Éléments pour une théorie de la justice transitionnelle," article publié dans La vie des idées.fr, 23 mars 2009, *Les Classiques des sciences sociales*, 15.

65 Gutmann and Thompson, "The Moral Foundations of Truth Commissions," 33.

66 Direction de la communication de la présidence du Faso. 2019. *Haut Conseil pour la Réconciliation et l'Unité nationale (HCRUN) au Burkina: remise du rapport d'activités 2018 au président du Faso.*

67 Ludovic O. Kibora, "Réactions populaires aux attaques terroristes de janvier 2016 à Ouagadougou," *Mande Studies* 21 (2019): 64–5; M. Malagardis, *Attentat au Burkina: un lien avec le régime déchu de Compaoré?* (2018); Bruno Jaffré, *L'insurrection inachevée Burkina Faso 2014* (Paris: Éditions Syllepse, 2014), 283–6.

68 Dakuyo, "Insurrection populaire et justice transitionnelle au Burkina Faso."

69 James L. Gibson, "Does Truth Lead to Reconciliation? Testing the Causal Assumptions of the South African Truth and Reconciliation Process," *American Journal of Political Science* 48, no. 2 (2004): 202.

70 See, for example, Obissa J. Mien, "Réconciliation nationale au Burkina Faso: 'L'Appel de Manéga' lance le concept 'Je donne ma main,'" Le Faso. net, 3 July 2022, https://lefaso.net/spip.php?article114717; Firmin Ouattara, "Réconciliation nationale: 'Que la justice ne prenne pas en otage le processus,' Ablassé Ouédraogo," L'Express du Faso, 23 June 2021, www.lexpressdufaso-bf.com/reconciliation-nationale-que-la-justice-ne-prenne-pas-en-otage-le-processus-ablasse-ouedraogo/; "Burkina: La réconciliation nationale est 'une comédie institutionnelle,' selon le Balai Citoyen," Le Faso.net, 3 July 2022, https://lefaso.net/spip. php?article102704.

71 James Hughes and Denisa Kostovicova, "Introduction: Rethinking Reconciliation and Transitional Justice after Conflict," Ethnic and Racial Studies 41, no. 4 (2018): 618.

72 David A. Crocker, "Punishment, Reconciliation, and Democratic Deliberation," *Buffalo Criminal Law Review* 5, no. 2, (2002): 525–30.

73 Elin Skaar, "Reconciliation in a Transitional Justice Perspective," *Transitional Justice Review* 1, no.1 (2013): 65.

74 Susan Dwyer, "Reconciliation for Realists," in *Dilemmas of Reconciliation: Cases and Concepts*, ed. Carol A.L. Prager and Trudy Govier (Waterloo: Wilfrid Laurier University Press, 2000), 54–5.

75 Jonathan Sisson, "A Conceptual Framework for Dealing with the Past," *Politorbis*, no. 50 (2010): 12–16.

8

Mali's Truth, Justice, and Reconciliation Commission: Truth Seeking and Peacebuilding across Borders

Janine Lespérance

The global proliferation of truth commissions over recent decades creates learning possibilities for new ones. They can draw upon challenges encountered and solutions adopted in other contexts to build their knowledge about post-conflict justice, truth-seeking processes, and reparations, and develop structures and practices adapted to their specific context. Third-party individuals or organizations can play a role in this process by sharing expertise and facilitating information exchanges.

One such organization is Avocats sans frontières Canada (Lawyers without Borders Canada, henceforth referred to as ASFC). ASFC is a non-governmental, international co-operation organization headquartered in Quebec City, Canada. It is active in various Latin American and African countries, working in partnership with human rights lawyers and organizations to facilitate access to justice for marginalized groups. ASFC has been present in Mali since 2012 and has directly supported one of the key institutions in Mali's transitional justice process: the Commission Vérité, Justice et Réconciliation (Truth, Justice, and Reconciliation Commission, henceforth referred to as CVJR). Created on 15 January 2014,[1] the CVJR's role of furthering national reconciliation was recognized in the 2015 Algiers Peace Accord (henceforth, Peace Accord).[2] The CVJR became operational in 2017. ASFC and the CVJR signed a partnership agreement in July of the same year.

ASFC's experience in support of the CVJR demonstrates there are opportunities for impactful international collaboration in peace-building processes and for developing a common transnational approach to peacebuilding through truth commissions. With a primarily descriptive approach, this chapter illustrates how an international non-governmental organization (NGO) can contribute to the work of a truth commission and how practices and experiences shared across borders can help a truth commission make strategic decisions. This chapter also aims to shed light on some of the practical challenges truth commissions and their technical and financial partners face. It encourages further reflection on the transmission of knowledge between truth commissions to contribute to the development of best practices.

This chapter first introduces the Malian CVJR, examining some of the obstacles it faces as a truth commission operating in a difficult context. Next, it presents an overview of ASFC's work in Mali, identifying some of its contributions and challenges in supporting the CVJR.

MALI'S MAIN TRANSITIONAL JUSTICE
INSTITUTION: THE CVJR

Context of the CVJR's Operations

Since gaining independence from French colonization in 1960, Mali has been confronted by multiple armed rebellions (1963, 1990, 2006, 2012) and coups d'état (1968, 1991, 2012, 2020, 2021). This recurrent instability has various intertwined historical, social, political, and economic causes. The multidimensional crisis that emerged in 2012 involves secessionist Touareg groups in the north that declared the independence of the Azawad region,[3] a political and constitutional crisis instigated by a military coup d'état in 2012, the incursion of Islamic extremist armed groups, and inter-community violence.[4] Various forms of trafficking, corruption, and the weakness or absence of the Malian state, especially in the north, have contributed to the feasibility of conflict and thus its continuation.

The international community has intervened in Mali in response to the crisis. Notably, French military forces first intervened in January 2013, as well as the Economic Community of West African States through its African-led International Support Mission to Mali. The United Nations (UN) Multidimensional Integrated Stabilization Mission in Mali (MINUSMA) was established on 25 April 2013[5] and has been deployed since July 2013. Its mandate has been renewed and, as of the time of writing, extends until 30 June 2023.[6]

Despite the presence of international forces and the signature of the Peace Accord, violence has continued. In central Mali, there has been an increase in inter-community violence, including massacres, especially since 2018. The conflict has involved a range of serious human rights violations, including murder; arbitrary detention; use of children by armed groups; restriction of civil liberties, particularly through the strict imposition of Sharia law, with threats of severe punishment for contraventions;[7] rape and other forms of sexual and gender-based violence, including forced marriage; torture; and the destruction of cultural heritage. One non-state actor has been convicted by the International Criminal Court (ICC) for the destruction of cultural heritage,[8] and another faces charges before the ICC for war crimes and crimes against humanity committed in Timbuktu, including sexual violence.[9] While non-state actors have committed many violations, almost all parties in the conflict are alleged to have committed abuses, including Mali's defence and security forces.[10]

Structure and Mandate of the CVJR

The CVJR is one of the principal transitional justice mechanisms established in Mali to contribute to peacebuilding and reconciliation, as recognized by the Peace Accord signatories. They agreed to "promote a true national reconciliation founded on [...] the establishment of transitional justice mechanisms, notably through the operationalization of the CVJR."[11]

The CVJR had the mandate of "contributing to the instauration of a durable peace through the search for truth, reconciliation, and the consolidation of national unity and democratic values."[12] Accomplishing this mandate involved investigations of individual and collective violations of human rights and attacks on cultural heritage; creating conditions for the reinsertion of displaced people; facilitating dialogue within and between communities, as well as between the population and the state; promoting respect for the rule of law, republican, democratic, and socio-cultural values, and the right to difference; and making recommendations for preventing conflicts and for reparations for victims.[13] The CVJR's internal regulations specified, in a non-exhaustive list, the broad range of crimes it could investigate: murder and arbitrary execution; arrests or arbitrary detention; removal and kidnapping; forced conscription and attempted forced recruitment; rape and other sexual violence;

pillaging, theft, and destruction of property; enforced disappearance; torture and other cruel, inhuman, or degrading treatment; and destruction of cultural heritage.[14]

The CVJR had a relatively large number of leaders: twenty-five commissioners, including a president, Ousmane Oumarou Sidibé, and two vice-presidents. These commissioners represented a broad cross-section of Malian society, including human rights organizations, the private sector, and – to the chagrin of many victims of human rights violations[15] – armed groups signatory to the Peace Accord. Various commissioners presided over sub-commissions focusing on gender issues; raising awareness and reconciliation; studies, reports, and documentation; support for victims and reparations; and searching for truth.

The plenary assembly of the CVJR, composed of its commissioners, discussed and adopted internal regulations, action plans, and reports.[16] A general secretariat assisted the president with financial and administrative management and relations with the government and other institutions and partners. Apart from its main headquarters in Bamako, the CVJR had regional satellite offices in Bamako, Kidal, Mopti, Gao, Ségou, and Timbuktu.

Two principal aspects of the CVJR's mandate discussed here are truth seeking and the development of a reparations policy.

Truth-Seeking Functions of the CVJR

With respect to truth seeking, the CVJR aimed to contribute to reparative justice by shining light on human rights violations and their context, with a focus on the post-colonial period.

A number of studies and reports allowed the CVJR to analyze the causes of violent conflict in Mali and identify and classify rights violations. The CVJR also collected individual declarations from victims across the country who presented themselves to the CVJR, often at its regional satellite offices. These declarations were gathered on hard-copy statement forms and later entered into a database, which involved considerable effort given the number of declarations being processed. As of December 2022, the CVJR had collected 32,797 victim declarations.[17]

In addition, the CVJR established an investigations team in March 2019, tasked with the responsibility of selecting emblematic cases, carrying out additional investigations to fill information gaps, and corroborating existing information.[18] However, the CVJR's investigations did not establish individual criminal responsibility, and its activities did not involve an amnesty process; its findings were not intended to be used in judicial proceedings. As of the first trimester of 2019, CVJR records indicated that no author of crimes had presented themselves to the CVJR to provide their testimony.

Public Hearings

The CVJR held five different thematic public audiences with a limited number of attendees.[19] The hearings focused on violations of the right to liberty; violations of the right to life; torture and other cruel, inhumane, or degrading treatment; enforced disappearances; violations of property rights (for example, pillaging); women victims of sexual violence; and child victims of conflicts. Only a limited number of victims – chosen in advance according to established criteria, through the collaboration of the CVJR's offices – were able to testify at the public hearings.[20] For example, thirteen victims testified at the first hearing, on 8 December 2019. The limited nature of the public hearings meant that choosing themes and specific victims to testify were sensitive political decisions underpinned by the CVJR's intention for the hearings to be as representative and well-balanced as possible.

In comparison to some truth commissions, public hearings were less central to the CVJR's investigation strategy. The CVJR did not give alleged perpetrators of crimes the opportunity to speak. For the CVJR, public hearings were envisioned primarily as a means of helping the public understand the plight of victims of grave human rights violations through the presentation of emblematic cases, and contributing to the dignity and healing of victims, drawing particular attention to certain groups that are often marginalized. The hearings were intended to serve a public communications purpose and contribute to shaping the collective narrative on the conflict in Mali.

The CVJR's communications strategy for the hearings involved the production of video and audio documentaries, graphic material, public broadcasting, and translation into Malian languages – Peul, Arabic, Bambara, Tamashek, Songhay – as well as French and sign language. The five hearings were broadcast on national radio and television channels and on social media. Presumably, more Malians are likely to have access to the public hearings than to the final written report of the CVJR.[21]

Developing a National Reparations Program

Proposing a reparations policy to the Malian government for adoption was a key part of the CVJR's mandate. It was accomplished on 3 November 2022, when the CVJR announced that its proposed national policy was adopted by the interim legislative body.[22]

For the development of the reparations policy, the CVJR had at its disposal victims' declarations and the various analyses and reports prepared through its truth-seeking activities. Another source of information was a major victims' consultation organized by ASFC and carried out in collaboration with its Malian partners.[23] Consultation sessions involving individual interviews and discussion groups were held with 3,755 Malians in 2017. The results were published in January 2018. Although this consultation was not intended solely for the CVJR, it was instrumental in the commission's development of a reparations policy. Building upon that work, the CVJR carried out its own consultations of women and children in order to be better equipped to take their needs into account in developing the reparations policy.

In developing its reparations framework, the CVJR faced the delicate strategic quandary of finding the appropriate balance between ambitiously advocating for an extensive reparations policy that fully responded to victims' needs and the gravity of harms committed, and a more conservative, restricted approach that would perhaps be more realistic in a context of limited government resources and capacity. The CVJR opted for an intermediate approach and recommended the creation of a body to manage the allocation of reparations.

The CVJR shared its draft policy on reparations in events with victim[24] and government representatives,[25] prior to it being finalized.

Practical Challenges

One of the principal challenges for the CVJR was the security situation in which it operated. Far from being a truth commission investigating crimes committed well in the past, the CVJR carried out its work in an environment of ongoing abuses. After the CVJR came into operation, the situation worsened, particularly in central Mali. Freedom of movement was restricted for people in the north and centre of the country due to security conditions, and the CVJR endeavoured to collect victims' statements without jeopardizing their safety. Illustrating this challenge, the CVJR's first semester activity report for 2018 states that 1,783 declarations were collected in the regional offices between 1 January and 30 June 2018, and the report notes this number is lower than the numbers for the first and second semesters of 2017, at 4,516 and 2,487 respectively. The report also notes this trend can be explained in part by "the recurring insecurity and the difficulties of travelling to regional antennas experienced by communities in remote and less accessible areas."[26] In certain areas, namely Bamako, Timbuktu, and Ségou, the CVJR's regional satellite offices deployed mobile teams to allow victims to make their declarations more easily. In the region of Mopti, the strategy adopted due to ongoing insecurity was to transport victims to the regional office.

In addition, the ongoing conflict meant there was no obvious time to end the investigations of the CVJR. Originally, the CVJR mandate was to investigate human rights violations committed between 1960 and 2013. However, since violations continued to occur, the CVJR's plenary voted in early 2018 to reinterpret its mandate as extending from 1960 until the present day. It must be noted that gathering, organizing, and analyzing information about human rights violations committed in a vast territory over sixty years is a monumental undertaking.

Another challenge for the CVJR was generating the political will to support its work. While the CVJR was generally not obstructed in its work and had its mandate renewed, its work was not necessarily a priority of the Malian government. For example, when the Malian government introduced a bill for an amnesty law in 2018, known as the "Loi d'entente nationale" (National Accord Law), it contained provisions on reparation and other measures that did not consider the responsibilities and ongoing work of the CVJR. The bill proposed a limited form of reparation available to only certain victims and did not reflect international standards, as well as imposing certain measures without consultation, including a national day of pardon, a national reconciliation week, and the drafting of a general inclusive history of Mali by a committee.[27] Due to changes and instability in governance after its creation, the CVJR had to continuously seek to create and maintain political support – often with new interlocutors – to ensure its priorities, conclusions, and recommendations were taken seriously.

At the same time, public engagement was an ongoing challenge. The CVJR had to build awareness of its activities and approach among victims of the conflict and among Malians more broadly, many of whom have low trust and negative perceptions of Malian state institutions.[28] ASFC's aforementioned consultation in 2017 revealed a lack of knowledge about the CVJR or misunderstanding of its mandate among victims. For example, some people thought the CVJR was a judicial institution that would establish criminal responsibility.[29] Similarly, a mission of the CVJR in December 2017 revealed there was widespread ignorance or confusion about the CVJR in the Timbuktu region, particularly among nomadic or semi-nomadic groups.[30] The CVJR worked to build alliances with human rights organizations and victims' associations. Such partnerships are crucial for the inevitable advocacy required to ensure that the government properly implements the CVJR's recommendations and reparations framework.

ASFC'S SUPPORT OF THE CVJR

ASFC's projects contributing to the transitional justice process in Mali supported the CVJR both directly and indirectly.[31] ASFC has worked to facilitate the participation of women, girls, and other persons in situations of vulnerability in the construction of durable peace in Mali, and it encouraged the adoption of a cross-cutting gender perspective in the CVJR's activities. As one of the CVJR's principal international partners, ASFC supported the CVJR in some of its main areas of concern: recommendations and proposals, investigation capacity, institutional capacity, ensuring increased confidence of victims, and drafting the final report. Coordination with the CVJR occurred principally through ASFC's country director, legal adviser, and transitional justice coordinator, located in Bamako. ASFC has both Malian and international staff in Mali.

Some of the specific activities supported by ASFC included:

- organization of interviews with a specific list of special witnesses (known as *les grands témoins*, which can be understood as "major witnesses"), carefully pre-selected by the CVJR for their particular knowledge of the underlying structural causes – historical, social, political, economic – of conflict in Mali,[32] and the subsequent analysis and reporting of the information collected;
- a comprehensive, scientific mapping, including verifying and corroborating incidents of human rights violations in Mali since

1960 using open sources, carried out through a partnership with
Université Laval's Clinique de droit international pénal et humanitaire (International Criminal and Humanitarian Law Clinic,
CDIPH), with which ASFC has a long-standing relationship;[33]
· a historical narrative and legal analysis based on and accompanying the mapping work;
· training on methodology for producing reports;
· recruitment and training of the CVJR investigations team, design
of the investigation's strategy, and consolidation of the investigation team's reports;
· provision of psychological support to victims in urgent need of
assistance;
· facilitation of the equitable development of reparations
programs through the organization of consultations with women
and children;[34]
· development of the reparations policy;[35]
· development of recommendations for preventing future conflicts
(guarantees of non-repetition);
· deployment of mobile teams to collect declarations from
displaced persons in the M'Bera refugee camp in Mauritania;[36]
· organization of an awareness-raising workshop for victims'
associations and civil society actors on the future public hearings
of the CVJR; and
· organization of the public hearings.

One of the significant ways ASFC provided technical support to the
CVJR was the deployment of volunteer legal advisers who worked
directly with the CVJR in Bamako for six-month renewable mandates.[37] They developed or participated in the development of most
activities and tools made available to the CVJR, working in coordination with ASFC's legal and programmatic team in Bamako and
Quebec City. ASFC also organized several short-term missions of
international transitional justice expert consultants to carry out
capacity-building training sessions with the CVJR and contribute
to the activities listed above. ASFC coordinated with other international actors that supported the CVJR, and developed all project
plans in collaboration with the CVJR to ensure they responded to the
commission's needs.

ASFC sought to contribute to the CVJR's progress and success,
while not replacing any of the commission's core functions. As for

ASFC's activities more broadly, the organization sought to support and reinforce – not supplant – the CVJR. Subsidiarity and complementarity are, in fact, two of ASFC's main guiding principles.[38] These involve a commitment to capacity building; respect for the experience, knowledge, and agency of local actors; sharing information; and coordinating with other organizations.

Of course, the line between reinforcement and replacement may not always be clear. In supporting a truth commission, an international NGO should be careful to avoid potential pitfalls like reproducing colonial power dynamics or gender hierarchies, hampering local creativity, or disproportionately using limited resources for international consultants. It is important to be mindful of avoiding a detrimental impact on levels of engagement and ownership of results within a commission. Commissioner commitment and leadership are crucial for a truth commission's success and effective contribution to state-building, notably with respect to the advocacy role of commissioners vis-à-vis the government and society more broadly, during and after the completion of the commission's mandate.

ASFC's Broader Contributions to Transitional Justice in Mali

Apart from its projects supporting the CVJR directly, ASFC has contributed to the transitional justice process in Mali through activities in the areas of access to justice (through legal advice and representation); strategic litigation (bringing emblematic cases to court to foster change); social dialogue; preventing violence against women; the fight against corruption; and knowledge of transitional justice mechanisms. Generally, these activities aim to ensure that the CVJR's truth-building efforts are accompanied by the reduction of impunity, which is entrenched in Mali. These activities also aim to create a network of actors empowered to ensure human rights are respected and contribute to the transitional justice process.

ASFC's projects in Mali are complementary, and their results have mutually contributed to the realization of their objectives. Some examples of the ways ASFC's broader work contributed to the CVJR include:

· Identification of ways the mandate for a proposed commission on dialogue was insufficient and not in accordance with international standards for truth commissions,[39] which led to the

creation of the CVJR with its mandate more reflective of international standards.
- Legal analysis and advocacy – working with a coalition of Malian civil society organizations – regarding the aforementioned amnesty law.
- Major consultation of victims, resulting in data on victims' views, needs, and expectations, including reparations and the mandate, structure, and work of the CVJR. These consultations and subsequent sessions organized to present the results to participants helped raise awareness and dispel misunderstandings about the CVJR.

In general, ASFC seeks to create an environment conducive to the CVJR's success and, more generally, a successful transitional justice process in Mali.

SHARING LESSONS ACROSS BORDERS

The Value of Inter-context Learning

Many of the activities organized by ASFC in support of the CVJR involved opportunities to learn from the experiences of truth commissions elsewhere, primarily via experts with direct work experience in other truth-seeking mechanisms or transitional justice processes, or who otherwise accumulated expertise. Even across widely differing contexts, useful lessons can be found. Learning from other contexts is useful for truth commissions, such as the CVJR, which have some commissioners with no experience as leaders in truth commissions, transitional justice processes, or human rights related work more generally. Practices can be adopted or adapted to fit the local context.

Through the support of ASFC and other institutional partners, the CVJR had the opportunity to learn from the experiences of African and non-African countries, such as Algeria, Canada, Chile, Colombia, Gambia, Morocco, Mozambique, Peru, Rwanda, South Africa, and Tunisia. For example, in the planning of the CVJR's public hearings in Mali, South Africa and Peru were particularly identified as examples to assess. One training session at the CVJR introduced the South African strategy for public hearings, including the careful consultation of civil society actors to determine the themes of public hearings and the inclusion of a broad cross-section of society to aim for strong representation of different communities.

In many cases, experts went to the CVJR's headquarters in Bamako for exchanges facilitated by ASFC. However, the CVJR also conducted missions abroad facilitated by ASFC. Although costly, missions abroad permit participants to meet with a wide range of actors and thus gain a more comprehensive understanding of dynamics in another context. Practical challenges associated with these types of missions include choosing the proper representatives of the commission for the planned mission and ensuring that the lessons learned abroad are properly shared and disseminated within the commission upon return.

A South-South Cross-Continental Exchange: The CVJR in Colombia

On a mission in Colombia organized by ASFC, two commissioners of the CVJR had the opportunity to meet with, and thus learn directly from, diverse actors involved in the transitional justice process there. These included: institutional representatives from the Colombian Commission for Truth, Coexistence, and Non-repetition; the Special Jurisdiction for Peace;[40] the National Centre for Historical Memory; and the Monitoring, Promotion, and Verification Commission for the Implementation of the Final Agreement (with a representative of the Revolutionary Armed Forces of Colombia).[41] They also met with civil society representatives from the Centre for Research and Popular Education,[42] the José Alvear Restrepo Lawyers' Collective, the Colombian Commission of Jurists, Humanas, the Council for Human Rights and Displacement, and Afro-Colombian groups.

As an organization with staff in Colombia, and a long-standing presence in the country, ASFC drew upon its institutional expertise and contacts to facilitate the CVJR's visit. ASFC acted as a bridge between the Malian CVJR and a truth commission in a different context, as well as other actors whose experience the CVJR could learn from.

In particular, the mission in Colombia demonstrated the importance of having an integrated system of sophisticated transitional justice institutions, including mechanisms for truth, justice, and reparations.

It also reinforced the importance of a truth commission building strong relationships with civil society and the critical role that civil society actors play in transitional justice processes. Leveraging that experience, the CVJR made efforts to adopt an inclusive approach. For example, in its work to develop realistic and adapted recommendations aimed at the prevention of the resurgence of conflict in Mali, it held multi-stakeholder workshops in March 2022.[43]

A South-North Exchange: Learning from Canada's Truth and Reconciliation Commission

For some, Canada may not be the most obvious example of a country undergoing a transitional justice process or in need of a truth commission. However, Canada is arguably in a transitional justice process to overcome the legacy of colonialism and ongoing discrimination against Indigenous peoples. Canada's Truth and Reconciliation Commission (TRC) operated from 2009 until the publication of its final report in December 2015. It examined the history and impact of the Indian Residential School system of the Canadian government, which existed for over 150 years in Canada and had the underlying goal of coercive assimilation. For many children, the residential school experience was alien and dehumanizing. In addition to cultural loss and poor educational and health conditions, many children experienced severe physical and sexual abuse. The residential school system has had profound and lasting negative impacts at the individual, family, community, and societal levels.

Created in 2015, the National Centre for Truth and Reconciliation (NCTR) continues the TRC's work for education and dialogue with regard to the system and its impacts. Located at the University of Manitoba in Winnipeg, it houses the archives for all statements, documents, and other materials gathered during the operation of the TRC.[44]

ASFC organized a week-long mission to the NCTR in May 2018 for five of the CVJR's commissioners, including the president.[45] Their week at the NCTR covered various subjects, including the history of colonialism and residential schools in Canada, Indigenous values and culture, survivors' experiences, psychosocial support for survivors, archives and education strategies, truth commission logistics and operational decisions, communications and public relations strategies, leadership and truth commissions, the challenges faced by the TRC,[46] forms of reparation, and developing recommendations. The commissioners learned from the NCTR staff, many of whom had been a part of the TRC, former TRC chief commissioner Murray Sinclair, residential school survivors, and Elders. They also visited the Canadian Museum for Human Rights.

The differences between the Canadian and the Malian contexts are obvious. Nonetheless, several lessons learned and practices adopted by the Canadian TRC are relevant for Mali. For example – as shared with the commissioners during their week in Winnipeg – the integration of Indigenous cultural practices and creating a welcoming space at hearings was crucial for the Canadian TRC; Indigenous ceremony, symbolism, and values imbued the TRC's structure and actions. Respect for survivors was at the core of operational decisions. Measures adopted included allowing people to testify in their language of choice insofar as possible and allowing survivors to decide whether they would like their statement recorded or written. Similarly, health and security were at the core of the TRC's preoccupations. A holistic strategy was adopted, including the integration of cultural, spiritual, social, and psychological support; forms of support before, during, and after hearings; and recognition of the importance of providing support to anyone potentially impacted, whether directly or indirectly, by the information shared at hearings, including commissioners, members of the public, facility staff, family members, and survivors.

Regarding reparations, the Canadian example illustrates how different mechanisms can be integrated for a more holistic reparations scheme. For the harms inflicted by the Indian Residential School system, the settlement agreement included: a straightforward application process for a general category of victims (the "common experience payment"); a more intensive process with special private hearings for the most severe rights violations (the "independent assessment process"), involving the determination of amounts on a scale in accordance with the gravity of the violence experienced;[47] funds for special health and healing programming; and the creation of the TRC.

The TRC, in turn, called for structural and collective reparative measures to address the legacy of residential schools and promote reconciliation between Indigenous and non-Indigenous peoples in Canada. Some of the lessons the NCTR shared with the visitors from the CVJR included: collective reparation is important when harm has been committed against a community; it may be important to provide assistance with respect to the management of monetary reparations; and, crucially, truth commission processes should not re-victimize survivors of human rights violations.

One of the most important lessons shared during the mission in Winnipeg, and taken to heart by the participating commissioners from the CVJR, was the need to plan for the period after the termination of the truth commission's activities. Commissioners were encouraged to reflect on the creation of a permanent institution or network of institutions that will continue to work for reconciliation despite any changes in staff, leadership, or government. Ideally, such a body would have a stable source of funding, an appropriate structure, and a clear mandate.

Such an institution could continually monitor and push for the implementation of the truth commission's recommendations ("calls to action" in the case of Canada's TRC, a label that emphasizes their imperative nature). It could also accept declarations from survivors who had been unable or unprepared to testify during the limited period of operation of the truth commission, and continue investigative work the truth commission was unable to complete.[48] Other important functions for a post-commission institution are maintaining archives that achieve a balance between access to information and the protection of privacy, and pursuing educational initiatives. Creating an institution, or institutions, to follow a temporary truth commission is vital, since reconciliation is usually a long-term, multi-generational project.

Hearing about one truth commission's challenges regarding the implementation of recommendations may prompt leaders of another truth commission to reflect on and change their strategic approach during their mandate. In Mali, the CVJR decided it would publish its policy for a national reparations program in advance of the final report. This decision responded to the pressing needs of victims and enabled the CVJR to advocate for the implementation of an appropriate rights-based reparations policy before the end of its mandate.

On a less tangible level, missions such as that of the CVJR to Canada can serve as a motivator and a reminder of the shared purposes of truth commissions worldwide and the importance of commissioners' work. International exchanges can promote leadership, solidarity for human rights, and networks of support.

CONCLUSION

It can be said that Mali's CVJR had some noteworthy achievements: collecting tens of thousands of victim statements in extremely difficult security conditions, holding public hearings, having its mandate renewed despite political instability, and having its reparations policy accepted. The support of international partners, including ASFC, played a role in these outcomes, and the CVJR's cross-cultural exchanges and learning experiences contributed significantly to its approach and work.

The CVJR ended its activities in December 2022. However, at the time of writing, its final report has not yet been made public. The publication and dissemination of a balanced and methodologically robust final report that Malians accept is a significant remaining step for the fulfillment of the CVJR's mandate. If the CVJR puts forward strong and relevant recommendations that respond to victims' needs and can feasibly be implemented, it should contribute to local perceptions of the CVJR's credibility. A successor institution could certainly play an important role in promoting effective implementation.

Working toward reconciliation and the rule of law is a long-term project. At this stage, it is likely too soon to measure the CVJR's impact and success. Moreover, the CVJR has an important role, but it is only one mechanism among many in the transitional justice process in Mali. The ultimate success of this process, as for any transitional justice process, will depend on a multitude of interrelated contextual factors, initiatives, and developments. Crucially, if the CVJR's truth-seeking efforts are not accompanied by other advances, such as in the equitable implementation of the reparations scheme and in holding perpetrators of serious crimes accountable, victims of the conflict, who trusted the CVJR with their statements, may be left resentful, disillusioned, and in situations of persistent insecurity – despite the commission's considerable efforts to be inclusive, support victims, and build unity.

In presenting a brief overview of Mali's CVJR, and ASFC's support of it, the discussion above has touched on various issues regarding truth commission operations, including how a broad truth commission leadership composition can impact activities and outcomes; the ideal timing for the creation of a truth commission; strategies for carrying out commission activities in situations of ongoing insecurity; how best practices are shared and disseminated between different contexts; and finally, how international co-operation organizations can responsibly and effectively contribute to transitional justice processes by supporting truth commissions, as ASFC has sought to do for the CVJR. These issues all merit continued study and analysis to continue the development and improvement of truth-seeking strategies in transitional justice contexts in Africa and around the world.

NOTES

1 The CVJR was created by Ordinance no. 2014-003/P-RM of 15 January 2014, ratified by Law no. 2014-001 of 7 April 2014. Ordinance no. 0884 of 31 December 2015 set out the organization and methods of operation of the CVJR. The CVJR replaced a previous institution, the Commission for Dialogue and Reconciliation, which had been criticized for factors related to its independence and its mission, said to be focused on quick dialogue at the expense of truth seeking and the fulfillment of victims' right to reparations.

2 The *Accord pour la paix et la réconciliation au Mali issu du processus d'Alger* (Accord for peace and reconciliation in Mali emanating from the Algiers process) [Peace Accord], was signed on 15 May 2015 by the government of Mali, the pro-government Platform alliance, and two groups forming part of the Coordination des mouvements de l'Azawad (Coordination of Azawad Movements, or CMA). The remaining CMA groups signed the accord on 20 June 2015.

3 In January 2012, a secessionist rebellion broke out, formed by young Touaregs and Arab students from the north of Mali and Touareg combatants returned from Libya after the fall of the Muammar Gaddafi regime. They created the "Mouvement national pour la libération de l'Azawad" (National movement for the liberation of the Azawad), the vast territory of the north of Mali (covering the regions of Kidal, Gao, and Timbuktu).

4 Notably, in 2012, Ansar Dine, Al-Qaïda au Maghreb islamique, and the Mouvement pour l'unicité et le jihad en Afrique de l'Ouest. In 2014, various armed groups formed two movements: the CMA and the Platform.

5 UN Security Council, Resolution 2100, S/RES/2100 (2013), 25 April 2013.

6 UN Security Council, Resolution 2640, S/RES/2640 (2022), 29 June 2022, at para 15.

7 Such as restrictions on drinking, smoking, listening to music, interactions between men and women, clothing (especially for women), and
   so forth.

8 See The Prosecutor v Ahmad Al Faqi Al Mahdi, *CMoS* 14.276 ICC-01/12-
   01/15-171, Judgment and Sentence (27 September 2016) (International
   Criminal Court (ICC), Trial Chamber 8, www.icc-cpi.int/CourtRecords/
   CR2016_07245.PDF.

9 See ICC, "Opening of the Confirmation of Charges Hearing in Al Hassan
   Case: Audio-visual Materials and Photographs," press release, 8 July
   2019, www.icc-cpi.int/Pages/item.aspx?name=pr1467.

10 Victims of the conflict consulted by ASFC identified a range of actors as
   responsible for serious violence. See: Avocats sans frontières Canada, *Pour
   une justice transitionnelle efficace et inclusive, Rapport de consultation sur
   les perceptions, attentes et besoins exprimés par les victimes du conflit
   armé au Mali* (2018), 45–50, 75–81, https://asfcanada.ca/wp-content/
   uploads/2022/06/rc_victimes_mali_18-02_lr.pdf. The International
   Commission of Inquiry for Mali had reasonable grounds to believe Malian
   forces committed war crimes. See UNSC, S/2020/1332, *Report of the
   International Commission of Inquiry for Mali* (19 June 2020), Annex to
   the letter dated 17 December 2020 from the Secretary-General addressed
   to the president of the Security Council (29 January 2021), "Executive
   Summary," at paragraphs 36–46, and paragraphs 53–7.

11 Peace Accord, *supra* note 2 at Title 5, Chapter 14, Article 46. The CVJR is
   one of many initiatives and guiding principles set out in this article. Others
   include development of a National Charter for Peace, Unity and National
   Reconciliation; creation of a commission to fight against corruption and
   financial delinquency; creation of an International Investigation
   Commission; and "non amnesty for authors of war crimes, crimes against
   humanity, and grave human rights violations, including violence against
   women, girls, and children, linked to the conflict."

12 See Ordinance no. 2014-003, at Article 2, http://cvjrmali.com/data/docu-
   ments/ordce_cvjr-.pdf (site discontinued).

13 Ordinance no. 2014-003, at Article 2.

14 Translation by author. See "Règlement Intérieur de la Commission vérité,
   justice et réconciliation," at Article 5, http://cvjrmali.com/data/documents/
   REGLEMENT-INTERIEUR-CVJR-FINAL-1.pdf (site discontinued).

15 In ASFC's consultation, many victims who expressed a lack of confidence
   in the CVJR cited the fact that armed groups were part of the CVJR. See
   ASFC, *Pour une justice transitionnelle efficace et inclusive*, 86.

16 Decisions were taken by consensus, or alternatively, by determining a sim-
    ple majority of commissioners present through open vote or secret ballot.
    The president broke ties.

17 CVJR, "Situation des dépositions du 26 au 30 décembre 2022," Plenary
    assembly, 30 December 2022.

18 For its investigations, the CVJR applied the standard of "reasonable
    suspicion" to confirm an incident. The definition for reasonable suspicion
    was taken from the UN High Commissioner for Human Rights mapping
    report on grave human rights violations in the Democratic Republic of the
    Congo. The definition is: "a body of reliable indications corresponding to
    other confirmed circumstances tending to demonstrate that an incident or
    event happened."

19 See CVJR, "La CVJR recrute une agence de communication : Cahier
    des charges pour la communication autour des audiences publiques de
    la CVJR," www.fichier-pdf.fr/2019/03/18/cvjr-recrute-agence-de-
    communication/cvjr-recrute-agence-de-communication.pdf. The hearings
    were held in Bamako, and in preparation for hearings, victims were
    assisted by the CVJR through its regional offices, and notably its experts in
    psychosocial support. Six hearings were originally planned.

20 Their testimony is available on YouTube, on the CVJR's account: CVJR
    MALI, https://www.youtube.com/channel/UCcl7CJ8t7LpGRaRbJAdm
    6RA. According to a methodological note of the working group on public
    hearings, criteria for selecting witnesses for hearings included: physical and
    psychological aptitude to testify, educational value of the witness's story, reli-
    ability of information known about the violation, verifiability of unknown
    information about the violation, threats or risks affecting the victim, and the
    diversity of cases, including historical, regional, ethnic, gender, category of
    victims, category of authors (institutional affiliation, regional, ethnic).

21 This is particularly the case given the low literacy levels in Mali. In ASFC's
    consultation carried out in 2017, over 60% of victims participating were
    illiterate (38%) or had not gone to school beyond Koranic school (29%).
    See ASFC, *Pour une justice transitionnelle efficace et inclusive*, 39.

22 It is known as the National Transition Council.

23 ASFC, *Pour une justice transitionnelle efficace et inclusive*, 10. The
    partners for the consultation were l'Association des femmes africaines
    pour la recherche et le développement; Women in Law and Development
    in Africa; la Coalition malienne de défense de droits humains; le Groupe
    de recherche, d'étude, de formation femme-action; l'Association des
    juristes maliennes; l'Association pour le progrès et la défense des droits
    des femmes; and Environnement et développement tiers monde.

24 A meeting supported by PASP/GIZ with victims' representatives was held on 22 and 23 May 2019. See CVJR (@CVJR_MALI), Twitter, 22 May 2019, https://twitter.com/CVJR_MALI.

25 A meeting was held on 14 June with various government authorities, including technical and independent administrative authorities. See CVJR (@CVJR_MALI), Twitter, 14 June 2019, https://twitter.com/CVJR_MALI.

26 CVJR, *Rapport du 1er semestre 2018 de la Commission vérité, justice et réconciliation (janvier-juin)*, 4–5 [First semester report 2018].

27 Note that the provisions on reparation were amended in the adopted version of the law, in response to mobilization by CSOS. Nonetheless, the adopted amnesty law still has many problematic elements that remain unchanged, notably with regard to its scope of application and the procedure for authors of crime to gain the benefit of the amnesty. For example, the law does not provide for a transparent procedure and does not require authors of crime to contribute to reparations. See ASFC, "La loi d'entente nationale: Une menace pour la paix, la réconciliation et les droits des victimes au Mali," September 2019, https://asfcanada.ca/wp-content/uploads/2022/06/loi-entente-nationale-menace-paix-droits-victimes.pdf.

28 See, for example, ASFC, *Pour une justice transitionnelle efficace et inclusive*, 58, 62, 66.

29 ASFC, *Pour une justice transitionnelle efficace et inclusive*, 15.

30 "Rapport du 1er semestre 2018 de la Commission vérité, justice et réconciliation (janvier- juin)," 27. See also Friedrich-Ebert-Stiftung, "Mali-mètre 10, political survey: What Do the Malians Think?," October 2018, 117–18, www.fes-mali.org/images/FES_MM10.pdf. This study, involving over 2,000 participants from all regions of the country, revealed that although 81% of those who knew the CVJR considered its work important, only 34% of the participants actually knew about the CVJR.

31 As of June 2022, ASFC had three projects in Mali. They are: Justice and Peace in Mali; Supporting the Fight against Impunity in Mali; and Youth Committed to Sustainable Peace: Support for Youth Participation in the Reconciliation Process in Mali. These build on ASFC's previous projects in Mali: Justice, Prevention, and Reconciliation for Women, Minors, and other Persons Affected by the Crisis in Mali (JUPREC); Reinforcement of the Truth, Justice, and Reconciliation Commission(RCVJR); and Stabilizing Mali through the Truth, Justice, and Reconciliation Commission (SCVJR). JUPREC was a five-year project with a budget of Can$20 million, funded by Global Affairs Canada and carried out in consortium with the Centre d'étude et de coopération internationale and the École nationale

d'administration publique of Québec. It ended in March 2020. RCVJR and SCVJR were funded by the Peace and Stabilization Operations Program of the government of Canada. SCVJR ran from 2019 to 2021.

32 These interviews were carried out between 26 April and 26 May 2018 in Gao, Bamako, Timbuktu, Taoudénit, Tessalit, Gossi, Ménaka, Ségou, and Kidal.

33 ASFC's and the CDIPH's work together was facilitated by the Canadian Partnership for International Justice (CPIJ), funded by the Social Sciences and Humanities Research Council of Canada for five years (2016–2021). The CPIJ is a unique partnership that brings together academic and practitioner members focused on international justice issues, to increase co-operation and communication between the academic and NGO spheres. See https://cpij-pcji.ca.

34 These consultations were held over four days in May 2018. Thirty children and thirty women were consulted.

35 The other main actor supporting the CVJR in the development of its reparations policy was GIZ, the German Agency for International Cooperation.

36 Testimonies from 521 Malian refugees were collected.

37 ASFC's volunteer legal advisers tend to be young lawyers with expertise in international human rights law.

38 See ASFC, "Nos principes d'action," https://asfcanada.ca/medias/nos-principes-daction/. The other principles are collegiality, respect for human rights, professionalism and responsibility, and risk management.

39 See ASFC, *De la crise à une paix durable: La justice et les droits humains dans un contexte de transition au Mali*, 2 August 2013, 46–7, www.lwb-canada.ca/documents/file/asf_rapport_malie_v5_web.pdf.

40 Jurisdicción Especial para la Paz, in Spanish. This special judicial system was established by the Colombian peace accords and provided reduced sentences for those who admitted their responsibility and clarified facts.

41 In Spanish, the Comisión de Seguimiento, Impulso y Verificación a la Implementación del Acuerdo Final.

42 In Spanish, the Centro de Investigación y Educación Popular.

43 ASFC participated in these workshops.

44 The Indian Residential Schools Settlement Agreement mandated the TRC to create a permanent archive for the materials collected. The NCTR plays this role. See National Centre for Truth and Reconciliation, "Our Mandate," https://nctr.ca/about/about-the-nctr/our-mandate.

45 The author of this chapter accompanied the commissioners for the week at the NCTR.

46 One particular challenge described was getting the Canadian government
    to broadly disclose documents to the TRC. The TRC had to bring court
    challenges against Canada in order to obtain documents and received
    many of these late in its mandate.

47 IAP hearings were private and involved an adjudicator asking questions of
    the claimant, in the presence of their lawyer if represented, and a govern-
    ment of Canada lawyer, in order to determine the amount of reparation
    the person would obtain. Although intended to be a streamlined
    approach, and less adversarial in relation to regular litigation, some sur-
    vivors found this process humiliating, intrusive, and harmful as they were
    probed about their experiences of sexual and physical abuse.

48 In Canada, work has continued, in particular, on the identification of clan-
    destine graves of Indian Residential School students and commemoration
    activities.

9

Post-Authoritarianism, Truth Seeking, and the Judicial Accountability Gap: Lessons from Nigeria

Hakeem Yusuf

While it has been recognized that the judiciary plays an important role in contemporary governance,[1] the judiciary's accountability for its role in authoritarian polities remains a largely elided issue in transitional justice arrangements, designed as part of the efforts to build democratic states. The role of the judiciary in Nigeria's truncated experience of truth seeking draws attention to the need for accountability for its role in post-authoritarian societies and potential pitfalls inherent in the continued lack of focus on the issue in transitional contexts. As a matter of policy, the purview of the truth-seeking process, as a transitional justice mechanism, ought to be extended to scrutiny of the judiciary's role as a key organ of the state and a key component of state building.

Judicial accountability for its role in past governance is important. On the one hand, it has emerged that the judiciary plays a significant role in governance in authoritarian societies.[2] On the other, experiential accounts strongly suggest that the judiciary usually assumes a strategic role in post-authoritarian transitions and processes of democratic state building.[3] This is especially the case with regard to issues of human rights, governance, efforts at democratic consolidation, and (re)institution of rule of law.[4] The accountability gap on the judicial function saddles the transitional society with an untransformed judiciary, challenged by unresolved legitimacy questions. The set of dynamics at play in post-authoritarian contexts suggests the need for more critical focus on the judicial function in transitional justice processes in the building of a democratic state.

This chapter argues that neglect of judicial accountability for the past has resonance for achieving the aims of truth and justice for victims of gross violations of human rights, as well as broader issues of transitional justice. Moreover, the contextual analysis suggests that neglecting judicial accountability for its role in past governance as a measure of transitional justice threatens institutional transformation, an important aspect of post-authoritarian state building.[5] The absence of transformation at times of political change threatens not only the rule of law but also the transition project.

The rest of the chapter is organized in the following manner. First, the authoritarian past of Nigeria is examined, providing a glimpse of the contextual background to the discussion. It briefly describes the circumstances that necessitated the truth-seeking process in Nigeria. The process of political change to civil rule and the transitional justice measures that accompanied it, especially the course of the truth-seeking process embodied in the Human Rights Violations Investigation Commission (the commission or Oputa Panel), is examined next. Third, the focus turns to the tension generated by the interaction between the judiciary and the truth-seeking process. The discussion here sets the foundation for advancing the need to incorporate judicial accountability for the past into transitional justice arrangements. Fourth, the case for judicial accountability in post-authoritarian societies is argued. Normative arguments for and against the case for judicial accountability for the past are analyzed. Fifth, the chapter extends the foregoing discussion to consider an experiential account of the Nigerian situation. The chapter concludes that the neglect of judicial accounts, apart from providing an incomplete account of the past, are ill-suited to position the judiciary for the usually challenging responsibilities it must shoulder in societal transformation and democratic state building, following the experience of authoritarianism.

THE AUTHORITARIAN PAST OF NIGERIA

Like many other countries in sub-Saharan Africa, most of Nigeria's post-independent political experience was authoritarian rule. The military ruled the country for nearly three decades with two short intervals of civil governance.[6] Military authoritarianism virtually destroyed the fabric of state and society. The economic and social well-being of the people plummeted as the military acted like an army of occupation misruling captured territory. All institutions of civil governance suffered debilitation as the military ruled with draconian decrees that undermined the constitution. These "laws" either suspended parts of or asserted supremacy (and were judicially so upheld) over the constitution.[7]

Gross violations of human rights were rampant to the extent that the country acquired pariah status within the international community. State security agencies, the armed forces, and police alike commonly applied lethal force against the civil populace, especially those actively engaged in organized opposition to authoritarian rule. Journalists, labour unions, student groups, political associations, market associations, human rights activists and organizations, and the Nigerian Bar Association were usual targets of state violence. Government measures against these and similar groups included proscription, illegal arrests, detention, seizure of property and arson, mysterious disappearances, as well as state-sponsored murder.

There were public executions in violation of constitutional provisions on due process. The execution of leading environmental activist and renowned author Kenule Saro-Wiwa and some other members of the Movement for the Survival of the Ogoni People referred to as the "Ogoni Nine" particularly caught international attention leading to the suspension of Nigeria from the Commonwealth. The administration of General Sani Abacha (November 1993–June 1998) was especially noted for its ruthlessness toward political opposition and the struggle for democracy in the country.

Successive military regimes perfected the plunder, compromised all institutions of the state, and generally directed them toward flagrant violations of human rights. Regime after regime declared an intention to pursue a development agenda, economic rectitude, unity, and peace in the country. None of these commendable objectives were achieved by the numerous putsches and coups. Rather, the military institutionalized corruption even as the country moved rapidly down the ladder of development, descending into one of the twenty poorest nations in the world, despite abundant human and natural resources.[8] Predictably, the rule of law took the uncomfortable back seat in affairs of governance.

POLITICAL CHANGE AND TRANSITIONAL JUSTICE IN NIGERIA

The sudden death of General Sani Abacha in June 1998 provided an opportunity for political change. His successor, General Abdusalami Abubakar, embarked on an accelerated civil transition program. This culminated in the election and handover of power to political office holders at the three levels of governance and the exit of the military on 29 May 1999. Even as the political transition program of the Abubakar regime progressed, the foregoing situation in the country established the imperative to implement some measure of transitional justice to counter impunity. It had become important to ensure state acknowledgment for the misrule of the country by the military and secure reparations for victims of gross violations of human rights.

The first measure took the form of prosecution. This was a half-hearted attempt by the departing Abubakar regime to prosecute a handful of some of the most prominent actors in the Abacha regime generally believed to be involved in gross violations of human rights. There was also, at the time, a largely symbolic internal lustration of "political" military officers from active service – those who had participated in governance at various levels in the country – and were still serving in the armed forces. However, the truth-seeking process initiated by the then newly inaugurated civil administration of President Olusegun Obasanjo remains the notable transitional justice mechanism adopted in the post-authoritarian period.

Barely two weeks after assuming office, President Obasanjo announced the establishment of the Oputa Panel to investigate gross violations of human rights that took place in the country during the period of military rule.[9] Addressing these violations, ensuring justice for victims, as well as the need to "heal the nation" had featured as topical issues in the presidential election campaigns. Not surprisingly, at his inaugural address to the country, Obasanjo could not ignore them. He commended "home-based fellow Nigerians" for their fortitude in bearing "unprecedented hardship, deprivation of every conceivable rights and privileges [sic] that were once taken for granted."[10]

The Oputa Panel was established under the hand of President Obasanjo through Statutory Instrument No. 8 of 1999[11] pursuant to Tribunals of Inquiry Act (TIA).[12] Its mandate was principally to ascertain all incidents of gross violations of human rights committed in Nigeria between 15 January 1966 and 28 May 1999, the last day of military rule in the country. It was also to recommend appropriate measures to redress past injustices and prevent future violations of human rights in the country. The Oputa Panel was further mandated to suggest measures to foster rule of law, which had been violently displaced during the years of military dictatorship.[13]

The Oputa Panel's mandate did not include violations committed during the colonial period. Indeed, its initial remit was to investigate human rights violations committed during the period from 1 October 1979 to 28 May 1999, which excluded the military regime of then general Obasanjo as head of state, focusing only on the period after he had handed power to a civilian government until his return to power as civilian president. Civil society organizations (CSOs), the human rights community, victims and survivors of human rights violations, politicians and the public at large strongly criticized this term mandate for several reasons. Apart from the fact that it excluded several periods of military authoritarian rule, it also notably thereby excluded the period of Nigeria's civil war, which had remained a thorny issue in the body politic. The government bowed to public pressure and extended the term mandate of the Oputa Panel to cover these periods.

In interpreting its mandate, the Oputa Panel did not expressly offer a definition of gross human rights violations. However, it did declare that it considered the South Africa Truth and Reconciliation Commission (TRC) as its model.[14] It had recourse, among others, to the definition of the term in section 1 of the South African TRC Act, international human rights instruments, and the Nigerian Constitution, which guaranteed the rights it identified to be in issue. In the words of the chairman, "*Our quo warranto is the search for this reconciliation.*"[15] This approach of the Oputa Panel was at least in part linked to the statement of President Obasanjo at the inauguration of the panel, that he was establishing it in view of his government's "determination to heal the wounds of the past ... for complete reconciliation based on truth and knowledge of the truth in our land."[16] Nonetheless, expectations were high that the Oputa Panel would contribute extensively to social reconstruction in Nigeria, as it was empowered to make any other recommendations which were in the public interest and were necessitated by the evidence.

Constrained by factors like limited personnel, time, and financial resources, the Oputa Panel heard only 200 petitions at its public hearings out of some 10,000 it received. There was thus a great disparity between the petitions submitted to the panel and those heard in public. While the number of cases selected for the public hearings was limited, it took testimony from some 2,000 witnesses, received 1,750 exhibits related to them, and publicly named alleged

perpetrators of gross violations of human rights. In recognition of
the need to address the large number of unheard cases of human
rights violations, the Oputa Panel commissioned research reports
by experts. These reports played an important part in the work of
the truth-seeking process since they reached out to areas and victims
the Oputa Panel did not cover, thereby providing a vital voice to an
otherwise "voiceless" majority.

The public hearings were of a general and institutional nature.
They were held in the six geopolitical zones of the country from
24 October 2000 to 9 November 2001. The general hearings centred on individual complaints. The institutional hearings were
organized for CSOs, human rights groups, and specialized professional organizations. The latter hearings featured testimonies and
submissions from the National Human Rights Commission, the
armed forces, the police, State Security Service, the Nigeria prisons,
about ten CSOs and human rights organizations, and a few individuals. The choice of state institutions, with the notable exception of
the National Human Rights Commission, may have been informed
by the popular view that they constitute notorious sources of human
rights violations. The National Human Rights Commission, for its
part, was set up precisely to monitor human rights implementation
in various aspects of national life, ironically by the Abacha junta.
The hearings on the police and the Prisons Service, institutions inti-
mately connected to the criminal justice system, highlighted the need
for the third key player, the judiciary, to be brought to accounts for
its role in governance, but the Oputa Panel neglected to advert to it.

A broad spectrum of stakeholders, including the political elite,
journalists, legal practitioners, former political officer holders (and
CSO) leaders took their turn to give testimony at the public hearings).[17] The human rights violations they suffered were allegedly
perpetrated by the army, the security agencies, and the police. There
were also some claims against corporate bodies. By the time it left
office, the military establishment had instituted a "vicious cycle" of
violence exhibited in domestic violence, armed robbery, brigandage,
religious riots, impunity, and lawlessness in the polity.[18]

In view of the expansive mandate, expectations were high that the
Oputa Panel would contribute extensively to social reconstruction
in Nigeria. With awareness of the nature of public expectations and
the benefit of its liberally worded mandate, the Oputa Panel's recommendations extended beyond investigations of alleged violations

of human rights to include a propositional agenda for transforming Nigerian society. It proceeded on the premise that the truth-seeking process provided an opportunity to lay the foundations for social reconstruction and reconciliation. However, the aftermath of the truth process was disappointing.

It is important to mention an apt feature of the TIA under which the Oputa Panel was set up. This is the power to subpoena witnesses and documents. The Oputa Panel also had powers to order the arrest of any individual it determined had acted in contempt of it. These "coercive" powers, as discussed below, led to contentious litigation against the panel by former military rulers. Wary of the accountability process, their challenge of these powers laid the foundations for the egregious judicial role in truncating the implementation of the Oputa Panel's wide-ranging recommendations.

UNDOING TRUTH AND JUSTICE: THE DELE GIWA PETITION AND THE JUDICIARY

The judiciary remains not only unaccounted for its role in the period of authoritarian rule but also played a significant part in the current experience of a failed transitional justice process in the country. This came about by its jurisprudential choices in the litigation generated by the Dele Giwa petition.

Dele Giwa was a Lagos-based investigative journalist, editor in chief, and publisher of *Newswatch*, renowned for seminal and credible reporting of sensitive matters of public interest in the 1980s. His professional career was cut short in 1986 by a letter-bomb allegedly delivered by military intelligence on the orders of the then military ruler, General Ibrahim Babangida. The police investigation into the matter was abandoned and closed prematurely. Efforts by Giwa's solicitor, Gani Fawehinmi, to investigate and secure private as well as public prosecution of the alleged perpetrators of the dastardly act were obstructed by the military government through the passage of special legislation.[19]

Fawehinmi submitted a petition on the matter to the Oputa Panel, calling for the murder investigation to be reopened. The latter issued summons for the appearance of the ex-military ruler and his two security chiefs accused of complicity in the matter. To stave off the summons, the generals rushed to the High Court with an *ex parte* application to restrain the Oputa Panel from having them testify before it. This was in *Justice Chukwudifu Oputa (Rtd.) and Human Rights Violations Investigation Commission and Gani Fawehinmi v General Ibrahim Babangida, Brigadier Halilu Akilu and Brigadier Kunle Togun* (the *Oputa Panel* case).[20] They sought, among other things, a declaration that the president lacked the powers to act under the existing law to establish a body like the Oputa Panel for the whole country. They also claimed the summons contravened their right to liberty.

Meanwhile, a legal team applied to represent the generals at the public hearing. This move, opposed by the petitioners, raised important questions about the proper role and capacity of legal counsel in the truth-seeking process. The contention was whether the Oputa Panel had the power to issue and serve summonses on them, and having objected to appear, could the generals give and cross-examine evidence by proxy? The issue as framed by the Oputa Panel itself was whether proceedings before a truth commission constituted a suit at law or a judicial proceeding. The Oputa Panel took the view that proceedings before a truth-seeking commission like itself did not constitute adversarial proceedings. Thus, the personal attendance of the summoned generals was required for the proper fulfillment of its mandate. It maintained that witnesses were bound to attend in person to be entitled to the rights of legal representation and (cross-)examination.

The foregoing appeared to be novel issues when they were raised in objection before the Nigerian court during the proceedings of the Oputa Panel. It is unclear whether they have been raised in objection to any other truth-seeking process after the Oputa Panel. The TIA did not provide for proxy representation of witnesses. However, if the settled position of the law (at least in common law jurisdictions) on witnesses in civil and criminal litigation can be extrapolated, legal counsel cannot take the place of witnesses. In other words, testimony is a personal issue that cannot be delegated and stands apart from the right to legal representation.[21] It arguably would have amounted to a fundamental contradiction in terms in a *truth-seeking* process for alleged perpetrators of rights violations to testify by proxy.

Nonetheless, the generals, with the sanction of an injunction granted by the trial court, held out throughout the public hearings.[22] The matter eventually found its way to the Supreme Court (the Court). It held that the constitution does not confer powers on the National Assembly to enact a general law on tribunals of inquiry for the whole country, and so it was a matter within the competence of the states only. The president exceeded his jurisdiction in establishing the Oputa Panel with a remit to carry out a national inquiry into the violations of human rights in all parts of the country. The Court also upheld the lower court's finding that certain sections of the enabling statute were unconstitutional and invalid for conferring the power on a tribunal of inquiry to compel attendance or impose a sentence of fine or imprisonment.[23] The sections, the Court held, contravene sections 35 and 36 of the Constitution of Nigeria 1999 that provide for the right to liberty and fair hearing, respectively.

The *Oputa Panel* case eloquently calls attention to two of a number of unsettling features of the legal and statutory framework of governance in Nigeria's political transition. First is the extensive reliance by all branches of government on autocratic legislation deriving from the colonial past and authoritarian military regimes. This is reflected in the way an elected civil government placed reliance on the TIA, a pre-republican legislation to set up a truth commission by executive fiat at a time it had become standard practice to do so under purpose-specific legislation.[24] Second is a customary, uncritical adherence to judicial precedent by the courts, even at the highest level. The courts relied on and referred extensively to *Sir Abubakar Tafawa Balewa & Others v Doherty & Others (Balewa)*,[25] in which the then Federal Supreme Court (FSC) and the Privy Council had both upheld objections to the compulsory powers and the jurisdictional reach of the TIA. The contentious value of judicial precedents, particularly in the common law legal tradition, is outside the scope of this work.[26] Suffice to note, however, that since 1963,[27] the Court is neither bound in fact nor law by the decisions of both authorities. On the one hand, the FSC from that year became the Court of Appeal and the then newly constituted Supreme Court, not the Privy Council in London, was constitutionally designated the highest judicial forum for the country. Thus, in relying on the Balewa case, the Court effectively relied on a lower court's decision to deny the opportunity for truth and justice for victims of gross violations of human rights in the country.

Clearly, the political branch, in its failure to inaugurate the truth-seeking process through a purpose-designed legislation, bears considerable responsibility for the shaky legal foundations of the Oputa Panel. Such reliance in the aftermath of three decades of authoritarian rule that earned the country international censure[28] raises fundamental questions. It raises doubt about the administration's commitment to justice, human rights, and the reinstitution of the rule of law in the country. Notwithstanding the neglect of the political branch, there is cause to question the attitude of the transition judiciary. Considering its opportune institutional memory, its continued preference for legal formalism is out of step with the times.

The preference for legal formalism with its emphasis on plain-fact jurisprudence[29] is at the heart of judicial imperviousness to the dynamics of transition that ought to be a paramount consideration in the *Oputa Panel* case. The approach of the judiciary, in this case, betrayed the fundamental lack of engagement with the socio-political circumstances of the country and legal developments in the international arena. It reflected judicial resistance to the much-desired need for socio-political change. In coming to a decision that struck at the root of the truth-seeking process, the Nigerian judiciary in the *Oputa Panel* case arguably undermined the rule of law at an important juncture in the country's transition to civil governance.

The Court accorded primacy to protecting the *federal character* of the polity over the rights of victims of gross violations of human rights. Moreover, there is the part of the Court's decision that held mandatory attendance at a truth commission as contrary to the right to personal liberty. This aspect of the decision in the *Oputa Panel* case, even from a purely formal legal point of view, is, with respect, not sustainable. The Court held that constitutionally only a court of law can make an order to deprive a citizen of the right to liberty.

However, under the Nigerian Constitution of 1999 as well as earlier constitutions, and indeed in line with international human rights law and practice, the right to liberty can be derogated from in defined circumstances. One such context is where there is reasonable suspicion of the commission of an offence, which was precisely in issue before the Oputa Panel. Section 35(1)(b) of the constitution provides in part that personal liberty may be curtailed *to secure the fulfillment of any obligation imposed upon him by law.*[30] The Court, on the basis of this proviso, ought to have upheld the "coercive" powers of the Oputa Panel under the 1999 Constitution. After all, the Oputa Panel was constituted under law, and the duty to attend its summons, challenged by the plaintiffs, was a statutory one.

In this regard, it is essential to recall that a truth commission has an extended form of inquiry as its core function. This function can

be easily frustrated or defeated if it lacks the power to summon witnesses and issue subpoena to produce evidence. Indeed, as a matter
of practice, such power is not at all novel for quasi-judicial bodies in
the Nigerian context. Similar powers are statutorily conferred and
exercised with judicial sanction by some professional disciplinary
bodies in the country.[31]

It was also imperative in the context of the *Oputa Panel* case to
consider the imperatives of the *transition moment*. The need for
restoring the rule of law, securing reparations for victims of gross
violations of human rights, and transformation of societal institutions required an activist consideration of the issues arising from
the truth-seeking process. It is pertinent that in the context of the
transition in Nigeria, the rights of victims to obtain a remedy in
view of executive choices devolved largely on the outcome of the
truth-seeking process. The Court, in handing down the Oputa Panel
decision the way it did, neglected to reckon with the fact that the
nation was at the threshold of history, in transition and making a
decisive break with a past of human rights violations. The Oputa
Panel was quite open to the Supreme Court as the judicial forum of
last resort to have taken the expansive view of the facts and law and
opt for a jurisprudence reflecting not a "legalistic" consideration of
the issues in contention but rather an activist posture sensitive to the
"ideals of the nation."

Indeed, the socio-political circumstances of the country at the time
required the courts to adopt a reflexive jurisprudence in the determination of the *Oputa Panel* case. A broader perspective commends
the view that the issues involved may no doubt "offend" individual
rights.[32] Yet, they also border, even if implicitly, on the obligation of
the country to ensure that victims of gross human rights violations
are provided both an opportunity to be heard and an effective remedy. The Court's position could have been different if it had taken a
purposive approach to the legislation in question. Such an approach
would have allowed it to uphold the establishment of the Oputa
Panel for investigating past human rights violations as a measure for
ensuring "order and good government of the Federation or any part
thereof." [33] This power is conferred on the federal government by
section 4(1) of the Nigeria Constitution of 1999.

Objectionable still is the finding that the powers of the commission
contravened fair-hearing provisions of section 36 of the Nigerian
Constitution. It is a basic procedural practice judicially upheld (in

Nigeria and elsewhere) that evidentiary rules weigh against a party who fails to utilize reasonable opportunity provided to present their case. In such circumstances, the defaulting party cannot be heard to complain about lack of fair hearing. In vindication of this position, the Court was to hold in a later case that such a defaulting party cannot "turn around to accuse the court of denying him fair hearing."[34] It is a matter of the records that in the *Oputa Panel* case, the generals roundly and publicly rebuffed all available opportunities to testify before the panel.

The *Oputa Panel* case brought to the fore the tension that may arise between the truth-seeking process and the judiciary in transition. It highlights the dangers inherent in the existence of an accountability gap for the past with respect to the judiciary. Such a gap bequeaths a polity with a judiciary that may be immune to the changes taking place in the transition environment all around it.[35] In short, the *Oputa Panel* case laid bare the pitfall constituted by the neglect of judicial accountability for past governance in post-authoritarian societies.

JUDICIAL ACCOUNTABILITY FOR THE PAST

The Judiciary, Power, and Governance

Any institution or group that can influence how others experience the "vulnerabilities" of existence, both as individuals and groups wield "social power."[36] This ability to change an existing situation is the defining feature of power. In the power game, there are different groups in an active contest for dominance, each utilizing specific inherent advantages to achieve supremacy. The different power bases in the struggle to undermine the influence of others become constrained in that quest by certain self-limiting factors.[37] Notwithstanding the self-limiting aspect of the judiciary, namely that it does not initiate the process for exercising its power, contemporary social experience demonstrates this body is endowed with the resources to influence society.

The judiciary wields power in governance of a nature that cannot be ignored. It hardly stands to contest that the executive and legislature exercise political power. However, the judiciary, in furtherance of its interpretational role, mediates political power. In the mediatory role, the judiciary stands between the executive and the citizen in resolving conflicts in the same way it adjudicates between individuals. It is empowered to review the actions of the executive to determine their legality. This important role of the judicial function is not obliterated, even in authoritarian societies.[38] For the most part, however, transitional justice research, particularly with reference to institutional accountability, has focused on the role of the executive and the legislature in societies that have witnessed gross violations of human rights and impunity with scarce attention paid to the judicial function. Yet, so critical is the judiciary's role in the exercise of powers in the modern state that "a government is not a government without courts."[39]

One of the marked failures of the current transition paradigm is the commonly articulated transition reform agenda that focuses on the political branches of government at the expense of attention to the judicial dimension in transitioning polities.[40] But the very nature of its role constitutes the judiciary as a major element in the machinery of the state. From that vantage, the judiciary "cannot avoid the making of political decisions"[41] in upholding the rule of law in society.

THE JUDICIARY AND THE RULE OF LAW

Transformation of the judiciary is central to the repositioning of the rule of law as a beneficial rather than exploitative principle for the organization of society, and specifically, the (re)building of a democratic state. It is certainly the case that some understanding of the rule of law was deployed by erstwhile tyrannical regimes in the exercise of power, as in Nazi Germany; apartheid South Africa; and authoritarian military regimes in Africa, Eastern Europe, and Latin America. In each case, specific instrumental understandings of law were deployed to foster undemocratic, immoral, and inhuman policies of discrimination, repression, and gross violations of human rights. Discrimination laws, for example, were institutionalized and legitimated in Nazi Germany and apartheid South Africa.

It is suggested that a conception of the rule of law that emphasizes or relies on people power, or, in more formal terms, popular sovereignty holds strong promise for enduring fundamental changes aspired to in transitioning societies. The American transition from colonialism, the struggle for independence, and the pivotal role of the people in its constitutional development in the late eighteenth

century provide strong precedent for societies seeking to assert popular power in transitioning states.[42]

It can be argued that institutional accountability for the past
with a view to strengthening weak or transforming dysfunctional
state institutions is one of the fundamental ways to foster the
viability of democracy and rule of law. Such accountability facilitates acknowledgement of institutional shortcomings crucial to
achieving transformation of state institutions. It also constitutes
a definitive progression to democratic governance and movement
away from repression.[43]

Proceeding on our adopted view of rule of law, a publicly accessible process of scrutiny offered by the *truth-seeking* mechanism
can be expected to restore some measure of judicial credibility and
public confidence in the judiciary in such post-authoritarian contexts. To insist otherwise, namely that any institution is beyond
public scrutiny conducted in a *plainly public* manner afforded by a
truth-seeking process, amounts to conceding to the judiciary "a real
omnipotence."[44] This is precisely a privilege the judiciary has been
all too ready to deny the political branches of government through
the instrumentality of judicial review. More crucially, such a proposition is tantamount to a direct inversion of popular sovereignty and
the imposition of "judicial supremacy."[45] Further, the truth-seeking
mechanism offers opportunity for obtaining comprehensive accounts
for past governance and the institutional role of the judiciary in it.

INTEGRITY VERSUS ACCOUNTABILITY:
TWO NORMATIVE ARGUMENTS

Many possible objections can be raised against the case for judicial
accountability for its role in past governance as part of transitional
justice arrangements. The most important are essentially of a normative character. Foremost in this category is the integrity argument. For
clarity, this is considered from two related but distinct perspectives: the
need for institutional independence and immunity of judicial officers.

Judicial Independence

Arguably, there is evident tension between the doctrine of judicial
independence and the truth-seeking mechanism, even in the context
of transition. In other words, the imperative of judicial independence

cannot be reconciled with bringing the judiciary to account for its role in past governance through a public mechanism like a truth commission. The fundamental doctrinal basis of the principle of judicial independence is the desire to obviate potential constraints to the exercise of judicial power. Institutional independence is necessary to secure the role of the judiciary as the institution charged with the protection of the individual from oppression. In view of this essence of the judicial function, public accountability of the nature proposed here has the potential to erode if not critically subvert the integrity of the judiciary.

Judicial integrity is a value that needs to be maintained perhaps even more in the context of transitional societies than any other. This was, in fact, a major argument in the resistance of the South Africa judiciary to the attempt to bring it to account for its role in apartheid before the TRC.[46] In David Dyzenhaus's analysis of the South Africa experience, he offers valuable insight that challenges this position. The judicial branch, he argues, ought to be scrutinized on its allegiance to law or what he refers to as "fidelity to law." This is what the judicial oaths of office require. What is considered as law and fidelity, to which judges are bound, is an approach that "accords recognition to reciprocity between the rulers and the ruled."[47]

The point then is that judicial independence should not be constituted into a shield against giving public accounts of the judicial role during an authoritarian period. Rather, an account of the judicial role during such a period provides opportunity for an assessment of whether the judiciary did maintain its independence at the relevant time. Public scrutiny of the nature afforded by a truth-seeking mechanism offers a chance to examine whether the judicial function was performed in a manner that accorded primacy to law as required by judicial (oath of) office. Or, in the converse – and this is the crux of the matter – did any extraneous but contextual factor intervene to compromise judicial independence *properly* conceived? The necessity for this would appear self-evident. Stated differently, judicial independence as a shield against accountability of the judiciary for the past can be challenged on its own terms. Despite its importance for the adjudicatory role and dispensation of justice, judicial independence ought not to be allowed to override the need for accountability for powers conferred on the judiciary in terms of the process and outcomes of the exercise of such powers.

In its conception, judicial independence, like judicial power itself, is designed for the benefit of citizens.[48] While the argument for judicial independence may be strong, it ought to be borne in mind that such independence is not a perquisite of judicial office. It is commonly recognized that respect for courts is essentially directed at the institution and not the person of the individual judge. Respect for and compliance with judicial decisions rest (at least to an appreciable extent) on the belief in the impartiality and independence of the judiciary. It is not designed to cast a sanctimonious cloak around individual judges. This is central to any power or authority the judiciary can aspire to have in society.

Judicial Immunity

The other aspect of the argument, as stated earlier, is the related but distinct case for protecting judges from fear (of suit) in the discharge of their duties. This is the principle of judicial immunity. Legislation, statutory or constitutional, barring litigants or other interested parties from taking legal action against judicial officers is one of the most potent measures for securing the independence of judicial officers. Political office holders are also sometimes protected from suit in the discharge of their functions. But this is normally for a limited period. Judicial immunity from suit is, however, usually more comprehensive and enduring in its operation, commonly extending beyond the tenure of judicial office.

The principle has been institutionalized to extinguish any threat of litigation on the judge for performing the normal functions of the office. Discernible in the entrenchment of judicial immunity is the view that the nature of judicial function requires an independence of "mind" that addresses itself to ensuring justice according to *law*. The position is further strengthened by the view that judicial misconduct is appropriately addressed through "structural" mechanisms of appeal procedure and, in extreme cases, dismissal from office.[49]

The judicial calling must stand outside the whims of individuals as well as institutions, and particularly one that trumps the commonweal. Where it is possible to surmise that the judiciary has been complicit in the violations of human rights by the state under an illiberal regime, this supports a case for accountability for what could well amount to judicial abdication of its role. In other words, there ought to be a valid departure from the norm of traditional conceptions of judicial independence in troubled societies where there are ample causes to believe judges have deviated from keeping faith

with their judicial oaths of office. This should be the case where such
oaths – as they commonly do – required the discharge of the functions in a manner consistent with the constitutional values of the
country as against the wishes of authoritarian rulers. Whether this is
factually the case or otherwise must be tested through a process of
public accounting, at the least, to set the records straight.

Scrutiny of the judiciary through a *truth-seeking* process during a
period of fundamental political change as proposed here is distinct
from subjecting individual judges to the indignity of civil suits for
their judgments. In the event there is some measure of consensus
that the judicial function has been conducted in some inappropriate
manner, the need to reach beyond the shield of judicial immunity
assumes an imperative. This is important for achieving societal
transformation and reconstruction, pivotal objects of transitional
justice in societies with an experience of authoritarianism or conflict. It serves to scrutinize further the validity of these normative
objections to public accountability of the judiciary for the past in the
context of the Nigerian post-authoritarian experience.

AN UNACCOUNTED JUDICIARY
AND A TROUBLED TRANSITION

The military left the Nigerian Public Service structures intact throughout the period of authoritarian rule.[50] But it took over the executive
and legislative functions all over the country along with a ban on
political activities. Throughout the period of authoritarian rule, the
judiciary remained the only institution that survived the suspension
and takeover of the institutions of governance.[51] The military did
arrogate to itself the power to appoint judges, but the judiciary did
not experience any institutional truncation. By default, the judiciary
took an active part in governance throughout the period. It is thus
arguably complicit in the misgovernance and violations of human
rights in the country in the three decades of military rule.

The Judiciary in Authoritarianism

Despite their disdain for constitutionalism and human rights, authoritarian rulers usually exhibit a paradoxical interest in obtaining
some veneer of legality for their illegitimate hold on power.[52] Even
the military class, in its foray into governance, is obliged to secure

a veneer of legitimacy for the effective exercise of political power. In the pursuit of that objective, they usually leave the judicial institution intact, unsuspended like the political branch.[53] The military finds an opportunity for legitimation through retaining the judicial institution. And this was the case in Nigeria. The self-serving motive has been aptly described by Tayyab Mahmud: "Usurpers appear to recognize that judicial pronouncements about the nature and merits of the change and quantum of their legislative capacity have an impact on the legitimacy of the new regime because words like 'law' and 'legality' function as titles of honour ... *Securing judicial recognition appears to be the key to gaining political legitimacy.*"[54]

Apart from the legitimacy value, there is the unavoidable necessity for the judicial institution even in authoritarian societies. In contrast to executive and legislative governance, the more nuanced requirements of adjudication or judicial governance are well beyond the disposition or capacity of military adventurers in power. The incapacity on the part of the military to administer the judicial function necessitates the retention of the judiciary in governance. The specialized nature of the judicial function constitutes a positive force which the judiciary ought to have utilized in the quest to maintain its institutional integrity, uphold human rights and the rule of law, irrespective of the *duress* constituted by authoritarian military rule.[55]

Successive military administrations foisted untold hardship and suffering on the mass of the people.[56] What role did, or could have, the judiciary played in that suffering? This ought to have constituted an important thematic focus of the truth-seeking process in Nigeria in view of its broad terms of reference. Part of its remit was to "identify the person or persons, authorities, institutions or organizations which may be held accountable" for gross violations of human rights and determine the motives for these violations or abuses. The judiciary had become largely impotent in upholding the rights of individuals in the era of military rule in the country. In frustration, a Justice of the Supreme Court boldly advised victims of rights violations to seek redress through means other than the judicial process. He concluded that the military left no one in doubt as to the inviolability of their decrees.[57]

Such judicial apologia was borne as much out of a sense of the courts' frustration with the importunate and contemptuous treatment of judicial decisions (and the institution as a whole) by successive military administrations as from an attempt at self-preservation. In a way though, it reinforces the need for accountability for the nature of judicial governance during the years of authoritarian rule. How or why was this possible? The root of judicial apologia in the Nigerian context is not unconnected with the legitimation of military rule in the first instance by the judiciary.

On the onset of military rule, the courts, after a brief and, in retrospect, weak resistance, upheld the illegal putsch as a "revolution." The Supreme Court held that the *coup d'état* legitimately upstaged the *Grundnorm* as represented by the country's republican constitution of 1963.[58] The legitimation of authoritarian rule then came back in its turn to haunt the judiciary. As the Oputa Panel found, at the end of military rule, the courts and judges had become "toothless bulldogs."[59] This ought not to have been the case considering the judges always owed a duty to the constitution. In this regard, it is significant for instance that the judicial oaths of office were always contained in the constitution. All the constitutions in operation throughout the period of authoritarian rule contained supremacy clauses. All judges were, in fact, sworn on the constitution rather than military legislation, hence the legal and moral justification for holding them to their constitutionally prescribed oaths of judicial office.

It is thus arguable that the empirical record of the Nigerian judiciary in the period of authoritarian rule commends the imperative of accountability for the performance of the judicial function. This situation in turn commends the need for an enquiry on why the judges took to the path of compromise when their judicial oaths of office require fidelity to law as stated by the constitution rather than military legislation. The compromised status of the Nigerian judiciary is further exacerbated by a legacy of questionable appointments characterized by nepotism and prebendalism. The compromised and corrupt judicial function generated a lacklustre attitude within the public for recourse to due process of law in the resolution of disputes. Such was the state of the judiciary at the point the country moved to civil governance on 29 May 1999.

The Judiciary in the Post-Authoritarian Period

Governance in Nigeria is confronted by several complexities in this period of its longest experience of civil rule in its post-independence. A good number of the complexities derive from the peculiar dynamics of a post-colonial, post-authoritarian state with heterogeneous identities. These complexities include rising crime rates, poverty, unemployment, the deplorable state of social infrastructure, and the failure of transitional justice measures for past victims of gross violations of human rights in which the judiciary, as discussed above, is implicated. Further, the fallouts of a grossly manipulated electoral process and the legitimacy deficit concomitant to it have deep resonance for the emergence of the judicialization of politics as a prominent feature of governance in the country, particularly from 2003 to date.

However, the most serious challenge to Nigeria's continued viability as a functional state has been posed by intergovernmental disputes over spheres of power in a lopsided federation.[60] These have been accompanied by unhealthy wrangling for power among the political elite, pervasive corruption, and the absence of effective dialogue to foster a consensual basis for the continued existence of the polity among various stakeholders. The judiciary, particularly the appellate courts, has been inundated with "political cases" and has become a strategic actor in policy decision-making and governance at a level unprecedented in Nigeria's history.[61]

One can conveniently cite over a dozen remarkable cases of judicialization of politics in the country in the context of the democratic transition at the intergovernmental level.[62] A topical survey would include *Attorney General of the Federation v Attorney General of Abia and 35 Ors*,[63] dealing with disputed claims between the federal and littoral states for oil resources derivable from the continental shelf of the country; *Attorney General of Ondo State v Attorney General of the Federation and 35 Ors* (the ICPC Case)[64] dealing with the establishment of a monolith anti-corruption agency in the federation; *Attorney General of the Federation v Attorney General of Abia and 35 Ors* (No. 2)[65] and *Attorney General of Ogun State v Attorney General of the Federation*[66] both dealing (again) with fiscal federalism and allegations of illegal withholding of funds by the federal government.

Attorney General of Lagos State v Attorney General of the Federation[67] centred on disputations over the propriety of inherited military legislation that conferred ultimate planning powers on the federal government, possessed only of complete geopolitical control over the federal capital territory. All the states of the federation challenged the constitutionality of certain sections of the Electoral Act (promulgated by the National Assembly), in as much as it sought to make provisions for elections into local (government) authorities in *Attorney General of Abia and 35 Ors v Attorney General of the Federation.*[68]

The disputations over the appropriate spheres of power and control in the country between the federal government on the one hand and the states on the other were so frequent. Consequently, there was a seeming endless recourse to the judiciary for resolution. Customization of this approach to governance and the extensive judicialization of politics it generated attracted notice and *obiter dicta* of the Supreme Court. In one case, it observed that "this is yet another open quarrel between the State and Federal Government" with which it had become "thoroughly familiar."[69] The situation in the country is attributable to the un-negotiated transition from decades of military rule. This has forced to the centre stage of governance unresolved and unmediated tensions arising from the country's de jure federal status that has witnessed a transformation to a de facto unitary state. These remain critical issues left unaddressed in the process of political change.

However, the impact of the judicialization of politics has raised serious concerns on the decisional independence and integrity of judicial officers. In Nigeria, the most prominent of the concerns centres on judicial ineptitude and corruption (or simply apprehensions of it), especially in the lower courts and throughout the system.[70] It is instructive that the recent decision of the Presidential Elections Petition Tribunal on the 2007 elections did not escape the allegations of corruption that dogged the steps and seriously compromised the adjudication of the 2003 elections in the country.[71] Even the Supreme Court, which finally decided the matter, was not spared. This led Justice Tobi, one of the justices who sat on the panel of the decisive final appeal in the highly contentious election petition[72] to warn litigants (politicians) to stop calling judges "all sorts of names." In obvious exasperation, the learned justice wondered why judges are not trusted by the public in the administration of justice.[73]

It is suggested that the persistence of real or imagined corruption in the judiciary is a product of the existential continuity of the institution in the transition process. It is arguable that ambivalence toward the courts will persist in the country, if judicial accountability for past complicity in misgovernance during the country's authoritarian past remains completely ignored, or under-addressed.

CONCLUSION

At all times, but especially in the circumstances of transition and political change from an authoritarian past, the judiciary must be wary of designs through recourse to the judicial process to frustrate transitional justice measures. This is particularly important for restoring and fortifying rule of law in a transitional setting as the foundation for building a democratic state. Such awareness appears to have been lost on the Nigerian courts in the *Oputa Panel* case. The judiciary thus fostered a situation whereby the strong determination of the generals not to appear before the Oputa Panel introduced a twist to the truth-seeking process from which it never recovered.

The role of the judiciary in governance in authoritarian societies raises the need for scrutiny of the judicial function as an integral aspect of transitional justice arrangements in building democratic states. This is because a critical assessment of judicial impact on the course of governance and the exercise of state powers provides a comprehensive account of the past. Such accountability for the past also confronts the judiciary with its role in governance, facilitates acknowledgment, and opens the way for the desired institutional transformation necessary to build a democratic state. This is premised in part on contemporary social experience that the judiciary as an institution of the state always participates in governance. The conduct of that role in authoritarian societies merits account at times of socio-political change.

What emerges from the Nigerian experience is that accountability for the role of the judiciary in governance during an authoritarian period is relevant because of certain standards and societal expectations of the institution. Where such expectations are not met, it leads to the lack of public trust and confidence in the judicial system, which is fatal to societal cohesion, peace, and development. Since the judiciary commands neither the money controlled by the legislature nor the force at the service of the executive, public confidence is at the heart of obedience to judicial decisions.[74] It is not at all challenging to establish such a situation in transitional societies that had laboured under authoritarian rule, war, institutionalized discrimination like apartheid, or other forms of substantial social displacement. Hence the significance of incorporating judicial accountability into transitional justice processes designed as part of the building of democratic states.

The judiciary in post-authoritarian societies is usually privileged in at least two ways, which accentuate the need for accountability for the past. First, it actively participates in governance and may, by the reason of such participation, be complicit for misrule and violation of human rights. Thus, unlike the political institutions which invariably suffer from suspension or abrogation by authoritarian rulers, it benefits from an institutional memory in the post-authoritarian period. This gives it an edge in governance over the political organs of the state at the crucial period of consolidating political change in transitional societies. Indeed, it usually takes the strategic position of mediator in state-society, intra- and intergovernmental disputations, and rights claims. Second, and connected to the first, is the need by authoritarian regimes for the judicial function despite their dubious claims to messianic executive and legislative capabilities, as was commonly the case in military regimes in Nigeria. This strategic positioning of the judiciary makes more compelling the case for judicial accounts for its role in past governance.

The dynamics of transitional justice lends itself to Pamela Karlan's argument that the claim to judicial independence must be balanced against actual judicial outcomes.[75] The positive values of judicial immunity (and more broadly, independence) notwithstanding, an absolutist interpretation of it could seriously undermine other equally important societal values.[76] Society, as a body corporate, stands above its institutions. It is entitled to an account as principal for the exercise of powers devolved to any of its agents, parts, or institutions as surrogates in furtherance of the commonweal. The judiciary as one such surrogate is thereby not excluded. The operation of normative or other principles as a shield for judicial accounts for the past in post-authoritarian contexts, no matter how important, simply lack legitimacy.

The gap in governance created by a transition's peculiar political power dynamics accentuates the need for a judiciary committed to construct an agenda of state rebuilding. Such an agenda is ideally the hallmark and legitimizing justification for the transition in the first place. This is particularly relevant in the context of a transition that has resulted not in a real (as is the aspiration of the people and mantra of the elites now in power) but a virtual democracy: in other words, a situational dynamic in which the ruling elite have perfected the art of manipulating the transition process in a way to secure their hold on power and still create the impression that *liberal* democracy has been instituted.

NOTES

1 For an interesting sample of the expanding body of literature on "judi-cialization of politics" and "Constitutionalization of politics" in liberal democracies as well as authoritarian societies see Lee Epstein et al., "The Role of Constitutional courts in the Establishment and Maintenance of Democratic Systems of Government," *Law & Society Review* 35, no. 1 (2001): 117; Ran Hirschl, *Towards Juristocracy: The Origins and Consequences of the New Constitutionalism* (Cambridge: Harvard, University Press, 2004); Ran Hirschl, "The New Constitutionalism and the Judicialization of Pure Politics Worldwide," *Fordham Law Review* 75, no. 2 (2006): 721; Tom Ginsburg, *Judicial Review in New Democracies* (New York: Cambridge University Press, 2003); Samuel Isaacharoff, "Democracy and Collective Decision Making," *International Journal of Constitutional Law* 6, no. 2 (2008): 231–66; and Heinz Klug, *Constituting Democracy: Law, Globalism and South Africa's Political Reconstruction* (Cambridge: Cambridge University Press, 2000).

2 Moustafa Tamir, *The Struggle for Constitutional Power: Law Politics and Economic Development in Egypt* (New York: Cambridge University Press, 2007); Tom Ginsburg and Moustafa Tamir, *Rule by Law: The Politics of Courts in Authoritarian Regimes* (New York: Cambridge University Press, 2008).

3 John Morison, Kieran McEvoy, and Gordon Anthony, eds, *Judges, Transition and Human Rights* (Oxford: Oxford University Press, 2007), 2.

4 Morison, McEvoy, and Anthony, *Judges, Transition and Human Rights*, 2–3; Wojciech Sadurski, *Rights Before Courts: A Study of Constitutional Courts in Post Communist States of Central and Eastern Europe* (Dordrecht: Springer, 2005).

5 Rami Mani, "Dilemmas of Expanding Transitional Justice or the Nexus between Development and Transitional Justice," *International Journal of Transitional Justice* 2, no. 3 (2008): 253–65; Natascha Zupan and Sylvia Servaes, "Transitional Justice and Dealing with the Past," FriEnt Guidance Paper, Working Group on Development and Peace (Bonn: FriEnt, 2007), 1–32.

6 The country was under civil democratic rule from 1 October 1960 to 15 January 1966 and from 1 October 1979 to 31 December 1983.

7 Hakeem O. Yusuf, "Calling the Judiciary to Account for the Past: Transitional Justice and Judicial Accountability in Nigeria," *Law & Policy* 30, no. 2 (2008): 194–226, 207–19.

8 World Bank in Nigeria, "Overview: Political Context," accessed 10 December 2020, www.worldbank.org/en/country/nigeria/overview.

9 It was inaugurated on 14 June 1999.

10 Nigeria World "Inaugural Speech by His Excellency, President Olusegun Obasanjo following his Swearing-in as President of the Federal Republic of Nigeria on May 29, 1999," accessed 10 December 2020, www.dawodu.com/obas1.htm.

11 This was amended by Statutory Instrument No. 13 of 1999. See "Foreword" by Hon. Justice Chukwudifu A. Oputa CFR, Justice Emeritus Supreme Court Of Nigeria, chair, *Synoptic Overview Oputa Panel Report: Conclusions and Recommendations*, May 2002, accessed 10 December 2020, www.dawodu.com/oputa1.htm. The site also has the full report.

12 No. 447, Laws of the Federation of Nigeria, 1990, was originally enacted as colonial legislation.

13 For a detailed account of the work and challenges that confronted the Oputa Panel, see Hakeem O. Yusuf, "Travails of Truth: Achieving Justice for Victims of Impunity in Nigeria," *International Journal of Transitional Justice* 1, no. 2 (2007): 268–86.

14 *Human Rights Violations Investigations Commission Report (Oputa Panel Report)*, vol. 2, 34, www.dawodu.com/oputa3.pdf.

15 *Synoptic Overview, supra* note 11 at 8.

16 "Address by His Excellency the President, Commander-In-Chief of the Armed Forces, Chief Olusegun Obasanjo, G.C.F.R at the Inauguration Ceremony of the Human Rights Violations Investigations Panel on Monday 14 June 1999."

17 Included in the ranks were former president Shehu Shagari, the country's first executive president, and President Olusegun Obasanjo in his erstwhile capacity as military head of state.

18 *Synoptic Overview, supra* note 11.

19 Despite the frustrations he has met with in his quest to bring the killers of the prominent journalist to justice, he has remained undaunted. See for instance, O. Ojo, "21 Years after Dele Giwa's Murder – Fawehinmi to Govt: Reopen Case," *Guardian* (Lagos) (online), 20 October 2007.

20 [2003] M.J.S.C 63. This is the report of the defendants' appeal to the Supreme Court following the victory of "the generals" at the Court of Appeal. Reference will however be made in a composite manner to the matter through the court of first instance (Federal High Court) through to the Supreme Court. Reference to 'Courts' in the following context will cover all three courts except as specifically stated. For discussion of the case and others in the context of transformative constitutionalism, see

Hakeem O. Yusuf, "The Judiciary and Constitutionalism in Transitions: A Critique," *Global Jurist* 7, no. 3 (2007): 1–47.

21 This position is consistent with practice elsewhere. For example, Legal Notice No. 5 of 1986 in Uganda created the country's current truth commission, which provides that "any person desiring to give evidence to the Commission shall do so in *person.*" Emphasis added.

22 The first decision in the matter, by the Court of Appeal, was delivered on 31 October 2001, ten days after the conclusion of the public hearings.

23 Tribunals of Inquiry Act No. 447, sections 5(d), 11(1)(b), 11(4), and 12(2).

24 Thus, the South Africa and Ghana Truth Commissions, which closely preceded and succeeded the Nigerian truth-seeking process respectively, were set up pursuant to tailor-made legislation.

25 (1963) 1 WLR 949.

26 For a succinct discussion of the role of precedent in the work of judges, see Lee Epstein and Jack Knight "Courts and Judges," in *Blackwell Companion to Law and Society*, ed. Austin Sarat (Malden, MA: Blackwell Publishing, 2004), 184–7.

27 When the country became a republic.

28 Stuart Mole, "The 2003 Nigerian Elections: A Democratic Settlement?" *The Round Table* 92, no. 370 (2003): 423, 424.

29 David Dyzenhaus, *Judging the Judges, Judging Ourselves: Truth, Reconciliation and the Apartheid Legal Order* (Oxford: Hart Publishing, 2003), 16.

30 Emphasis mine.

31 See for instance, the Medical and Dental Practitioners Act Cap 221 (now Cap M8, 2004) Laws of the Federation of Nigeria 1990 establishes the Medical and Dental Council of Nigeria and empowers this council to enact rules of professional conduct for medical practitioners as well as establish the Medical and Dental Practitioners Disciplinary Tribunal. This tribunal is mandated to determine cases of professional misconduct against medical personnel, and appeals from its decisions go straight to the Court of Appeal. It is thus accorded the status of a High Court, a superior court of record in the country.

32 Brigadier-General Togun (Rtd.) v Hon. Justice Chukwudifu Oputa (Rtd.) & 2 others and General Ibrahim Babangida & 1 Other [2001] 16 NWLR pt 740, 597 at 662 (cases consolidated on the orders of the court). Hereafter, *Togun v Oputa* (No. 2), 645.

33 For a discussion of the sometimes progressive but wavering judicial construction of this constitutional provision, see Hakeem O. Yusuf, "The

Judiciary and Political Change in Africa: Developing Transitional Jurisprudence in Nigeria," *International Journal of Constitutional Law* 7, no. 4 (2009): 654.

34 See the position of the Court in Hon. Muyiwa Inakoju & 17 Ors v Hon. Abraham Adeolu Adeleke & 3 Ors [2007] 4 NWLR pt. 1025, 423 and (2007) 7 NILR 136, per Justice Niki Tobi 35. Emphasis mine.

35 See generally Yusuf, *supra* note 7.

36 Gianfranco Poggi, *Forms of Power* (Cambridge: Polity Press, 2001), 203–4.

37 Poggi, 203–4.

38 Tamir, *supra* note 2.

39 Henry M. Hart and Herbert Wechsler, *Federal Courts and the Federal System*, 2nd ed. (Mineola, NY: Foundation Press Inc., 1973), 6.

40 H. Kwasi Prempeh, "Judicial Review and Challenge of Constitutionalism in Contemporary Africa," *Tulane Law Review* 80 (2006): 1299.

41 John A.G. Griffith, *The Politics of the Judiciary*, 5th ed. (London: Fontana, 1997), 292–3.

42 Larry K. Kramer, *The People Themselves: Popular Constitutionalism and Judicial Review* (Oxford: Oxford University Press, 2004).

43 Fionnuala Ni Aolain and Colm Campbell, "The Paradox of Transition in Conflicted Democracies," *Human Rights Quarterly* 27, no. 1 (2005): 172, 184, 207.

44 Ni Aolain and Campbell, 178.

45 Williams J. Watkins Jr., "Popular Sovereignty, Judicial Supremacy and the American Revolution: Why the Judiciary Cannot be the Final Arbiter of Constitutions," *Duke Journal of Constitutional Law and Public Policy* 159 (2006): 1, 41.

46 Dyzenhaus, *supra* note 29.

47 Dyzenhaus, *supra* note 29 at 183.

48 Murray Gleeson, "The Right to an Independent Judiciary" (14th Commonwealth Law Conference London, September 2005). www.hcourt.gov.au/assets/publications/speeches/former-justices/gleesoncj/cj_sept05.html.

49 Pamela S. Karlan, "Two Concepts of Judicial Independence," *Southern California Law Review* 72 (1999): 535, 539; and Robert C. Waters, "Judicial Immunity vs. Due Process: When Should a Judge be Subject to Suit?" *Cato Journal* 9, no. 2 (1987): 461, 470.

50 Abiola Ojo, *Constitutional Law and Military Rule in Nigeria* (Ibadan: Evans Brothers Nigeria Publishers Limited, 1987), 116.

51 Ojo, 116.

52 Anthony W. Pereira, "Of Judges and Generals: Security Courts under Authoritarian Regimes in Argentina, Brazil and Chile," in *Rule by Law*, ed. Ginsburg and Tamir, 23–57, 55.

53 Tayyab Mahmud, "Jurisprudence of Successful Treason: Coup *d'état* & Common Law," *Cornell International Law Journal* 27 (1994): 49–140, 103; and Lisa Hilbink, "Agents of Anti-Politics: Courts in Pinochet's Chile," in *Rule by Law*, ed. Ginsburg and Tamir, 102.

54 Mahmud, "Jurisprudence of Successful Treason," 103–4. Emphasis mine.

55 Tunde I. Ogowewo, "Why the Judicial Annulment of the Constitution of 1999 is Imperative to the Survival of Nigeria's Democracy," *Journal of African Law* 44 (2000): 135–66, 157–9.

56 *Synoptic Overview, supra* note 11.

57 Nwosu v Environmental Sanitation Authority [1990] 2 NWLR Pt.135, 688.

58 E.O. Lakanmi and Kikelomo Ola v The Attorney–General (Western State), The Secretary to the Tribunal (Investigation of Assets Tribunal) and the Counsel to the Tribunal (1971), *University of Ife Law Reports*, 201.

59 *Synoptic Overview, supra* note 11 at 39.

60 Sola Akinrinade, "Constitutionalism and the Resolution of Conflicts in Nigeria," *The Round Table* 92, no.368 (2003): 49.

61 Hakeem O. Yusuf, "Robes on Tight Ropes: The Judicialisation of Politics in Nigeria," *Global Jurist* 8, no. 2 (2008): 8–9.

62 And that number is by no means exhaustive of this line of cases.

63 (2002) 4 SC Pt I, 1.

64 (2002) 6 SC Pt I, 1.

65 (2002) NWLR 542 S.C.

66 (2002) 12 SC Pt II, 1.

67 (2003) 6 SC Pt I, 24.

68 (2003) 3 SC 106.

69 Attorney General of Abia & 2 Ors v Attorney General of the Federation & 33 Ors (2006) 7 NILR 71, 1, 2.

70 USAID, *Democracy and Governance Assessment of Nigeria* (Washington, DC: USAID, 2006), 11 and 28, accessed 10 December 2020, http://pdf. usaid.gov/pdf_docs/PNADI079.pdf.

71 "How the Presidential Elections Petition Tribunal Came to its Decision," Sahara Reporters, New York (website) https://saharareporters.com/ 2008/10/05/how-presidential-elections-petition-tribunal-came-its-controversial-verdict.

72 This is reflected in the decision by a bare majority of 4–3 upholding the earlier unanimous decision of the Presidential Elections Petition Tribunal.
73 Atiku Abubakar GCON & 2Ors v Alhaji Umar Musa Yar'Adua & 6Ors (2008) 36 NSCQR 231, 402–3.
74 Gleeson, *supra* note 48 at 1–2.
75 Karlan, *supra* note 49 at 558.
76 Karlan, *supra* note 49 at 539.

SECTION THREE

Documents and Archives

TRCs and the Archival Imperative

Abena Ampofoa Asare

More than fourteen African countries have established Truth and Reconciliation Commissions (TRCs) over the past three decades, and more are currently proposed.[1] Fuelled by both international investment and local pressures, the TRC form, originally used in South America in the waning days of the Cold War, has proliferated on the African continent. Since the 1996 South African TRC captured the global imagination, the subsequent adoption of commissions around the world established the TRC as a transitional justice instrument with transnational value. Diverse governments and populations embrace truth and reconciliation as a path toward political stability, to signal compliance with international norms, pursue national cohesion, and increase respect for human rights, among other motivations. Myriad and sundry reach for this concept, with varied expectations, to navigate the consequences of historical violence.[2] However, for communities that have held truth and reconciliation processes, the consequences are decidedly ambivalent. In the space between the high hopes attached to the global TRC form and the uneven reality, the African continent's TRC trajectory is an invaluable guide.

One of the lessons from the global TRC experience is the importance of preserving, processing, and publishing TRC records. Creating effective archives is a substantive, albeit overlooked, part of the political transformation that TRCs pursue in the world. These archives are neither supplemental nor incidental to a truth commission's goals of cohesion, restoration, stability, education, and reparation. Although truth commissions are often evaluated based on what they accomplish over the course of their mandate period, when a commission finishes its work, its contribution is only just beginning.[3] The political transformation TRCs pursue depends on how the narratives about political violence are received, utilized, and consolidated; the timeline for a truth commission's impact may extend even farther than we can imagine.

Archives untether the political promise of any given truth commission from the present moment; they preserve the possibility that the records of suffering and violence emerging from these commissions are not limited by the political moment of their creation. One lesson from the global history of truth commissions is that governments are often unable or unwilling to immediately "make good" on the rhetoric of historical justice. Governments may authorize truth commissions as part of political performance or in an uneasy state of transition; the state that inaugurates the TRC may be unable to pursue the structural and political shifts needed for reparation or restoration.

For example, Chile's National Commission for Truth and Reconciliation, established in 1990, worked in the shadow of the Pinochet government's amnesty law, meaning that the documents it gathered were unable to be used in criminal prosecutions. After the arrest of Pinochet in 1998, Chilean judges and courts responded to the changed political context and the commission's records were utilized more expansively by domestic courts.[4] After the UN-commissioned Salvadoran Truth Commission released its 1993 report, "From Madness to Hope: The 12-Year War in El Salvador," the commission's political vitality was stymied when its archives ended up under lock and key with the UN Secretary-General.[5] More than twenty years after the commission released its report, US courts utilized information within it to justify the deportation of two officials in Salvadoran high command who were named by the commission as accomplices to torture and extrajudicial killing.[6]

In advocating for robust TRC archives, this chapter suggests that the full consequences of truth commissions may well be "a question of the future," meaning, "if we want to know what it will have meant, we will only know tomorrow."[7] By building strong TRC archives we acknowledge that the full audience for these stories, testimonies, and insights may not yet have been born. The healing and transformation that a truth commission promises may occur long after its mandate has expired; these records may be useful in the hands of future generations.

However, another lesson of the African continent's TRCs is that there is often considerable distance between the existence of a TRC and the creation of robust and useful archives. The materials gathered together and created by various truth commissions tend to *disappear* in the aftermath of the process. Disappearance does not only refer to the erasure or destruction of these records, although these types of physical losses do occur. Disappearance also refers to the absence of these records in the public sphere, the high barriers separating the TRC materials from the public, and the various ways the substance of these records is shrouded from public view. The value of truth commission records and the need for their preservation is not, on the face of it, controversial.[8] Human rights organizations such as Amnesty International describe archiving as a duty and advise states that embark on truth and reconciliation processes to make adequate provision for the preservation of the associated archives.

The International Center for Transitional Justice, in its 2013 guide to best practices, encourages architects of truth commissions "to hand over" the extensive materials that will be created to a "national archival authority or another institution."[9] Beneath this brief prescription lies a world of complexity. As a result, careful thinking about the physical and political afterlives of truth commission materials should precede their inauguration of a truth commission.[10] The rhetorical support for archiving TRC records must be juxtaposed against an empirical reality where these materials' fate is anything but assured. Technological gaps, lack of political will, insufficient resources, among other factors, often hinder African Truth Commissions from producing robust archives that might reach toward a future justice.

Below I explore the contours of truth commission archives and describe how the complexity of these is neglected, forgotten, and disappeared in different national contexts. Using examples from the African continent's TRC trajectory, specifically Ghana's National Reconciliation Commission, this chapter considers the consequences of the trend of archival disappearance and the potential of archival reappearance. Archives are imperative for truth and reconciliation's pursuit of a comprehensive vision of historical justice. They insulate the transformational potential of the TRC from the compromises of the neo-liberal present through acts of preservation, processing, and publication. Speaking of archives claims the truth and reconciliation process as a planting of seeds; it affirms the ongoing labour of transitional justice that must inevitably "extend far beyond the so-called transition" and will require the "healing and repair work of several generations."[11]

TRC ARCHIVES, IN PART *AND* IN WHOLE

Everywhere there is a truth commission it leaves in its wake a trail of documents. These materials may "include audio and video recordings, letters written from jails and sneaked out by sympathetic guards, court documents being produced daily, cassette tapes of perpetrator confessions, newspaper articles; ephemera such as pamphlets, posters, and mimeographed leaflets; professional records of promotions, firings and complaints; documents produced by local bureaucrats; and of course, the written and oral testimony of those who have suffered or witnessed suffering." Along with describing the actions and experiences of individuals, communities, and institutions, these documents also reveal the commission's practices and organizational identity. These materials can productively be read together as an archive with all the attendant complexity that this status carries with it.[12]

The archive, this "montage of fragments that creates an illusion of totality and continuity,"[13] then serves as a vector and consolidator of power.[14] There is a duality, a play between revelation and obfuscation in the practice of the African continent's national TRCs. These processes valorize disclosure as a force for political transformation; yet, in practice, concealment and erasure are also organizing features of these national truth commissions. That which is ignored, glossed over, and battened down in the course of a commission's work is palpable and substantial; this too forms a bulk. The stories that are not told, the perpetrators who remain unnamed, the organizing frameworks not used, the types of restoration that victims cannot imagine, let alone ask for; these all dance into view just outside the frame whenever a TRC does its work. The silences that surround the work of Africa's national truth commissions are palpable, and often extend to the treatment of the TRC records after the fact.[15]

Truth commission records have conventionally been processed, preserved, and publicized in part, not in whole. The full body of investigative reports, testimonies and petitions, administrative documents, and other materials are rarely gathered together in archives that are straightforward, easy to locate and consult.[16] Usually, at a minimum, the truth commission's official report is the most visible part of the archive. Meant to distill the initiative's work, these final reports are written to summarize the truth commission's work for a broad domestic and international public.

However, even these final reports do not always make it before the public eye. Nigeria's Human Rights Violations Investigation Commission, commonly called the Oputa Panel, was halted before its eight-volume, 15,000-page report was released to the public. After the sponsoring government of Olusegun Obasanjo annulled the report and the commission's work, the Oputa Panel's secretary, Matthew Kukah, insisted that releasing the report was a political obligation. "Releasing the report would not have, and will not solve our problems. It will not put bread on the table but would have helped to establish confidence that government is sincere."[17] Although the report was eventually leaked to the public three years after it was submitted to the president, the fact of its disappearance highlights the ambivalence with which many governments embrace TRCs. It is not only in Nigeria where governments who once sponsored a truth commission might choose to later disappear the final report. In Oceania's Solomon Islands, the TRC report (2008) was also disappeared by the executive branch and then leaked into the public's hands.[18]

Even a long delay of a TRC report can function as a disappearance of sorts. Côte d'Ivoire's Commission for Dialogue, Truth and Reconciliation (2012) collected numerous statements (72,000) about the crisis surrounding the country's 2010–2011 national elections. After the commissioners submitted their work, President Alassane Ouattara delayed the report's release; no public explanation was offered.[19] Instead, the Ouattara government created a successor commission to deal strictly with reparations, thus appearing to close the door on the truth commission's work without ever making it available to the public. Although this four-year gap between the commission's completion and the release of its report undoubtedly dampened public engagement, the Côte d'Ivoire report was ultimately released by the government.

Importantly, truth commission reports do not constitute the full archive. Written and collated by the official commissioners, these reports rarely reflect or transmit the complexity of the citizen narratives gathered together, often for the first time, by a TRC. In this way, even when the report is made available, the full archive may still be obscured in the public view. The accumulated interviews, petitions, witness statements, and other materials associated with a commission's work and functioning have their own logic. Citizens transmit information about the texture, impact, and consequence of political violence in their word choice and syntax, the supporting materials they carry before the commission, and the other choices through which they turn the TRC into a space for the amplification of their voices.[20]

For this reason, researchers insist that the report is the beginning, not the end, of TRC archives. Five years after Togo's Truth, Justice, and Reconciliation Commission released the summary of its final report, researchers Jeremy Sarkin and Tetevi Davi wonder when the "many thousands of witness statements" gathered will become available to the public.[21] The Mauritius Truth and Justice Commission (2009) insists that its archival plan is not only for the final report but also for the other materials gathered by the commission. In Mauritius, the archival plan explicitly provides for "retain[ing] and mak[ing] accessible ... written documents (transcripts, questionnaires, census recording and other written sources), audiovisual recordings (oral interviews and hearings) and other materials for both legal reasons and research purposes."[22] The expansive political possibility of a truth commission often lies in the space between a partial and full view of TRC archives, that is, between the streamlined final report and the unruly and complicated citizen narratives.

The administrative documents that tell the story of a commission's origins, its funding streams, internal debates, and compromises are also critical parts of a TRC archive. In the case of the Sierra Leone TRC (2002), Megan MacKenzie and Mohamed Sesay challenge the "grassroots" nature of the process by examining the provenance of the organizing documents and concepts. The International Center for Transitional Justice, a transnational non-governmental organization, provided training to the Sierra Leone government about what a truth commission is and how it should function. The UN Office of the High Commissioner for Human Rights (OHCR) drafted the statute establishing the TRC.[23] Moreover, the bulk of funding for the Sierra Leone TRC came from international donors.[24] The administrative documents detailing the practical foundations of any truth commission provide crucial insight into a commission's identity and outcomes. These background documents, separate from the report or even the citizen petitions and testimonies, are also significant parts of the archive.

CASE STUDIES OF DISAPPEARANCE AND APPEARANCE

Even the famed South African TRC has faced difficulties in the preservation and publication of its records and material. The prominence of this TRC – and its records – in national and global circulation is undeniable. In its foundational documents, this TRC articulated a "commitment to transparency and public scrutiny," identifying its records as "a national asset which must be both protected and made accessible." Even with this archival directive, there have been some difficulties in fulfilling the mission.

The praiseworthy collaboration between the independent South African History Archive (SAHA) and the South African Broadcasting Corporation to catalogue, contextualize, and develop appropriate technologies to further public engagement with the variety of TRC records has not always been successful in preserving materials for posterity. For example, an eighty-seven-part *Truth Commission: Special Report* TV series created and run by the broadcasting corporation during the period of public hearings became largely unavailable after its initial broadcast. SAHA later discovered that some of the original master videos had gone missing from the archives over the years and were permanently lost to the public.[25] In addition, the sheer technical and labour difficulties of processing the 3,000+ cubic metres of material transferred from the TRC offices to the South African National Archives meant the majority of these records were unavailable to the public for a number of years.[26]

The gap between a rhetoric of accessibility and a reality of disappearance also shapes the afterlife of the Ghana National Reconciliation Commission (NRC). In Ghana, the NRC was perceived – and is still remembered – as just another innovation in an ongoing partisan contest between the country's two largest political parties. As such, the NRC is reduced, by supporters and critics alike, to a referendum on the parties and leaders who have occupied the national political imagination since independence.[27] However, the bulk of NRC testimonies and petitions focused on ordinary Ghanaians and featured narratives that evade and exceed the polemical political contest between the two competing parties.[28] The NRC is remembered and discussed as a redundant piece of an ongoing power struggle, but the petitioner narratives display a vision of suffering, revelation, and recourse that is broader, deeper, and wider than the so-called "big men" pursuing state power at any given moment.

To understand the difference between the Ghanaian NRC final report and the petitioner testimonies and records, I focus on one petition that propels us quickly past the understanding of the NRC as solely a partisan referendum and allows a glimpse into the depth of the NRC archive. I encountered the Plange file in a box of other petitions from the NRC's Accra office. Arranged in alphanumerical order, the Plange file was one of the many NRC documents deposited at the University of Ghana's Balme Library in the Africana reserved section. In a slim folder, written in long-hand, this petition details the story of a young man hit by a stray bullet shot by an overzealous soldier at a traffic stop in the early 1980s Ghana, in the time of military rule under the Provisional National Defence Council. Although the young man, Nii Ayi Plange, was rushed to the hospital, he suffered losses and sought redress with the commission.

The first page of the Plange petition begins, "I, Nii Ayi Plange, cannot speak when I am called to testify because I am mute. I have therefore delegated my sister, Madam Grace Plange, to do the talking for me." From this very first sentence, the Plange petition calls into question one of the primary conventions of the truth commission format. TRCs "draw from a model that holds that speech is cathartic," that prioritizes the act of disclosure as the foundation for individual and collective healing.[29] When Nii Ayi declares his inability to speak, to participate in this TRC as it is structured, his simple confession brings into view those in the body politic who, for any number of reasons, cannot make this move toward public articulation. Human rights enforcement mechanisms, built on a foundation of court and court-like instruments, all depend on an assumed articulate plaintiff. However, Nii Ayi's testimony underscores the exclusion that happens when accountability depends on public declarations of suffering. What of those types of suffering that are, for physical, social, or economic reasons, unspeakable? What of those victims who can never be plaintiffs?

In this file, Madam Grace, Nii Ayi's sister, is supposedly the mouthpiece for her brother's pain; she is the intermediary who is supposed to translate his experiences to the commissioners and the

Ghanaian public. However, the substance of the petition belies the idea of Madam Grace as amanuensis. In speaking for her brother, she also speaks for herself, drawing attention to the way a single event devastates a family over time. "I am the only family he has, I have sold everything I have to take care of him ... to the extent that my own children do not have school fees."[30] The amalgamated harm of a single event is revealed in Madam Grace's anguish at her brother's pain and her own plight trying to support him over the years. In the context of a truth commission, Madam Grace's petition highlights the intricacy and expansiveness of the reparations program needed to staunch the wounds of political violence. If harm is social, any attempts to repair must also be social; true redress would confront political violence that ripples through families and communities, pulling many into its wake.

Reading the Ghana NRC Report alone, as well-written as it is, does not reveal the complex analyses of harm and redress that are part of the Plange file or allow comprehension of the limits of a truth commission structure that depends on an assumed articulate plaintiff. The reader of the NRC Report would not see the last two pages of the Plange file. One page is a photocopied photograph of Nii Ayi Plange seated cross-legged, a smile on his face; they would not have a chance to see the eyes and features of a handsome young man whose potential was limited so abruptly. The last page is a death certificate for Nii Ayi Plange. In the course of the NRC's work, before any determination had been made by the commissioners, Nii Ayi Plange passed away. There is perhaps no clearer insight into the gaps and inadequacies of the truth commission process than this.

Perhaps this is one of the most important distinctions between an expanded TRC archive and a truth commission report: the multiple documents produced over the course of a truth commission's work push past sanitized and/or streamlined depictions of the search for truth and the path to reconciliation. In the case of Ghana, citizen narratives held critiques of the commission's framework and presentation, revealing the "epistemic injustice," that Dietlinde Wouters identifies as a consequence of transitional justice processes embedded in the conventions and languages of international law.[31] In the Ghana archive, there are many different perspectives on the Ghanaian past. Citizens shared narratives highlighting the continuity of suffering despite the rapid transitions in political leadership. Their stories often exposed violence that could not be simply laid at the feet of one political party or the other. In this fuller archive, the national reconciliation process was more than a site for political campaigning by other means; it was also a place where diverse citizens lodged their stories and perspectives into the public record. But what if there is no public access to this fuller archive, particularly over time?

The gulf between the way the NRC is remembered in Ghana and the substance of the full archive is not inconsequential. Citizens and researchers who never encounter the full NRC archive may never grasp the value of this time-consuming and expensive truth and reconciliation process. The disappearance of the full TRC archive furthers a narrative of stagnancy and impossibility around the concept of historical justice. Who feels reconciled because of the Ghana NRC? critics ask. What was the value of the process? skeptics muse. The reality is that critics of the NRC usually have received only a partial view of the commission's outcomes and consequences. The brief afterlife of the NRC reflects the limitation and inattention given to the archive. The NRC Report itself was poorly disseminated in the years following the commission due to the shifting priorities of the sponsoring government and the directives of the subsequent administration that wanted little to do with a process that had already been dismissed as partisan antics.[32] Researchers continue to struggle to access the documents and materials stored at the Balme Library. These records are not completely processed and preserved, and consulting them is not straightforward. In this way, the substance of the NRC archive is rarely seen, let alone analyzed.

The disappearance of a complex truth commission archive, due to limitations of technology, access, and political will is more common than not when considering the afterlives of African TRCs. Take, for instance, the Kenya Truth, Justice, and Reconciliation Commission Report (TJRC, 2008). Apart from the final report, pieces of the broader archive existed on the Kenya TJRC's excellent website. Eventually, this internet site, seemingly public and accessible to all, became defunct after the end of the commission's work. The assumption that electronic data sites will last forever creates a context where much of this information is quickly lost, as websites are pulled and changed.[33]

Using the service of the Internet Archive's Wayback Machine, a concerted effort to try to combat the permanent loss of digital material on the Web, Columbia University Archive preserves pieces of the

Kenya TJRC's once-thriving website, including a newsletter featuring citizen testimony, a map showing the location and itinerary of public hearings, and photo gallery. On the Columbia University Archive website, the last date for which the Internet Archive captured the Kenya TJRC's populated webpage was 23 June 2014. The next entry in the Wayback Machine, 1 October 2014, shows a blank webpage at the TJRC address. By 2015, the page now features Japanese script advertising real estate, and by December 2018, the page has gone dark with only thin English script announcing "FORBIDDEN." It is unclear where the interviews, maps, documents, photo gallery, newsletters – all the content generated for the TJRC webpage – have gone and there is no evidence that these are stored in physical copy somewhere else.

The loss of parts of the Kenyan TJRC website to the ether is also not inconsequential. Much like Ghana, public analyses of the value of the Kenyan Truth Commission reflect an engagement with only a partial archive. Some scholars have criticized the Kenyan TJRC for presenting only a "sanitized" official narrative that did not engage with the economic and structural violence underlying Kenya's political woes.[34] However, the records of the TJRC website preserved by the Columbia University Archive's Wayback Machine challenge the idea that the Kenyan commission only dealt with a sanitized and individual notion of harm. Although the TJRC website is now defunct, on 2 December 2011, there was a report from the TJRC hearings in Bungoma. Under the headline "Land Has Made Us Poorer!" there is a report of testimony from three co-operative societies who insist that poor families who were holders of "public, community, and trust land" were targeted and subject to exploitation by political, military, and civil service elite. The structural violence embedded in Kenyan society was not obscured in these citizen testimonies; on the contrary, the TJRC website featured challenging citizen narratives of collective economic harm.

These few case studies highlight the acts of commission and omission that hinder public engagement with TRC materials. Truth commissions may face challenges of preservation and access, *even when* the sponsoring government has identified these as a precious national resource. Technology, shifting political fortunes, neglect, and economic scarcity are some of the factors that may be used to justify the disappearance of truth commission materials from the public gaze. In this way, the constraints, fears, and ideological commitments of the present moment limit the work of truth commissions when they are formed and in the immediate aftermath. The archival imperative seeks to establish a process that would enable these commissions to find light, audience, or presence in the future.

Truth commissions have always had to strike a balance between revelation and concealment. Privacy concerns are routinely addressed when planning TRC public hearings. There are numerous reasons why individuals may resist disclosing the violence they have endured in a public forum. Privacy and security concerns also justify archival practices that deliberately shroud or disappear the truth commission in a particular context or time. Guatemala's Commission for Historical Clarification promptly shipped all of its documents outside the country and quarantined them in a secret US location at the commission's conclusion. These records are entirely sealed for fifty years. In El Salvador, there were competing visions of where the commission's archives should ultimately be stored and whether the records might be safely stored within the country or should be sent to George Washington University's International Rule of Law Institute to be administered by an international board of directors.[35] Truth commission archives are embroiled, rightly so, within debates about individual privacy, community ownership of knowledge, and global information economies. Acknowledging the disappearance of TRC archives is also a call to consider and confront the institutional trust and mistrust that surround the work of truth and reconciliation. Developing a robust archival practice requires combating the idea of a truth commission as a performative event or cathartic ritual, and instead highlighting the enduring value of the documents, narratives, stories, and critiques located within.

CONCLUSION

One lesson that all those who would embrace the TRC form would do well to learn is the importance of planning to preserve, process, and publish truth commission archives. In these expansive archives, the unruly and complex parts of political violence are made plain. Prioritizing the archive releases a truth commission's work from the contemporary context; it bequeaths the commission's insights and fallacies to future generations. In places where more parts of TRC archives are preserved, processed, and thus able to be utilized, these records have remarkable afterlives. The Chilean TRC report was referenced in international trials and also in domestic prosecutions. Chilean judges relied on this detailed and meticulous TRC report to build thousands of domestic human rights cases more than a decade after the commission had officially concluded its work.[36] In South Africa, because of public access to the archive, the "strange" testimony of a political prisoner's mother was heard again, and found its place in the national record after being initially dismissed.[37] Now, the record of the Plange file illuminates the critiques of transitional justice's exclusionary norms already embedded in survivor testimony.

This paper describes the contours of truth commission archives that extend beyond the report, beyond the testimonies and petitions, and includes all the records, however disparate and/or contradictory, associated with the commission's functioning. By describing how African truth commission documents are disappeared, in part or in whole, this chapter encourages vigilance and forethought regarding the archive as key aspects of the planning and implementation of the truth and reconciliation formula.

If the African continent's trajectory with truth commissions offers a cautionary tale about the swift disappearance of TRC archives, it also offers guidance in terms of pursuing this archival imperative. Gambia's Truth, Reconciliation and Reparations Commission (TRRC, 2017) embraced the future of the archive perhaps more than any other commission that has preceded it. Gambia's TRRC demonstrated a strong commitment to public access by streaming the public hearings live on YouTube, Facebook, and national television. Witnesses testified in English, Wolof, Mandinka, and other local languages; sign language interpretation was also included. In addition, some of the commission's organizing documents, such as the guidelines for the appointment of commissioners, are posted on the commission's website.

By insisting on the public gaze as a fundamental part of the TRRC's work, the Gambian process embraces the possibility of a future justice. The communities, institutions, and advocates around the world who now clamour for the TRC as a useful tool in various struggles must learn from the Gambian commission and consider, humbly, that their work might be the planting of seeds they may not see harvested. Prioritizing the preservation, processing, and publication of the whole truth commission archive ensures that the political and economic capital, the time, and most importantly, the energy and stories of those who participate, are not expended in vain.

252 Abena Ampofoa Asare

NOTES

1 Those countries with TRCs include: Democratic Republic of Congo, Truth and Reconciliation Commission, 2004; Gambia, Truth, Reconciliation and Reparations Commission, 2018; Ghana, National Reconciliation Commission, 2001; Kenya, Truth, Justice, and Reconciliation Commission, 2008; Liberia, Truth and Reconciliation Commission, 2005; Mauritius, Truth and Justice Commission, 2009; Morocco, Equity and Reconciliation Commission, 2004; Nigeria, Human Rights Violation Investigation Commission, 1999; Rwanda, National Unity and Reconciliation Commission, 2009; Sierra Leone Truth and Reconciliation Commission, 1999; South Africa, Truth and Reconciliation Commission, 1995; Togo, Truth and Justice Commission, 2009; Tunisia, Truth and Dignity Commission, 2014; Côte d'Ivoire, Dialogue, Truth, and Reconciliation Commission, 2012; Burundi, Truth and Reconciliation Commission, 2012.
2 Ethiopia: Solomon Ayele Dersso, "Ethiopia's Experiment in Reconciliation," US Institute of Peace (website), 23 September 2019, www.usip.org/publications/2019/09/ethiopias-experiment-reconciliation; United Kingdom: Kojo Koram, "Britain Needs a Truth and Reconciliation Commission, not Another Racism Inquiry," 16 June 2020, www.the-guardian.com/commentisfree/2020/jun/16/britain-truth-reconciliation-commission-racism-imperial.
3 Sandra Rubli and Briony Jones, *Archives for a Peaceful Future: Essential* (Bern: Swisspeace, 2013), 6.
4 Anita Ferrara, "Archives and Transitional Justice in Chile: A Crucial Relationship," *Human Rights Review* 22, no. 3–4 (2021): 264.
5 Ann M. Schneider, "Truth Commissions and Their Archives in El Salvador, Peru and Brazil," in *The Brazilian Truth Commission: Local, National and Global Perspectives*, ed. Nina Schneider (Berghahn Books: 2019), 270.
6 Schneider, "Truth Commissions and Their Archives," 270.
7 Jacques Derrida, *Archive Fever: A Freudian Impression* (Chicago: University of Chicago Press, 1996), 36.
8 Proscovia Svärd, "The Role of Archives in Enhancing Accountability and Transparency – The Case of Sierra Leone," ESARBICA *Journal of the Eastern and Southern Africa Regional Branch of the International Council on Archives* 27, no. 1 (2009): 3.
9 Eduardo González, *Drafting a Truth Commission Mandate: A Practical Tool*, International Center for Transitional Justice, 20 June 2013, www.

ictj.org/sites/default/files/ICTJ-Report-DraftingMandate-Truth-Commission-2013_0.pdf.

10 Rubli and Jones, *Archives for a Peaceful Future: Essential*, 8.

11 Moses Chrispus Okello et al., *Where Law Meets Reality: Forging African Transitional Justice* (Pambazuka Press, 2012), xix.

12 Achille Mbembe, "The Power of the Archives and its Limits," in *Refiguring the Archive*, ed. C. Hamilton et al. (Dordrecht: Springer, 2002), 20.

13 Mbembe, "The Power of the Archives and its Limits," 20.

14 Michel-Rolph Trouillot, *Silencing the Past: Power and the Production of History* (Boston: Beacon Press, 1995); Michelle Caswell, *Archiving the Unspeakable: Silence, Memory, and the Photographic Record in Cambodia* (Madison: University of Wisconsin Press, 2014), 27; Kirsten Weld, *Paper Cadavers: The Archives of Dictatorship in Guatemala* (Durham, NC: Duke University Press, 2014), 6.

15 Belinda Bozzoli, "Public Ritual and Private Transition: The Truth Commission in Alexandra Township, South Africa 1996," *African Studies* 57, no. 2 (1998): 193; Valji, *Centre for the Study of Violence and Reconciliation*, 1; Sean Field, "Beyond 'Healing': Trauma, Oral History and Regeneration," *Oral History* 34, no. 1 (2006): 33.

16 Trudy Huskamp Peterson, *Final Acts: A Guide to Preserving the Records of Truth Commissions* (Baltimore, MD: Johns Hopkins University Press, 2005); Rubli and Jones, *Archives for a Peaceful Future: Essential*.

17 Ikenna Emewu, "The Legal Implications of Harbouring Charles Taylor," *Niger Delta Congress*, 2003, http://www.nigerdeltacongress.com/karticles /legod_implications_of _harborin.htm (site discontinued).

18 Louise Vella, "Translating Transitional Justice: The Solomon Islands Truth and Reconciliation Commission," State, Society and Governance in Melanesia Discussion Paper 2, 2014, www.academia.edu/7329642/Translating_Transitional_Justice_The_Solomon_Islands_Truth_and_Reconciliation_Commission.

19 Saskia Brechenmacher, "From The Hague to Abidjan: Whither Transitional Justice in Côte d'Ivoire? | Reinventing Peace," World Peace Foundation (website), 21 April 2016, https://sites.tufts.edu/reinventing-peace/2016/04/21/from-the-hague-to-abidjan-whither-transitional-justice-in-cote-divoire/; Human Rights Watch, "To Consolidate This Peace of Ours: A Human Rights Agenda for Côte d'Ivoire," 8 December 2015.

20 Abena Asare, *Truth Without Reconciliation: A Human Rights History of Ghana* (Philadelphia: University of Pennsylvania Press, 2018), 77.

21 Jeremy Sarkin and Tetevi Davi, "The Togolese Truth, Justice, and

Reconciliation Commission: Lessons for Transitional Justice Processes Elsewhere," *Peace and Conflict Studies* 24, no. 1 (2017): 5.

22 *Mauritius Truth and Justice Commission Report*, 2009, Appendix 2.01, https://hmcwordpress.humanities.mcmaster.ca/Truthcommissions/wp-content/uploads/2019/01/Mauritius.TJC_.Report-FULL.pdf.

23 Megan MacKenzie and Mohamed Sesay, "No Amnesty from/for the International: The Production and Promotion of TRCs as an International Norm in Sierra Leone," *International Studies Perspective* 13, no. 2 (2012): 157.

24 Ibid., 159.

25 Catherine Kennedy, "Opening the TRC Archive: A SAHA Case Study," Archive and Public Culture (website), 7 August 2014, www.apc.uct.ac.za/apc/projects/archival_platform/opening-trc-archive-saha-case-study.

26 Piers Pigou, "Accessing the Records of the Truth and Reconciliation Commission," in *Paper Wars: Access to Information in South Africa*, ed. Kate Allan (Johannesburg: Wits University Press, 2009), 18.

27 Nahla Valji, "Ghana's National Reconciliation Commission: A Comparative Assessment," Occasional Paper series (The International Centre for Transitional Justice, 2006): 6, www.ictj.org/sites/default/files/ICTJ-Ghana-Reconciliation-Commission-2006-English_0.pdf; S. Pillay and H. Scanlon, *Peace Versus Justice? Truth and Reconciliation Commissions and War Crimes Tribunals in Africa* (Cape Town: Centre for Conflict Resolution, 2008), 23.

28 Asare, *Truth Without Reconciliation*, 13; Akosua Adomako Ampofo, "'My Cocoa Is between My Legs': Sex as Work among Ghanaian Women," in *Women's Labor in the Global Economy: Speaking in Multiple Voices*, ed. Sharon Harley (New Brunswick, NJ: Rutgers University Press, 2007), 203.

29 Gina Ross, *Beyond the Trauma Vortex into the Healing Vortex* (Los Angeles: The International Trauma-Healing Institute, 2010), 75.

30 Ghana National Reconciliation Commission, NRC File ACC.

31 Dietlinde Wouters, "There Was This Goat: The Archive for Justice as a Remedy for the Epistemic Injustice in Truth Commissions," *International Journal of Human Rights* 25, no. 3 (2021): 7.

32 Felix Odartey-Wellington and Amin Alhassan, "Disseminating the National Reconciliation Report: A Critical Step in Ghana's Democratic Consolidation," *African Journal of Political Science and International Relations* 10, no. 4 (2016): 40.

33 P.T. Panos, "The Internet Archive: An End to the Digital Dark Age," *Journal of Social Work Education* 39, no. 2 (2003): 343.

34 Catherine Muhoma, "Versions of Truth and Collective Memory: The Quest for Forgiveness and Healing in the Context of Kenya's Postelection Violence," *Research in African Literatures* 43, no.1 (2012): 171.
35 Schneider, "Truth Commissions and Their Archives," 270.
36 Anita Ferrara, *Assessing the Long-Term Impact of Truth Commissions: The Chilean Truth and Reconciliation Commission in Historical Perspective* (London: Routledge, 2014), 141.
37 Dietlinde Wouters, "There Was This Goat: The Archive for Justice as a Remedy for the Epistemic Injustice in Truth Commissions," *International Journal of Human Rights* 25, no. 3 (2021).

Nation and Narration: Creative Imaginaries of Truth and Reconciliation

Paul Ugor

A cursory examination of the proliferating literature on Truth and Reconciliation Commissions (TRCs) suggests there is now indeed an international transitional justice industrial complex comprised of several TRC commissions, research institutes, and an expanding academic community of reconciliation specialists and forgiveness entrepreneurs/contractors in the global public domain. In my view, however, what often gets lost in the massive industry of critique that has taken shape around reconciliation discourse is the fact that as legal mechanisms instituted to facilitate processes of memorialization, non-retributive justice, and national healing, the arduous work of restorative justice is often rooted in storytelling.

As Claire Moon has noted, projects of truth and reconciliation are founded on the culturalist idea that "reconciliation is a story or narrative about transition that legitimizes ... certain political decisions (such as amnesty) and proscribes others (such as punishment), and brings into being particular protagonists (or subjects and agents, namely 'victims' and 'perpetrators') as central to that story. This story, by definition, attempts to unify disparate and, sometimes, conflicting social, political, individual perspectives on the past."[1] Moon's observation illuminates the centrality of narratology in projects of truth telling, memorialization, and individual/collective reconciliation. National reconciliation and truth-telling processes are often anchored in personal and collective narratives, which are frequently marked by a certain *constructedness* or structuration whereby each victim, perpetrator, or witness weaves or frames a narrative of their past actions and experiences for both national and international audiences. I use *narrativity* here in referring not only to what is being recounted in a story but also how that story is emplotted to yield certain meanings, and thus have a certain effect on the listening audience.

Kerry Bystrom has noted how TRCs' guiding tropes of truth telling, forgiveness, and reconciliation are discursively underlined and powered by a well-known slogan: "revealing is healing."[2] But revelation, which emphasizes and presupposes access to a hidden or a buried past, can only happen through a process of narrativization. Thus, transitional justice endeavours are habitually an exercise in storytelling. The South African TRC, for example, was constituted to hold hearings that gave victims the opportunity to recount their stories of horrific trauma, anguish, and loss. It also offered opportunities for victimizers to tell stories of their roles in the victims' traumatic lives. Archbishop Desmond Tutu, chair of the commission, reinforced the centrality of storytelling to the entire process when he insisted that far beyond the search for justice, transitional or retributive, the commission's greatest task was to "listen to the unknown victims – those who have never received any attention from authorities or the media – and to provide a forum for the exposure of their experiences."[3] More than anything else, the commission sought to privilege the stories of ordinary people. Thus, the work of TRCs is often premised on the spiritual principle that healing and reconciliation happen only after confession, which itself demands recounting a past in the form of a story-narrative.

It is this unique and crucial aspect of national truth telling and reconciliation as an exercise in storytelling that fascinates me as a literary-cultural studies scholar. I am particularly invested in exploring certain questions: what kinds of stories were told in the South African TRC hearings? Who told those stories, and how were they recounted? What kinds of rhetorical strategies were deployed by the respective actors in the reconciliation saga in telling their stories, and what were the effects of these strategies? How were these stories, in turn, reported by the media that covered the events? What discourses were embedded in these varied narratives of the reconciliation actors? And perhaps most importantly, how did these public performances or dramatizations of storytelling function as acts of democratic state making?

In attempting to answer these questions, I draw on the tools of literary and cultural analysis in examining how storytelling as a process of national reconciliation and healing in South Africa played out as a wired system of discursivity, which mobilized certain motifs, signs, symbols, and idioms (oral, written, and embodied) in varied forms of textual practice that sought to legitimate certain historical claims, ideological positions, individual interests, and national aspirations. By closely examining the rhetorical practices of the testimonies of perpetrators of apartheid violence in the commission hearings, in particular, I want to demonstrate how state violence was narratively whitewashed as an unavoidable and necessary exercise in nation building. I also aim to show how the rhetorical strategies used in the testimonies by apartheid state agents functioned as a narrative practice in evading culpability and its accompanying sanctions. As a number of scholars have noted, the outcome is that particular ways of telling stories during the South African TRC process undermined, rather than promoted, reconciliation and restorative justice.

The literary-cultural studies approach I bring to bear on my reading of the TRC's work in South Africa is not unique by any stretch of the imagination. Several scholars have not only addressed Antjie Krog's engagement with the complex processes of truth tell-ing, national reconciliation, and empathy, they have specifically addressed the conjunction between poetics and politics in *Country of My Skull*.[4] The essays by Alexandra Effe and by Patricia Ewick and Susan Silbey particularly interrogate the role of narrative struc-ture in the novel's critique of the dynamics of hegemonic power in post-apartheid South Africa, especially the multiple ways in which it shows how certain approaches to narrativizing the past weaken the South African healing and reconciliation process. Through thought-ful analysis of the hybrid literary testimony in *Country of My Skull*, Alexandra Effe for example, addresses "how specific narra-tive strategies enable perspective-taking, facilitate identification and empathy, foster collective identity, and forge a realm where stories retain truth-value beyond verifiability and falsifiability."[5] Focusing specifically on the Human Rights Violations Committee hearings, Catherine Cole has also shown the captivating affinities between the TRC's public hearings and conventional proscenium theatre. She argues that the hearings played out as forms of political theatre, with "moments of direct conflict between perpetrator and victim – conflict being one of the central features of the genre of drama."[6] As a formal process of adjudicating transitional justice and collective healing and redemption, Cole ultimately demonstrates how the TRC's work played out as a form of public ritual in which various protagonists were engaged in public performances or enactments of individual and collective confession, penitence, and forgiveness.

Concentrating specifically on the genre of drama, Kerry Bystrom further offers an insightful cultural analysis of John Kani's 2015 play *Missing*,[7] in which she argues that the text is a powerful critique of the lingering inequities in post-reconciliation South Africa. In validating her argument, she quotes one of the protagonists in the play, Robert Khalipa:

> What happened? We fought for freedom, we ended up with democracy. What the hell is democracy? We lost our blood, our comrades, for this democracy? Yes, we won the elections; can someone tell me who lost? The rich are still rich, the poor even poorer now than they have been before. When I want justice, when I want revenge, I am told about truth and reconciliation. I am told to forgive. I saw the people who tortured me, who killed my brothers. I want what I fought for. I want justice.[8]

According to Bystrom, this speech by Robert, a high-profile African National Congress (ANC) member and activist who feels betrayed by the movement, "telescopes the many disappointments that grew within South Africa between 1994, when over forty years of institutionalized and violently extractive racism known as apartheid officially ended, and 2014, when *Missing* premiered."[9] As a form of commentary on post-apartheid, post-TRC South Africa, Robert's damning utterance reveals a looming sense of betrayal and disillusionment among the majority of Black South Africans who were (and still remain) the primary and direct victims of apartheid's brutal policies. Apartheid's Black victims still feel trapped in the same racially toxic and socially oppressive environment that denied them dignity and their basic human rights. Rebecca Saunders has noted how evidence presented by trade unions, opposition parties, and scholars all point to a devastating post-apartheid neo-liberal order that "has made very meagre progress in alleviating South Africa's suffering – the country's Gini-coefficient remains second only to Brazil as the most unequal society in the world – and has mostly functioned to enrich a minuscule black elite."[10]

What the studies of cultural representations of reconciliation in South Africa reveal then is that narratives now function as powerful forms of national dialogue that exert influential critiques of a new rainbow nation founded on faulty principles and values – on amnesty, transitional justice, and national reconciliation – and in the process, compromise the desired search for restorative and redistributive justice. It is no wonder that the South African cultural critic Sarah Nuttall has drawn interesting connections between cultural representations about the TRC and the recent explosions of protest culture in South Africa by young people. Nuttall notes how "student activists, artists and performers, writers and poets" are all finding radical ways of bringing about epochal change to a new democratic state and its system that continues to draw on the old repertoires of oppression associated with the apartheid state.[11]

Taken together, these mounting cultural critiques of imaginative works on truth and reconciliation in South Africa constitute what author/cultural critic Zakes Mda now calls "fictions of reconciliation," that is, creative imaginaries that address and problematize national reconciliation and healing in South Africa.[12] The broader point I make in my contribution is how particular narratives about the South African TRC function to reveal ways that national healing and resolution place unfair expectations on certain populations, who are burdened with the weight of collective trauma, forgiveness, and nation building, in the process relieving others of accountability and their own painful contributions to national reinvention.

THEORETICAL AND METHODOLOGICAL FORMULATION

What I seek to accomplish in this chapter is to triangulate the complex links between processes of storytelling, truth telling and reconciliation, and state building. I am interested in exploring the work of the South African TRC as a public performance of storytelling, but one particularly invested in "gathering the past in a ritual of revival; gathering the present."[13] I am particularly invested to explore how the fictional representations of the testimonies at the South African TRC hearings tell us something about the skewed "remaking" of the new rainbow nation. I proceed from the well-established notion and premise in the humanities that a nation is essentially a cultural object, that is, it is often systematically constructed through all kinds of narratives, representations, and symbols. In doing so, I draw on several cultural thinkers who have forged connections between storytelling and nation making.

The French cultural theorist Ernest Renan argues in his essay "What Is a Nation?" that a nation is not so much a collective of people in one designated geographical territory and with a shared ancestry and culture such as history, language, arts, food, and so forth. He insists instead that a nation is actually held together by what he calls a "soul" or "a spiritual principle," which gets tested in a periodic referendum. This soul consists of two crucial elements: "One lies in the past, one in the present. One is the possession in common of a rich legacy of memories; the other is present-day consent, the desire to live together, the will to perpetuate the value of the heritage that one has received in an undivided form."[14]

In formulating a soul for the nation, however, its subjects must routinely determine which past they want to forget and which they want to remember. So, the ritual of a referendum functions mainly to ascertain whether all the constitutive elements of that union agree on the version of history/past that defines its consciousness. This question of which past to remember and which one to forget, I think, was at the very centre of the South African TRC hearings. By revisiting and recounting its violent past, South Africa was engaged in the process of national reinvention through the retrieval and reorganization of the collective history that will serve as a foundational glue for holding the state together. A singular and grand-meta Afrikaner narrative was being replaced by a multi-racial and plural history that accounted for the blood and sweat of other ethnicities whose narratives also make up the rainbow nation.

In forging links between personal narratives and national reconstruction, therefore, I draw inspiration from Fredric Jameson's theorization of Third World literature as a national allegory, "where the telling of the individual story and the individual experience cannot but ultimately involve the whole laborious telling of the collectivity itself."[15] The personal individual experience not only becomes political, but it also functions as a metaphor for the collective national experience. Carli Coetzee sees the discourse of nationhood in *Country of My Skull* when she contends that the text "invites the reader to acknowledge the interconnectedness between the author and her country, the country of her 'skull,' which is described in terms of her physical being. Yet in the title, *Country of [M]y Skull*, can also be found some doubt as to the author's claim to an identification with the country, her country of birth."[16]

Recognizing the powerful relations between personal and collective experiences, Homi Bhabha has made a strong connection between the idea of a nation and the process of narration. In making a case for the nation as a work of textuality, Bhabha insists that as a form of cultural elaboration, a nation is essentially "an agency of *ambivalent* narration that holds culture at its most productive position, as a force for 'subordination, fracturing, diffusing, reproducing, as much as producing, creating, forcing, guiding.'"[17] Drawing theoretical insights from Benedict Anderson, Bhabha thus makes a persuasive case for the particular ways in which a nation ought to be understood not by aligning it with what he calls "self-consciously held political ideologies, but with large cultural systems that preceded it, out of which – as well as against which – it came into being."[18]

In other words, a nation ought not to be understood by its current ideological rhetorics, but by the expansive work of cultural formulations it constructs of itself through representations, mostly in the form of narratives in historical, fictional, filmic, and others kinds of imaginative work. Informed by the ideas of Patrick Wright's *On Living in an Old Country* (1985) and Paul Gilroy's *There Ain't No Black in the Union Jack* (1987), Bhabha embraces a unique approach to the political idea of a nation as an exercise in narrativization, which depends heavily on "textual strategies, metaphoric displacements, subtexts and figurative stratagems."[19] This approach to the project of nationhood that understands a nation as an exercise in metaphorization, in which state making is more symbolic, rhetorical, mythological, and collective, is what I bring to bear on my reading of Antjie Krog's *Country of My Skull*. It is a narrativist approach to transitional justice work, especially as a process in state making that displaces the usual historicism that accompanies the discourse of nation as a political entity and rather perceives it as a by-product of cultural or symbolic work.

State building as a process of textualization is also connected to the process of archivization that Abena Asare hints at in chapter 10 of this volume. Not only do truth commissions work with historical archives, but they also build elaborate archival material that can be used as legal evidence in courts, which is why they often disappear, as Asare has suggested. But it must be noted that archival work is not random; it is a science, for it involves a methodical and systematic process of structuration and symbolic ordering that includes the identification of artifacts, their naming, classification, unification, codification, and postulation. It is these varied activities associated with archival work that Derrida calls *archivization*. The authority assigned to the archivist, what Derrida calls *archontic power*, involves a systematic arrangement of the past and what he describes as the power of *consignation*. "By consignation, we do not only mean, in the ordinary sense of the word, the act of assigning residence or of entrusting so as to put into reserve (to consign, to deposit), in a place and on a substrate, but here the act of *con*signing through *gathering together signs*."[20] By this analysis, the process of archivization is likened to historiography, and it is also a semiotic exercise, essentially a meaning-making enterprise, that is, a cultural or representational act implicated in epistemological work. This process of knowledge making entails the power to affect the organization of society through the knowledge of the past or historical signs that archives purvey.

There are two major conclusions that can be drawn from this framing of the archive. First, archiving or archivization is an epistemic act – an exercise in knowledge creation. Second, the products of its work in the form of historical documents, photos/images, maps, and other cultural artifacts of historical significance are readable texts deserving of interpretation for what they say about the past and how they frame that past. Thus, if the process of archivization involves consignation, the ascription of meaning, its associated processes of taxonomy, synchronization, and postulation are textual and interpretative practices that people interested in public records/ archives must heed. Because archives are sites of historical information, knowledge, and political and cultural power, what Achille Mbembe calls "an instituting imaginary," we should pay serious attention to their particular textual practices.

Examining a variety of historically relevant sources left by the South African writer Miriam Tlali, Sarah Nuttall has also shown how the archive of fictional writers – their manuscripts, letters, interviews, and other documents – can function as archival materials.[21] Ronald S. Roberts has made a strong case for the links between art and the archive, demonstrating convincingly how the intersections between the two genres trouble the conventional "binary opposition between creativity and conservation,"[22] noting the oneness shared by "archival and human materiality" and thus insisting that "the artist's enhancement of society's archival recognition(s) is an enhancement of the range and scope of human being itself."[23] Citing

Nadine Gordimer, who insists the novelist is a "walking archivist" with "a facility that works upon while it stores fragments of perception," Roberts surmises that the "novelist becomes [the] explorer of previously unknown reaches of an existential archive, opening up new vistas of farsightedness, expanding society's sense of what its archives, the components of its collective selfhood, can be."[24]

In this sense, the archive is not just a mausoleum but the collective communal memory and record. It is a disciplined form of narrative history that finds expression in all kinds of cultural representations that are visual, oral, performative, and written. In my contribution, therefore, I examine the ways in which Antjie Krog's novel about the South African TRC functions as an archive to address the imbalances and inequities associated with the process of national healing and reconciliation in Africa.

STORYTELLING AND STATE FORMATION: TESTIMONIES AND NARRATIVE STRATEGIES

Antjie Krog was the head of the radio team of the South African Broadcasting Service that covered the proceedings of the South African TRC. Set between March 1994, when its legal framework was being put in place by the Justice Portfolio Committee, and October 1998, when its interim report was submitted to President Nelson Mandela, *Country of My Skull* is an exhaustive account of Krog's coverage of the TRC hearings and activities. Combining her multiple skills as writer, investigative journalist, and public intellectual, the work transcends generic boundaries, drawing on a wide range of genres that include oral and written testimonies; media reportage and analysis; political and social commentary; personal meditations; fragments of literary pieces such as poems and music lyrics; conversations with colleagues and family members; and personal family history. Divided into six segments, a significant chunk of the narrative draws on the long and direct testimonies by victims, perpetrators, and witnesses during the Human Rights Violations sub-Committee hearings between 1996 and 1998. In many ways, therefore, the work is an imaginative account of the testimonies of egregious and horrific violence, unbearable pain, unrelenting guilt, and mounting anger expressed at the TRC hearings.

As Susan Gallagher has rightly noted, "Many of the grim dispositions of victims poured out before the TRC are once again brought into the public sphere in Krog's text. [But] these stories appear now as literary testimony, reinforcing their earlier manifestation as legal testimony."[25] So Krog's work of non-fiction is not just about the stories of victims, perpetrators, and witnesses testifying to their experiences and actions in the infamous era of apartheid, it becomes her own story about her thoughts (metaphorized by the term *skull*) about her "country" of birth, South Africa.

The structuralist narrative deployed in Krog's work is reminiscent of Hayden White's insistence on the centrality of narrative in historiography, if we understand the process of transitional justice as an exercise in historical mapping. In sketching out the inextricable links between story, plot, and arguments in historical narrative – histories that tell stories – White contends that what is crucial to the narrative elements of historiographical work is not so much the story as it is their explanatory effect, often achieved through the conscious "emplotting procedures used in it to make of the events it describes a comprehensible dramatic unity."[26] Although White insists that he was more concerned with explaining the central role of historiography in narrative than the significance of narrative in historiography, he ironically argues that "historiography is a species of the genus narrative, rather than the reverse."[27] Tracing the etymology of the term *narrative* in Latin, Greek, and Sanskrit, White surmises that used in its proper sense, "the term 'narrative' denotes an account of something that is known or is knowable, or that was once known and has been forgotten and therefore can be recalled to mind by appropriate means of discourse."[28]

What is crucial to the epistemological function of the narrative is the plotting – the way the story is told or how the materials are organized – more so than the content of the story itself. I mobilize this idea about the structure of the historical narrative only to highlight what the unstable narrative structure of *Country of My Skull* says about South Africa as a national entity. The text's non-linearity, which has a direct impact on the reader's ability to comprehend the piece as a coherent artistic whole, very much mirrors the psychological trauma and consequent instability that plagues South Africa. To skip from one genre, stylistic form, narrative trope, linguistic form, idiom, and cultural history to another is an experience in fragmentation, very much like an ailing, fragmented, and unstable South Africa. My point here being that even the form of the text is crucial to its discourse of national crisis.

The form of the narrative is important in figuring out the book's discourse of a disjointed national psyche, but even the story content of the work is imbricated in this narrative structuring of a collective psychosis. Each account by a victim, perpetrator, witness, or translator is a version or an incomplete, and at times, incoherent account of the full story. Nowhere is this narrative relativity encapsulated than in the amnesty testimonies regarding the murder of Black police officer Richard Mutase and his wife, Irene Mutase, in November 1987.[29] While each of the Vlakplaas five involved in the murder agreed on who killed Richard, they provided two different accounts of who killed his wife. Captain Jacques Hechter and Paul van Vuuren claimed it was Mamasela, a Black police officer attached to the hit squad, who killed Mutase's wife because he feared she had seen his face and would recognize him later. But Mamasela accused Hechter of the murder, claiming that he was in the room pacifying Irene while her husband was being killed, when Hechter walked in, placed a pillow on the poor woman's head and shot into her face.

Antjie Krog herself observes, as each of the Vlakplaas five told their stories of the chilling murders they committed, "their stories became part of a whole circuit of narratives: township stories, literature, Truth Commission testimonies, newspaper reports ... The murder was the clay. The political climate, the amnesty conditions, the presence of Tshidiso Mutase and his grandmother, the lawyers – all these were the hands forming the clay. So, there are actually two stories: the story and the understory, the matrix, the propelling force determining what is left out, what is used, how it is used."[30] The murder, like apartheid itself, was the meat/clay of the narrative, but it was being instrumentalized, crafted, and narrativized differently by different actors/narrators.

What the unique episodic structure and content of the novel reveal then is that although the TRC was commissioned to seek out South Africa's historical "truth" through a process of storytelling, the "truth" it was presented with, and the one it surmised from its findings, is still an incomplete version of "history" susceptible to fragmentation and questioning, depending on who is doing the telling. It is perhaps for this reason that Hayden White added a cautionary tale to the understanding of historical narrative, noting that its comprehension should be rooted in the consciousness of the multiple "ways that traditionally provided modes of storytelling function to inform us of the ways that our own culture can provide a host of different meanings for the same set of events."[31]

Beyond form, it is in the actual testimonies of perpetrators, victims, witnesses, party leaders, and even the commentaries of the TRC's officials that we come to witness the rhetorical strategies that weld storytelling with state formation. Krog's very first chapter presents an episode recounting one of the Justice Portfolio Committee hearings featuring General Johan van der Merwe, a former head of the Security Branch and commissioner of the South African Police Service from 1990 to 1995, and Freedom Front leader General Constand Viljoen. The latter notes that although the TRC's ultimate aim was to bring lasting reconciliation between the Afrikaner and the African and other ethnicities in South Africa, he warns that this could only "happen if the Truth Commission does not vilify the Afrikaner into being worse than we are," adding that both factions in the struggle failed. "We all used violence to get what we wanted. The terror of the tyrant invited the terror of the revolutionary."[32]

Viljoen's testimony emblematized the unique mode of testimony or storytelling that dominated the TRC hearings. It prescribed the conditions under which the Afrikaner could participate in the process of truth telling and national reconciliation, a condition that demanded exoneration even before the process of historical inquest began. Moreover, it heralded a narrative structure/pattern in which the plot – the way of telling the story and organizing the historical material – was more important than truth telling itself and historical retrieval as a process of national healing. It was a rhetorical move that did not deny culpability but rather invoked the collective guilt of both Afrikaner and anti-apartheid forces, creating a coeval status for victims and victimizers, meaning no one had to be sanctioned for the actions of the past, however violent those actions were.

In Charlayne Hunter-Gault's introduction to *Country of My Skull*, she notes how "even Archbishop Desmond Tutu's most eloquent pleas could not persuade whites to come forward to testify in significant numbers."[33] The few that ultimately testified in the amnesty hearings did so without the slightest compunction (and hence the first chapter's title "They Never Wept, the Men of My Race"), and they framed the stories of their in/actions as nationalist pursuits. Two examples will buttress this nationalist slant in the TRC testimonies. Brigadier Jack Cronje, one of the Vlakplaas five who sought amnesty for the bloody activities that led to more than forty murders, said the following during his testimony: "This is what my life has come to ... All that I have, my best years, all that I know of loyalty and honour, I gave to the police. Now I find myself disgraced by politics. When I drove back in the mornings after an operation, and people passed me on their way to work, I thought, I did it for you and for you ... you could sleep safe and sound because I was doing my job. This country would not have held a week if it weren't for the security forces ... For myself, I didn't do it, also not for my pocket. I did it for my country."[34]

Cronje, who was already sixty at the time of his testimony and suffering from Alzheimer's, did not deny the brutal acts committed under his watch against fellow South Africans. But the way he recounts his story rationalizes these violent actions, locating them within the context of certain social norms and values, according to Antjie Krog, one "buffered by an Afrikaner culture in power" in which nothing was spared in protecting the interest of the Boer nation.[35] Cronje not only frames himself as a victim who is being punished for doing his job with "loyalty" and "honour," he dismisses any guilt by justifying his violent actions as part of the general stuff of state making. While others slept safely at night, he and his team prowled like monsters to mete out indispensable violence that they believed kept the nation safe.

Cronje's testimony offers important insight into how to make sense of political violence in post-colonial Africa and how to explain what Mahmood Mamdani describes as a modern sensibility that understands "political violence as necessary to historical progress."[36] More like the soldiers in Napoleon's army, the Vlakplaas five saw themselves not as state mercenaries engaged in senseless violence but as patriots, "those who killed for a cause, who were animated by sentiments, by what we have come to recognize as civic religion: nationalism."[37] Subjective violence by oppressed Black South Africans is considered senseless because it is not underwritten by a nationalistic cause, but apartheid violence, even if undertaken by a rogue operative, is meaningful because it aims to prop/protect the nation-state.

Susan Gallagher has noted how the commotions of the 1980s and the resultant transformations of the 1990s in South Africa brought about a renewed interest in the confessional mode of writing among Afrikaner writers. This new creative or artistic investment in the confessional mode associated with genres such as memoirs, autobiographies, and creative non-fiction can be attributed to the belief that "Afrikaner confessional narratives may ... contribute to the

creation of a plural yet unified national identity that moves away
from one form of ethnonationalism without resorting to another."[38]
The earlier forms of non-confessional Afrikaner writing were
informed by a particular Boer sensibility/culture in which, as J.M.
Coetzee notes, people are seen as representative of types or social
categories, rather than as people.[39] This tendency toward social
categorization, especially when informed by what Mamdani calls
"race-branding," leads to the formation of political identities along
group lines, "whereby it is possible not only to set a group apart
as an enemy but also to annihilate it with an easy conscience."[40]
Nowhere is this dynamic in South Africa more clarified than in the
discussions Antjie Krog had with the psychiatrist Dr Sean Kaliski.

Desperate to make sense of the horrific actions of the Vlakplaas
five, Krog took her interviews with them to Kaliski. His response is
telling and insightful: although ANC and Pan Africanist Congress
(PAC) struggle activists were often framed as threatening commu-
nists, Kaliski insisted that apartheid's violence was not rooted in
the fear of communism. He argued that the violence was founded
on a particular cultural environment in which "we believed black
people were not human; they were a threat, they were going to kill
us all and then waste away the country until it was nothing but
another African disaster area."[41] Kaliski locates this violence in the
cultural force or "legitimacy constructed in the past around these
extreme forms of violence. The lawgivers made the laws, the lawyers executed them, and there were assisted by a whole lot of other
professions. This created a normative structure that legitimized the
killings."[42] Kaliski's explanation at once grounds absurd political
violence in notions of "country," and reveals how that violence
works as part of political identities constituted and underpinned by
group dynamics, an "us" versus "them" mindset, in which individual acts of violence are often understood as acts in the pursuit of
collective interests, in this case, the Afrikaner nation.

This mindset invokes Robert I. Simon's book *Bad Men Do What
Good Men Dream* (1996), a title implying that "while some men
were out killing black people, many whites were busy dreaming of a
life without black people: separate laws, separate amenities, separate
churches, separate homes, separate towns, separate countries ..."[43]
The testimonies of the violent acts by the agents of the South African
security apparatus thus had to be understood as brave acts of state
formation, valiant acts of a courageous few who ensured that the

collective invisible Afrikaner interest is protected. Which is why, for most of the white apartheid security operatives who testified, the real people that needed to be publicly interrogated were the National Party politicians because they made the laws that the security apparatuses implemented.[44]

This idea of perpetrators of political violence as 'victims' who paid a price for their loyalty to the nation is best illustrated by the case of police captain Jeffrey Benzien.[45] Infamous for his torture and interrogation techniques, Benzien was a captain with the murder and robbery unit of the police, who was later promoted and transferred to the security police. Some of the horrendous techniques he used during interrogation included the "wet bag" method (suffocating victims in a wet plastic bag which denied them oxygen and burned their lungs); shocking victims with an electric equipment in the nose, ears, genitals, and rectum; and shoving his hands into his victim's anus with a broom to sweep out hidden evidence in their stomach.[46] All of Benzien's victims who testified confirmed that during apartheid he "was feared nationally – he could get the information he wanted in less than thirty minutes."[47] He was so feared by the anti-apartheid activists that even when he appeared at the TRC hearings, he still held tremendous psychological control and power over his former victims. In his testimony to the Amnesty Committee, Benzien was defiant: "Cape Town had the same potential as Johannesburg, Pretoria, and Durban for shopping Mall bombs – But I, with respect, Mr. Chairman, did my work well."[48] He saw himself as a conscientious policeman who was fighting terrorists that sought to destabilize his nation. At the hearings, he was now presented as a victim suffering from post-traumatic stress disorder, auditory hallucinations, and memory loss.

For the first time in the amnesty hearings, a psychologist (Ria Kotze) was invited and cross-examined. Kotze had been treating Benzien's wife for depression but was called sometime in 1994 to attend to her husband when he had a nervous breakdown. Kotze recounts a particular incident in which "Benzien was sitting on his veranda one evening, smoking a cigarette, and then he had a flashback – so intense and real that he burst into tears." His wife called Kotze and told her that when she asked Benzien what was wrong, he kept on saying, "I cannot tell you – I'm too ashamed." Kotze says Benzien "suffers from a severe form of self-loathing."[49] The tables had turned – the ill-reputed torturer was now "a victim" of the cold-hearted working conditions of apartheid. "He was a good cop at Murder and Robbery. But he was so good that he was moved to Security, where he had to create these torture methods to fulfill the expectations about him. This destroyed his whole sense of self."[50]

Benzien, like the victims he tortured and violated, had become a victim of state formation, "destroyed" by the work he did to build a nation. Benzien's sensational testimony, and the empathetic medical evidence mobilized to legitimate it, revealed the real dangers of transitional justice work. As Rebecca Saunders has noted, national reconciliation could become an empty gesture that not only "benefits perpetrators," but also victimizers could deploy their own trauma and the pervasive rhetoric of "forgiveness as a way to circumvent justice."[51]

The South African TRC, from the forty plus truth commissions that have been established around the world in the past three decades, stands out in the grand history of international transitional justice. It was the first time that career politicians appeared and made submissions before the commission. And when they did, the parties, like their security operatives, framed their testimonies or narratives around the project of nationhood. As Krog notes, the submissions by the political parties to the TRC were a radical departure from the commission's earlier public focus. It was "a shift from individual tales to the collective, from victims to the masterminds, from the powerless to those in power."[52] The parties were being asked to tell stories of their respective roles in a ghoulish national history in which citizens were engaged in a free-for-all extravaganza of murder, torture, and dehumanization. And the TRC hearings presented an invaluable opportunity to the political parties because, as Krog observes, "politicians are opportunistic enough to realize that a political party can get more mileage out of a very public, highly moral forum than out of any number of mass rallies. Or that the richness of the victims' testimonies has moved political parties to want to tell their side of the story."[53] For the parties, it was not so much about truth telling as it was about rationalizing their political ideologies and gaining political legitimacy in the process.

Chief Mangosuthu Gatsha Buthelezi, leader of the Inkatha Freedom Party and Eugene Terre'Blanche, the leader of the far-right nationalist Afrikaner Weerstandsbeweging, did not show up at the TRC proceedings, for reasons all connected to their dissatisfaction with the ways in which they thought the new South African

national imaginary was being reorganized. But Frederick W. de
Klerk appeared on behalf of the National Party, and his account of
his party's activities was straightforward. Although he agreed the
party sanctioned the use of unconventional methods in dealing with
anti-apartheid activists, "they never included the authorization of
assassination, murder, torture, rape, assault. I've never been part of
any decision taken by cabinet, the State Security Council, or any
committee authorizing the instruction of such abuses. I personally
also never such actions."[54] He continued, acceding, "There is that
which was wrong with the NP past and that which was right. It is my
responsibility to admit to that which was wrong."

De Klerk's testimony is fascinating, marked by a denial of both
responsibility and apology to the victims of state violence. But by
denying knowledge of the activities of overzealous and negligent
agents of the apartheid state, he suggests that as the key administra-
tor of the apartheid machinery, the country the NP ran was founded
on respect for due process and the dispensation of retributive justice.
This is an expurgated version of a nation's past that was in fact
based on racial prejudice and capitalism. Almost fifty years of apartheid's brutality on its citizens, those it considered to be "other," was
simply and superficially explained away by claiming ignorance.

The ANC presented a more detailed account of its own past
actions, including acknowledgment of the many deaths of activists
in their training camps in Angola and Mozambique. But as Krog
notes, "The ANC's whole submission centers on the notion of a just
war. Because the war was just, the battles were just. Necklacing,
they say, was never part of official policy. And they avoid spelling
out the chain of command that led to incidents like the Magoo's Bar
bombing."[55] ANC's own account of its past is very easy to explain,
for it is a classic example of what Mamdani calls "derivative violence—the violence of victims turned killers."[56]

Drawing on Frantz Fanon's work, *The Wretched of the Earth*,
Mamdani shows how the Martinican-born psychiatrist theorized
the liberationist actions of "the native turned perpetrator, of the
native who kills not just to extinguish the humanity of the other but
to defend his or her own, and of the moral ambivalence this must
provoke in other human beings like us."[57] ANC's testimony then was
a particular historical narrative that framed its actions around the
attempt to constitute a new nation. In that context of state formation struggles, especially for a just and equal society, native violence

makes sense precisely because it is, "the violence of yesterday's victims, the violence of those who had cast aside their victimhood to
become masters of their own lives,"[58] of their own nation and future.

Perhaps the most illuminating testimony of a political official that
captures the argument I've made so far is that of the Freedom Front
leader, Constand Viljoen:

> When the realization sank in that black people actually wanted
> what we had ... that the black liberation struggle already had
> links with communism ... for the ethnic Afrikaner, it spelt athe-
> ism and dialectical materialism. There was no turning back – we
> were with our backs against the wall. We were reminded about
> past atrocities in Africa and already experienced a visible decline
> in the quality of our lives. Yet ... as the rich and the liberal
> moved to safer and more lucrative homes elsewhere on the globe,
> the Afrikaner braced himself to stay in Africa, to which he was
> indigenous. Naturally, he dug in his heels. But don't blame him
> for not being concerned and for not being able to show sensitiv-
> ity at a moment when his world was turned upside down.[59]

Viljoen's testimony is a particular rhetorical framing of a national
historiography grounded in the epic struggles between competing
nations, Black Africans vs. Afrikaner, a ruthless competition for
survival and dominance. But it is also a particular hi/story of state formation that aligns with organized forms of group power. Mamdani
has argued that "if we are to make political violence thinkable, we
need to understand the process by which victims and perpetrators
become polarized as group identities. Who do perpetrators of violence think they are? And who do they think they will eliminate
through violence?"[60] Viljoen's narrative privileges a unique colonial
history of the formation of disparate identities between settlers and
natives in South Africa, but those identities, rooted in racial/ethnic
prejudice, come to inform and energize national political identities. It is a narrative that buttresses how cultural markers, that is,
race and ethnicity, can come to inform political identities, which
are then distilled, formalized, and then instrumentalized as the basis
for social discrimination between groups, which is what happened
under apartheid in South Africa.

Women were important protagonists in the South African transitional justice process, so crucial that not only were specific "women's

hearings" held as part of the TRC's public testimonies, but also three chapters in Krog's book are dedicated to testaments by women.[61] Their emotional stories offer chilling accounts of mindless acts of violence against Black South African women such as rape, physical, verbal, and psychological abuse, and the most horrendous forms of human violations. According to Thenjiwe Mtintso, the chair of the Gender Commission, in her opening remarks at the hearings for women in Gauteng, "Women had to do star-jumps naked, breasts flying, fallopian tubes were flooded with water until they burst; rats were pushed into vaginas ... Women have been made to stand the whole day with blood flowing down and drying on their legs." This harrowing account of egregious violence is revealing because what it does show is that in the toxic environment of racial hate and angst fuelled by apartheid, "men use[d] women's bodies as a terrain of struggle – as a battleground" of the forces of both Boer nationalism and anti-apartheid liberationist activism.[62]

As women recounted horrific tales of how they were *disciplined* with rape; how rats went into their holding cells to eat soiled pads and tried to get in between their legs; how bullets were left in their bodies; and how pregnant women were *disembowelled*[63] it becomes blatantly obvious that the epic struggle for the soul and future of South Africa was fought not only in the treacherous battlefields of internal and transnational borders but also on the borders of women's bodies – the sanctity of their bodies, the sacredness of their biology and reproductive capacity, and their human dignity. The battle over South Africa as nation expressed itself as a struggle for domination over the anatomy of women.

It is no wonder that Krog's chapter on Winnie Mandela's testimony to the commission is entitled, "Mother Faces the Nation." The "Winnie Hearing," the biggest news story in the global media in the last week of November 1997, turned out to be an epic saga, perhaps more sensational than the testimonies of top national political leaders. Winnie Mandela was accused of masterminding the kidnapping of three young ANC activists by members of the Mandela United Football Club, a youth collective/security gang created, sponsored and mentored by her. One of the kidnapped victims, Stompie Seipei, was later brutally murdered. In Winnie's testimony to the commission, she denied the accusations levelled against her, claiming lack of knowledge of what the young members of her club did as individuals. I am interested in neither the sensationalism surrounding

Winnie's trial nor the vociferousness of her denial; I am invested in the ways in which she framed her response to the accusations.

In a manner reminiscent of all apartheid victims, Winnie Mandela noted the following: "I am an ordinary human being – they did things to me that is not acceptable." But in a nationalist rhetoric that resonates powerfully with so many others who appeared before the commission, she was defiant, insisting that "while many sat comfortably in their houses, we fought a just war."[64] Winne Mandela, the living symbol of Nelson Mandela, the ANC, and by extension, all Black and anti-apartheid struggles, invoked the nation-making rhetoric of her white male counterparts, insisting that the violence of her youth club was in pursuit of a just course – survival, that is, the liberation of Black and other marginalized South Africans from the shackles of apartheid's inhuman oppression. Her defence was a rhetorical move that justified political violence in pursuit of a future for a new nation, a new rainbow South Africa in which all human beings – white, Black, coloured – were equal before the law and entitled to all political, economic, and social rights as global citizens in a free, liberal, and democratic world. It was a rhetorical move in tacit support of what Bhabha calls "Fanonian violence," which sought to redeem Black South Africans from invidious colonial violence that violated Black bodies and souls.

CONCLUDING REMARKS: NATION MAKING AS CULTURAL SIGNIFICATION

So far, I have limited my analysis to the testimonies of apartheid security operatives, political party officials, and some women. The textual evidence I have amassed to this point, however, should allow us to make a persuasive case for the unique ways in which *Country of My Skull* triangulates the links between storytelling, national reconciliation, and democratic state building. And in doing so, I return to my point of entry in the chapter. In making the argument for a nation as a work of cultural signification, Homi Bhabha notes that this process of national mythification often produces an ambivalent national imaginary constituted from competing narratives. He observes that in "the absence of their merging into a new identity they have survived as competing dogmas – *societas* cum *universitate* – imposing a particular ambivalence upon all the institutions of a modern state and a specific ambiguity upon its vocabulary of discourse."[65] If the nation is an ambivalent cultural entity because of its contested history, its competing narratives, what effect might this have on the nation as a unified entity?

The ambiguity that Homi Bhabha theorizes was made clear in the case of South Africa by a young philosophy professor, Dr Wilhelm Verwoerd. After the testimonies by the infamous Vlakplaas five, Krog and her colleague bumped into the young Verwoerd while on a tea break. They asked him what he thought of the Vlakplaas five, and he responded with a wry smile and gave a quote from Paul Russel: "'If truth is the main casualty in war, ambiguity is another ...' One of the legacies of war is a habit of simple distinction, simplification, and opposition ... which continues to do much of our thinking for us." When Krog and her colleague asked him for clarification, he responded, "It means that in the past we had no choice but to live by simple white and black guidelines. But we shouldn't continue being dictated to by oversimplified credos during times of peace. We must try and make space for ambiguity."[66] Interestingly, this dense philosophical response came from the grandson of Dr Verwoerd (the architect of apartheid), who was now a staff of the TRC.

Part of what I argue in this chapter then is the crucial reality of the ambiguity of the nation-space as a product of cultural work is what Krog addresses in *Country of My Skull*. And what she reveals is a project of state formation in which the particular narratives mobilized by powerful voices to bring the new rainbow nation into being were marked by a lack of fixity, or what you might call the relativity of truth. Truth telling actually became a process of masking the truth. In ruminating on the testimonies and the work of the TRC, and the versions of "truth" it has elicited, Krog notes: "The truth is validated by the majority, they say. Or you bring your own version of the truth to the merciless arena of the past – only in this way does the past become thinkable, the world become habitable. And if you believe your own version, your own lie, how can it be said that you're being misleading? To what extent can you bring yourself not to know what you know? *Eventually it is not the lie that matters, but the mechanism in yourself that allows you to accept distortions.*"[67]

I therefore argue that as a creative treatise that captures and problematizes a nation as the by-product of a signifying practice, the novel's final submission on the transitional justice process in South Africa is that not only was it an exercise in cultural signification, it was also what Neville Alexander calls "the moment of maneuver." It was a historic exercise in national reconciliation in which perpetrators of state violence ingeniously avoided culpability for their crimes by invoking the rhetoric of forgiveness and nationhood. Rebecca Saunders has observed that while the exercise in public confession and its use of rights language "functioned in powerful ways to establish a previously unacknowledged history in South Africa, assign meaning to cultural trauma, identify and grant dignity to victims, and occasionally designate responsibility, it often proved more useful to perpetrators than to victims, functioned to prioritize national over individual forms of healing, and allowed the South African government to substitute spiritual and symbolic forms of reparations over material ones."[68] Thus, what Krog's *Country of My Skull* reveals is how a process of national narrativization, of translating and codifying past experiences of human rights abuse in a controlled environment and language, played into a dominant discourse of national reconciliation and healing that whitewashed the urgent and palpable need for material and moral justice.

Aside from creating a national archive of a malevolent past and public rituals of symbolic atonement, the novel shows how the process of national reconciliation became an exercise in cultural adjudication, that is, in passing judgment on a national culture. After listening to the hi/story of the horrific crimes committed by Afrikaner security officials in the service of the apartheid regime, Krog realized that all the perpetrators looked and sounded familiar, like most of her uncles, brothers, and white neighbours, and what she has "in common with them is a culture—and part of that culture over decades hatched the abominations for which they represent." So, for Krog, it was not these men that were asking for amnesty, it was a national culture that was asking for forgiveness. I use the term *culture* here not just in the limited anthropological sense of "a whole way of life," but as Clifford Geertz has argued, as a text, as a meaning-making system in which all the signs, codes, metaphors, idioms, and myths that shaped the organization of South African national life prescribed, nurtured, and legitimated racial violence and the exploitation of Black bodies.

NOTES

1 Claire Moon, *Narrating Political Reconciliation: South Africa's Truth and Recompilation Commission* (Lanham: Lexington Books, 2008), 6–7.

2 Kerry Bystrom, "Reassessing South African Truth and Reconciliation: John Kani's Missing and Performative Demands for Justice," in *The Culture of Dissenting Memory: Truth Commissions in the Global South*, ed. Véronique Tadjo (London: Routledge, 2019), 2.

3 Antjie Krog, *Country of My Skull: Guilt, Sorrow, and the Limits of Forgiveness in the New South Africa* (New York: Three Rivers Press, 1998), 30.

4 See, for example, Alexandra Effe, "Postcolonial Criticism and Cognitive Literary Studies: A New Formalist Approach to Antjie Krog's Country of My Skull," *Journal of Postcolonial Writing* 56 (2020): 97–109; Chielozona Eze, *Race, Decolonization, and Global Citizenship in South Africa* (Rochester, NY: University of Rochester Press, 2018); Taiwo Adetunji Osinubi, "Abusive Narratives: Antjie Krog, Rian Malan, and the Transmission of Violence," *Comparative Studies of South Asia, Africa and the Middle East* 28, no. 1 (2008): 109–23; Laura Moss, "'Nice Audible Crying': Editions, Testimonies and Country of My Skull," *Research in African Literatures* 37, no. 4 (2006): 85–104; Patricia Ewick & Susan S. Silbey, "Subversive Stories and Hegemonic Tales: Toward a Sociology of Narrative," *Law and Society Review* 29, no. 2 (1995): 197–226.

5 Effe, "Postcolonial Criticism," 98.

6 Catherine M. Cole, *Performing South African Truth and Reconciliation Commission: Stages of Transition* (Bloomington: Indiana University Press, 2010), 13.

7 John Kani's earlier play, *Nothing but the Truth* (2012), deals with the same theme of post-reconciliation disappointments in South Africa.

8 John Kani, *Missing* (Johannesburg: Wits University Press, 2015), 17–18.

9 Bystrom, "Reassessing South African Truth Commission," 1–2.

10 Rebecca Saunders, "Questionable Associations: The Role of Forgiveness in Transitional Justice," *The International Journal of Transitional Justice* 5 (2011): 62.

11 Sarah Nuttall, "The Shock of the New-Old," *Social Dynamics: Journal of African Studies* 45, no. 2 (2019): 280–5.

12 See Zakes Mda, "The Fiction of Reconciliation: Creating Dialogue through Verbal and Performance Art in South Africa," *Journal of Human Rights* 8, no. 2 (2009): 121–32.

13 Homi Bhabha, "DissemiNation," in *Nation and Narration*, ed. Homi Bhabha (London: Routledge, 1990), 291.

14 Ernest Renan, "What is a Nation?" in *Nation and Narration*, ed. Homi Bhabha (London: Routledge, 1990), 19.

15 Fredric Jameson, "Third-World Literature in the Era of Multinational Capitalism," *Social Text*, no.15 (1986): 65–88.

16 Carli Coetzee, "They Never Wept, the Men of My Race: Antjie Krog's 'Country of My Skull' and White South African Signature," *Journal of South African Studies* 27, no.4 (2001): 685.

17 Bhabha, "Introduction," in *Nation and Narration*, 3–4.

18 Ibid., 1.

19 Ibid., 2.

20 Ibid., 3.

21 Sarah Nuttall, "Literature and the Archive: The Biography of Texts," in *Refiguring the Archive*, ed. C. Hamilton et al. (Dordrecht: Springer, 2002), 291.

22 Ronald S. Roberts, "Keeping the Self: The Novelist as (Self-)Archivist," in *Refiguring the Archive*, ed. C. Hamilton et al. (Dordrecht: Springer, 2002), 301.

23 Ibid., 302.

24 Ibid., 321.

25 Susan Gallagher, *Truth and Reconciliation: The Confessional Mode in South African Literature* (Portsmouth, NH: Heinemann, 2002), 155.

26 Hayden White, "The Structure of Historical Narrative," *The Fiction of Narrative: Essays on History, Literature, and Theory 1957–2007*, ed. Robert Doran (Baltimore, MD: The Johns Hopkins University Press, 2010), 112.

27 Ibid., 112.

28 Ibid., 119.

29 Krog, *Country of My Skull*, 103–14.

30 Ibid., 107.

31 Ibid., 125.

32 Ibid., 6.

33 "Introduction," in *Country of My Skull*, vii.

34 Krog, *Country of My Skull*, 116.

35 Ibid., 117.

36 Mahmood Mamdani, "Making Sense of Political Violence in Postcolonial Africa," *Experiments with Truth: Transitional Justice and the Processes of Truth and Reconciliation*, ed. Okwui Enwezor et al. (Ostfildern-Ruit, Germany: Hatje Cantz Publishers, 2002), 21.

37 Ibid.

38 Gallagher, *Truth and Reconciliation*, 146.

39 J.M. Coetzee, "The White Tribe," cited in Gallagher, *Truth and Reconciliation*, 145.

40 Mamdani, "Making Sense of Political Violence," 25.
41 Krog, *Country of my Skull*, 118.
42 Ibid.
43 Ibid., 118.
44 Ibid., 6 and 118. This sentiment was expressed by General Johan van der Merwe and Captain Jacques Hechter, both former members of the South African Police Service.
45 For a full account of Benzien's hearings, see 92–9.
46 Benzien was forced by one of his former victims, Tony Yengeni, who later became a member of the TRC, to demonstrate the infamous "wet bag method" at one of the amnesty hearings.
47 Krog, *Country of My Skull*, 95.
48 Ibid., 95.
49 Ibid., 98.
50 Ibid., 98–9.
51 Saunders, "Questionable Associations," 128.
52 Ibid., 134
53 Ibid., 132.
54 Krog, *Country of My Skull*, 136.
55 Ibid., 137.
56 Mamdani, "Making Sense of Postcolonial Violence," 25.
57 Ibid., 25–6.
58 Ibid., 26.
59 Krog, *Country of My Skull*, 138.
60 Mamdani, "Making Sense of Political Violence," 26.
61 See chapter 7, "Two Women: Let us Hear It in Another Language"; chapter 16, "Truth is a Woman"; and chapter 20, "Mother Faces the Nation" all in Krog, *Country of My Skull*.
62 Krog, *Country of My Skull*, 235.
63 Ibid., 235–49.
64 Ibid., 337.
65 Bhabha, "Introduction," in *Nation and Narration*, 2.
66 Krog, *Country of My Skull*, 126.
67 Ibid., 112, emphasis mine.
68 Rebecca Saunders, "Lost in Translation: Expressions of Human Suffering, The Language of Human Rights, and the South African Truth and Reconciliation Commission," *International Journal of Human Rights*, no. 9 (2008): 51.

The South African Truth and Reconciliation Commission and Access to its Documentation

Proscovia Svärd

This chapter examines the extent to which the documentation generated by the South African Truth and Reconciliation Commission (TRC) was being used to promote an understanding of its work. The South African government established the commission according to the terms of the Promotion of National Unity and Reconciliation Act No. 34 of 1995. Based in Cape Town, the TRC concluded its work in 1998, when it presented its final report. Its mission was to uncover the truth about the atrocities that were committed during the apartheid era and to reconcile the people of South Africa.[1] As with most truth commissions, the South African TRC offered a platform for victims and perpetrators to share their experiences with the apartheid system in an endeavour to repair the deeply impacted social fabric. TRCs are believed to help post-conflict societies transition from a past of human rights violations to a democratic society that holds respect for human rights.[2] James Gibson has argued that TRCs aim to transform societies by changing beliefs and attitudes.[3] Therefore, it is essential that they capture people's attention and are credible information sources that inform about the past and guide societies into future political activities.

Clint van der Walt, Vijé Franchi, and Garth Stevens argue that national unity and reconciliation in South Africa were pursued at the expense of economic, social, and psychological reparations to the majority of South Africans.[4] Archbishop Tutu, chair of the South African TRC, stated that although reconciliation was complex, it was the foundation that allowed the transition from apartheid to democracy.[5] Tutu argued further that the conclusion of the

TRC should have been the beginning of the reconciliation process. The commission's last assignment was to hand over its findings and recommendations to the government. The commission realized sustainable reconciliation was a long-term societal process; therefore, its recommendations included addressing the racial and socio-economic injustices and prosecuting perpetrators who either did not seek or were not granted amnesty. However, the government has not implemented these recommendations, thereby hindering national reconciliation. Bishop Tutu noted that victims of apartheid abuses have not received justice. Moreover, South Africans who were privileged during the apartheid regime had not paid their dues by contributing to the financial circumstances of those who were denied the right to be lifted out of poverty. Tutu lamented that the same socio-economic injustices prevailed twenty years later, especially among Black South Africans.[6]

Gearoid Millar's chapter in this volume, titled "The Long-Term Legacies of Transitional Justice: Understanding the Paradox of Peace in Sierra Leone," demonstrates that reconciliation is a long-term project that requires long-term commitment. Reconciliation is not attainable through a single process, that is, the conducting of a TRC. Rather, it must be pursued in an ongoing manner that can address the unfinished business of a TRC, such as the payment of reparations and the meting out of justice. A lack of an inter-generational conversation regarding the apartheid system has been identified, highlighting the importance of both history and critical dialogue to reconciliation. Research confirms the need for people to understand their history to meaningfully engage in the democratic transition of their society.

Jonathan VanAntwerpen holds the view that the South African TRC master narrative has been vigorously and repeatedly criticized because of the commission's approach that embraced amnesty and forgiveness. He has argued that there are two ways of looking at reconciliation: one connotes a transformation of social relations, and the other is some form of resignation to the existing order of things.[7] The TRC was also critiqued for creating sophisticated amnesia regarding the greater structural and historical violence of apartheid by only focusing on human rights violations from 1960 onwards.[8] To avoid this amnesia, the past must be documented. International organizations such as the United Nations Human Rights Commission have ensured that records documenting human rights violations are captured and preserved. Measures like the Joinet/Orentlicher Principles were adopted by the UN General Assembly and relate to the protection and promotion of human rights, and include the collection, preservation, and access to the records.

As other scholars have stated, one of the key functions that had unexpected repercussions at the end of the South African TRC's work was record-keeping. Filing systems for both paper and electronic records had been implemented, and policies had been adopted in the TRC case. However, compliance was uneven, and a lack of clarity during the handover process meant that a significant number of staff members were left with the records in their possession. It was confirmed that access to the TRC documents was far from optimum.[9] The documentation of human rights abuses should be managed and used to foster remembering and understanding of the conflict – the very foundation for forgiveness and reconciliation.

Human rights archives can help societies deal with the painful past and build a peaceful future. However, for this to happen, the documentation should be used to promote meaningful dialogue and debate to promote the rights and healing of the victims.[10] Although the South African TRC has been widely researched, its archive calls for deeper scholarly engagement. The TRC has been used as a template upon which other African truth commissions have been based; the Sierra Leonean TRC is a good example.[11] The members of the Kenyan Truth Commission visited South Africa for experience sharing two decades after the South African TRC finished its work.[12] It is relevant to establish how its documentation has been used to promote an understanding of its work.

The National Archives of South Africa is the custodian of the South African TRC archives, but as of 2016, when this study was conducted, the Department of Justice (DOJ) was responsible for granting access to the documentation. The TRC recommended the optimal use of its documentation by all South Africans, with the understanding that the past was expected to help the country avoid the same mistakes and regress to conflict. This understanding facilitates building a new society that promotes democratic values and respect for human rights.[13] The effective use of the archived documentation was supposed to promote understanding of the TRC's work and, thus, encourage reconciliation. However, research shows that TRCs in general have a poor record when it comes to the dissemination of their findings and use of their documentation by those they document.[14]

DOCUMENTING THE SOUTH AFRICAN TRC

The South African TRC provided a forum for thousands of ordinary citizens to recount their experiences of human rights violations and abuses. Additionally, through the gathered testimonies, the commission created an officially recognized archive of the apartheid past, thereby offering a template for excavating a traumatic history and initiating a debate on reconciliation. Janine Clark has argued that within transitional justice literature, there is much speculation about the relationship between truth and reconciliation but little empirical evidence.[15] For reconciliation to occur, finding the truth is not enough; the truth must also be diffused in society to bring about fundamental change in people's lives and how they relate to each other. Several transitional justice scholars have postulated that the truth process in South Africa did indeed contribute to reconciliation, a crucial factor in democratization. To promote reconciliation, the South African TRC made extensive recommendations to address the rule of law, human rights practices, transparency, accountability, and corruption which were documented not only in the commission's final report but also in the thousands of primary documents from its investigations and public hearings.[16]

Because TRCs are structured differently, and are conceived and created under different jurisdictions, they confront different legal, political, and archival challenges regarding the documentation they generate. Michele Pickover has argued that the documentation is central to promoting people's understanding of the past;[17] therefore, management of and access to it are of crucial importance. In their 2019 study of the documentation and archiving process of the Canadian TRC, Cynthia Milton and Anne-Marie Reynaud have noted that all TRCs face challenges of managing their afterlife materials.[18] My study of the documentation processes of the Sierra Leonean and Liberian TRCs in 2007 and 2009 respectively identified challenges such as a lack in the areas of information management skills, storage facilities, financial and human resources, and political will as hindering factors in the dissemination of the TRCs' work. These challenges are omnipresent, despite the critical role documentation is supposed to play in post-conflict countries.

Other studies have confirmed the National Archives of South Africa has experienced major problems regarding the preservation of both paper and audiovisual records. This has hindered full access to the documentation. The South African TRC's ambition was to make the documentation it generated widely available to South Africans. The commission had even developed guidelines for the administration of access to its records. However, according to Lekoko Kenosi, the main challenge facing the National Archives is the management of electronic records. He argues that the TRC records' true contribution to accountability can only be achieved through citizens' access to them. He has lamented that lack of access was likely to have long-term repercussions regarding issues such as compensation to the victims.[19] The records contain names of perpetrators who have not yet been tried and are vital to the rule of law and political accountability in post-apartheid South Africa. Although governments are custodians of the information they collect, that information belongs to the people. In the case of the South African TRC, problems persist in accessing the apartheid-era security establishment records and identifying apartheid spies and assassins due to a culture of secrecy.

Access to the TRC documentation was vital to the commission's unfinished business, such as the provision of reparations to the victims, persecution of perpetrators who ignored the commission's amnesty process, and ongoing truth recovery efforts to understand more about the hidden and unacknowledged aspects of the past. It has been noted that the South African TRC archives are housed in the under-resourced National Archives of South Africa, even though they are under the DOJ's jurisdiction. One study of the National Archives conducted in 2014 revealed there were neither plans nor budget to process the documentation, nor were there plans to create an archival repository. This was contrary to the TRC's recommendation that the government allocate money to the National Archives to preserve and maintain its documentation and create decentralized memory centres to facilitate public access.

Although the South African TRC has been internationally applauded for its work because its approach was based on the principles of transparency and public participation, its impact seems to have stalled due to what one writer describes as "apartheid fatigue." Even though many South Africans are not conversant with the commission's findings, there were calls to stop unearthing the past and encouragement to look toward the future. Yet, the people as a collective have an obligation to acknowledge the past and bear witness to violations of the apartheid regime. To do this, people need to have knowledge of their oppressive history, which becomes part of their heritage that enables them to remember. This explains why the TRC recommended its archive be made accessible to all South Africans.

Vivian Bickford-Smith, Sean Field, and Clive Glaser have argued that the emotional costs of the apartheid system needed to be recorded and interpreted by oral historians. They have wondered if the TRC, as a generator of the official history, has silenced alternative stories. Given South Africa's conflictual past, they have recommended alternative stories be recorded and disseminated as a contribution to the democratization of the society. They lament the government's failure to implement the South African TRC recommendations, especially the reparation payments that had been promised to victims of human rights violations.[20]

Similarly, Verne Harris has problematized the way we look at representations of events through documentary evidence and demonstrated the possibility for the oppressors to silence certain stories. He has argued that archives are constructed windows into personal and collective processes, and as such they constitute only a sliver of the documentary record.[21] Harris has unique insights on this question since he represented the National Archives during an investigation that the TRC carried out into the destruction of public records. The investigation exposed a large-scale and systematic sanitization of public memory, which had been authorized by high levels of the apartheid government. This was an attempt to hide its darkest secrets. Other recent studies indicate that the TRC archives are hard to access, even for historians. One scholar has noted: "Many South Africans – especially those faced with the country's notorious socio-economic inequality – consider the idea of a post-apartheid present a bitter joke and find themselves standing at the other side of the bridge."[22]

One motivation for this study is the point Briony Jones and Oliveira have made about the paucity in the literature that focuses on TRCs' archives. These authors confirm that what is missing in the growing literature on TRCs and their practices is a discourse on the archives they generate.[23] They hold the view that archives that document human rights abuses are part of broader social and political contexts. Since access and use were problematic, Jones and Oliveira have proposed an alternative conceptualization of the TRC archives as new democratic spaces. The documentary and archival access gaps that have been identified demonstrate a need to address the impediments to accessibility. The generated documentation needs to be managed in a manner that promotes an understanding of the TRC's work. If it is to function in making the TRC's work meaningful to the victims, promote reconciliation, and understand the past, the commission's archives must be democratized.

UNDERSTANDING OF THE SOUTH AFRICAN TRC'S WORK

To understand the intersections between the commission and the documentation of its work, I employed a case study approach. I collected data in 2016 through twelve interviews that I conducted with five men and seven women aged twenty-five to seventy. The small sampling of interviewees means the results are not representative of all South Africans, which is a limitation of the study. Those interviewed regarded themselves within three racial identities: white South Africans, Black South Africans, and people of colour. I found the ways in which respondents understood the work of the TRC varied, depending on whether or not they were directly affected by the apartheid system. Some respondents were still young at the time the TRC was established, and they did not remember exactly what had transpired. And some white South Africans who lived in the rural areas did not experience the atrocities of the apartheid system as directly. For example, one respondent contended: "Despite what was happening in South Africa during the apartheid regime, I and even some Black people did not know the gravity of the atrocities that were being committed. The TRC opened an ugly wound."

A young respondent asserted that she did not fully understand why there was racism in the country and could not say much about the TRC process. She noted, however, that people ought to be made aware of their history to understand the present. The respondents who were young when the TRC was established had no understanding of the commission's process. Another respondent stated the TRC did not cover all angles of the conflict and some cases remained unclear. This respondent gave an example of the case of Chris Hani. Hani was the leader of the South African Communist Party and chief of staff of Umkhonto we Sizwe, the armed wing of the African National Congress, who was assassinated on 10 April 1993. The respondent also mentioned Dr Wouter Basson, who was head of the country's secret chemical and biological warfare project during the apartheid era. The press had nicknamed Basson "Mr Death"

because he killed people even though he was trained as a cardiolo-
gist. This respondent observed: "'Mr Death' and some other people
who appeared before the TRC were not granted amnesty because
they did not tell the whole truth, but they are still free." Basson's
court case, which occurred during the time I conducted my interviews in South Africa, was well-publicized in the media since the
medical council was trying to revoke his licence because of his
actions during apartheid.

The interviews revealed the popular interpretation and predominant view of the TRC was that it was a waste of time and it changed
little. According to one of the respondents, the TRC effectively
enabled a blanket amnesty, the reparations were not forthcoming, and people's lives had not changed. Furthermore, although
the South African TRC recommended wide-ranging reparations
and systematic prosecution of people who did not get amnesty,
the government failed to implement these. A special investigation
unit was established, but only three prosecutions had so far been
carried out at the time of my interviews. One of the respondents
posited that "South Africa had a leadership, which was satisfied
with an elite transition and no meaningful redistribution of wealth.
The new elite did not really want the truth to get out because too
many of them would be compromised."

THE PRESERVATION AND USE OF SOUTH AFRICAN
TRC DOCUMENTATION

The TRC recommended its documentation as an instrument to support reconciliation work, but this has not been the case. The TRC
further recommended digitization for that documentation and the
establishment of centres of memory around the country. One of the
respondents informed me that when the TRC offices were closed,
the records were secured and transferred to the National Archives.
There, a strong room adjacent to the public reading room was identified as a place to have a permanent exhibition of the materials and
offer guided tours so that people could see the materials, but this
was not happening.

Several civil society organizations (CSOs), such as the South
African History Archive (SAHA), have been working toward getting
TRC records into the public domain. SAHA had managed to publish
a database of victims of human rights violations. The database was

a public record that could help people do all kinds of searches and analyses. SAHA and other NGOs had put a lot of materials online that were utilized in several educational kits. These initiatives have allowed for some access to the documentation but not on a scale that was envisaged in the 1990s, and they certainly were not supported by the state. Rather, many of these initiatives have been supported by NGOs funded by donors and accessed by privileged academics and students from the West. The research done on the South African TRC, including books, journal articles, and theses, has been overwhelmingly produced by North American scholars.

Although the National Archives provided access to the TRC records, the DOJ determined whether accessibility to requested documents would be granted. The DOJ controlled access because, technically; the legislation that established the TRC had a clause indicating all its assets were to devolve to the DOJ. And the assets included the TRC documentation. The National Archives of South Africa Act allows the transfer of the documentation after twenty years. Two decades after the TRC ended its work, the hope is that the National Archives will take complete control of the documentation, thereby making it more accessible to the public.

Reuse of TRC documentation has been encouraged. People have written documentaries and plays based on the TRC documentation. Activists and politicians who were incarcerated under the apartheid regime and a few other interested persons who visited the National Archives have requested access to the documents in search of personal information. Some relatives of victims of the apartheid regime also consulted the archives. Broadcasting companies, producers of documentaries, playwrights, and CSOs have also used the documentation. The National Prosecution Authority was an active user of the TRC archives for missing person cases.

Documentation access was regulated by the Promotion of Access to Information Act in 2000.[24] TRC documentation that was not in the public domain could only be accessed with permission from the DOJ. Researchers could access audio and audiovisual materials at the National Archives. The Government Communication and Information System made copies of such materials on CD/DVDs. There were also post-TRC television programs of special cases. Researchers were allowed to watch the programs only at the National Archives but could not secure a copy due to copyright laws. Request for access to the TRC documentation was usually granted, except for the sensitive records regulated by the DOJ, such as sensitive information related to bomb-making. Several respondents interviewed for this study stated that many ordinary people did not know about the TRC process and were unfamiliar with how to access TRC documentation.

Although plans to digitize the South African TRC documentation have not been carried out, the documentation was well taken care of in an archival setting with properly regulated temperatures. It was stored in two strong rooms. Organizations such as SAHA had an approach of copying records and securing them. All these materials ultimately needed to be deposited with the National Archives because they are public records that had to be accessible as part of the more extensive collection of TRC documentation. An interview respondent informed me that professional and efficient personnel at the National Archives were doing their best to preserve the records. Still, they were working in an environment that was extremely hostile toward any work on the TRC documentation. This respondent argued that the state did not want to hear about the TRC issues.

The interview data revealed that the real worry was the electronic records. The National Archives had the paper and audiovisual records, but the electronic records were kept by the DOJ. A respondent stated that at the end of the TRC work, a team went around the country to every TRC office and simply downloaded information from hard drives, servers, and people's desktops, and this was hurriedly done. The electronic records might no longer be readable because, as far as the respondent knew, the last audit was done in 2003, and already at that point, several of the files were not readable. He could not imagine the state of the records as of 2016.

CONCLUSION

This chapter has examined the extent to which the documentation generated by the South African TRC was being used to promote an understanding of its work. TRCs are regarded as transitional justice mechanisms because they have the potential to deal with the complexities of reconciliation and the democratization of post-conflict societies. To achieve reconciliation, these societies must address the past, which entails using the documentation that TRCs generate to create a culture that respects human rights. The goal of documentation is to promote an understanding of the conflict. TRCs create a platform for both the victims and the perpetrators to recount their experiences, facilitating a common narrative about a conflict that can inform political speculations. The literature reviewed confirms that even though all TRCs faced the challenge of managing their materials, the South African TRC's ambition was to make its documentation available to the people.

Michelle Caswell argues that human rights archives can only help post-conflict societies if they are meaningfully utilized.[25] The South African TRC recommended the South African Human Rights Commission and the National Education Centre to create projects to encourage children to keep the past alive and looked upon its database as a rich electronic resource that was to be made available to the people for further use through the National Archives. The TRC further recommended the establishment of a secretariat in the presidency that was to oversee the implementation of its recommendations. However, the major impediment to access the TRC documentation is lack of political will.

Several respondents in my study pointed out that although they lived in South Africa during apartheid, they did not fully understand the gravity of the atrocities committed by the regime. This is what makes having TRC documentation in the public domain of paramount importance – so that the public can stay informed. Society has an obligation to remember apartheid's oppressive history. The South African TRC documentation is a form of collective memory that should be used to keep the apartheid history alive.

The major challenge for information management amid post-conflict reconstruction is lack of political will to implement an information management infrastructure that would include computerized systems for the dissemination, long-term preservation, and reuse plans of the TRC documentation. The issue of record-keeping has not been a key element during the conduct of TRCs, and this study, among other reviewed studies, confirms that without proper record-keeping, challenges for the use of the TRC documentation will persist, and meaning from these records will continue to elude the victims and the post-conflict societies at large.

Based on my research findings, I conclude that TRC documentation has not been proactively used as the commission recommended. The post-apartheid regimes have not promoted access by all citizens to the documentation, except for a few who can afford the access process. One of the young interview respondents did not know the apartheid history, but she believed it should be a right for people to know their history. Though the South African TRC is looked upon as a successful model that is recommended to other nations endeavouring to achieve a peaceful transition to democracy, its recommendations have not yet been fully implemented by the post-apartheid governments. Hence, reconciliation is still beyond the reach of many South Africans, especially those still living in abject poverty. TRC records and archives are a rich resource that should be effectively used to promote an understanding of the commission's work, which in turn empowers citizens with the knowledge to comprehend their history and push the government to implement TRC recommendations toward a more democratic state.

NOTES

1 South African History Archives, *Truth Commission Special Report*, n.d., http://sabctrc.saha.org.za/reports/volume6/section5/chapter7/subsection1. htm.
2 John Braithwaite, "Survey Article: Repentance Rituals and Restorative Justice," *The Journal of Political Philosophy* 8, no. 1 (2000); K. David Androff, "Truth and Reconciliation Commissions (TRCs): An International Human Rights Intervention and Its Connection to Social Work," *The British Journal of Social Work* 40, no. 6 (2010).
3 James L. Gibson, "On Legitimacy Theory and the Effectiveness of Truth Commissions," *Law and Contemporary Problems, Group-Conflict Resolution* 2, no. 2 (2009): 123–41.
4 Clint van der Walt, Vijé Franchi, and Garth Stevens, "The South African Truth and Reconciliation Commission: 'Race,' Historical Compromise and Transitional Democracy," *International Journal of Intercultural Relations* 23 (2003): 251–67.
5 Desmond Tutu, "Self-Reflection and Reconciliation Recipe for a Tired World (Självreflektion och försoning receipt för en prövad värld)," *Svenska Dagbladet*, Stockholm, 25 February 2018, 10–11.
6 Tutu, "Self-Reflection and Reconciliation."
7 Jonathan D. VanAntwerpen, "In the Shadow of the Secular: Theories of Reconciliation and the South African TRC" (PhD diss., Graduate Division, California Digital Library, University of California, Berkeley, 2011).
8 Van der Walt, Franchi, and Stevens, "The South African Truth and Reconciliation Commission."

9 Goethe Institute, Nelson Mandela Foundation, and Rosa Luxemburg Foundation, *Workshop: Truth, Reconciliation and Transparency in South Africa and Kenya Lessons Learned*, 2009.

10 Michelle Caswell, "Defining Human Rights Archives: Introduction to the Special Double Issue on Archives and Human Rights," *Archival Science* 14, no. 3–4 (2014): 207–13.

11 Proscovia Svärd, "The Challenges of Documenting War Atrocities in Post-Conflict Sierra Leone: A Study of the Truth and Reconciliation Commission (TRC)," *African Journal of International Affairs* 10, no. 1&2 (2007): 55–72.

12 Goethe Institute, Nelson Mandela Foundation, and Rosa Luxemburg Foundation, *Workshop*.

13 Priscilla Hayner, *Unspeakable Truths: Confronting State Terror and Atrocity* (New York: Routledge, 2002).

14 Trudy H. Peterson, *The Final Acts: Preserving the Records of Truth Commissions* (Woodrow Wilson Center Press with Johns Hopkins University Press, 2006); Svärd, "The Challenges of Documenting War Atrocities," 55–72; Proscovia Svärd, "Archiving Challenges in Africa: The Case of Post-Conflict Liberia," *IASA Journal* 32 (2009): 38–55.

15 Janine N. Clark, "Reconciliation via Truth? A Study of South Africa's TRC," *Journal of Human Rights* 11, no. 2 (2012): 189–209.

16 Drew Cottle and Sunil Thapa, "The Role of Truth and Reconciliation Commission in Peace Building: Nepal," *International Journal of Social Sciences* 3, no. 3 (2017): 218–38.

17 Michele Pickover, "Negotiations, Contestations and Fabrications: The Politics of Archives in South Africa Ten Years after Democracy," *Innovation* 30 (2005): 1–11.

18 Cynthia E. Milton and Anne-Marie Reynaud, "Archives, Museums and Sacred Storage: Dealing with the Afterlife of the Truth and Reconciliation Commission of Canada," *International Journal of Transitional Justice* 13, no. 3 (2019): 524–45.

19 Lekoko S. Kenosi, "Records, the Truth Commission, and National Reconciliation: Accountability in Post-Apartheid South Africa" (PhD diss. School of Information Sciences, University of Pittsburgh, 2008).

20 Vivian Bickford-Smith, Sean Field and Clive Glaser, "The Western Cape Oral History Project: The 1990," *African Studies* 60, no. 1 (2001): 5–23.

21 Verne Harris, "The Archival Sliver: Power, Memory, and Archives in South Africa," *Archival Science* 2, no. 1 (2002): 63–86.

22 Rafael Verbuyst, "History, Historians and the South African Truth and Reconciliation Commission," *New Contree*, no. 66. (2013): 15.

23 Briony Jones and Ingrid Oliveira, "Truth Commission Archives as New Democratic Spaces," *Journal of Human Rights Practice* 8, no. 1 (2016): 6–24.

24 PAIA, Act No. 2 of 2000.

25 Caswell, "Defining Human Rights Archives, 207–13.

The Gambian TRRC: Toward a "Comprehensive Model" of Truth Commissions

Baba G. Jallow

On 22 July 2019, exactly thirty months after Gambia's Yahya Jammeh was forced out of power and into exile in Equatorial Guinea, and precisely twenty-five years since he seized power in a military coup on 22 July 1994, the first member of the former dictator's death squad (the Junglers) walked into the hearing hall of the Truth, Reconciliation and Reparations Commission (TRRC). He solemnly took the oath, sat on the witness chair, and guided in his testimony by the commission's lead counsel, narrated in chilling detail how he and other Junglers arrested and murdered several individuals. Over the next three days, two other Junglers appeared before the TRRC and a bewildered nation to confess their participation in at least seventy murders under the direct orders of Yahya Jammeh.

The Junglers were a group of commandoes selected from the State Guards, a unit of The Gambia National Army responsible for the president's security. Officially called The Patrol Team, their primary duty was to patrol the area of The Gambia-Southern Senegal border near the president's home village of Kanilai. In reality, they were mainly engaged in the nocturnal arrests, tortures, and killings of victims identified by Jammeh as posing a threat to the security of the state. They were told that whoever they were asked to "deal with" was an enemy of the state, and it was their duty as soldiers to protect their country. By the time the TRRC was held, the dictator had fled, as had some of the Junglers' commanders. The rest had been arrested after the change of government. Feeling aggrieved that they had been left behind to suffer for merely obeying the orders of a man who lived conveniently in exile, they told everything they knew, describing in graphic detail how each victim was arrested, executed, and disposed of.

The whole nation had been in shock since the TRRC's first public hearing on 7 January 2019. With the testimonies of the Junglers, there was a renewed state of shock in the country. For while people knew of their existence and that they had killed and disappeared many people on the direct orders of Yahya Jammeh, few knew the details about how and where victims were arrested, how they were treated after arrest, where they were taken, how they were killed, by whom, and how their bodies were disposed of. Now the unfailingly gruesome details assailed the minds of the people at the TRRC hearing hall, through live radio broadcasts, on television screens, through YouTube and social media, and in taxi cabs, restaurants, and bars. Dressed in full military fatigue, the Junglers who had been in detention at Fajara and Yundum military barracks for over two years confessed to their participation in the murders of several dozen victims, including fifty-four Ghanaian and other West African nationals in July 2005. The bodies were disappeared either by abandonment in the forest, burial in mass graves in the forest, or dumping in old wells situated in the Senegalese region of Casamance, just across the border from Kanilai.

As Gambians watched and listened in horror, they heard accounts of how Dawda Nyassi was lured via a phone call to the Junglers car, taken to a bush around Banjul International Airport, shot dead by four men, and his body left right there in the darkness. Gambians heard how the prominent journalist Deyda Hydara, whom the Junglers referred to as "the magic pen" was pursued and sprayed with bullets while driving home on the night of 16 December 2004. Gambians heard how nine death row inmates, including one woman and one mentally unstable person, were taken from their prison cells in the middle of the night, driven to the bush across the border in Casamance, suffocated to death with plastic bags, and dumped into an old well. Gambians heard how Haruna Jammeh, a close relative of the dictator, was picked up from the headquarters of the National Intelligence Agency in Banjul, taken to the bush, strangled with a rope, had his neck stamped on, and his body dumped into an old well.

The Junglers revealed how Haruna Jammeh's sister and the former president's cousin Marcie Jammeh were both taken to the forest and shot point-blank in the head for demanding to know where Haruna was. They revealed how forty-four Ghanaians and eight other West African nationals suspected of being mercenaries were arrested on the orders of Yahya Jammeh, taken to the bush in Casamance, shot one by one execution style, and dumped into an old well. Among other painful stories, the Junglers revealed how two young Gambian-American citizens were picked up on their way home from a local restaurant, taken to see the dictator at his palace in Kanilai, then taken to the bush, suffocated, beheaded, and dumped into an old well. According to the Junglers, Yahya Jammeh's order was to kill the two young men and cut their bodies into pieces. The people could not fail to notice that all these arrests and executions were committed at night.

It was not the first time that perpetrators had confessed their crimes at the TRRC's public hearings. As of 22 July 2019, ninety witnesses – both victims and perpetrators – had testified before the commission. Fourteen of these witnesses were alleged and self-confessed perpetrators whose testimonies contained graphic details of killings and tortures. On 28 February 2019, Alhagie Kanyi, alias *mofaala* (the killer), confessed to participating in the execution of fourteen soldiers on 11 November 1994, and the brutal murder by battering of former finance minister Ousman Koro Ceesay in the compound of a senior military official in June 1995. The high point of the hearings before the appearance of the Junglers was the voluntary appearance before the commission of former junta number two man, Sanna Sabally, on 24 April 2019. In a marathon two-day testimony that almost brought The Gambia to a standstill, the once feared individual readily admitted to committing all the crimes attributed to him, including the killing of eleven fellow soldiers after a foiled coup attempt on 11 November 1994. Sabally also told of the almost unimaginable torture he suffered after falling out with Jammeh and under detention at Mile 2 Prison, a jail Jammeh proudly called "my five-star hotel." Neither Kanyi nor Sabally was a Jungler, and neither was arrested after their testimonies. The Junglers, however, had been held under military detention since early 2017.

A day after they confessed to participating in horrible tortures and at least seventy extrajudicial killings, then justice minister Abubacarr Tambadou announced his intention to release from detention three of the Junglers who testified before the commission, pending the recommendations of the TRRC. The minister said these Junglers had been truthful before the commission and that their release was a

way of encouraging other Junglers – especially those who had fled
into exile – to come forward and help the country know the truth
about what happened under the Jammeh dictatorship. He also suggested that many families still wanted to know what had happened
to their loved ones. The more the Junglers testified, the more likely
that families would get some healing and closure about the fate of
their loved ones. It was not an announcement many Gambians were
ready to hear. And it was not an announcement they were going to
keep quiet about.

In fact, Gambians had stopped keeping quiet since 1 December
2016. On that day, they went to the polls and voted their brutal dictator of twenty-two years out of power. The following day, visibly
confused at his unexpected defeat, Jammeh called Coalition candidate Adama Barrow to congratulate him and concede defeat. A
week later, on 9 December, the former dictator appeared on national
television to announce he had rejected the results of the elections
and that Gambians must go back to the polls. His announcement
was met with uncharacteristic defiance in the spontaneous eruption
of public condemnation, and the appearance of The Gambia Has
Decided hashtag. No amount of intimidation by way of threats and
the deployment of heavily armed soldiers in the streets of Banjul
could shake the people's resolve to have Jammeh step down. The
ensuing impasse lasted six weeks before Economic Community of
West African States troops crossed the border from northern Senegal
and forced him into exile in Equatorial Guinea.

THE GAMBIAN TRRC

A year after those historic elections, the TRRC was established by an
Act of the National Assembly in December 2017 to fulfill President
Barrow's campaign promise to investigate human rights violations
committed by the ousted president. In fulfillment of its mandate,
the commission was tasked to create an impartial historical record
of violations and abuses of human rights from July 1994 to January
2017, in order to promote healing and reconciliation. The TRRC also
had the following mandates: respond to the needs of victims; provide
victims with an opportunity to relate their own accounts of the violations and abuses suffered; establish and make known the fate or
whereabouts of disappeared victims; grant reparations to victims in
appropriate cases; address impunity; and prevent a repetition of the

violations and abuses by making recommendations for the establishment of appropriate preventive mechanisms, including institutional
and legal reforms. The act gave the TRRC subpoena authority and
empowered the commission to grant interim reparations.

The passage of the TRRC act came after a short but rigorous process of both national and international consultations and study tours
organized and coordinated by the Gambian Ministry of Justice. In
August 2017, the ministry, in collaboration with The Gambia office
of the United Nations Development Programme, the Dakar-based
Office of the High Commissioner for Human Rights, UNICEF, and
some civil society organizations (CSOs) embarked on a ten-day
nationwide consultation process. According to the report subsequently released on this activity, "the objective of the consultations,
which took place from the 14th to the 24th of August 2017, was to
solicit the views and opinions of Gambians on a wide range of issues
on the objectives and functions of the proposed TRRC."[1] Opinions
and ideas shared at these national consultations informed the establishment by the Ministry of Justice of a Technical Committee on
Transitional Justice composed of representatives from government
and non-governmental institutions to actively work together on
shaping the proposed TRRC. This technical committee held regular
consultative and brainstorming sessions at the Ministry of Justice
and contributed to the conceptualization and formulation of the
TRRC act and guidelines for selecting commissioners, which were
widely publicized in the media.

Shortly thereafter, in September 2017, a team led by Attorney
General and Minister of Justice Tambadou embarked on a study
tour to Sierra Leone and South Africa, with a view to exploring how
their truth commission experiences could "inform Gambia's policy,
strategy and implementation of its transitional justice mechanisms."[2]
Through information gathering and consultations, the Gambian del-
egation hoped to share experiences on challenges, lessons learned,
and best practices in the establishment of a comprehensive transitional justice process incorporating truth, justice, reconciliation,
reparations, and guarantees of non-recurrence.[3] The report on these
study tours indicates that important lessons were learned on, among
other things, victim and witness participation, witness protection,
information management and communications strategies, women
and gender mainstreaming, challenges of reconciliation and reparations, and the extent to which truth commissions have been able to

guarantee non-recurrence of human rights violations. Lessons from these study tours were useful in formulating the TRRC act and setting up the commission in subsequent months.

The first part of 2018 saw the appointment of an executive secretary and the drafting of guidelines for the selection and appointment of commissioners of the TRRC. In accordance with these guidelines, calls for the nomination of commissioners from the urban areas, the Gambian Diaspora, and all five regions of the country were issued and widely publicized. One commissioner was to be appointed from each of the five regions following widespread consultations in each district of each region. Coordinated by the regional governors, the selection of regional commissioners was conducted by seven-member politically neutral Regional Selection Panels (RSPs) made up of representatives of youth and women's groups, CSOs, NGOs working in the field of human rights, religious and community leaders in each of the country's five regions.

Following consultations with the inhabitants of all districts in each region, each RSP selected three candidates, including at least one female from among the majority ethnic groups in the region whose names were submitted to the governors. Nomination criteria for appointment as TRRC commissioner included personal integrity, high moral character, no criminal record, no known active involvement in a political party, residency in the region, and Gambian nationality. After receiving the nominations from their respective RSPs, the regional governors transmitted their lists of finalists to the Ministry of Justice with a report identifying members of the RSPs and certifying that the nomination process complied with the guidelines for the selection and appointment of commissioners.

The Ministry of Justice then selected eleven finalists from the list of regional, urban, and Diaspora nominees. The finalists' names were published in the media, and the public was given ten days to raise any objections they might have regarding any of the candidates. In the absence of any serious objections, the president conducted the last set of consultations on the candidates with key CSOs before appointing them commissioners of the TRRC. In October 2018, these eleven commissioners were sworn in, and the TRRC was officially launched by President Barrow at a ceremony at the commission's new headquarters at Dunes Resort (a hotel that used to belong to the ousted dictator and was now under receivership).

Three months later, on 7 January 2019, the TRRC held its first
public hearing on the causes and consequences of the military
coup of 22 July 1994, that brought Yahya Jammeh and his Armed
Forces Provisional Ruling Council into power. By the end of the first
three-week session of public hearings on 24 January, the TRRC had
irreversibly captured the imagination of the Gambian public and
generated a national conversation that grew increasingly vehement
as the process unfolded. The conversation only intensified with the
appearance and graphic confessions of the first three Junglers.

THE CONTROVERSIES OF THE GAMBIAN TRRC

The justice minister's announcement of his intention to release three
Junglers as a way of encouraging others to come forward and testify
reignited and heightened the simmering controversy over the alleged
primacy of criminal prosecutions over truth, amnesty, and reconciliation that had characterized the TRRC process since its inception.
From the very beginning, some Gambians called the TRRC "a joke,"
a "money-making venture," and "a smokescreen" behind which the
new government was hiding to score political points and deny victims their right to justice. There is always the persuasive refrain:
no reconciliation without justice, or, we want justice, not reconciliation. The two concepts are juxtaposed as mutually exclusive. It
is either justice – understood as the arrest and prosecution of all
alleged perpetrators – or reconciliation – understood as a denial of
justice for victims.

The argument is made that since the perpetrators are known, why
not just arrest and prosecute them rather than waste scarce public
resources on an expensive truth commission? This, of course, is easier said than done, as most truth commission and transitional justice
scholarship shows. In many cases, only a few perpetrators bearing
the greatest responsibility for the most serious violations are ever
prosecuted. In The Gambia, the sequence is that the TRRC will be
allowed to complete its work and then make recommendations for
prosecutions and pardon – and the state will then consider which
cases to take forward.

States like The Gambia that establish truth commissions are often
accused of neglecting justice and trying to force reconciliation down
the throats of victims. Yet, it is the difficult task of such commissions to promote reconciliation, here understood as the restoration

of peaceful relations between victims and perpetrators. Where this form of reconciliation is possible, there is release from guilt for perpetrators and relief from bitterness for victims and their families. For perpetrators, confessing or accepting their crimes, showing remorse, and asking and receiving forgiveness offer a chance for social rehabilitation and a new lease on life. Such processes also hold perpetrators publicly accountable for their actions.

For victims, having an opportunity to confront their tormentors by telling their stories or hearing what happened to their loved ones and forgiving perpetrators, where possible, can bring a certain measure of relief and closure that eases their abiding pain. A good measure of humanity is restored when victims get some measure of recognition and closure, perhaps letting go of their anger, and perpetrators are relieved from the unrelenting burden of a guilty conscience. Society ultimately benefits and, to some extent, feels reconciled to itself when the truth about past atrocities is acknowledged, and the mistakes of the past are laid bare before the public eye. In the final analysis, the TRRC's mandate does not permit justice before reconciliation because justice (prosecutions) could only occur after the TRRC process ends and the commission's recommendations are submitted to the government.

The narratives that emerge from truth commission hearings have a way of capturing the public imagination and generating robust national conversations about the human capacity for cruelty and the resilience of the human spirit in the face of unspeakable odds. More broadly, these narratives encourage public conversations about the past: what happened, how, and to some extent, why. The narratives contain lessons that, though not necessarily new in the wider scheme of things, have a way of inspiring ideas and questions on the nature of the human mind and the often incomprehensible banality of atrocity.

During the TRRC's public hearings, the testimonies of both victims and perpetrators suggested that in most cases of victimization, the victims were innocent of any crime. On the contrary, the evidence suggested that people were arbitrarily arrested, detained, tortured under interrogation, and often killed without committing any crime whatsoever. Entire communities are traumatized and whole families destroyed in the process, often reduced to abject poverty, permanent physical impairment, and unspeakable challenges of day-to-day survival. Depending on how well the process is managed, a truth commission may reopen old wounds, re-traumatize victims, traumatize entire nations, but at the end of the day, it will facilitate the conversations that need to happen for national healing and reconciliation to take place.

Despite their vast potential as vehicles for positive social transformation, truth commissions are often very unpopular. Some see them as worthless institutions whose recommendations will never be implemented. In post-authoritarian societies like The Gambia, supporters of the regime under investigation called the truth commission a deliberate witch hunt against the ousted leader. Cognizant of the importance of a truth commission acting fairly and with integrity – and to be seen doing so – the TRRC found itself repeatedly making the argument or reiterating to journalists and the general public that the commission was not a witch hunt. That refutation may have reassured some members of the public, but diehard loyalists of the ousted regime still declared their loyalty and defended Yahya Jammeh, even in the face of overwhelming evidence of the atrocities committed under his watch.

Among other outlandish claims made by Jammeh supporters was that witnesses, especially perpetrators, were paid by the TRRC to lie against the former president in a deliberate witch hunt by the current government. Despite the denials and accusations, Jammeh's support base took a severe hit from the painful narratives emerging from witness testimonies. However, neither Jammeh's declining popularity nor the public's appreciation of the value of the truth coming out of the TRRC hearings made it any easier to navigate the problematic waters of justice versus truth and reconciliation.

Closely related to the controversy over justice versus truth and reconciliation is the difficult question of reparations. Especially where a truth commission has the term in its name, such as in the Gambian TRRC, reparations evoke high expectations of monetary compensation in transitional societies. As most victims of atrocity are poor, these expectations offer an opportunity for relief, however temporary, from persistent poverty. The TRRC experience shows that many victims come forward to testify not only because they want justice but also because they expect some form of monetary compensation for the wrongs they suffered. The question of reparations is rendered more difficult to address for most truth commissions because they can only recommend payment of reparations by the government. And whereas most commission reports include such recommendations, governments are generally either unwilling or unable to pay reparations for the majority of victims.

Post-transitional societies are therefore often marked by noticeable levels of discontent at the legacies of truth commissions. A good part of the truth is known. Perhaps some perpetrators are punished, and some victims compensated. But many victims remain bitter that justice has not been done because they have not been compensated for their pain and losses. The situation is easier to handle when, as in the Gambian TRRC, the commission is empowered by its founding legislation to grant reparations. This was one unique feature of the Gambian model that could be replicated by other truth commissions.

One of the obvious ways to manage high expectations over reparations is to tirelessly explain, at every possible opportunity, that these can take many forms and are meant to provide some relief to victims and victim communities. Reparation is thus not synonymous with monetary compensation, although it might include such compensation. Reparation can also consist of assisting victims in getting urgent medical treatment, scholarships to the children of victims, memorials and monuments, training, and assistance to find gainful employment. This message needs to be widely shared in transitional societies through the media especially, but also through town hall meetings, village dialogues, men's and women's listening circles, school visits, training sessions, and even in one-on-one conversations. The narrative that emerges in transitional societies must be infused with the understanding that reparations are not only about monetary compensation.

At the same time, as the narrative unfolds and settles into a pattern, it must be demonstrated that these other forms of reparation are taking place and that some people benefit from them. This can happen only when interim reparations are provided as part of a commission's operations, as was the case with the TRRC. The best way to facilitate this is to empower truth commissions to directly grant reparations without taking orders or directives from the government or outside parties and without waiting to include them in their final reports.

THE COMPREHENSIVE APPROACH OF THE
GAMBIAN TRRC TO TRUTH AND RECONCILIATION

An overriding rationale for creating truth commissions is to prevent recurrence, as famously articulated in the title of Argentina's National Commission on the Disappeared report *Nunca Mas* (*Never Again*). While this may or may not be spelled out in truth commission mandates, there is always an underlying desire in societies emerging from conflict or repression to ensure that what happened in the past does not happen again. The mixture of pain, outrage, and horror often palpable in societies transitioning from violent conflict or repressive dictatorship engenders a widespread desire, if not determination, to prevent the past repeating. In many instances, the expectation is that exposing human rights violations through the truth-seeking process and including recommendations for institutional reforms in a commission's final report will help prevent recurrence.

Since violations are generally committed through the agency of the police, the secret service, the military or other armed groups, the expectation is that security sector reforms would remove the bulk of factors responsible for the performance of atrocity. In the Gambian context, we found that over and above abuses by security forces, the nature of the country's political culture was one significant factor as to why Yahya Jammeh was able to silence dissent and commit atrocities against the people for so long. For this reason, we agreed early on with Nanci Adler that "removing the repressor from the society" does not necessarily "remove the repression from the society."[4] That requires deliberate, targeted effort.

Because they have not taken concrete steps to address how cultural factors have enabled dictatorship and human rights violations, most societies that have witnessed truth commission processes have not experienced the kind of socio-political and cultural transformation that can prevent a recurrence of dictatorship or widespread human rights violations. Neither prosecutions, where they occur, nor institutional reforms, where they are implemented, are enough to prevent recurrence. Therefore, governments, policymakers, and transitional justice scholars are challenged to look beyond policy lapses and institutional failures when crafting truth commission mandates. Some transitional justice experts attribute the relative lack of truth commission success to a lack of inclusivity in commission processes.[5]

With the benefit of hindsight, a rich body of scholarship on transitional justice, and a welcome level of interpretative discretion granted by the act establishing it, the Gambian TRRC adopted a comprehensive approach to truth commission work in response to some observed limitations of these commissions. The defining characteristic of this comprehensive approach is inclusivity, premised on an ethic of empowerment. To demonstrate this point about inclusivity and empowerment, and as we have seen above, Gambians from all walks of life and all regions and districts were involved in the selection and nomination of the eleven commissioners of the TRRC. Unique to the Gambian model, this meant that The Gambia had no serious complaints or accusations of bias or corruption in the appointment of commissioners. There were a few complaints that only four out of the eleven commissioners were women, but also praise for the fact that all the major ethnic groups of the country were represented on the commission, as were the two major religions in the country – Islam and Christianity. The eleven commissioners included a bishop and two imams. The commission also had a children and youth representative and a gender representative. Significantly, two of the eleven commissioners had no form of Western education, but simultaneous interpretation was provided for them through all hearings and other major commission functions.

A look at the work of most truth commissions suggests that the great majority of the commission's work is carried out by the commissioners themselves, often assisted by a secretariat and a team of researchers, investigators, and other support staff. The commissioners hear testimonies, conduct some of the research and investigations, collect statements from witnesses, and embark on community outreach activities. This means that however effective the commissioners may be, they can only do so much within their limited mandate periods. Even with abundant resources at their disposal, which is often not the case, a dozen commissioners or fewer cannot carry out all the work necessary for the meaningful social transformation required by transitional justice processes. The TRRC addressed this challenge through another unique approach.

To ensure non-recurrence, it was determined from the beginning that the TRRC secretariat must be well-equipped to do more than serve as mere backup support to the commissioners, as was the case in previous African truth commissions. For this reason, and thanks to the welcome interpretative discretion accorded by the TRRC act, especially regarding the functions of the executive secretary, several specialized units were created within the secretariat to ensure maximum engagement with and inclusion of both victims and the general public. Thus, in addition to its Research and Investigations Unit, the TRRC secretariat had a fully staffed and functional Victim Support Unit, which acted as an interface between the commission and victims, providing medical, educational, psychosocial, and livelihood support to all victims who needed it; a Women's Affairs Unit to ensure women and gender issues were mainstreamed in the transitional justice process; a Reconciliation Unit whose responsibility was to promote reconciliation in all sectors of Gambian society; and a Communications and Outreach Unit, which coordinated with all units during outreach activities and implemented the commission's communication strategy.

There was even a Youth and Children's Network Coordination Unit, whose primary function was to engage young people, schoolchildren, and older students at all levels of the education system across the country in conversation on the rights and responsibilities of citizenship, the nature of the social contract, and the need for young people to be actively engaged in the politics of the country, especially by getting ID and voters cards and participating in elections. Students from schools around the Greater Banjul Area were routinely invited to attend the commission's public hearings. The result of this inclusion of the secretariat was that the TRRC pursued its mandate via two parallel processes: while hearings of witness testimonies were ongoing at the commission's head office in the suburbs of Banjul, various units of the secretariat were out in the field, engaging in community outreach activities across the country as part of the TRRC's #NeverAgain Campaign.

During the commission's mandate period, the TRRC's Youth and Children's Network Coordination Unit conducted over sixty outreach activities targeting young adults and schoolchildren in communities and schools across the country. The unit visited 55 schools and engaged an estimated 60,000 students across the country. The unit also brought 95 young people, including non-students and students from secondary schools, the University of The Gambia and other institutions, to attend some commission hearing sessions. Four of the five-unit staff were men and women in their twenties. All four of these Youth Empowerment Officers were university students, poets, and well-known youth activists in the country.

In collaboration with communications and other units, the TRRC's Unit conducted several town hall meetings and village dialogues across the country during the commission's existence. During the month of Ramadan in 2019, the Reconciliation Unit engaged several Muslim communities around the Greater Banjul Area. The conversations conducted over *Iftar* – or the breaking of the fast – dwelled on the commission's work and the need for forgiveness, reconciliation, and healing, even as we sought justice and reparations for victims of human rights violations. During the weekend of 27–28 July 2019, the unit visited several churches in Banjul and surrounding areas and engaged Christian communities in conversations about the commission's mandate and especially how to promote justice, healing, and reconciliation in The Gambia.

At least fifteen women's listening circles targeting women across the country were organized and coordinated by the TRRC's Women's Affairs Unit. These circles were designed to provide a safe space for women to share their experiences of human rights violations, especially those of a sexual nature. The TRRC encouraged women, especially victims of sexual violence, to reach out and share their stories with the commission according to modalities that safeguarded their privacy and their integrity. Women were given the option to testify either publicly, as protected witnesses, or behind closed doors with only the commissioners and counsel present. Or they could choose to submit statements that would be part of the commission's record.

The TRRC has had a noticeable impact on Gambian society and political culture. It became, in a relatively short period, ensconced as part of the Gambian social consciousness, through the high-profile public hearings, the town hall meetings, village dialogues and listening circles, the robust school outreach program, and songs composed by various artists about the commission and the Never Again slogan. When a former member of Jammeh's military junta refused to testify before the commission in June 2019, a spontaneous public demonstration erupted at the TRRC headquarters and a nearby police station. Demonstrators chanting "Never Again" insisted that the witness must appear before the commission, earning the TRRC the flattering sobriquet, #ThePeople'sCommission.

By the time the commission submitted its final report on 25 November 2021, and eventually closed its doors on 28 February 2022, the Gambian public narrative had noticeably shifted from one of oppression, fear, and an all-powerful state, to one in which citizens were determined to hold their government accountable and ensure justice for victims of human rights violations. The country also saw the mushrooming of victims' organizations focused on working to ensure that the commission's recommendations, including those for reparations and the prosecution of alleged perpetrators, are implemented by the government. The work of the TRRC played a key role in bringing about this social transformation in the country's civic culture.

In the final analysis at the present time, the commission seems to have left a lasting and positive legacy in Gambian society. First, the TRRC must be among few truth commissions in which a good number of perpetrators willingly appeared, to testify and confess their crimes that included torture and murder. Second, the robust conversation on the rights and responsibilities of citizenship, the limits of state power and authority, and the need to stand up to any signs of repression or abuse of state authority continues in the post-TRRC period. Already, there is a critical mass of Gambian citizens engaged in this conversation, and the trend is likely to endure.

CONCLUSION

By way of conclusion, I emphasize a few points on the value and limitations of the truth commission model as a transitional justice mechanism in Africa, and I make a few suggestions on how we can maximize its impact on transitional societies.

Truth commissions are valuable avenues for healing and closure for victims and their loved ones. Whether or not perpetrators are prosecuted, victims benefit from an opportunity to confront their painful past, address their tormentors, know the fate of their disappeared and murdered loved ones, or receive some form of acknowledgment and compensation. Despite their very practical limitations and the persistent controversy surrounding their existence and mandates, truth commissions engender narratives that help societies come to terms with their painful past and cement their determination to build a better future. They, therefore, remain a viable option for societies in transition from conflict or dictatorship to peace and democracy.

In light of practical context-specific challenges, scholars, policymakers, and practitioners of transitional justice in Africa must learn to think beyond conventional notions of what a truth commission should look like and what its specific roles should be. In essence, a truth commission in the African context must be considered both a quasi-judicial transitional justice mechanism and an institution for civic education and popular empowerment. Dictatorship in Africa emerges largely because of people's lack of both civic education and knowledge that power resides in them, and not in the government. Within the African context, an effective truth commission process must include robust civic engagement and popular empowerment. Dictatorship thrives and human rights violations are committed with impunity largely because, in Africa, the great majority of citizens are not empowered enough to resist their governments. A politically empowered citizenry is the best guarantee against oppression and political impunity.

An effective truth commission process must be Janus-faced in both theory and practice. Its investigations of past human rights abuses must go hand in hand with practical efforts at building a better and brighter future. An effective truth commission must be inclusive in practical terms, both at the level of the commission as an institution and at the national level. Truth commission secretariats must be adequately equipped in terms of manpower and resources to be active participants in executing the commission's mandate, especially through conducting outreach activities and delivering practical day-to-day help to victims. At the national level, as many local actors as possible – religious and secular, artists, CSOs, and the media – must consciously engage as partners in the transitional justice process. As well, an effective truth commission must be transparent in the execution of its mandate. All its public hearings must be open and accessible to the public. With the exception of protected witnesses and witnesses testify behind closed doors, truth commission hearings should be covered by the media and preferably streamed live on both broadcast media and social media. This transparency complements the inclusivity aspect of its work and makes the truth-seeking process more credible.

Finally, an effective truth commission must jealously guard its independence and integrity. There must be zero tolerance for interference by the state and staunch resistance to external actors wanting to impose their own ideas on proceedings. Indigenous realities and objectives must both shape the commission's structure and determine its strategies of operation. Context absolutely matters.

NOTES

1 Ministry of Justice, *The Gambia: Report on the National Consultations for the Truth, Reconciliation and Reparations Commission, 14th–24th August 2017.*

2 The Institute for Human Rights and Development in Africa, *Report to the Working Group on Death Penalty, Extrajudicial, Summary or Arbitrary Killings and Enforced Disappearances in Africa on the Protection of Victims of Enforced Disappearances in The Gambia*, October 2020, 2, www.ihrda.org/wp-content/uploads/2021/03/Report-on-ED-EJK-in-The-Gambia-to-ACHPR-WG-on-ED-EJK-Oct-2020.pdf.

3 The Institute for Human Rights and Development in Africa, *Report to the Working Group*, 1–2.

4 Nanci Adler, *Understanding the Age of Transitional Justice: Crimes, Courts, Commissions and Chronicling* (New Brunswick, NJ: Rutgers University Press, 2018).

5 Seth Kaplan and Mark Freeman, "Inclusive Transitions Framework," (Barcelona: Institute for Integrated Transitions, 2015).

SECTION FOUR

Outcomes and Legacies

14

Ghana's National Reconciliation Commission:
A Retrospective

Robert K. Ame and Seidu M. Alidu

Truth and Reconciliation Commissions (TRCs) have become one of
the most widely used mechanisms to address issues of human rights
abuses and foster reconciliation among victims and perpetrators of
human rights violations. These commissions are largely restorative
in their approach and use techniques designed to reconcile societies
in the aftermath of major conflicts or atrocious authoritarian rule in
order to bring about healing and closure. They also aim to establish
the truth about human rights violations, which helps communities
understand the causes of past abuses to facilitate the restoration of
personal dignity and bring closure to stigmatization and trauma.
Yet, in many parts of the world, TRCs have encountered enormous
challenges, including a lack of funding and transparency, political
interference, and an unwillingness or inability of governments to
implement the recommendations resulting from the commissions'
work. These challenges manifested in the works of the Commission
of Inquiry into the Disappearances of People in Uganda and the
National Commission of Inquiry into Disappearances established in
1971 and 1982 in Uganda and Bolivia, respectively,[1] and the recent
examples in DR Congo, Nepal, Kenya, and Sierra Leone.[2]

Ghana's experience with civil conflicts pales in comparison to
its neighbours, considering the types and magnitude of conflict in
the West African sub-region in recent times. However, Ghana has
had its fair share of military dictatorships, often characterized by
gross human rights violations in which killings, abductions, disappearances, detentions, and illegal seizure of properties that occurred

during both constitutional (i.e., democratically elected or civilian) as well as unconstitutional (i.e., military) regimes. Robert Ameh has argued that the disagreements between the two main factions among the nationalists who fought for Ghana's independence have resulted in "unfinished business," which has created a "cycle of vengeance and vendettas," the execution of which translates into gross human rights violations and abuses of political opponents in both constitutional and unconstitutional regimes.[3] When Ghana's perennial problems of ethnocentrism, nepotism, and elitism are factored in to these challenges, a virulent recipe of political antagonism that stifles development is produced.

True to their campaign promise, the New Patriotic Party (NPP) government championed the passage of the National Reconciliation Commission Act (Act 611), in the Ghanaian parliament in December 2001. This act gave birth to the National Reconciliation Commission (NRC), which was inaugurated by His Excellency John Agyekum Kufuor, then president of Ghana, in May 2002. Commencing in September 2002, the NRC completed its work in July 2004 and submitted a five-volume report to the president on 12 October 2004.[4]

This chapter assesses the work of the NRC and its legacy as part of the process of consolidating the building of a democratic state in Ghana. The chapter is divided into two parts. The first part briefly reviews the NRC's work, covering the (1) mandate, (2) methodology, (3) membership of the commission, (4) findings, (5) recommendations, and (6) implications of the report for the NRC's objectives. The second part addresses the NRC's legacy by reviewing the past fifteen years since the commission's work ended and is guided by the following questions: Did the NRC achieve its goals? Was it able to uncover the truth about various conflicts and human rights violations? Have the types of conflicts and human rights violations examined ended or at least subsided? Has the work of the NRC resulted in reconciliation among Ghanaians? The qualitative research methods of secondary data analysis of government reports, media reports, and pertinent literature review are utilized. We have already commented extensively on the mandate, the appointment of members, and the methodology of the NRC elsewhere.[5] In this chapter, we therefore only briefly mention a few salient points regarding these aspects as they pertain to the overall achievements of the NRC and its legacy.

THE WORK OF THE NRC

The overarching aim of the NRC was to investigate human rights abuses by military regimes as a way of promoting reconciliation among Ghanaians for the consolidation of the democratic state. To that end, the NRC was to investigate the context, causes, and circumstances of human rights violations by the state or persons acting on behalf of the state; identify the individuals and state organs involved; establish accurate and complete records of the violations; identify the victims; and make recommendations for compensation. In addition, the NRC had as its mandate to "investigate any other matter which it considers require[s] investigation in order to promote and achieve national reconciliation."[6] Although the act specified investigation of only six types of human rights violations,[7] this clause introduced enough flexibility for the NRC to work without unnecessary constraints regarding mandate, even if it was entirely left to the commission's discretion.

The mandate of the NRC would have been curtailed by section 3(2) of the act, which sought to circumscribe the commission's jurisdiction to investigating only unconstitutional regimes, unless someone specifically petitioned it to investigate violations during constitutional regimes. This would have meant that only military regimes would have been investigated by the NRC, excluding civilian regimes, which equally perpetrated gross human rights violations. This attempt to limit the NRC's work became known as the "door of opportunity versus window of hope" controversy in Ghana's reconciliation debate. Fortunately, members of the commission gave a positive interpretation to that clause and basically made no distinctions between petitions from military or constitutional regimes.[8] So overall, the mandate was neither too rigid nor too flexible, thus conforming to Priscilla Hayner's best practices on reconciliation commissions' mandate.[9]

Members of the NRC were appointed by the president on the advice of the Council of State. While some had suggested NRC members be appointed and vetted by parliament generally, there was little controversy surrounding their appointment.[10] As Ameh has pointed out, the classification and coding system adopted by the NRC was based on the model proposed by Patrick Ball.[11] This model enabled the commission to adopt a sound methodology in approaching its work and allowed for the capture and analysis of multiple violations, victims, and perpetrators. The model also made it possible for the NRC to identify what constituted each category of violation and opened the door for the commission to pose questions that reflected-the substance of the NRC's mandate.[12]

FINDINGS OF THE NRC

A key finding of the NRC was that human rights violations existed in all regimes – both constitutional and unconstitutional, justifying the demand of those who had argued that the work of the NRC should not be limited to unconstitutional (military) regimes. But the report also showed the violations peaked during military regimes, with the highest numbers recorded during the Armed Forces Revolutionary Council (AFRC) and Provisional National Defense Council's (PNDC) regimes, both led by former president Jerry J. Rawlings. Of all the violations the NRC recorded, 84% occurred during these two regimes, with as high as 68% taking place during the PNDC regime. The Convention People's Party regime, a democratically elected regime led by Ghana's first president, Kwame Nkrumah, recorded the next highest level of violations. The lowest number of violations was recorded during the People's National Party government, another civilian regime. This is presented in figure 14.1. In terms of types of violations, the pattern was the same for all six outlined in the NRC mandate.

Second, the NRC Report indicates the military forces, the police service, and the prison service were the main perpetrators. Together, they were responsible for almost 80% of all violations, with the military forces alone being responsible for about 53%. Figure 14.2[13] represents these statistics clearly.

Third, 79% of the victims within the mandated period were male, and 19% were female. The gender of the remaining 1% was not known. Under all the categories of violations investigated by the NRC, men were more likely to be victims than women, and no woman was subjected to execution-style killing. However, violations of women scored high in the categories of forced sale of goods (43.9%), sexual abuse (42.9%), and destruction of property (36.6%), head shaving (33.7%), and psychological torture (30.4%). Victims were mainly adults (99%); however, 4% of "other killings" and 4% of sexual abuses were against children. The report showed that the wealthy and influential suffered most (69%).

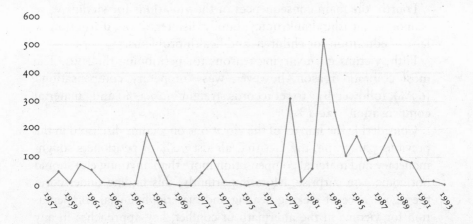

Figure 14.1 | Detention violations over the period

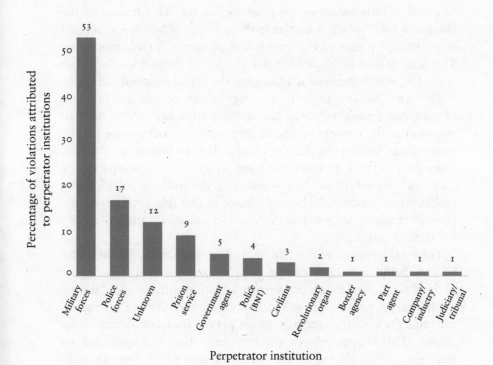

Figure 14.2 | Perpetrator responsibility for all violations

Fourth, the main consequences of the violations for victims were economic hardship/bankruptcy, family disintegration, disruption or lack of education for children, and health problems.

Fifth, victims gave varying reasons for petitioning the NRC. The most common reason, however, was "monetary compensation" (69%), followed by "to set records straight" (29.2 %) and "material compensation" (20.1%).[14]

Considering the impact of the violations on victims discussed in the previous paragraph, the fact that almost 90% of petitioners sought monetary and material compensation more than anything else should not come as a surprise. More importantly, this finding underscores the significance of seeking healing and material/financial compensation for victims in the aftermath of conflict, key approaches in any truth and reconciliation process, rather than criminal prosecution of perpetrators. Only 6.4% petitioned the NRC for reasons of seeking "justice against perpetrators." A key controversy in the TRC literature is whether nations should opt for a reconciliation approach or criminal prosecution in the post-conflict era. This finding of the Ghanaian NRC, which is similar to those from the South African and other TRCs,[15] points to the importance of opting for reconciliation. This finding also highlights the significance of the restorative justice approach, which focuses on addressing the varied needs of victims.[16]

The NRC Report finds that a significant percentage (29.2%) of petitioners sought "to set the records straight," confirming an assertion in the restorative justice literature that victims are mainly interested in finding out the truth about their victimization.[17] Often, a mandate of TRCs, and an underlying principle of restorative justice – as was the case for the NRC – is to seek the truth surrounding the violations in question.[18] The importance of this relates to setting the records straight, acknowledging the victimization, and validating the victims' stories.[19]

The establishment of the Ghana NRC was informed by the NPP's effort to fulfill its election campaign promise to its voters. The report of the NRC showed that human rights violations often peaked during the military regimes more so than the civilian, indicating the significant role the country's security forces play in terms of human rights abuses. This chapter shows the brutalities that were inflicted on innocent citizens during military regimes, and which were the subject of the NRC's investigations and public hearings, still continue in

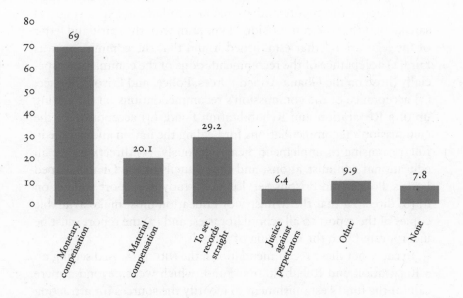

Figure 14.3 | Reasons for making statements to the commission

democratically elected governments and are still perpetrated mainly by the same national security institutions.

THE NRC RECOMMENDATIONS

The NRC recommended the president, the commander-in-chief of the Armed Forces of Ghana, and the heads of public institutions such as the security services should formally apologize, and monuments should be erected, and commemorative events should be held, such as an annual reconciliation lecture series. The NRC also recommended restitution that included the return of property seized from individuals as well as monetary compensation that included scholarships for the victims and/or their children and health insurance benefits for victims. Finally, the NRC recommended institutional reforms within the military, the police, the prisons, the judiciary, and civil society organizations, and wide dissemination of the NRC Report, including incorporating it in school curricula.

The government of Ghana issued a White Paper in April 2005 that accepted the report and its recommendations expressing: (1) satisfaction that the commission "kept faith with the spirit and letter of the legislation" that established it and that the commission was fair; (2) acceptance of the recommendations of the commission especially those on the Ghana Armed Forces, Police, and Prisons Service; (3) acceptance of the commission's recommendations on the setting up of a Reparation and Rehabilitation Fund; (4) acceptance of the commission's recommendations for healing the nation and people in full, promising to implement them vigorously; (5) directing that all educational administrations, and the councils of the Ghana Armed Forces, Police, and Prisons Service must study the report and act on it; (6) directing that the Ministry of Education must make available copies of the report to all school libraries; and (7) the report must be incorporated into the curricula of schools.[20]

To carry out these recommendations, the NRC proposed setting up a Reparation and Rehabilitation Fund, which went beyond a mere call for the fund's establishment to identify the sources for attracting money to it. The NRC suggested five different sources, including the government's national budget; a percentage of the Highly Indebted Poor Country funds the country was sourcing from the World Bank at the time, the Poverty Alleviation Fund; contributions from corporate bodies; voluntary donations from the public; proceeds from the sale of the NRC's report and memorabilia; and even contributions from willing perpetrators.[21] The NRC must be commended for considering the sources from which compensation would be paid to victims; this is uncharacteristic of many such commissions.

IMPLEMENTATION, OR LACK THEREOF, OF THE NRC'S RECOMMENDATIONS

In line with the NRC Act, the commission recommended various forms of compensation for petitioners, ranging from symbolic measures to restitution and monetary compensation. The symbolic measures, as indicated earlier, included an apology from the president, commander-in-chief of the Armed Forces of Ghana, and heads of the security services, the erection of monuments and holding of commemorative events. Our research did not turn up evidence of any of these symbolic recommendations having been implemented; there is no record of any of these having been done. There is also no evidence of wide dissemination of the NRC Report in public libraries, nor its incorporation into school curricula. One of the significant challenges of the work of TRCs has been the lack of power to ensure the implementation of their recommendations to the political leaders that authorize them. In their introduction to this volume, Bonny Ibhawoh, Jasper Abemia Ayelazuno, and Sylvia Bawa reiterate Archbishop Desmond Tutu's profound statement in the final submission of the report for South African TRC, by underscoring the significance of the TRC model in recommending amnesty and reparation, all embodied in the restorative justice approach.

Yet, they raise a deep concern about the efficacy of the TRC model when it could only recommend reparations and not grant them; where it could not go after perpetrators because of the enormous power they wield, and what happened when known perpetrators deliberately refused to participate in the TRC process? Even though these flaws were widely held against the South African TRC, it passes for the work of most known TRCs, including the Ghanaian case, albeit with some variations. However, according to Ken Attafuah, who served as the executive secretary of the NRC, when the commission submitted its report to former president Kufuor, it also made copies available to every public university in the country; the Balme Library at the University of Ghana alone was provided with ten copies. He lamented, however, that faceless people had removed the reports from the libraries and online portals.[22]

EXHUMATIONS AND COMMEMORATIVE ACTS

In line with its own recommendations and even before submitting its report, the NRC undertook exhumation of victims' bodies and handed them over to their families for befitting funerals in order to provide healing and redress to aggrieved families as part of the overall national reconciliation. Its first exhumation exercise occurred on 1 September 2003 at the Akwasa Cemetery, Mile 11, on the Accra-Cape Coast Road. On 29 April 2004, following a successful exhumation, the NRC handed over remains of the victims who were executed by firing squad in May 1986 to their respective families for an appropriate burial.[23] The families expressed their appreciation to the government for establishing the NRC.[24]

On 17 May 2004, the NRC, with the assistance of experts, undertook its second exhumation exercise at the Aboso Cemetery, near

Tarkwa, in the Western Region, where it exhumed the bodies of five victims and handed those over to their families.[25] The bodies went through post-mortem examination and other forensic tests, including DNA for their identification. This was necessary not only to promote the overall goal of reconciliation but also to dispel any doubts about the occurrence of those violations and victimizations.

REPARATIONS AND MONETARY COMPENSATION

Reparative measures constitute an important element within the content of every transitional justice policy that aims to achieve the goal of national reconciliation. As José Zalaquett has succinctly argued: "There is no real reparation of the loss of life or of the permanent physical or psychological sequelae of torture or of other repressive measures. However, within such inherent limitations, every possible effort should be made to compensate victims of human rights violations and their families."[26]

The NRC succeeded in meeting the needs and interests of victims by recommending a comprehensive reparative policy through the establishment of a reparative and rehabilitation fund. This recommendation was not only in accordance with the terms of reference of the NRC Act, international law, and treaties to which Ghana is a party and signatory but also in line with chapter 15 of the Fourth Republican Constitution.[27] The outcome of the NRC process, as mentioned, revealed that the overwhelming majority of victims (89.1%) petitioned the NRC because of compensation, both monetary and material, while only 6.4% demanded justice against their perpetrators, which was outside the commission's mandate anyway.[28]

The government's reparative program was largely tangible reparative measures in the form of monetary provisions and restitution of seized properties. Out of the 4,240 petitioners, more than half, comprising 2,514, were selected for the reparation measures. About 2,117 of the 2,514 qualified for monetary reparation, while the remaining 397 received other forms of reparation, including reinstatement to their previous jobs and the restitution of seized properties.[29] In 2006, the government began compensating victims, setting aside 13.5 billion cedis from the 2006 national budget to compensate the 2,177 victims. The government regarded monetary compensations as a way of identifying itself with the victims' suffering to facilitate their healing but not payment for their suffering. For instance, Joe Ghartey, the erstwhile Attorney General and minister for justice, told the beneficiaries that "no amount of money could pay for the suffering some of you went through." Indeed, the NRC itself emphasized the fact that no amount of reparation could fully compensate for the victims' losses.[30]

Individual payments ranged from about US$217 to US$3,300, depending on the extent of abuse or violation.[31] Seidu Alidu summarizes the detailed monetary compensation to victims as follows:

> Payments were made in two different currencies ... with 72 people paid in US dollars to the tune of $44,271.60 and 2,310 people paid in Ghana Cedis to the tune of 12,211,000,000. No reason has been given for this decision, but most of the beneficiaries who received US dollars were ex-military men. The breakdown for those who received their monies in Cedis are as follows: 31 people were paid 20 million each; 161 people received 15 million each; 297 people received 10 million each; 66 people received 7 million each; 564 people received 5 million each; 13 people were paid 4 million each; 227 people were given 3 million each; 466 people received 2 million each; and 186 people received 1 million each.[32]

Even with all these payments, former president Kufuor, whose government created the NRC, recently acknowledged that not all compensations were fully paid.[33]

DE-CONFISCATION OF ASSETS

Through the recommendations of the Confiscated Assets Committee of the NRC, 137 individuals benefited from the government's assets de-confiscation policy in October 2008. The government regarded the de-confiscation exercise as very important in achieving national reconciliation. The key beneficiaries among the list were four former heads of state: Dr Kwame Nkrumah, General Akwasi A. Afrifa, General Ignatius K. Acheampong, and General Frederick W.K. Akuffo.[34] The government, through the work of the NRC, was able to restore the rights of certain victims who suffered abuse and unlawful seizure of properties under authoritarian regimes.

Generally, the NRC contributed largely to the provision of restorative packages to victims, despite the anomalies that characterized the government's reparation exercise. The absence of an effective monitoring system called into question the genuineness and degree of transparency in the reparative exercise. The government's de-confiscation exercise raised some public concerns about the de-confiscation of properties of some individuals who were alleged to have plundered state coffers and thus acquired those properties illegally. Some members of the public also portrayed the restitution process as restoring the properties of only the then ruling political party (NPP) members, whose properties were confiscated under the PNDC regime.[35]

IMPACT OF THE NRC'S WORK

It takes a generation for reconciliation and other goals of TRCs to bear fruit. However, a period of fifteen years after a TRC concludes its work is sufficient time to provide an indication of the type of fruit, if any, that it will bear, which in turn could be indicative of the nature of its legacy. TRCs are broadly subsumed under the principles and ethos of restorative justice[36] and, therefore, do not punish offenders for crimes committed under the mandated period;[37] rather, they seek to uncover the truth surrounding mandated violations and abuses and recommend reforms that may lead to healing and final closure. Therefore, the work of TRCs is to reduce the number of "untruths" that are circulated uncontested and allow for self-retrospection and national reflection on ways that will prevent the recurrence of the violations.[38]

Gearoid Millar's contribution to this volume, chapter 15, presents contradictory findings and implications of the work of the Sierra Leone TRC to the peace and stability of the country. He had held the view that the Sierra Leone TRC failed to "connect local communities and promote reconciliation" in the country; a view contrary to that of Lyn Graybill who argues that the Sierra Leone TRC was quite "successful in generating reconciliation and peace within the country." These contradictory findings led Millar to re-examine his previous works and conclusion, and he realized that the source of the difference is the methodology. Indeed, it makes considerable difference, even in the Ghanaian case. While Graybill's conclusion had emanated from speaking to "elites" that were associated with the work of the commission, Millar's was based on interacting with grassroots leaders and community members.

In Ghana, the success and impact of the TRC is dependent on who the researcher samples. Unlike Sierra Leone, it is less about the class divide of elites and masses. Rather, it is a partisan divide. When you speak to either the elite or the masses who are members of and/or sympathetic to the ruling NPP that established the TRC, they will recount to you how successful and impactful the work of the TRC has been to contribute to healing, reconciliation, and nation building. You are likely going to get the reverse answer when you speak to the members of and/or people sympathetic to the opposition the National Democratic Congress at the time the commission was established. Thus, it became difficult to get an acceptable national truth/narrative about who were the victims and perpetrators of the crimes committed during the commission's working mandate. Invariably, one of the shortfalls of TRCs' work is their inability to provide an all-encompassing truth that bridges the compartmentalized versions still being circulated. Indeed, Michael Ignatieff (1996) argues that the work of TRCs assists in arriving at an acceptable version of truth that reduces the number of many untruths circulating unchallenged.

TRCs do not have the mandate to prosecute and the testimonies given before them are inadmissible in court;[39] therefore, there is less expectation that the work of a commission would lead to grand prosecutions. In recent times, the trend in international practice has been that where a TRC unearths grave human rights violations (including genocide, crimes against humanity, and war crimes or torture), the state concerned, or the international community, would resort to the International Criminal Court (ICC) (or prior to the ICC, to ad hoc national or international criminal tribunals) for complete prosecution, as happened in several countries around the world such as Liberia[40] and Sierra Leone.[41]

In the Ghanaian case, the work of the NRC did not lead to any prosecutions at the ICC or in a special national tribunal. However, victims often spoke of the TRC process as providing them a cathartic experience and that, therefore, they were able to gain closure. These findings overlap with those of Paul Ugor's, in chapter 11 of this volume, that TRCs provide the "guiding tropes of truth telling, forgiveness, and reconciliation" through a "process of narrativization." Narrativization, according to Ugor, is a discursive process that allows victims of conflict or grave human rights violations to get healing through publicly narrating what they have been through. He concludes that "transitional justice endeavours are habitually an exercise in storytelling."[42] Deductively, transitional justice processes must put a premium on self-reconciliation and self-healing of victims by creating opportunities for them to ventilate their grievances more than achieving a nationally acceptable truth.

The hearing process of the NRC also brought some success stories that allowed for the symbolic expression of reconciliation through apology and forgiveness. The commission created a congenial atmosphere in which victims had the chance to interact with offenders, creating the opportunity for offenders to show remorse and acknowledge their wrongdoings while victims, or their relatives, showed a willingness to forgive. Although it is problematic to translate this form of reconciliation at the individual level to the national level, a professor of law at the University of Ghana and a commissioner to the reconciliation process in Ghana, now Supreme Court Justice Henrietta Mensa-Bonsu, reiterated the principle of multiple effects. She has argued that the creation of the conditions that increased the possibility of forgiveness constituted a positive step in the national reconciliation exercise. She stressed that since the victims and perpetrators were all part of the larger political community, the national platform created by the NRC for the entire nation contributed to national reconciliation.[43] While these impacts are difficult to measure, they are certainly among the intangible achievements of any reconciliation process.

A victim of the 24 February 1966 coup on the first day of the public hearing raised the curtains on forgiveness when he declared that he had forgiven all those who played a role in his ordeals of the past.[44] An ex-military officer, Mathew Adabuga, who was a key player in the 31 December 1981 coup that ushered the PNDC government into power, used the same platform to render his apology to the nation. He stated, "I am truly sorry, and I, from the bottom of my heart, apologize to all the people of Ghana, particularly those I offended in those sad days in our country. In the name of the Almighty God, I humbly ask for forgiveness."[45]

The most emotional instance during the NRC proceedings was when Benson Tongo Baba, a former director of the Prisons Service, appeared before the commission and openly apologized to Rexford Obeng, a victim of human rights violations during the military era in Ghana. Baba had allegedly supervised his torture at both the Ussher Fort and Nsawam Prisons and had therefore asked for forgiveness from him. Baba apologized: "I am sorry for the unfortunate incident

that fateful night, but I was only carrying out my official duty ...
I am not a bad person as people think."[46] Obeng walked to Baba
and embraced him, generating applause from the audience in the
NRC's auditorium. Also, Osahene Boakye Djan, who was the deputy
chair of the AFRC that overthrew the Limann government, rendered
an unreserved apology to Justice Dixon Kwame Afreh, a retired
Supreme Court judge, for inadvertently linking him to the execution
of eight army generals in 1979.[47]

However, these incidents occurred at the public hearings of the
NRC, raising doubts that it might have been stage-managed. At the
larger community level, experiences and attitudes differ fifteen years
after the commission's work. Largely, and unfortunately too, only
members of the opposition party, generally regarded as enemies of
the government in power in Ghanaian politics, are held accountable
for acts of corruption and for perpetrating human rights violations
and abuses. It should be emphasized that corruption, the practice
of selective justice, and the blatant abuse of power are not limited to any particular government, as is clearly shown by the NRC
Report that covered such issues from 7 March 1957 to December
1991. Rather, these infractions have occurred under every type of
government Ghana has had in the past, whether constitutional or
unconstitutional, with the former usually formed by either of the
two main political parties (NDC and NPP) and their forebears. So,
the following examples are only the most recent incidents, which
decidedly illustrate that fifteen years after the NRC's work the very
same abuses that led to its creation are still occurring in the country.

At the height of the NPP's election victory in 2017, vigilante groups
associated with the new government – including the Invincible
Forces, the Delta Force, and the Kandahar Boys – openly seized public facilities from perceived NDC supporters and also locked up state
institutions, including the National Health Insurance Scheme and
Youth Employment Authority, among others, without recourse to
the law.[48] When these incidents became embarrassing and unbearable, the president and his ministers for the interior and national
security asked the inspector general of police (IGP) to arrest members of these groups who fell afoul of the law. The IGP was reluctant
to act because, in Ghana, the position is appointed by the president
in consultation with the Council of State. The decision to consult
with the Council of State is just a formality, making the IGP position
a political office. Therefore, the Ghana police, headed by the IGP,

kowtow to the dictates of the political executive and clearly lack the independence to impartially perform their duties. Many Ghanaians believe the call from the president and the interior minister for the arrest of pro-government vigilante forces was more a gesture meant to save face for the government in light of the violence orchestrated by these partisan vigilante groups rather than a serious order to be acted upon.[49]

This reality became quite apparent after the violent by-election in the Ayawaso West Wuogon constituency, when the Ghana Police Services personnel stood idle while innocent voters, including an opposition Member of Parliament for Ningo-Prampram, were shot at and physically assaulted by pro-government party vigilantes. The Ayawaso West Wuogon constituency by-election was held on Monday, 31 January 2019, following the death of the NPP Member of Parliament, Hon. Emmanuel Kyeremateng Agyarko. Typical of most by-elections in Ghana since the beginning of the Fourth Republic, each of the two dominant political parties (i.e., the NDC and the NPP) allegedly deployed their party security forces to "protect the ballot" and intimidate their opponents. As the government White Paper – issued after submission of the report of the commission set up to investigate the brutalities that had occurred that day – stated, the national chairman of the opposition NDC, Samuel Ofosu-Ampofo, alleged the Invisible Forces (a vigilante group affiliated to the governing NPP) "had been given national security uniforms ... [and] numbering about ten at every polling station [were] shooting indiscriminately, attacking people and intimidating people [who had come out to vote]."[50]

The NDC Member of Parliament for Ningo-Prampram, Samuel Nartey George, corroborated the NDC national chairman's account and had himself endured beatings. Recordings of these violent incidents were widely circulated on social and mainstream media, prompting the president of Ghana to appoint a commission of inquiry to investigate the matter, pursuant to article 278, clause (1), paragraph (a) of the 1992 Constitution. The commission was chaired by Emile Francis Short, a former judge, an academic, and first commissioner for the Commission on Human Rights and Administrative Justice, Ghana's National Human Rights Commission. The commission of inquiry became known as the "Justice Emile Short Commission."

The commission of inquiry submitted its report to the president on 14 March 2019, and the government issued a White Paper pursuant to article 280, clause (3) of the constitution. The White Paper rejected the majority of recommendations of the Justice Emile Short Commission that was struck to investigate the violence that had occurred during the by-election because it implicated the party vigilantes associated with the government. The government's White Paper stated: "the Report failed to address the first and most critical of the terms of reference which was to make full, faithful and impartial inquiry into the circumstances of, and establish the facts, leading to the events and associated violence that occurred in the Ayawaso West Wuogon by-election on the 31st Day of January 2019."[51]

Considering about 80% of the atrocities recorded in the NRC Report were perpetrated by security services during the military regimes of the AFRC/PNDC era and that the abduction of the judges and army officers highlighted the violence from that era, we consider it an unspeakable horror when a vigilante group affiliated with the ruling party storms a lawfully constituted court and releases the accused persons. This act was roundly condemned by well-meaning Ghanaians, including the traditional ruler, Asantehene Otumfuo Osei Tutu II. Even though some of the perpetrators of this heinous act were later arrested and put before the court, they were acquitted and discharged with only a minor fine to pay because of their affiliation to the ruling party.[52] The highly respected king lamented the fact that everything is politicized in Ghana,[53] as he weighed in on the inability of the government to effectively address the vigilante menace in the country two years later, and he argued that politicization had prevented the application of the existing criminal laws to the majority of perpetrators, their identification, and arrest. As if the preceding was not enough, the recent demolition of Raymond Archer's $12 million business at the Trade Fair Center, in Accra, by national security personnel at dawn[54] smacks of the era of military regimes in Ghana's past, one of the very reasons for which the NRC was established.

IMPLICATIONS OF POST-RECONCILIATION HUMAN RIGHTS VIOLATIONS FOR THE NRC'S WORK

The TRCs' core mandate of forging national reconciliation seems to have eluded the Ghanaian reconciliation process fifteen years after its completion. This is evident in the country's current deeply divided partisan condition. Indeed, the accusation of partisan influence on the work of the NRC started the very day the NRC Act was passed.[55] The minority NDC party boycotted the passage of the act, citing political fears that it would be used to witch hunt the founder of their party.[56] As indicated earlier, the chair of the commission was in a conflict-of-interest position. Hence, the acronym for the National Reconciliation Commission, NRC, was sarcastically referred to as "Nail Rawlings Commission," in an apparent reference to the founder of the NDC, Flight Lieutenant Jerry J. Rawlings. He was the leader of both the AFRC and the PNDC regimes that accounted for over 80% of all violations investigated by the NRC, as mentioned.[57]

Different opinions started to emerge from the beginning of the NRC's work and that affected the unanimous acceptability of the commission's report. Many NDC supporters of former president Rawlings still believe the work of the NRC was meant to embarrass him. Former president Kufuor has revealed that "the motive behind the establishment of the NRC was to prevent victims of military atrocities from trying to take revenge."[58] This raises the question as to whether this was why his administration initially wanted the commission to investigate only military regimes. The contestation of victims' and perpetrators' truth following the work of the NRC continues to divide the country fifteen years later.

Further evidence that undergirds this assertion lies with two recent documentaries, *Who Killed the Judges?* aired in October 2018, and *The Scars of the Revolution*, aired in December 2019, both produced by Raymond Acquah, an employee of a private radio station (Joy FM) in Accra. Both documentaries sought to answer the questions regarding the NRC's investigation of the abduction and murder of three High Court judges and an army officer in 1981. The investigation of this case was one of the highlights of the NRC's work, which compelled the appearance of former president Rawlings at the hearings of the commission, as this crime occurred under his watch as head of the PNDC government. Discussions around the documentaries gained traction in national media and presented an opportunity for Ghanaians to re-examine the work of the NRC.

The overwhelming reactions (emotional outbursts, new revelations, and surprises on the poor implementation of the NRC's findings) left many Ghanaians more confused than educated. The release of the second documentary even led to the coming together of some victims and perceived perpetrators, unlikely bedfellows, to form a group with the aim to lobby "the government to implement all the recommendations of the NRC report." While former president Kufuor has claimed that the NRC's work brought closure, the conflicting reactions to the documentaries suggest this was not the case.[59]

It is not only the citizens who are still searching for answers over the impact of the NRC's work on Ghanaian society. The security agencies who were guilty of most of the atrocities within the commission's mandate period are busily repeating their actions that caused the establishment of the NRC in the first place. These actions do not show any evidence of the NRC's recommendations for reforms within the security services and the inculcation of human rights principles into their training. Brutalities meted out to citizens from state security forces have become a daily occurrence, as shown in multiple examples circulated in the media. In October 2019, students from the Ghana School of Law who were legally protesting a mass failure in their entrance exams from their school were met with brute force by armed police officers. Even though this action was widely condemned, no police officer has been arrested, charged, or reprimanded over that action.[60]

The following year, there was an audio recording of a civilian being brutalized by police officers in Koforidua. Aglebe Dodzi was handcuffed and beaten by General Sergeant Patrick Amoako and General Lance Corporal Isaac Marfo for stealing.[61] Since 2006, there have been attacks by security agencies on over twenty-five journalists and media employees who were doing their job.[62] These attacks have inflicted considerable harm to many journalists, leaving some with serious medical conditions, including Victor Kwawukume, who lost his sense of smell following an attack by the Ho police in the course of his lawful duty.[63] Similarly, Latif Iddrisu, a Multimedia journalist, was left with a fractured skull in July 2018 after being assaulted in front of the Criminal Investigations Department Headquarters in Accra during his station's coverage of protests by the opposition National Democratic Congress.[64]

In the end, it would seem reasonable to argue that the case of Ghana's NRC, as discussed in this chapter, validates Bonny Ibhawoh's argument that "truth commissions have fallen short of their mandate to objectively investigate human rights abuses, deliver justice to victims, and foster national reconciliation. If anything, truth commissions have served more as vehicles for legitimizing political power and reinforcing statist agendas."[65]

CONCLUSION: "HIGHLY CONTESTED
TRUTHS AND NO RECONCILIATION"

It is evident fifteen years on that the Ghanaian reconciliation encountered challenges that every other truth commission would have faced
at the time of its work. Still, it managed to achieve some remarkable
feats, including the payment of compensation, exhumation of victims' bodies and the provision of befitting burial to same, restoration
of confiscated properties to their owners, and, more importantly,
provision of opportunity for victims to ventilate their grievances.
The NRC even garnered some intangible benefits, such as some perpetrators publicly receiving forgiveness from victims. However, all
these processes were not an end in themselves. They were meant to
prepare the grounds for reconciliation and the healing of the country
as part of the processes of building a democratic Ghanaian state.
This includes recommendations for more professionalism from the
security services in dealing with citizens and the law; enforcement
agencies being just in the face of partisan pressure; and the government uplifting the economic status of citizens in order for them to
live decent and cherished lives.

Unfortunately, in the context of the NRC and its attempt to foster
rehabilitation in Ghana, these recommendations are not met. The
success of the NRC was short-lived, and the long-term goal of preventing the issues that necessitated the commission has been tenuous.
Without even discussing the impacts of ethnocentrism, nepotism, and
elitism, factors which could muddy further the reconciliation efforts
discussed above, this chapter shows how highly divisive Ghanaian
society has become, how selective our law enforcement practices
continue to be, how brute our security institutions have become
without recourse to the law, and how poverty continues to put the
vulnerable and poor in harm's way of human rights violations.

In the short term, the work of the NRC satisfied the partisan interest of quick dividends, but in the medium to long term, the NRC's
objectives remain elusive. Hence, further to Abena Asare's argument as suggested by the title of her book which assesses the work
of Ghana's NRC, *Truth Without Reconciliation*, our conclusion is
that fifteen years later, the commission's work did not lead to the
attainment of its objectives. Rather, it provided Ghana with highly
contested truths and failed to promote reconciliation. Despite
being hailed as a model of electoral democracy and democratic

peace in Africa, the recent violence and violations of human rights discussed above reveal that Ghana remains a deeply divided country characterized by selective justice, impunity, and acrimonious partisan politics. The democratic state the NRC expected to help consolidate is shaken to the foundation by political fissures in the post-reconciliation era.

NOTES

1 Pricilla Hayner, "Fifteen Truth Commissions: A Comparative Study," *Human Rights Quarterly* 16, no. 4. (1994): 597–655; Joanna Quinn, "Constraints: The Un-Doing of the Ugandan Truth Commission," *Human Rights Quarterly* 26 (2004): 401–27; Joanna Quinn, "Transitional Justice" in *Human Rights: Politics and Practice*, 3rd ed., ed. Michael Goodhart (Oxford: Oxford University Press, 2016), 389–404.

2 International Center for Transitional Justice (ICTJ), "Challenging the Conventional: Can Truth Commissions Strengthen Peace Processes?" (2014).

3 Robert Ameh, "Doing Justice after Conflict: The Case for Ghana's National Reconciliation Commission," *Canadian Journal of Law and Society* 21, no. 1 (2006): 85–109; Robert Ameh, "Uncovering Truth: Ghana's National Reconciliation Commission Excavation of Past Human Rights Abuses," *Contemporary Justice Review* 9, no. 4 (2006).

4 NRC Report, 2004. https://hmcwordpress.humanities.mcmaster.ca/ Truthcommissions/wp-content/uploads/2018/10/Ghana.NRC_.Report-FULL.pdf.

5 Seidu Alidu, "The NRC and Reconciliation in Ghana: An Assessment," *The Review of International Affairs* 1138–1139 (2010): 153–77; Seidu Alidu, David Webb, and Gavin Fairbairn, "'Truths' and 'Re-Imaging' in the Reconciliation Process," *Journal of Peace Review* 21, no. 2 (2009): 135–42; Seidu Alidu and Robert Ame, "Civil Society Activism and the National Reconciliation Commission of Ghana: A Case of the Civil Society Coalition on National Reconciliation," *Transitional Justice Review* 1, no. 1 (2012): 103–35; Robert Ame and Seidu Alidu, "Truth and Reconciliation Commissions, Restorative Justice, Peacemaking Criminology and Development," *Criminal Justice Studies* 23, no. 3 (2010): 253–68; Ameh, "Doing Justice after Conflict," 85–109; Ameh, "Uncovering Truth."

6 Republic of Ghana, *National Reconciliation Commission Act*, Act 611, section 4(f), 2002.

7 Killings, abductions, disappearances, detentions, torture, ill treatment, and seizure of properties.

8 For a more detailed discussion of this controversy, see Ameh, "Doing Justice after Conflict."

9 Priscilla Hayner, "Truth Commissions: A Schematic Review," *International Review of the Red Cross*, no. 862 (2006).

10 Hansard (Ghanaian parliamentary debates) vol. 30, no. 21, November 2001.

11 Patrick Ball, "Who Did What to Whom? Planning and Implementing A Large-Scale Human Rights Data Project," (Washington, DC: American Association for the Advancement of Science, 1996).

12 Professor Ken Attafuah, Executive Secretary of the Commission, earned a PhD in criminology from the School of Criminology, Simon Fraser University, Burnaby, British Columbia. He is, thus, well-versed in methods of scholarly research, which he brought to bear on the work of the commission.

13 NRC Report, 160.

14 NRC Report, 167–8. Figures add up to more than 100% because some victims cited multiple reasons for petitioning the commission.

15 Nahla Valji, "Ghana's National Reconciliation Commission: A Comparative Assessment," ICTJ *Occasional Paper Series* (ICTJ, 2006); R.C. Slye, "Amnesty, Truth and Reconciliation: Reflecting on the South African Amnesty Process," in *Truth V. Justice: The Morality of Truth Commissions*, ed. Robert I. Rotberg and Dennis F. Thompson (Princeton: Princeton University Press, 2000), 22–44; Ken Attafuah, "An Overview of the Ghana National Reconciliation Commission and its Relationship with the Courts," in *Criminal Law Forum* 15, no. 1–2 (2004): 125–34.

16 David Bloomfield, *On Good Terms: Clarifying Reconciliation*, Report No. 14 (Berlin: Berghof Research Centre for Constructive Conflict Management, 2006); John W. De Gruchy, *Reconciliation: Restoring Justice* (London: SCM Press, 2002).

17 Howard Zehr, *The Little Book of Restorative Justice* (Intercourse, PA: Good Books, 2002); Howard Zehr, "Retributive Justice, Restorative Justice," in *A Restorative Justice Reader: Texts, Sources, Context*, ed. Gerry Johnstone (Devon: Willan Publishing, 2003): 69–82; Roger Graef, *Why Restorative Justice? Repairing the Harm Caused by Crime* (London: Calouste Gulbenkian Foundation, 2001); James L. Gibson, "The Contribution of Truth to Reconciliation: Lessons from South Africa," in *Journal of Conflict Resolution* 50 (2006): 409–32.

18 P. van Zyl, "Unfinished Business: The Truth and Reconciliation Commission's Contribution to Justice in Post-Apartheid South Africa," in

Post-Conflict Justice, ed. M.C. Bassiouni, (New York: Transnational Publishers, 2002), 745–60; M.C. Bassiouni, "Accountability for Violations of International Humanitarian Law," in *Post-Conflict Justice*, ed. M.C. Bassiouni (New York: Transnational Publishers, 2002): 3–54.

19 William Schabas, "A Synergistic Relationship: The Sierra Leonean Truth and Reconciliation Commission and the Special Court for Sierra Leone," in *Truth Commissions and Courts: The Tension between Criminal Justice and the Search for Truth*, ed. William A. Schabas and Shane Darcy (Dordrecht, Netherlands: Kluwer Academic Publishers, 2005); John P. Lederach, *The Journey Toward Reconciliation* (Scottdale, PA: Herald Press, 1999).

20 The government White Paper on the NRC Report was signed by then minister of justice and Attorney General, Ayikoi Otoo, on 22 April 2005, www.ghana.gov.gh/dexadd/WHITE%20PAPER%20ON%20NRC.pdf (site discontinued).

21 NRC Report.

22 My Joy Online. "Faceless Persons Removed NRC Reports from Libraries, Online Portals – Prof. Attafuah," 21 December 2019, www.myjoyonline. com/news/2019/December-21st/faceless-persons-removed-nrc-reports-from-libraries-online-portals-prof-attafuah.php. While implicitly confirming that the records of the NRC have been deposited at the Balme Library, the main library at the University of Ghana, a TRC researcher, Abena Asare, mentioned "limited access and close monitor[ing] ..." while using those records. Abena Asare, *Truth Without Reconciliation* (Philadelphia, University of Pennsylvania Press, 2018): ix.

23 The victims were Godwin Mawuli Drah Goka, Yaw Brefo-Berko, Kyeremeh Gyan, Samuel Boamah Payin, Samuel Charles Aforo, and Richard Charles Koomson.

24 NRC Report, 15.

25 NRC Report, 15.

26 José Zalaquett, "Confronting Human Rights Violations Committed by former Governments: Principles Applicable and Political Constraints," in *Transitional Justice: How Emerging Democracies reckon with former Regimes*, ed. Neil J. Kritz (Washington, DC: United States Institute of Peace 1995), 10.

27 CDD-Ghana, "Never Again: Summary and Synthesis of the National Reconciliation Commission Report," (Centre for Democratic Development, 2005).

28 NRC Report.

29 Alidu, "The NRC and Reconciliation in Ghana."

30 NRC Report, 174.

31 The New Humanitarian. "Ghana: Reparations for victims of human rights abuses," 17 October, 2006, www.thenewhumanitarian.org/report/61353/ghana-reparations-victims-human-rights-abuses#:~:text=The%20US%20%241.5%20million%20in,independence%20from%20Britain%20in%201957.

32 Alidu, "The NRC and Reconciliation in Ghana," 172.

33 My Joy Online. "Kufuor Defends Establishment of National Reconciliation Commission," 24 January 2020, www.myjoyonline.com/kufuor-defends-establishment-of-national-reconciliation-commission.

34 "Four Former Heads of State, 133 Others Get Back Assets," *Daily Graphic*, Wednesday, 22 October, 2008, 1.

35 A. Ateku, "Human Rights and Ghana's Fourth Republic, 1992–2008: An Assessment" (Master of Philosophy thesis, Department of Political Science, University of Ghana, 2009), 131.

36 Zehr, "Retributive Justice, Restorative Justice"; Gerry Johnstone, ed., *A Restorative Justice Reader: Texts, Sources, Context* (Devon: Willan Publishing, 2003); G. Johnstone and Daniel W. Van Ness, eds, *Handbook of Restorative Justice* (Devon: Willan Publishing, 2007).

37 Priscilla B. Hayner, *Unspeakable Truths: Confronting State Terror and Atrocity* (New York: Routledge, 2001).

38 Mahmood Mamdani, *Citizen and Subject: Contemporary Africa and the Legacy of Late Colonialism* (Princeton University Press, 1996).

39 Bassiouni, "Accountability for Violations of International Humanitarian Law"; Schabas, "A Synergistic Relationship."

40 See Trial International's dossier on Charles Taylor's trial, accessed 2 June 2020, https://trialinternational.org/latest-post/charles-taylor/ (site discontinued).

41 See the Trial International's dossier on Foday Sankoh, accessed 2 June 2020, https://trialinternational.org/latest-post/foday-sankoh (site discontinued).

42 Chapter 11, Ugor, "Nation and Narration," this volume.

43 Henrietta Mensa-Bonsu, "Reconciliation and National Integration," in *Ghana Academy of Arts and Sciences and the Friedrich Ebert Stiftung, Public Forum on Reconciling the Nation* (Accra: British Council Hall, 2005).

44 GhanaWeb, "Reconciliation, How Did it Go?," 12 October 2004, www.ghanaweb.com/GhanaHomePage/features/artikel.php?ID=67547.

45 GhanaWeb, "Reconciliation, How Did it Go?"

46 See "Accused and Victim reconcile at Commission," 16 January 2003,

www.ghanaweb.com/GhanaHomePage/NewsArchive/Accused-And-Victim-Reconcile-At-Commission-31659.

47 See GhanaWeb, "Boakye Gyan at NRC Again," 24 November 2003, www.ghanaweb.com/GhanaHomePage/NewsArchive/Boakye-Djan-at-NRC-again-47235.

48 A. Abubakari-Sadik, "State Institutions and Political Party Vigilantism: The Case of National Health Insurance Authority (NHIA) and the Youth Employment Agency (YEA), in the Northern Region from 2009–2017" (Master of Philosophy thesis, Department of Political Science, University of Ghana, 2019).

49 Seidu Alidu, "Political Vigilante Groups and Rationalism in Ghana's Electoral Democracy," in *Contemporary Issues in Ghana: Politics, Security, Conflicts and Identity*, ed. Seidu Alidu, Awaisu Braimah, and Cletus Mbowura (Accra: Woeli Publishers, 2020): 33–51.

50 Republic of Ghana, *White Paper on the Report of the Commission of Inquiry into the Ayawaso West Wuogon Events*, WP. No.3/2019 (Accra: Government Printer, Assembly Press).

51 See GhanaWeb, "Government White Paper on Short Commission Unfortunate," www.ghanaweb.com/GhanaHomePage/NewsArchive/Government-White-Paper-on-Short-Commission-unfortunate-Aning-782558.

52 GhanaWeb, "Asantehene Questions Quality of Justice Delivery after Delta Force Saga," 21 November 2017, https://www.ghanaweb.com/GhanaHomePage/NewsArchive/Asantehene-questions-quality-of-justice-delivery-after-Delta-Force-saga-602479.

53 GhanaWeb, "Let's Boldly Deal with Lawlessness to Avert Violence in 2020 – Asantehene," 14 July 2019, https://ghheadlines.com/agency/ghana-web.

54 GhanaWeb, "Trade Fair Demolition: 'I Thought these Things Stopped even in Hell'– Franklin Cudjoe," 18 February 2020, www.ghanaweb.com/GhanaHomePage/NewsArchive/Trade-Fair-Demolition-I-thought-these-things-stopped-even-in-hell-Franklin-Cudjoe-869740.

55 Alidu, "The NRC and Reconciliation in Ghana."

56 Ibid.

57 Ameh, "Doing Justice after Conflict."

58 My Joy Online, "Kufuor Defends Establishment of National Reconciliation."

59 Ibid.

60 See Delali Adogla-Bessa, "Police Brutality against Law Students Totally

Unacceptable – Gov't," CNR Citi Newsroom, 8 October 2019, https://cit-
inewsroom.com/2019/10/police-brutality-against-law-students-totally-
unacceptable-govt/.

61 See CNR Citi Newsroom, "Victim Brutalized by Police Officers at
    Koforidua Speaks Out [Audio]," 2 October 2019, https://citinewsroom.
    com/2019/10/victim-brutalised-by-police-officers-at-koforidua-breaks-
    silence-audio/.

62 See Jonas Nyabor, "Police/Military Brutalities on Journalists: No
    Prosecutions since 2006," CNR Citi Newsroom, 19 March 2019.

63 Nyabor, "Police/Military Brutalities on Journalists."

64 Ibid.

65 Bonny Ibhawoh, "Human Rights and the Politics of Regime Legitimation
    in Africa: From Rights Commissions to Truth Commissions," in
    Expanding Perspectives on Human Rights in Africa, ed. M. Raymond
    Izarali, Oliver Masakure, and Bonny Ibhawoh (New York: Routledge,
    2019), 21–38.

The Long-Term Legacies of Transitional Justice: Understanding the Paradox of Peace in Sierra Leone

Gearoid Millar

It has been quite some time since I started studying the Sierra Leone Truth and Reconciliation Commission (TRC). After comparing the Sierra Leone TRC to the case of South Africa for my master's thesis, I developed a PhD proposal to conduct a much more in-depth study of the role of cultural and religious ritual in the public hearings process administered by the Sierra Leonean TRC. I started my PhD studies in 2006, two years after the commission submitted its final report. As I described recently in a paper reflecting on my research methodology during that project,[1] this initial proposal proved unworkable on the ground, and I ended up instead focusing more generally on local non-elite experiences of the TRC, and its public hearing processes in particular.[2] Over the past decade, since completing my twelve months of fieldwork for that project over two trips between 2007 and 2009, I have returned to Sierra Leone for further research projects, written many peer-reviewed articles about the case, and contributed (I like to think) quite actively to the scholarly work on transitional justice and peacebuilding to which TRCs are thought to contribute.

But it is only in the last few years that I have had the time to reflect on the longer-term legacies of peacebuilding and transitional justice in Sierra Leone and on the specific contribution (or the lack thereof) of the TRC within that. As discussed below, I have written quite extensively about local experiences of the TRC in the short- and medium-term (five to ten years) aftermath of the conflict. Much of what I wrote was quite negative about those experiences and pessimistic about the sustainability of peace in the country. These publications echoed the tone of the findings from scholars such as Tim Kelsall and Rosalind Shaw,[3] which described the failure of the TRC's truth-telling process to connect with local communities and promote its stated goal of "social harmony and reconciliation." Indeed, when combined with the emergence of ethnic blaming and scapegoating during election periods in the years following the conflict, I certainly was not optimistic that Sierra Leone would remain at peace.

However, we have now passed the twentieth anniversary of the end of the war, and for all the negative findings related to the impacts and experiences of the TRC, we have not seen a return to mass organized violence. Even as the country has clearly failed to "build back better" as resilience authors would hope,[4] as it continues to float along the bottom of the UN's Human Development Index (in 2022 it was 181st out of 191 ranked countries),[5] as it has experienced repeated disruptions and disasters (such as the Ebola crisis in 2014/2015 and the Freetown mudslide in 2017), as hints of political impropriety have stirred protest and dissent,[6] as the country has experienced the unknown impacts of the Covid-19 pandemic,[7] and, most recently, as protests have emerged in response to the cost of living crisis,[8] peace has generally been maintained. In line with this sustained period of peace which was, of course, the ultimate aim of the TRC, a substantial contribution to the literature by Lyn Graybill argues that the claims of more critical scholars regarding the failures of the TRC to connect with local communities and promote reconciliation were misplaced.[9] Instead, Graybill has argued that the TRC was quite successful in generating reconciliation and peace within the country, a conclusion which runs counter to my own findings in the past. This chapter, therefore, seeks to address this apparent paradox and functions, as a result, as a somewhat self-reflective and self-critical reconsideration of my past work.

In the pages that follow, I first summarize some of my own findings regarding the TRC and articulate why these drove deep concerns about the sustainability of peace in Sierra Leone. I then turn to a discussion of the paradox between the apparent failures of peacebuilding and transitional justice in Sierra Leone within an economic and political context seemingly ripe to inspire further conflict, and the somehow prevailing peace. In this section, I also discuss the inherent limitations of assessing individual transitional justice or peacebuilding processes, such as the TRC, which are always interacting and articulating with other interventions, and argue that more scholars must acknowledge and accept the ongoing turn toward complexity theory for understanding the long-term legacies of post-conflict interventions writ large. But this section also makes clear the difficulty of observing and understanding such complex interactions between interventions and over time. It is in this context that the final section concludes by promoting Ethnographic Peace Research (EPR) as one way to approach this challenge.

LIMITS AND FRICTIONS OF THE SIERRA LEONE TRC

The TRC model has been developing and changing now for decades. Early truth commissions in Latin America were largely tasked with investigating and recording the truth in order to promote *acknowledgment* of the past abuses of the state, or what Martha Minow has called an "affirmation of atrocity."[10] In these cases, where many victims had been disappeared with no acknowledgment by the perpetrators, such acknowledgment of wrongdoing was thought to be a form of justice in and of itself, and it was in the light of these early truth commissions that the "right to truth" became a core demand of human rights advocates at the turn of the century.[11] In short, in these early cases, truth seeking was thought to lead to justice because it overcame impunity by uncovering the truth about what had previously been denied. However, following the ground-breaking South African case, this process of *truth seeking* was largely supplanted by more performative processes of *truth telling* within the setting of public hearings.[12] These performances were theorized to provide a new form of restorative justice to victims and perpetrators of violence that went beyond simple acknowledgment of abuses on the part of the state and promoted what Arie Nadler and Nurit Shnabel called "socioemotional" healing.[13]

The aims of the TRC fell somewhere between the two. As clearly spelled out in its 2004 report, these were: (1) "to create an impartial historical record of violations and abuses of human rights and international humanitarian law"; (2) to "promote healing and reconciliation"; and (3) "to prevent a repetition of the violations and abuses suffered."[14] The TRC therefore sought to provide a clear record of the past violence and, through public truth-telling performances, promote socioemotional healing for the purpose of sustainable peace. These goals, in short, were interrelated, reflecting the long theorized positive interaction of truth (an impartial record), reconciliation (often also associated with healing), and peace (or non-repetition of violence).[15] But as even the South African TRC recognized, there is no single and universal definition of "truth" in post-conflict situations,[16] nor are there clear or universal definitions of healing, reconciliation, or peace. Indeed, conceptions of what these three concepts mean clearly differ, however marginally or substantially, between contexts and cultures.[17] Further, it is this difference between the concepts, which planners and practitioners of TRCs hold in their heads and those local "beneficiaries" hold in theirs, that undermined the potential positive influences of the Sierra Leone TRC.[18]

A key reason these conceptual discrepancies can undermine the potential positive contribution of TRCs is that the communication that frames a TRC's work (shaped by the narrative of the intervening actors) interacts with the worldviews of local communities to generate *expectations* among beneficiaries, which may diverge substantially from what the intervening parties consider the proper implementation of the TRC. As I have described in multiple publications, in the case of Sierra Leonean TRC, there were consistent messages, primarily through the radio but also in newspapers and on posters promoting the process, that the Disarmament, Demobilisation and Reintegration (DDR) program had helped the perpetrators, and now the TRC had come to "help" the victims.

But the DDR program had provided former combatants with housing, distributed economic resources, and trained them for new careers in the post-conflict society. When the radio programs said that the TRC too had come to help, local people expected something similar; some form of housing, schooling, or direct economic benefit. As these expectations were then not met, and indeed, the TRC had no funding or mandate to make such provision, the actual implementation of the TRC – public performances of truth telling – fell far short of their expectations.[19] This mismatch between expectation and provision, driven largely by miscommunication and conceptual differences about what was required, served to undermine the positive contribution of the TRC.

The DDR process was not the only source of confusion. Indeed, the ongoing operations of the Special Court for Sierra Leone (SCSL) and those of scores of non-governmental organizations (NGOs) operating in the country in the aftermath of the conflict similarly served to confuse local expectations. The relationship between the SCSL and the TRC has been widely documented. Some argued that they had a synergistic relationship,[20] while others refute this and argued instead that there was considerable confusion between the mandates of the two institutions.[21] My findings certainly support this latter argument and strongly indicate that local people could not disentangle the goals and processes of the two institutions, instead becoming confused about what each intended to achieve and the processes they planned to administer.[22]

Similarly, the work of the many different international NGOs operating in the post-conflict period, providing relief in the form of medical services, housing, education, food, and so forth, caused a "great amount of misunderstanding among non-elites" between what other postwar processes did and what the TRC accomplished.[23] As I noted at the time, while the TRC's radio announcements and publicity campaign had done a very good job of informing local non-elites that it was coming to "help" them, it had done a terrible job of clarifying how that would be accomplished and the actual services it would or would not provide. This failure led, quite predictably, to increased expectations that then went unmet by the process itself.

The story is, of course, a bit more complicated than this. Some people did experience the TRC's processes positively and even lauded it for its positive effect within local communities. However, among my interviewees, those who reported such positive experiences, who felt that the TRC process had helped them or their country find peace and reconciliation, were not local non-elites, but rather were members of the relatively small local educated and English-speaking elite. The people who reported positive experiences of the TRC were overwhelmingly those who had either experienced some form of economic or career benefits from the processes, or who had participated in its training and sensitization activities through their work with religious organizations or in civil society.[24] So, for example, while local non-elites knew little of and had little interaction with the TRC, except what was broadcast via the radio adverts about its coming to "help" them, elites were often exactly those who were "able to take advantage of the large influx of funds that followed the war, gaining jobs, additional training, increased opportunities and additional sources of status from the peacebuilding process."[25] As such, the peacebuilding process, and the TRC, as one element of that, very much "helped" local elites, while generally providing little of value to local non-elites. Local elites were, therefore, much more likely to experience it positively.

Although these economic and career factors are very important in explaining the divergence between elite and non-elite experiences of the TRC, they do not tell the full story, and in fact, they can serve to conceal more fundamental problems with the truth-telling process. Why was truth telling not experienced – as the international experts theorized – as cathartic in itself, as a driver of "socioemotional reconciliation"?[26] Answering these questions requires closer scrutiny of religious and cultural dynamics specific to Sierra Leone.

The powerful faith of the Sierra Leonean people, for example, played an extremely interesting and underappreciated role in local experiences of the TRC process. The overwhelming belief in a power beyond the control of mere mortals certainly enhanced local willingness to forgive and reconcile with former perpetrators, but it also undermined the value of man-made psychosocial solutions to promote peace. To the vast majority of local "beneficiaries" I engaged with, whether Christian or Muslim, God had brought the war, and God had brought the peace.[27] They saw little value in the process the TRC implemented after religious leaders (pastors, priests and imams) had already been preaching peace and forgiveness for years prior to the TRC. Most, in short, had accepted forgiveness and reconciliation as their responsibility as Christians or Muslims and largely saw the efforts of the TRC as alien, imposed and, ultimately, unnecessary.

Similarly, at perhaps an even deeper level than their religious faith, most of my interviewees expressed unease about the process of truth telling and disclosing stories about violence committed or experienced during the conflict. This unease is rooted in what has been described by scholars as the "aesthetic of secrecy" by which Sierra Leoneans control information and knowledge. William Murphy, for example, describes how this operates in relation to spaces, some of which are assigned for secret knowledge and secret communication, while others are assigned for public or non-secret knowledge or events. As he explained, "The archetypal spatial contrast" in Sierra Leone "is the contrast between the 'village' as a public domain and the 'forest' as a hidden domain of secret ritual and clandestine meetings."[28]

This archetype is not only about space. It is internalized within individuals and frames social interaction in Sierra Leone, serving as a structure within which everyday communication and practice are performed. Within this aesthetic, knowledge is conceived as powerful, and keeping knowledge secret increases that power. As such, status and power are based on the control of information.[29] In a society where secrecy is of the utmost importance, "[a]ccess to secrets can mark the success or failure of individuals"[30] and, as a result, people do not divulge sensitive information needlessly. Into this environment waded the TRC, with assumptions about truth telling and disclosure as catharsis that were dissociated from the culture into which the process was injected.

These various dynamics, in the end, meant that experiences among the local non-elites diverged substantially from what is expected in response to TRC processes. The interaction between the international conceptions that dominate reconciliation and TRC theory on the one hand and the local conceptions of justice, reconciliation, and peace within the context of Sierra Leone on the other led to outcomes unexpected by the funders, planners, and implementers of that intervention. Theorists often describe a linear causal chain leading from acknowledgment, through apology, to forgiveness and reconciliation.[31] But local non-elites who participated in my study described much more complex dynamics than this.

As noted, many articulated a confusion about the process and how it did or didn't relate to the dozens of other transitional justice and peacebuilding interventions ongoing, parallel to the TRC.[32] Others just felt it was not pertinent to them, something that happened in the big towns for the Big Men, and with little influence on their lives. And still others described their dissatisfaction about the kind of "help" the TRC provided, and often anger at the wasted money spent talking at people instead of providing much-needed resources.[33] Most tellingly, there were those who felt it was an actively damaging or re-traumatizing experience. As I have described, some of my interviewees described the process as "pouring hot water over your head" or adding "pepper in my wound."[34] Although theorists of truth and reconciliation processes such as TRCs assume that audiences will be eager to express themselves and divulge their experiences, and that the process will be experienced as psychologically cathartic, this was simply not the case in Sierra Leone. These findings evidence, in short, the failures of the Sierra Leonean TRC.

THE PARADOX OF PEACE

At the time I was completing my PhD (in 2010), and then while drafting many of the publications cited above (between 2010 and 2014), these various findings painted a worrying picture. It seemed clear that the TRC had not managed to create the form of healing and reconciliation it had been designed to achieve. Further, during two later periods of fieldwork in 2012 and 2013 for a study examining the local experiences of a large development project that similarly claimed to be building the foundations of a sustainable peace in Sierra Leone (via investment, training, and jobs), I became even more concerned as I observed growing tensions and increasing inequalities in the country. This second project evidenced even more the way international interventions distributed opportunities and resources unevenly,[35] instigated conflict between local groups,[36] and implemented projects with unpredictable and disruptive outcomes driven by their misunderstanding of local lifeways and knowledge systems.[37] These findings also echo those of others who voiced concerns about the ongoing inequality and poverty a decade ago,[38] or noted worrying levels of misunderstanding and misjudgment on the part of development interventions.[39] Critical perspectives of intervention in Sierra Leone are, in short, hardly rare.

But this is where we find the paradox. For more than a decade now, it has seemed that Sierra Leone has been edging further into socio-economic and political territory that one would associate with rising chances of violent conflict. Just a few years after the end of the conflict, and along with the rest of the world, the country went through the economic tremors driven by the 2008/2009 financial crisis and the commensurate rise in the prices of food, fuel, and feed throughout the developing world.[40] Shortly after that, in 2014/2015 came the massive and unequal health and socio-economic impacts of Ebola,[41] and then in 2017, the Freetown mudslide, which again evidenced the inadequacies of the post-conflict infrastructure development and the inequality of housing and social security provision in the state.[42] More recently, tensions have developed between the political parties regarding the 2018 elections and the questionable anti-corruption reforms,[43] the unanswered questions regarding the true impact of the Covid-19 pandemic, and, as of this writing, the ongoing concerns regarding the cost of living crisis. This has all occurred within an economic context that has not substantially improved for the majority of people since the violence ended in 2002 and within a regional context of increasing precarity and insecurity.[44]

As noted above, Graybill seemed to find in the TRC a positive, peace-promoting institution that connected to the deeply held religious beliefs that dominate within both the Christian and Muslim communities in Sierra Leone. To Graybill, this consistency with the beliefs within faith communities allowed the TRC and its truth-telling process to inspire healing and reconciliation.[45] Graybill also noted the positive complementarity of the more locally driven *Fambul Tok* process, which encouraged "people at the grassroots to identify and draw upon their own traditions and resources to make themselves whole again."[46] But her narrative, which presents the TRC overall as a very positive influence and ignores many of the more provocative or problematic findings I have described above, generally avoids the paradox of peace in Sierra Leone by placing the TRC as one of the key agents of peacebuilding, as one of the foundations on which sustainable peace was built and, therefore, one of the primary reasons the various problems that have befallen the state in the post-conflict period have not resulted in further violence. To agree with Graybill, however, would be to ignore far too much of what I heard and saw in Sierra Leone, from the many survivors of and witnesses to violence, who contributed to my research. In the light of my own findings, the notion that the TRC was foundational to the sustained peace we have witnessed seem untenable.

A better explanation is found, I think, in the complex and longer-term *interactions* of the many post-conflict interventions that were applied in Sierra Leone and the non-linear and unpredictable ways that these many interventions contribute to post-conflict dynamics. By *non-linear* here I mean that we cannot assume, for example, that small interventions have small impacts (as they may, in complex systems, have larger than expected impacts), or that large interventions will have large impacts (as they may indeed have none). We may also not be able to assume that an intervention directly impacts an "outcome," as it may achieve such influence indirectly, through intermediary mechanisms and unpredictable pathways. While others have noted the positive effects of implementing parallel processes in post-conflict contexts, most specifically the very influential *Transitional Justice in Balance*,[47] my own perspective on this, as noted above, had always been that the

parallel implementation of various projects had caused confusion
and unmet expectations.[48] Others have similarly noted the down-
sides of such parallel implementation, with Cedric De Coning and
Karsten Friis, for example, lamenting the challenges of "coherence
and coordination" in such situations.[49]

However, in my recent effort to scrutinize this apparent paradox of peace in Sierra Leone, I have had to rethink this. I have
recognized, as a result, that although parallel implementation may
have negative implications for the local experiences of individual
processes (and I believe this was certainly the case for the TRC),
the complex collective influence of the various components of comprehensive peacebuilding interventions (that is, peacebuilding *writ
large*) may nonetheless have positive effects over the *long-term* due
to the non-linear interactions between interventions.

I realized, in short, that looking at the expectations and experiences of processes and programs individually, dissociated from the
interactions they inspire in the minds of "beneficiaries" (in the form
of unpredictable expectations and experiences), will always lead to
incoherent interpretations of what is happening more broadly within
post-conflict environments. Recent work in peacebuilding has been
making a forceful turn toward recognizing the non-linear, and therefore unpredictable, effects of intervention projects.[50] A key lesson of
such literature is the need to realize that through positive and negative feedback mechanisms, small inputs can have large outcomes,
large inputs can have minimal outcomes, positive effects from one
project can result in negative effects overall, and that there is even
the potential for negative effects from one or more projects to lead
nonetheless to positive effects overall.

Complex systems, in short, are contexts in which system elements
self-organize in response to the constant interactions between elements, leading in the end to emergent system properties that cannot
be predicted. What, in an evaluation of a single intervention, appear
to be negative outcomes, may, in the broader picture, result in positive
or peace-promoting influences through some unknown mechanisms
of interaction with other system elements, or just have little or no
effect in the grander scheme of things. Unfortunately, however, our
methodologies for observing, examining, and unpacking all these
interactions are extremely limited and very little thinking thus far
has been committed to the issue of assessing the long-term legacies of
peace interventions.[51] This remains one of the central problems for

transitional justice and peacebuilding scholarship and evaluation. In the long term, if the fields of peacebuilding and transitional justice fail to grapple with this challenge – that is, to develop methodologies that can better understand and assess the interactions between different post-conflict interventions within complex environments – they will continue to be unable to properly understand or assess their impacts or to propose and implement improved interventions.

CONCLUSION:
ASSESSING LONG-TERM LEGACIES WITH EPR

This essay was inspired by two significant realizations on my part. The first was recognition of the stark contrast between my own findings regarding the local experiences of the Sierra Leonean TRC and the more recent arguments made by Lyn Graybill,[52] as noted above. While my own study found the TRC to be redundant at best and provocative at worst, Graybill has argued that it fostered healing, reconciliation, and peace. Certainly, part of this divergence is found in the methods we each deployed, in that my own study relied primarily on in-depth interviews with local non-elites and long-term participant observation, while Graybill's data comes overwhelmingly from interviews with elites supplemented by secondary data from surveys. These different methodological choices led, not surprisingly, to very different findings. The second realization, however, was that my own rather pessimistic findings (both in my study of the TRC and then later of the large development project), which I had formerly been quite confident about, were undermined by the fact that peace in Sierra Leone has been maintained now, in a general sense, for more than twenty years. While Graybill's findings are consistent with this sustained peace, if my own findings are correct, then the peace itself presents us with a paradox.

As I developed this essay, however, it became clear that the problem may not be with my findings, or with Graybill's findings, but with any research that limits its focus to single temporally bounded interventions. As the turn to complexity theory has made clear, any intervention into a post-conflict society enters into an already complex socio-economic, political, cultural, spiritual, and geographic space that is almost always already host to dozens, if not hundreds, of other interventions implemented for related or tangential purposes. If we accept this as a given, then it should be assumed that

any specific project, program, or process will interact in unpredictable and unplannable ways with the many others already or soon
to be operating within that environment. Non-linear interactions,
positive and negative feedback loops, and the nature of complex
systems as constantly and dynamically self-organizing, dictate,
therefore, that there will be no clear causal relationships such as
those often assumed to pertain between acknowledgment, apology,
forgiveness, reconciliation, and sustainable peace. The apparent paradox, in short, is resolved when we view the problem through the
lens of complexity.

But this does raise substantial questions about exactly how scholars can observe and understand the impact of transitional justice
and peacebuilding interventions on peace writ large and over time.
In response, I would forcefully promote EPR as one component
of a much-needed methodological revolution in the field. EPR can
allow – in fact, demands – that local experiences of specific peace
intervention be taken seriously by engaging specifically not with
elites but with local non-elites who are the supposed beneficiaries of
most transitional justice and peacebuilding interventions. Further,
EPR requires that scholars understand the socio-cultural context
into which the intervention (as well as scholars themselves) are intervening, or what I have elsewhere called "ethnographic preparation."
Finally, it requires that scholars question their own conceptions and
understandings of the supposed aims of intervention (i.e., of "justice," "peace," "dignity," "security," "development," etc.), and
engage in what anthropologists describe as an "emic" or insider
perspective to attempt to understand, in essence, how local actors
perceive the interventions imposed upon them.[53]

Through these various strengths, EPR has already proven a valuable approach that can provide a robust methodology by which
transitional justice and peacebuilding scholars can examine and
understand the local experiences and impacts of specific interventions.[54] But I would extend this and argue that it should be a primary
tool for studying the impacts of interventions writ large and over
the long term. As I have described in much more depth elsewhere,[55]
EPR would be particularly valuable in this role for a number of reasons. First, EPR is a flexible approach incorporating a variety of
methods as needed in response to findings on the ground. As such,
it is suitable for collecting different forms of data pertinent to the
impacts and effects of many different forms of intervention. Second,

EPR is grounded in the pursuit of thick descriptions of interventions within complex socio-cultural contexts. As such, it is well suited to identifying and analyzing the complex interactions between intervention effects at the level of institutions, policies, practices, and experiences. Third, EPR scholars must engage closely with local actors in post-conflict contexts, building rapport and establishing trust. EPR, therefore, is very well suited to developing the kind of relationships that can sustain across time and allow evaluation of the long-term legacy of transitional justice and peacebuilding interventions. Although the challenges to understanding the long-term legacy of intervention writ large are substantial, EPR may provide a valuable tool in response.

NOTES

1 Gearoid Millar, "Ethnographic Peace Research: The Underappreciated Benefits of Long-Term Fieldwork," *International Peacekeeping* 25, no. 5 (2018): 653–76.
2 Gearoid Millar, *An Ethnographic Approach to Peacebuilding: Understanding Local Experiences in Transitional States* (London: Routledge, 2014).
3 Tim Kelsall, "Truth, Lies, Ritual: Preliminary Reflections on the Truth and Reconciliation Commission," *Human Rights Quarterly* 27, no. 2 (2005): 361–91; Rosalind Shaw, "Memory Frictions: Localizing the Truth and Reconciliation Commission in Sierra Leone," *International Journal of Transitional Justice* 1, no. 2 (2007): 207.
4 Sandeeka Mannakkara and Suzanne Wilkinson, "Build Back Better Principles for Post-Disaster Structural Improvements," *Structural Survey* 31, no. 4 (2013): 314–27.
5 UN Development Programme (UNDP), *Human Development Report 2022. Uncertain Times, Unsettled Lives: Shaping our Future in a Transforming World* (New York: UNDP, 2022), 274.
6 Institute for Peace and Security Studies, *Peace and Security Report: Sierra Leone, Conflict Insight* (2019).
7 New York Times, *A Covid Mystery in Africa*, podcast, 31:30, 7 April 2022, www.nytimes.com/2022/04/07/podcasts/the-daily/covid-cases-africa.html.
8 Umaru Fofana and Cooper Inveen, "Freetown in Shock after Dozens Killed in Sierra Leone Protests," Reuters, 11 August 2022, www.reuters.com/world/africa/six-police-officers-killed-sierra-leone-protests-police-head-2022-08-11/.

9 Lyn S. Graybill, *Religion, Tradition, and Restorative Justice in Sierra Leone* (South Bend: University of Notre Dame Press, 2017).

10 Martha Minow, *Between Vengeance and Forgiveness: Facing History after Genocide and Mass Violence* (Boston: Beacon Press, 1998), 4.

11 Thomas M. Antkowiak, "Truth as Right and Remedy in International Human Rights Experience," *Michigan Journal of International Law* 23, no. 4 (2002): 977–1013.

12 Gearoid Millar, "Performative Memory and Re-Victimization: Truth-Telling and Provocation in Sierra Leone," *Memory Studies* 8, no. 2 (2015): 242–54.

13 Ruti G. Teitel, "Transitional Justice Genealogy," *Harvard Human Rights Journal* 16 (2003): 78; B.A. Leebaw, "Legitimation or Judgement? South Africa's Restorative Approach to Transitional Justice," *Polity* 36, no. 1 (2003): 23–51; Arie Nadler and Nurit Shnabel, "Instrumental and Socioemotional Paths to Intergroup Reconciliation and the Needs-Based Model of Socioemotional Reconciliation," in *The Social Psychology of Intergroup Reconciliation*, ed. Arie Nadler, Thomas E. Malloy, and Jeffrey D. Fisher (Oxford: Oxford University Press, 2008), 37–56.

14 Sierra Leone Truth and Reconciliation Commission, *Witness to Truth: Final Report of the TRC* (Accra: Graphic Packaging, 2004): 24–5.

15 David Mendeloff, "Truth-Seeking, Truth-Telling, and Postconflict Peacebuilding: Curb the Enthusiasm?" *International Studies Review* 6, no. 3 (2004): 355–80.

16 Yasmin Naqvi, "The Right to Truth in International Law: Fact or Fiction?" *International Review of the Red Cross* 88, no. 886 (2006): 254.

17 Gearoid Millar, "Local Evaluations of Justice through Truth Telling in Sierra Leone: Postwar Needs and Transitional Justice," *Human Rights Review* 12, no. 4 (2011): 517.

18 Gearoid Millar, "Between Western Theory and Local Practice: Cultural Impediments to Truth-Telling in Sierra Leone," *Conflict Resolution Quarterly* 29, no. 2 (2011): 177–99; Gearoid Millar, "Disaggregating Hybridity: Why Hybrid Institutions Do Not Produce Predictable Experiences of Peace," *Journal of Peace Research* 51, no. 4 (2014): 501–14.

19 Gearoid Millar, "Expectations and Experiences of Peacebuilding in Sierra Leone: Parallel Peacebuilding Processes and Compound Friction," *International Peacekeeping* 20, no. 2 (2013): 195.

20 William A. Schabas, "Conjoined Twins of Transitional Justice? The Sierra Leone Truth and Reconciliation Commission and the Special Court," *Journal of International Criminal Justice* 2, no. 4 (2004): 1099.

21 Graybill, *Religion, Tradition, and Restorative Justice in Sierra Leone*, 43.

22 Millar, "Expectations and Experiences of Peacebuilding in Sierra Leone," 194.

23 Gearoid Millar, "Respecting Complexity: Compound Friction and Unpredictability in Peacebuilding," in *Peacebuilding and Friction: Global and Local Encounters in Post-Conflict Societies*, ed. Annika Björkdahl, Kristine Höglund, Gearoid Millar, Jaïr van der Lijn, Willemijn Verkoren (Abingdon: Routledge, 2016), 40.

24 Gearoid Millar, "Local Evaluations of Truth Telling in Sierra Leone: Getting at 'Why' Though a Qualitative Case Study Analysis," *International Journal of Transitional Justice* 4, no. 4 (2010).

25 Millar, "Local Evaluations of Truth Telling in Sierra Leone," 493.

26 Nadler and Shnabel, "Instrumental and Socioemotional Paths to Intergroup Reconciliation."

27 Gearoid Millar, "'Ah Lef ma Case fo God': Religious Belief and Personal Autonomy in Sierra Leone's Postwar Reconciliation," *Peace and Conflict: Journal of Peace Psychology* 18, no. 2 (2012): 136.

28 William P. Murphy, "Creating the Appearance of Consensus in Mende Political Discourse," *American Anthropologist* 92, no. 1 (1990): 27.

29 Millar, "Between Western Theory and Local Practice," 186–7.

30 C.H. Bledsoe and K.M. Robey, "Arabic Literacy and Secrecy among the Mende of Sierra Leone," *Man* 21, no. 2 (1986): 205.

31 Ronald J. Fisher, "Social-Psychological Processes in Interactive Conflict Analysis and Reconciliation," *Reconciliation, Justice, and Coexistence*, ed. Mohammed Abu-Nimer (Lanham: Lexington Books, 2001), 37.

32 Millar, "Expectations and Experiences of Peacebuilding in Sierra Leone."

33 Millar, "Performative Memory and Re-Victimization."

34 Millar, "Expectations and Experiences of Peacebuilding in Sierra Leone," 196.

35 Gearoid Millar, "'We Have No Voice for That': Land Rights, Power, and Gender in Rural Sierra Leone," *Journal of Human Right* 14, no. 4 (2015): 445–62; Gearoid Millar, "Investing in Peace?: Foreign Direct Investment as Economic Justice in Sierra Leone," *Third World Quarterly* 36, no. 9 (2015): 1700–16; Gearoid Millar, "For Whom Do Local Peace Processes Function? Maintaining Control through Conflict Management," *Cooperation and Conflict* 52, no. 3 (2017): 293–308.

36 Gearoid Millar, "Local Experiences of Liberal Peace: Marketization and Emerging Conflict Dynamics in Sierra Leone," *Journal of Peace Research* 53, no. 4 (2016): 569–81.

37 Gearoid Millar, "Knowledge and Control in the Contemporary Land
    Rush: Making Local Land Legible and Corporate Power Applicable in
    Rural Sierra Leone," *Journal of Agrarian Change* 16, no. 2 (2016): 206–
    24; Gearoid Millar, "Co-opting Authority and Privatizing Force in Rural
    Africa: Ensuring Corporate Power over Land and People," *Rural
    Sociology* 83, no. 4 (2018): 749–71.
38 Rosalind Shaw, "Linking Justice with Reintegration? Ex-Combatants and
    the Sierra Leone Experiment," *Localizing Transitional Justice:
    Interventions and Priorities after Mass Violence*, ed. Rosalind Shaw, Lars
    Waldorf, and Pierre Hazan (Stanford: Stanford University Press, 2010):
    111–32.
39 Augustin Palliere and Hubert Cochet, "Large Private Agricultural Projects
    and Job Creation: From Discourse to Reality. Case Study in Sella Limba,
    Sierra Leone," *Land Use Policy* 76 (2018).
40 Henk-Jan Brinkman et al., "High Food Prizes and the Global Financial
    Crisis have Reduced Access to Nutritious Food and Worsened Nutritional
    Status and Health," *The Journal of Nutrition* 140, no. 1 (2010): 153–61.
41 Emma-Louise Anderson and Alexander Beresford, "Infectious Injustice:
    The Political Foundations of the Ebola Crisis in Sierra Leone," *Third
    World Quarterly* 37, no. 3 (2016): 468–86.
42 Kenneth Lynch, Etienne Nel, and Tony Binns, "'Transforming Freetown':
    Dilemmas of Planning and Development in a West African City," *Cities*
    101 (2020).
43 Institute for Peace and Security Studies, *Peace and Security Report*, 11.
44 Robert B. Lloyd, "Ungoverned Spaces and Regional Insecurity: The Case
    of Mali," SAIS *Review of International Affairs* 36, no. 1 (2016): 133–41.
45 Graybill, *Religion, Tradition, and Restorative Justice in Sierra Leone.*
46 Lyn S. Graybill, "Traditional Practices and Reconciliation in Sierra Leone:
    The Effectiveness of Fambul Tok," *Conflict Trends* 3 (2010): 41–7.
47 Tricia D. Olsen, Leigh A. Payne, and Andrew G. Reiter, *Transitional
    Justice in Balance: Comparing Processes, Weighing Efficacy* (Washington
    DC: United States Institute of Peace, 2010).
48 Millar, "Expectations and Experiences of Peacebuilding in Sierra Leone,"
    189–203.
49 Cedric De Coning and Karsten Friis, "Coherence and Coordination: The
    Limits of the Comprehensive Approach," *Journal of International
    Peacekeeping* 15, no. 1–2 (2011): 243–72.
50 De Coning and Friis, "Coherence and Coordination"; David Chandler,
    "Peacebuilding and the Politics of Non-Linearity: Rethinking 'Hidden'
    Agency and 'Resistance,'" *Peacebuilding* 1, no. 1 (2013): 17–32; Gearoid

Millar, "Toward a Trans-Scalar Peace System: Challenging Complex Global Conflict Systems," *Peacebuilding* (2020); Gearoid Millar, "Ambition and Ambivalence: Reconsidering Positive Peace as a Trans-Scalar Peace System," *Journal of Peace Research* 58, no. 4 (2021).

51 Sukanya Podder, "Thinking about the Legacy of Peacebuilding Programmes," *Peace Review* 33, no. 1 (2021).

52 Graybill, *Religion, Tradition, and Restorative Justice in Sierra Leone.*

53 Birgit Bräuchler and Philipp Naucke, "Peacebuilding and Conceptualisations of the Local," *Social Anthropology* 26, no. 4 (2017): 432.

54 Gearoid Millar, ed., *Ethnographic Peace Research: Approaches and Tensions* (Basingstoke: Palgrave Macmillan, 2018).

55 Gearoid Millar, "Coordinated Ethnographic Peace Research: Assessing Complex Peace Interventions Writ Large and Over Time," *Peacebuilding* 8, no. 3 (2021).

Rebuilding Social Cohesion in Post-Genocide Rwanda

Jean Nepo Ndahimana

Since 1959, Rwanda has experienced human rights violations that escalated to genocide in 1994. The period between 1959 and 1990 was characterized by extreme violence against the Tutsi community. The persecution of the Tutsi has a deep history in Rwanda. The first republic, which ended in 1973, saw the beginning of massacres of Tutsi, and such violence and political persecution of the Tutsi continued into the second republic. None of the suspects of those killings were brought to justice or received punishment at that time, and no effort was made by successive governments to bring to justice those involved in the atrocities. The years of 1990 to 1994 constituted a period of extreme human rights violations in Rwanda, particularly from April 1994 to July 1994, when more than one million people perished within three months.

This period marked a conflict defined as the "liberation war" between the Rwandan Patriotic Army (RPA-Inkotanyi), the military wing of Front patriotique rwandaise (FPR-Inkotanyi), and the government forces (Forces armées rwandaises). This liberation war ended in July 1994 with the victory of RPA-Inkotanyi. On 19 July 1994, a new government of National Unity was formed, marking the official end of the war. The 1994 genocide devastated the Rwandan state socially, politically, and economically. In rebuilding the state after the genocide, establishing security, order, justice, and economic and political development policies and initiatives were among the country's main priorities. As with other societies that have undergone such horrific experiences, the Rwandan government had to find ways to deal with the mass scale of human rights abuses.

During the decade following the genocide, work by the Rwandan state and citizens focused on reconstruction and building sustainable peace. Part of the conversation centred on rebuilding a culture of trust and fostering societal repair. When shared culture is no longer the foundation of a society, that society is at risk of confronting violence. As Abraham Maslow has noted, "Sick people are made by a sick culture; healthy people are made possible by a healthy culture. But it's just as true that sick individuals make their culture sick and that healthy individuals make their culture healthy."[1] The new government's responsibility was to rebuild a healthy culture that could sustain healthy communities, which required reforming judicial, security, and social welfare systems. The expectation was that these reforms would restore the trust people had in their communities that had been damaged throughout violent episodes in the country's history.

The genocide rendered political and legal institutions such as parliament, the judiciary, the police, and prosecution services, fragile and ineffective. To address these gaps, the government adopted several initiatives as basic approaches to transitional justice that could lead to the rebirth of the nation. These initiatives were mostly state-led transitional justice responses to direct impacts and continuing legacies of the genocide. Transitional justice seeks recognition for victims and promotes possibilities for peace, reconciliation, and democracy. As several scholars have noted, transitional justice is not a specific form of justice, but rather justice adapted to societies transforming themselves after a period of pervasive human rights abuse. In some cases, these transformations happen suddenly; in others, they may evolve over many decades.[2]

This chapter explores the approaches and initiatives the Rwandan government adopted to rebuild social cohesion after the 1994 genocide, highlighting the impacts and challenges of those efforts in Rwandan political, social, and economic contexts. The Rwandan example is an important case in the debates over how to build social cohesion in the aftermath of genocide or mass human rights violations. Multiple transitional justice processes have been operating parallel to one another, and in some cases in succession. An examination of the range of transitional processes established in post-genocide Rwanda, as this chapter provides, offers an interesting case to explore these overlapping processes and their potential in other transitional societies to implement both local practices and international justice systems as time-bound and ongoing processes.

TRANSITIONAL JUSTICE APPROACHES IN RWANDA: REBUILDING SOCIAL COHESION

Rwanda has progressively adopted various approaches to address its history of human rights abuses as part of the process of promoting peace and reconciliation in the country. In March 1999, the Rwandan government created the National Unity and Reconciliation Commission (NURC) with the following objectives: prepare and coordinate national programs to promote national unity and reconciliation; implement ways and means to restore and consolidate unity and reconciliation among Rwandans; educate and mobilize the population on matters relating to national unity and reconciliation; carry out research, organize debates, disseminate ideas, and make publications relating to peace, national unity, and reconciliation; propose measures that can eradicate divisions among Rwandans and reinforce national unity and reconciliation; denounce and fight against acts, writings, and utterances intended to promote any kind of discrimination, intolerance, or xenophobia.

The work of the NURC was driven by a national quest for unity and reconciliation, two concepts central to understanding the current Rwandan context. Unity, defined as the state of being undivided with nothing wanting, is essential to reconnect the country with its past. The commission was given the responsibility of restoring unity among Rwandans. It is, of course, difficult to precisely evaluate the level of unity in any society. However, unity can be assessed through relationships, norms, interactions, behaviours, and institutions that bond society together. This is linked to the critical question of social cohesion, which the NURC has defined as "a status of affairs concerning both the vertical and the horizontal interactions among members of society as characterized by a set of attitudes and norms that includes trust, a sense of belonging, and the willingness to participate and help, as well as their behavioural manifestations."[3]

Another concept that has dominated the work of the NURC is reconciliation, also a complex notion that has been defined differently by a range of scholars. In the context of Rwanda, the NURC defines reconciliation as "conduct and practices of Rwandans that reflect the identity of the shared citizenship, culture, and equal rights manifested through interpersonal trust, tolerance, respect, equality, truth, and healing the wounds to lay a foundation for sustainable development."[4] The work of the NURC centred on reconciliation as a consensus practice of citizens who have common nationality, share the same culture, and have equal rights. The process of reconciliation entails building trust, tolerance, mutual respect, equality, complementary roles/interdependence, truth, and healing of one another's wounds inflicted by aspects of Rwanda's history, with the objective of laying a foundation for sustainable development.[5] The NURC's work was guided by this understanding of reconciliation.

Since its creation, the NURC has introduced several reconciliation initiatives and other peacebuilding activities aimed at fostering national cohesion. It has facilitated numerous workshops on its own and in collaboration with other civil society organizations (CSOs) that brought together survivors and perpetrators. NURC states its reconciliation initiatives are guided by the common contention that an essential ingredient of reconciliation after violence involves group processes of apology and forgiveness. Therefore, a successful reconciliation process in the aftermath of violence necessitates, on the one hand, the perpetrators voluntarily acknowledge and apologize for their wrongdoings. On the other hand, it is beneficial when the survivors' voluntary forgiveness is granted toward renewed relationships.[6] Based on this understanding, some initiatives of the NURC have sought to facilitate and document experiences of confession on the side of perpetrators and forgiveness on the side of victims. The commission has directly and indirectly supported many reconciliation groups countrywide, conducted several research projects on the topic of reconciliation, and supported other CSOs to launch programs and activities that promote trust building between victims and perpetrators.

The NURC approaches reconciliation as a process rather than a time-bound project. This process still faces some challenges that have not yet been adequately addressed. The commission measures its impact on national reconciliation in terms of citizen engagement and public attitudes. It has noted that citizens indicated the persistence of ethnic-based stereotyping (as expressed by 27.9% of citizens), genocide ideology (as expressed by 25.8% of citizens), and the wounds resulting from the divisive past and genocide in Rwanda that are not yet fully healed (as expressed by 4.6%

of citizens).[7] Despite these challenges, the commission's work in restoring peace, unity, and reconciliation is significant. The NURC is central to achieving the unity that Rwandans are still building, which is the cornerstone of the country's post-genocide reconstruction agenda.

THE GACACA COURTS

Another approach adopted to promote reconciliation and peace in Rwanda was the establishment of the Gacaca courts. This represented an attempt to rebuild justice institutions that would be locally and internationally trustworthy. It was not feasible for a retributive justice approach to efficiently handle all the genocide-related cases where all those accused of committing genocide could be brought to formal courts. Facing survivors' demands for justice, the Rwandan government had to dig deep into local practices to find ways to foster justice and reconciliation that did not exclude the possibilities of, or interfere with, using other transitional justice measures. In this regard, the Gacaca courts were established as a form of community-based justice, which would provide a second, parallel model for delivering justice.[8] The law governing the creation of the Gacaca courts and organization of criminal prosecution for genocide or other crimes against humanity was officially established on 26 January 2001. Gacaca jurisdictions had the following main objectives: reconstruct what happened during the genocide, expedite the legal proceedings by using as many courts as possible, and reconcile Rwandans to build national unity. The government positioned these Gacaca courts as a stepping stone for the country's reconstruction and called upon citizens to support them to achieve their justice and reconciliation objectives.

Gacaca courts opened in June 2002 as a response to the overwhelming number of genocide-related crimes. These courts allowed the same population that had experienced the genocide to guide and shape the Gacaca process. Gacaca courts carried out their activities over ten years, closing in 2012. In many ways, the implementation of these courts in Rwanda demonstrated the courage of Rwandan citizens, their will to reconstruct their nation, and their collective capacity to find solutions to their problems, especially those at the foundation of genocide. Observing the situation in Rwanda in the aftermath of the genocide, reconciliation and justice seemed to be impossible concepts to many people, especially regarding the country's ability to bring the overwhelming number of genocide suspects to justice. The mission of the Gacaca system was therefore to achieve "truth, justice, and reconciliation" amid widespread public distrust. It aimed to promote community healing by making the punishment of perpetrators more efficient and less expensive for the state. The Gacaca system challenged every Rwandan to engage in introspection and soul searching to contribute to the truth telling, national healing, reconciliation, and justice processes.

Much of Gacaca's success can be attributed to the fact that Rwandans ultimately believed in its potential. At the official closing of the Gacaca courts, President Paul Kagame stated Gacaca had empowered Rwandans in ways few could have envisaged. It illustrated the liberating value of truth. He emphasized this power of the "truths" revealed through the Gacaca courts stating: "When truth came out in court, from both the perpetrators and survivors of genocide, from witnesses and the community – freely, not at the prompting or tutoring of paid lawyers – it set everyone free. It prepared the ground for the restoration of social harmony."[9] Others have made similar assessments of the Gacaca system.

A report published by the Africa Research Institute authored by political scientist Phil Clark noted that "suspects and survivors often affirm that the opportunity to speak openly at Gacaca about events and emotions concerning the genocide has contributed to their healing." In interviews, "many suspects claim a sense of release from feelings of shame and social dislocation through confessing to – and apologizing for – their crimes in front of their victims and the wider community."[10] The report has stated that Gacaca has been "remarkably successful at fulfilling the Rwandan government's promise to deliver comprehensive prosecutions of genocidaires without exacerbating the dire overcrowding of jails that necessitated Gacaca in the first place. Far from being 'mob' or 'vigilante' justice, as many legal critics predicted, about a quarter of the sixty-seven Gacaca cases have resulted in acquittal. Many sentences have been commuted to community service, thereby facilitating the reintegration of detainees into society."[11] This report has drawn parallels between Gacaca and the International Criminal Tribunal for Rwanda (ICTR), observing that while Gacaca dispensed close to two million cases with a budget of US$40 million, the ICTR, which has completed sixty-nine trials, has used more than US$1 billion.[12]

In its own assessment, the National Service of Gacaca Courts (NSGC) has reported evidence of the positive values that manifested in the course of implementing the Gacaca program, such as opportunities it provided for upholding the spirit of hope and confidence to build a brighter future. Other positive attributes included trying all genocide cases within a short time, upholding human rights, supporting national unity and reconciliation, rebuilding the nation through community work to replace imprisonment, accepting guilt and seeking forgiveness, having the courage to hide those who were being hunted during the genocide, the survivors' courage to forgive those who committed inhumane crimes against them, and so many similar acts of selflessness.[13] The conclusions of the NSGC report indicate the Gacaca courts constituted an unforgettable landmark in the history of Rwanda that can serve as a guardrail and a tool to fight against divisionism and genocide ideology moving forward.

Despite this glowing assessment, the Gacaca system was not without problems. During the pilot phase some challenges were identified, including the persistence of genocide ideology; killing and intimidation of survivors, witnesses, and Inyangamugayo (Gacaca judges); cases of leaders accused of genocide who refused to testify; people moving to provinces where they were unknown in order to escape justice; refugees who fled Gacaca courts; and perpetrators who offered only partial confession of crimes. Although some of these challenges have had a long-lasting impact on the social cohesion of Rwandans, many were effectively managed. The ongoing issue of the perpetuation of a genocide ideology is among the major concerns that will take time to eradicate. Also, some suspected perpetrators of genocide outside the country were not tried for numerous reasons. The international justice system on genocide that supported the Gacaca court system has not operated as effectively as anticipated. International justice for these perpetrators has been slow and much remains to be done by the international community to bring them to justice.

NATIONAL COMMISSION FOR THE FIGHT AGAINST GENOCIDE

Established in 2007, the National Commission for the Fight against Genocide (Commission nationale de lutte contre le génocide, CNLG) is an independent and permanent institution with the mandate of commemoration. The commission has a specific mission of preventing genocide, the perpetuation of genocide ideology, and overcoming the long-term consequences. Since its creation, the commission has done significant work related to its mission. It has undertaken genocide-related research and initiated outreach programs around the country through platforms such as Café Littéraire. It holds public events in communities and partners with media, public, and academic institutions to educate the public about genocide and its consequences.[14]

The CNLG is responsible for genocide memorials and other related museums or symbols, more specifically national memorials such as the Kigali, Murambi, Bisesero, Nyange, Ntarama, Nyamata, and Nyarubuye Genocide Memorials. Other memorials are under district responsibilities and organizations on behalf of CNLG. Since its inception, this institution has confronted several challenges, which include addressing genocide deniers. However, genocide ideology is still perpetuated in Rwanda and by groups globally, primarily promoted through social media platforms beyond the control of state institutions and CNLG's work.

FUND FOR NEEDIEST SURVIVORS OF GENOCIDE IN RWANDA

Following the 1994 genocide, the government of National Unity embarked on ambitious development programs to rebuild a country that had undergone such systematic destruction of life and property. The government put in place several reparative initiatives to restore the lives and dignity of survivors. In this regard, the Genocide Survivors Support and Assistance Fund (Fond d'Assistance aux rescapés du Genocide, FARG) was created and given the task of prioritizing supporting the neediest survivors.[15] Among the priorities of the government of National Unity in 1994 was to rehabilitate and support the Tutsi genocide survivors who had undergone tremendous suffering during and after the genocide. Not only had their families and breadwinners been wiped out, most of the property of the survivors had also been lost or destroyed, leaving them vulnerable and in urgent need of assistance. This economic violence is an important aspect of genocide and other periods of mass human rights violations that is not always addressed or prioritized in transitional justice periods. In the Rwandan case, reparation programs and initiatives to help repair material and moral damages of the genocide were established by the state.

The rationale for the fund, as outlined in the law that established FARG in 1998, was to assist survivors of genocide perpetrated against the Tutsi in Rwanda from 1 October 1990 to 31 December 1994. Since 1998, the fund has expanded its scope of operation. The stated mission of the fund is to promote the social welfare of the neediest survivors of the genocide. In line with its mandate, FARG provides many services, including assistance with education, shelter, health, human rehabilitation, and income-generating activities. Many of these genocide survivors are orphans, widows, or widowers. Although much remains to be done to support survivors, FARG has had some impact since its establishment. As a state-sponsored initiative, the government invests 6% of the annual domestic revenues in FARG, with most of the budget spent on education and health services.

In dispatching its functions, FARG has prioritized education, given the significant number of the orphaned youth who needed to acquire quality education to ensure a better future. According to FARG officials, a total of RWF163.4 billion was spent on education from 1998 to 2017. FARG reported in 2017 that 97,677 students had completed secondary school and 12,524 students had completed higher learning education.

In relation to health, the genocide left thousands of survivors with physical and mental wounds that needed special attention. FARG reported 2,439,191 medical cases of genocide survivors who received treatment in different referral hospitals from 1998 to 2017. It also reported that 398 genocide survivors with complicated medical cases had been transferred abroad for further medical treatment during the same period. Officials estimated that over RWF 15.4 billion was spent on the treatment of genocide survivors, both in the country and abroad. In each financial year, at least 24,339 beneficiaries had been assisted under its medical care program.

FARG has also dispensed funds for housing and other poverty-reduction supports. Through its shelter program, 43,146 houses have been constructed and 46,551 beneficiaries have been assisted under its income-generating activities. Under the Girinka program, which aims to reduce extreme poverty in rural areas of Rwanda by providing families in need with a cow, 5,000 beneficiaries have been assisted. All these initiatives have helped survivors reintegrate into society. Creating opportunities for justice to be sought and for individuals and communities to be supported has contributed significantly to the social cohesion and development in post-genocide Rwanda.

Despite the successes as described in supporting the neediest genocide survivors, FARG did not manage to cater to all those who require
its support due to the genocide's large-scale devastating social and
economic consequences on people's lives. The designated budget is
still markedly insufficient to cover all the costs of health, education,
and shelter needs. Some of these challenges, especially those related
to health, are likely to persist for many years due to lack of funds
and also infrastructure.

MEMORIALIZATION EFFORTS

Memorialization efforts are considered crucial to forging social
cohesion in post-genocide Rwanda. Memorialization and commemoration endeavours have helped Rwandans, especially survivors,
deal with the past as part of a broader transitional justice program.
These efforts have included constructing memorials that preserve the
victims' public and personal memory and help educate them about
the past. As of 2021, at least 207 monuments had been constructed
countrywide to tell the story of genocide to the public. Preserving
memory helps build a strong foundation for a new generation, in
the hopes of fighting against the recurrence of genocide against the
Tutsi. Apart from the memorials already constructed, since 1994
the government has officially adopted, three months of commemoration of the 1994 genocide against the Tutsi in Rwanda, which is
observed both locally and internationally. The United Nations has
also designated 7 April as the International Day of Reflection on the
1994 genocide.

Different government institutions have played a substantial role in
positioning remembrance as an issue of national importance. Initially,
many Rwandans saw memorialization and commemoration as relevant only to government officials and survivors, but this mentality
has progressively changed. A report published by the Institute of
Research and Dialogue for Peace states that in the Rwandan context
"memory has an important educative role. It offers the opportunity
to measure the dimension and gravity of atrocities to provide the
community with strategies to fight against them. Furthermore, memory allows generations to come to have living proof of how cruelly
genocide was implemented. This is a tool to have a positive impact
on their behaviours and that of prospective leaders."[16] To keep the
memory alive for generations to come, initiatives that aim to preserve

the memory of victims, and the memory of the genocide in general, have been at the forefront of the actions of genocide survivors' organizations and the CNLG, in particular. As part of memorialization efforts, records of Gacaca proceedings and testimonies have been collected, indexed, and archived for future generations. The significance of archives after a transitional period are outlined in other chapters in this volume.[17]

Memorialization efforts have confronted many challenges. Survivors have passed away without their testimonies ever being recorded, and deep wounds keep some survivors from freely talking about their experiences, such as rape and other crimes of sexual violence. The generation that directly experienced the genocide is still with us, however, and collecting their oral history is a time-sensitive matter. Because of this, projects to record memories of the genocide need to be a priority. Without proper documentation, the story of genocide is susceptible to modifications and misinformation. It is essential, therefore, that the stories of victims and survivors be diligently documented and archived for future generations.

The documentation of the stories and narratives of Holocaust survivors provides a reference point. As Stephen Smith has noted: "With the passing of the baton, a significant change is taking place. Whatever we have heard, whatever evidence we have collected, whatever we have been told, the way we discuss the Holocaust will be very different without the survivor generation who have spoken to us firsthand. We all know that. But the question is, 'What will the memory be fifty years from now?'"[18] Promising and concerted efforts to collect and preserve the memory of genocide are still being made by the Rwandan government and partner non-government organizations, such as Aegis Trust through its Genocide Archive Rwanda, IBUKA (Remember),[19] and AERG (Student Survivors Association).[20] The role of CSOs is crucial to these ongoing efforts.

OTHER INITIATIVES AIMED AT RECONSTRUCTION AND RECONCILIATION

For the government to help rebuild a nation that will make the mantra "Never Again" a reality, careful consideration must be given to how Rwandans can be supported in learning from their past. One way the government has sought to do this is through the revision of the school curriculum. The national curriculum of Rwandan history has been revisited, and how it is taught to Rwandans, especially within the education system, has been re-examined. In terms of content, the history taught in schools before the genocide divided Rwandans instead of uniting them. To address this divisive approach, the reformed school curriculum includes new topics such as Peace and Values Education, which has been horizontally and vertically integrated throughout as a cross-cutting theme in the educational system.

Uniting Rwandans through youth engagement and reorientation has remained a priority of the government as well. Many new programs and initiatives to encourage unity have been aimed toward youth participation. These include a civic education program through the National Itorero Commission, Ndi Umunyarwanda,[21] youth camps, Rwanda Day, and the community work practice of *Umuganda*. Another interesting government project was to use the national identity card, a tool once used to exacerbate division because it specified one's ethnic group, now declares all citizens equal Rwandans.

SECURITY SYSTEM REFORM

Security system reform has also contributed to social cohesion in post-genocide Rwanda. Efforts to transform security organs from instruments of cruelty and corruption into institutions that serve the public with integrity have positively impacted social relations since the 1994 genocide. In this reform, many ex–Forces armées rwandaises members were reintegrated into the Rwanda Defence Force and Gendarmerie, which later became Rwanda National Police. Others were taken care of by the Rwanda National Demobilization and Reintegration Commission, which organizes trainings and workshops to help ex-combatants reintegrate into society. Even though this approach has been beneficial, some challenges persist, such as resistance to repatriation, perpetuation of genocide ideology, and genocide deniers spreading rumours about national security.

CONCLUSION

Given the foregoing analyses of reconstruction and reconciliation efforts in Rwanda, I outline below some recommendations to complement what has been accomplished in the effort at forging national unity and building social cohesion. First, state and civil society actors should work to increase outreach and awareness of peacebuilding and reconciliation initiatives. Amplifying and exemplifying the voices of those who have accepted forgiveness and reconciliation within the community creates an opportunity to inspire citizens who have not yet begun such a journey. Academics and civil society actors should conduct more in-depth research on the genocide. It is still essential to have more stories/books on genocide published, and empirical research needs to be carried out on the challenges to transitional justice approaches used in Rwanda. State and civil society actors should invest in collecting and archiving more stories about the genocide that will help to educate both the local and international public about the atrocities as a means of preventing reoccurrence.

It is also important to invest more in institutions established to support genocide survivors, such as FARG, to fulfill their mandate of providing rehabilitation and education, health care and other socio-economic support to victims and survivors. At the international level, all countries should commit to condemning genocide deniers wherever they are. Countries hosting genocide suspects should bring them to justice. Documents relating to ICTR proceedings should be handed over to the Rwandan government to be digitally archived. These should be considered the property of Rwanda.

Creating social cohesion in post-genocide society as the necessary foundation rebuilding the Rwandan state has been a complex and challenging task. It is true that there can be no single formula for dealing with a past marked by gross large-scale human rights abuse, as "all transitional justice approaches are based on a fundamental belief in universal human rights. But in the end, each society should – indeed must – choose its own path."[22] Rwanda has chosen its own path to address the devastation and legacies of genocide. The government has adopted culturally relevant strategies to help the country move forward, promote national unity, and rebuild trust between citizens that was destroyed by decades of divisive politics. This chapter has highlighted the ways in which different strategies and processes have the potential to create a more holistic approach to transitional justice, which in turn have contributed to rebuilding a sense of social cohesion. Though positive results have been observed through the initiatives described in this chapter, challenges remain. A greater intersection of such strategies, rather than the siloing of processes operating within the country, is one possible way to better address these challenges and support interrelating processes. The hope of many Rwandans is that these reconstruction and reconciliation initiatives will endure and sustain the efforts to rebuild the country.

NOTES

1 Maslow quoted in Mark S. Ferrara, *New Seeds of Profit* (Lanham: Lexington Books, 2019), 124.
2 International Center for Transitional Justice (ICTJ), "What is Transitional Justice?," 2009, www.ictj.org/sites/default/files/ICTJ-Global-Transitional-Justice-2009-English.pdf.
3 National Unity and Reconciliation Commission (NURC), *Rwanda Reconciliation Barometer* (Kigali-Rwanda, 2015), 9.
4 Ibid., 5.
5 Ibid.
6 Ibid., 87.
7 Ibid., 116.
8 Gacaca courts is a system of community justice inspired by Rwandan tradition. This traditional, communal justice was adapted in 2001 to fit the needs of Rwanda in the wake of the 1994 genocide against Tutsi in Rwanda whereby more than one million people were killed, tortured, and raped, simply because they were labelled "Tutsi."
9 Paul Kagame, "Presidential remarks during the official closing of Gacaca Courts," Kigali, 12 June 2012. http://paulkagame.com/?p=1355.
10 Phil Clark, "How Rwanda Judged its Genocide," Africa Research Institute (website), 2012, 8.
11 Ibid., 6–7.
12 Ibid., 7.
13 National Service of Gacaca Courts, *Administrative Report of the National Service of Gacaca Courts* (Kigali-Rwanda, 2012), 237.
14 More information can be found at www.cnlg.gov.rw/index.php?id=12 (site discontinued).
15 www.farg.gov.rw.
16 IRDP, *Rwandan Tutsi Genocide: Causes, Implementation and Memory*, Kigali (2006), 114.
17 See in this volume Abena Ampofoa Asare's chapter 10, titled "TRCs and the Archival Imperative," and Proscovia Svärd's chapter 12, titled "The South African Truth and Reconciliation Commission and Access to its Documentation."

18 Stephen D. Smith, *Never Again! Yet Again! A Personal Struggle with the Holocaust and Genocide,* (Israel: Geffen Publishing House, 2009).

19 IBUKA, which means "remember," is a non-government association. Its main mission is to preserve the memory of the genocide and to defend rights and interests of survivors.

20 AERG is the Student Survivors Association of the 1994 Genocide against Tutsi in Rwanda. See https://aerg.org.rw.

21 NDIUMUNYARWANDA is a national program initiated in 2013, with an ultimate goal of building a national identity and to foster a Rwandan community based on trust and unity. It was initiated as a way to strengthen the solidarity of the people, uphold their moral and spiritual values, as well as help them understand their fundamental rights as Rwandans.

22 ICTJ, "What Is Transitional Justice."

CONCLUSION

Assessing Truth Commission Impacts and Legacies

Bonny Ibhawoh

This book is a reflection on the role of truth commission practices in state building in Africa, where approximately a third of all truth commissions have been established. The chapters present studies of countries at different junctures of truth commission process or post–truth commission state building from multidisciplinary perspectives. While some chapters focus on the mandates, processes, and immediate outcomes, others investigate the long-term impacts and legacies. The perspectives offered in this book span a wide range of the work of truth commissions: civic engagement and public participation, institutional design and legal framework, redress for victims of sexual violence, gender inequities, post–truth commission peacebuilding, judicial accountability, social cohesion, creative narrativization, documentation, archiving, and memorialization.

The broad thematic range in this volume is accompanied by the varied perspectives of academics, policymakers, and practitioners that illuminate the complexities of truth commission mandates, processes, and outcomes. We conceived this book as a dialogue between academics, policymakers, and practitioners who are interested and involved in the work of truth commissions. While many of the chapters by academics address complex conceptual and theoretical questions relating to the work of truth commissions, others by practitioners and policymakers bring valuable practice-oriented and evidence-based perspectives to these questions. This multidisciplinary and cross-sectoral approach has allowed us to paint a more detailed picture of truth commissions than would have been possible if the conversation has been limited to academics. This nexus between concept, theory, and practice has also allowed for a comprehensive assessment of truth commissions not just as transitional justice mechanisms or restorative justice models but also as mechanisms of civic inclusion and state building. The broad thematic and diverse methodological approaches of the studies in this volume highlight the complexities of the two intersecting processes that frame this book, that of truth commission and state building.

Africa, which provides the backdrop for this study of truth commissions, is a continent of varied experiences with these commissions. Post-colonial state building has also played out in different ways across the continent. This book does not suggest a universal African experience, whether in relation to truth commission or state-building processes. Instead, our central argument is that truth commissions can and have been deployed as mechanisms of state building alongside their truth-finding function. This should be considered in assessing their outcomes and legacies. Thorough contextual and comparative studies of truth commissions that go beyond immediate outcomes allow us to understand better how they enhance or constrain state (re)building processes in post-conflict and post-authoritarian societies.

The studies in this book underscore the need for ongoing interdisciplinary, cross-sectoral, and comparative studies of truth commissions that go beyond their more explicit objectives of truth finding and justice to explore their implicit objectives and inadvertent outcomes. Truth commissions are better understood as long-term processes rather than time-bound projects. Long after the end of truth commission mandates and the submission of their final reports, their processes and outcomes continue to impact societies in various ways at different moments. As states and societies undergo political change, legacies of injustice have a bearing on what is deemed transformative.[1] This is true of all transitional justice mechanisms. However, because truth commissions are at once charged with digging into the past (to investigate the roots of abuse) and projecting into the future (with recommendations to prevent the recurrence of abuse) their long-term impacts on states and societies are likely to be more profound. Truth commissions also encompass a wide range of transitional justice measures, including acknowledgment through apologies, memorialization and public debates, restoration through reparations and restitution, and peacebuilding through criminal justice and amnesties.

The far-reaching ramifications of truth commission processes and outcomes for almost all sectors of society are evident in the wide range of contributions in this book.

A related theme that emerges from this volume is the centrality of narrative to truth-seeking processes. Perhaps the most significant value of truth commissions is the space they open for narrativizing public memory. Several chapters in this volume show that such narratives are central to the quest for justice and restitution. As Edward Said has noted, "Facts do not at all speak for themselves but require a socially acceptable narrative to absorb, sustain, and circulate them."[2] Because facts of abuse do not speak for themselves, we must rely on narratives that testify to human rights violations as the evidentiary foundations for redress and protection. Public participation in truth commission processes allows for the unleashing of otherwise constrained public narratives in ways that would be impossible within the legal formalities of regular courts or tribunals. In transitional states, the challenge of protecting and promoting human rights can only be met when the voices of victims and their interlocutors are heard, understood, and acted upon. Truth commissions provide a mechanism for doing this.

As we have also seen throughout this book, truth commissions privilege victims' voices and engender public debates about justice in ways that can be uniquely transformative and enduring. These transformations may be generational, changing the structures of states and the organization of societies. Public attitudes and scholarly assessment of truth commissions are bound to shift over time. Impacts and legacies of truth commissions that are not evident today may yet be revealed with time in ways that may shape state-building and nation-beginning trajectories for years to come. As more countries in both the Global South and North adopt the truth commission model to address contemporary human rights abuses and historical injustices, the dialogue between scholars, policymakers, and practitioners must continue to help us better understand how truth commissions work under different situations, their impacts on various constituencies, and their legacies over time.

UNIVERSALIZING THE RIGHT TO TRUTH

What is the future of truth commissions? How can the lessons we have learned from the past aid our understanding of truth seeking going forward? The growing popularity of truth commissions

as transitional justice mechanisms for dealing with past atrocities
reflects the increasing interest of governments, not simply in conflict transformation but also in managing public memory. Though
backed by state authority, truth commissions open up spaces for
non-state actors outside the realm of politics and the court to inject
cultural, ethical, and religious discourses into peacebuilding and
state-building processes.[3]

The future of the truth commission model of restorative justice points toward growing global acceptance and adaptation. As
more states and societies seek alternative mechanisms to investigate
present-day human rights violations and address historical injustices, official truth seeking is increasingly framed in terms of the
"right to truth." The right to truth places an obligation on states
to account for the truth about the circumstances of human rights
violations, preserve the memory of abuses, and work toward institutional reforms. The concept of the right to truth has developed in
the context of gross human rights violations and grave breaches of
humanitarian law. It is often invoked in the context of violations
such as arbitrary killings, forced disappearance, torture, and abductions. In these situations, the right to truth is founded on the need
for a full accounting of what happened to victims and survivors. The
right is enshrined in several human rights documents, including the
United Nations Declaration on the Rights of Indigenous Peoples
and the UN *Principles for the Protection and Promotion of Human
Rights through Action to Combat Impunity* (*Principles to Combat
Impunity*).[4]

The United Nations (UN) has affirmed that people subjected to
human rights violations have a right to know the truth as part of
their right to an effective remedy. In 2010 the UN General Assembly
proclaimed 24 March as the "Right to Truth Day."[5] The annual
observance pays tribute to the memory of El Salvadorian cleric
Oscar Romero who was assassinated in 1980 after denouncing
human rights violations. The day honours the memory of victims
of gross human rights violations and pays tribute to those who have
devoted their lives to, and lost their lives in, the struggle to protect
human rights.

The right to truth is now a well-established international human
rights principle. It is linked to the duty and obligation of states to protect and guarantee human rights, to conduct thorough investigations

of violations and guarantee effective remedies and reparations. Beyond remedying present-day human rights violations, the right to truth extends to historical abuses and injustices. The UN has affirmed that people have the inalienable right to know the truth about past events concerning the perpetration of heinous crimes and the circumstances and reasons that led, through systematic violations, to those crimes. The premise is that a full and effective exercise of the right to the truth provides a vital safeguard against the recurrence of violations.[6]

The right to truth is also linked with the "duty to remember." This human rights principle recognizes that a people's knowledge of the history of their abuse and oppression is part of their heritage and, as such, must be ensured by appropriate measures. This is required to fulfill the state's duty to preserve archives concerning human rights violations and facilitate knowledge of those violations. According to the UN "Principles to Combat Impunity," the aim of protecting archives is to preserve the collective memory of violation from extinction and guard against the development of revisionist and negationist arguments.[7]

Objective truth seeking within and beyond formal judicial processes is essential to establishing accountability for human rights violations. Accountability involves three interlinked rights: the right to truth, the right to justice, and the right to an effective remedy and reparation. Fulfilling these rights requires inclusive mechanisms and participatory strategies that involve all stakeholders in truth-seeking processes. Truth commissions provide spaces for such participatory truth seeking and truth telling. Despite their limitations, they can be effective mechanisms for establishing accountability for human rights violations and implementing the right to truth, particularly in relation to recognition, restitution, and memorialization.

NOTES

1   Ruti Teitel, *Transitional Justice* (Oxford: Oxford University Press, 2000), 6.
2   Edward Said, "Permission to Narrate," in *The Politics of Dispossession: The Struggle for Palestinian Self-Determination, 1969–1994* (New York: Pantheon Books, 1994), 254.
3   Ruti Teitel, "Transitional Justice Genealogy," *Harvard Human Rights Journal* 16 (2003): 69–94.

4 *United Nations Declaration on the Rights of Indigenous Peoples* (Geneva: UN, 2008); United Nations (UN), "Principles for the Protection and Promotion of Human Rights through Action to Combat Impunity" (Geneva: UN, 2005, ("Principles for Combating Impunity"), https://documents-dds-ny.un.org/doc/UNDOC/GEN/G05/109/00/PDF/G0510900.pdf. Also see UN, "Human Rights Council, Resolution 9/11. Right to the Truth, A/HRC/9/L.12; A/HRC/RES/12/12," Human Rights Council Resolution, Right to the Truth, 2009, www.daccess-ods.un.org/tmp/6330708.86135101.html.

5 UN, "International Day for the Right to the Truth Concerning Gross Human Rights Violations and for the Dignity of Victims," www.un.org/en/observances/right-to-truth-day.

6 "Principles for Combating Impunity."

7 Ibid.

Contributors

ABENA AMPOFOA ASARE is associate professor of Africana studies and history at SUNY Stony Brook University. Her research and writing span human rights, citizenship, and transformative justice in Africa and the African diaspora. She is the author of *Truth Without Reconciliation: A Human Rights History of Ghana* (University of Pennsylvania, 2018), selected as a Choice Outstanding Academic Title by the American Library Association.

JASPER ABEMBIA AYELAZUNO is a Ghanaian public servant and academic with more than thirty years of combined experience in law enforcement, teaching, and research. Before joining academia, he worked for the Ghana National Reconciliation Commission as a statement taker/investigator. Presently, he is associate professor of political science and vice dean of the Faculty of Communication and Cultural Studies, University for Development Studies (UDS), Ghana. His research interests are interdisciplinary in nature, encompassing land governance, capitalist farming, agrarian change, extractive industries, democracy/democratization, social justice, truth commissions, political agency, civic activism, and resistance. He has supervised students and published on these areas in top-tier journals. He is the author of *Neoliberal Globalisation and Resistance from Below: Why the Subalterns Resist in Bolivia and not in Ghana* (Routledge, 2019).

SEIDU M. ALIDU is currently a senior lecturer at the University of Ghana, Department of Political Science. He was a Donahue Institute Scholar on United States political thought at the University of Massachusetts in 2014. He is a visiting lecturer

to twelve Master of Research and Public Policy (MRPP) universities in Africa, including the University of Lagos, University
of Ibadan, University of Dar es Salaam, University of Nairobi,
and the University of Botswana. He was a Fellow at the Maria
Sibylla Merian Institute for Advanced Studies in Africa (MIASA)
on parliaments and democracy in Africa. He has worked closely
with and for numerous policy think tanks, including the Partnership for African Social and Governance Research (PASGR)
based in Nairobi, Kenya; Centre for International Development Issues Nijmegen based in the Netherlands; the Institute
for Development Studies at the University of Sussex; the Institute for Democratic Governance; the Friedrich-Ebert-Stiftung;
the United Nations Development Programme; the Varieties
of Democracy Project based at the University of Gothenburg,
Sweden; the Ghana Armed Forces Command and Staff College,
the German-African Governance Partnership Organization; and
the Social Science Research Council based in New York. He has
published widely on his subject area with his papers appearing
in *Peace Review*, *Criminal Justice Studies*, *Transitional Justice
Review*, *Journal of African Political Economy and Development*, and *Contemporary Journal of African Development and
Ghana Studies*.

ROBERT K. AME is associate professor of human rights and
criminology at Wilfrid Laurier University. His research interests
in human rights include Truth and Reconciliation Commissions
(TRCs) and children's rights. His work in criminology focuses on
the youth justice system in Ghana, crimes against humanity, and
restorative justice. His publications have appeared in academic
journals such as the *Contemporary Justice Review*, *Journal of
Global Ethics*, *Journal of Family History*, *Canadian Journal
of Law and Society*, *The International Journal of Children's
Rights*, and the *Canadian Journal of African Studies*, and as
chapters in numerous books. He is lead co-editor of *Children's
Rights in Ghana: Rhetoric or Reality?* (Lexington Books, 2011)
and co-editor of *Childhoods at the Intersection of the Local and
the Global* (Palgrave Macmillan, 2012).

SYLVIA BAWA is associate professor in the Department of
Sociology at York University. Bawa is a global sociologist

whose research links globalization, human rights, post-colonial feminism, and development theory. With a specific focus on women's rights and empowerment in sub-Saharan Africa, her work examines how historical forces and events shape current political, economic, cultural, and social circumstances while highlighting the particular contradictory and paradoxical outcomes they produce at national, global, and local levels.

ABOUBACAR DAKUYO is a doctoral candidate in law at the University of Ottawa Faculty of Law. His general research area focuses on the implementation of transitional justice mechanisms in post-conflict or post-authoritarian contexts in Africa. His doctoral research focuses on the implementation of a transformative approach to transitional justice in South Sudan. He holds an LLM in international law from the Université du Québec à Montréal (UQAM) and an MA in development studies from the Geneva Graduate Institute (IHEID). He is a member of the Human Rights Research and Education Centre (HRREC) at the University of Ottawa, where he coordinates the research group of the International Criminal Court Legal Tools and International Justice.

JEAN DE DIEU SIKULIBO works as a senior legal advisor at the International Humanitarian Law Resource Centre. He holds a PhD in international law from the University of Strathclyde, UK; an LLM in international law from the University of Cape Town, South Africa; and LLB from the National University of Rwanda. He has served as a legal assistant at the Supreme Court of Rwanda and as a legal officer at the Lawyers without Borders Mission in Rwanda. He also served as legal adviser at the United Nations and as visiting lecturer of international law at various universities in Rwanda. He has written and spoken widely on a broad range of international legal issues, primarily relating to the recent developments in international criminal justice, transitional justice processes in Africa, international humanitarian law, and human rights.

TEDDY FODAY-MUSA is a PhD candidate and Gerda Henkel Fellow in the Department of Political Science, University of Ghana, Legon. He has worked extensively in the fields of disarmament, demobilization, and reintegration of ex-combatants to restore peace to his country of Sierra Leone during the civil war. He erected *peace poles* across the country with the message *May Peace Prevail on Earth*, translated in all Sierra Leonean local languages. As an undergraduate student during the war, he developed an interest in post-conflict transformation, advocating for peace and reconciliation. His dissertation examined the relationship between the elements of reconciliation in conflict resolution strategies, using the South African TRC as a case study. He has a master's degree in international studies (MIS) in peace and conflict resolution from the University of Queensland in Australia. He is currently a lecturer in the Department of Peace Studies at Fourah Bay College – University of Sierra Leone.

BONNY IBHAWOH is professor and Senator William McMaster Chair in Global Human Rights at McMaster University. He researches and teaches in the fields of human rights, legal history, imperial history, development studies, and peace/conflict studies. He has taught in universities in Africa, Europe, the United States, and Canada. He has worked as a visiting professor, research fellow, or consultant with human rights organizations, including the Danish Institute for Human Rights, the Carnegie Council for Ethics and International Affairs, the Canadian Museum of Human Rights, and the Rapoport Center for Human Rights and Justice at the University of Texas at Austin. He chairs the United Nations Expert Mechanism on the Right to Development and has served on the board of human rights and development NGOs, including *Inclusive Development International* and *Empowerment Squared*. He is the author of the books *Imperial Justice* and *Human Rights in Africa*.

BABA G. JALLOW is executive secretary of The Gambia's Truth, Reconciliation and Reparations Commission (TRRC). He holds a PhD in African history from UC Davis, an MA in liberal studies from Rutgers University (Camden), and a BA in history and political science from the University of Sierra Leone. He has taught African and world history at Creighton University (2011–15) and La Salle University (2015–17), both in the United States. He was a journalist in his home country of Gambia for many years and spent seventeen years in exile in the United States (2000–17). In December 2017, he returned home to help establish and head the TRRC Secretariat at the invitation of the Gambian government.

JANINE LESPÉRANCE is a Canadian human rights lawyer. She currently has an independent oversight position in the Canadian correctional system to ensure inmates are not held in solitary confinement. At the time this article was initially drafted, in August 2019, she was a legal adviser for Lawyers without Borders Canada (usually known as Avocats sans frontières Canada, or ASFC). In that role, she worked closely with her colleagues in Mali to increase civil society participation in the peace process and build the capacity of the Truth, Justice, and Reconciliation Commission. Her experience includes project creation and leadership; legal research, analysis, and strategy development; and teaching. While based at the University of Ottawa, she taught human rights law as a part-time professor for the Faculty of Law, coordinated projects for the Human Rights Clinic of the Human Rights Research and Education Centre, and was executive director of the International Commission of Jurists Canadian Section. While completing her legal articles at Sack Goldblatt Mitchell LLP, she worked on public interest cases, and Independent Assessment Process claims for Indian Residential School survivors. She has also worked with the Canadian Centre for International Justice, Amnesty International, and the Rabinal Community Legal Clinic in Guatemala. She holds a JD, specialization in international law, from the University of Ottawa. She would like to thank her former colleagues from ASFC for their assistance with this article, in particular, Pierrick Rouat, Antoine Stomboli, and Philippe Tremblay.

GEAROID MILLAR is professor of sociology at the University of Aberdeen. His research focuses on the local experiences of international interventions for peace, justice, and development. He has published extensively about local experiences of the Truth and Reconciliation Commission and large development interventions in post-conflict Sierra Leone, and specifically on the complex and unpredictable interactions between international and local actors in post-conflict contexts. He has worked over the past decade developing the Ethnographic Peace Research (EPR) approach. He is the author of *An Ethnographic Approach to Peacebuilding: Understanding Local Experiences in Transitional States*

(Routledge, 2014) and editor of *Ethnographic Peace Research: Approaches and Tensions* (Palgrave, 2018). His current work focuses on twenty-first-century challenges to peace. Articles on these and other topics have appeared in journals such as the *Journal of Peace Research*, *Cooperation and Conflict*, *Peacebuilding*, *Third World Quarterly*, *International Peacekeeping*, and *Memory Studies*.

JEAN NEPO NDAHIMANA holds a BA from the University of Rwanda/ College of Education (UR-CE) in the department of Arts and Education. He is an MSc candidate in environmental and development studies at the University of Lay Adventists of Kigali, Rwanda. He currently works for Aegis Trust-Rwanda (an international NGO preventing crimes against humanity) as the Peace Schools coordinator. He has ample experience in Rwanda's peacebuilding process and skills and knowledge from the Auschwitz Institute for Peace and Reconciliation (AIPR) on Foundations of Mass Atrocity Prevention, Collective Memory, Memorialization, and Prevention. As a survivor of the genocide, his ongoing research is focused on the 1994 genocide against Tutsi in Rwanda. He contributes to the implementation of peace education by Aegis Trust in Rwanda and abroad.

UCHECHUKWU NGWABA joined the Lincoln Alexander School of Law, Toronto Metropolitan University, as assistant professor in 2021. Trained as a lawyer in Nigeria and Australia, he obtained his PhD from Macquarie University, Sydney, Australia and has taught in three Australian universities before joining Lincoln Alexander School of Law. His research program engages multidisciplinary, comparative and socio-legal methods in exploring complex questions affecting health governance frameworks in the Global North and South.

OBIORA C. OKAFOR is the Edward B. Burling Chair in International Law and Institutions at the Johns Hopkins University School of Advanced International Studies (SAIS). He was the inaugural York Research Chair in International and Transnational Legal Studies and a taught international law as a professor at the Osgoode Hall Law School of York University, Toronto, Canada. He is the UN Independent Expert on Human Rights and International Solidarity and a former chair of the UN Human Rights Council Advisory Committee. He has held the Gani Fawehinmi Distinguished Chair in Human Rights Law at the Nigerian Institute of Advanced Legal Studies and served as a visiting professor at several universities and institutes around the world. He received the Award of Academic Excellence of the Canadian Association of Law Teachers in 2010 and the Gold Medal for Exceptional Research and Major Contributions to Jurisprudence of the Nigerian Institute of Advanced Legal Studies in 2013. He is the author or co-editor of seven books and over one hundred articles and other scholarly pieces.

ROGER SOUTHALL is Emeritus Professor in Sociology, University of the Witwatersrand, and Professorial Research Associate, SOAS, University of London. He was formerly professor of political studies, Rhodes University. He is the author of *Liberation Movements in Power: Party and State in Southern Africa* (2013) and *The New Black Middle Class in South Africa* (2016) and various edited collections. He is presently concluding a manuscript, "Reluctant Democrats? Whites in Post-Apartheid South Africa."

PROSCOVIA SVÄRD is associate professor of records management and archival science history at Sorbonne University, Abu Dhabi. Previously an associate professor at the Faculty of Science, Technology, and Media, Department of Information Systems and Technology, Forum for Digitalization, Mid Sweden University, she is also a Research Fellow at the Department of Information Science, University of South Africa (Unisa), in Pretoria. She completed her PhD at the University of Amsterdam. She has a licentiate degree in computer and systems sciences. Her research interests include enterprise content management, records management, information culture, e-government development, public sector information (PSI) and Open Data, long-term preservation of digital information, Truth and Reconciliation Commissions and their documentation processes, the role of archives in enhancing accountability and transparency in government institutions, information access, and the link to democracy and development.

PAUL UGOR is a professor of English language and literature at the University of Waterloo. Previously, he was associate professor in the Department of English at Illinois State University. His research interests are in the areas of Anglophone world literatures, post-colonial studies, Black popular culture, and modern African literatures and cinema/video. His work has appeared in peer-reviewed academic journals such as *Africa: The Journal of the International African Institute; African Literature Today, Canadian Journal of African Studies, Postcolonial Texts, Journal of African Literature Association,* and several edited books.

JENNIFER WALLACE is a PhD candidate in the Department of History at McMaster University. Her research is centred around the intersection of transitional justice processes and memorialization. Her doctoral research explores how the Truth and Reconciliation Commission of South Africa simultaneously altered and maintained discourse around conceptions of history and memorialization practices. She has extensive experience working directly in museums, memorialization developments, and oral history projects. She has also presented and published through peer-reviewed journals, such as the *Canadian Association of African Studies* and the *Canadian Museums Association.* She further merges her academic interests and community engagement work as a member of Participedia and McMaster's Centre for Human Rights and Restorative Justice.

HAKEEM YUSUF is professor of global law at the University of Derby. His work in transitional justice and comparative constitutional law has won international recognition. In 2011, he served on a Truth and Reconciliation Commission in Osun State, Nigeria. His article in the *International Journal of Transitional Justice* provided a pioneering account of the truth-telling process in Nigeria (the Oputa Panel). His second book, *Colonial and Post-Colonial Constitutionalism in the Commonwealth: Peace, Order and Good Government* (Routledge Abingdon, 2014), was awarded the prestigious John T. Saywell Prize for Canadian Constitutional Legal History for 2015 and shortlisted for the Kevin Boyle Prize 2015 by the Irish Association of Law Teachers (IALT). His first book, *Transitional Justice, Judicial Accountability and the Rule of Law* (2010), was shortlisted for the 2010 Kevin Boyle Prize by IALT. His article "The Judiciary and Constitutionalism in Transitions: A Critique" won the Silver Medal in the Global Jurist 2007 Awards.

Index

Page numbers with an *f* refer to figures.
Page numbers with a *t* refer to tables.

Abacha, Sani (Nigeria), 210–11
Abubakar, Abdusalami (Nigeria),
    210–11
accessibility: and participation in
    truth commissions, 191–2, 246–
    7, 310; of records, 22, 244, 245,
    285–6, 289–90
accountability. *See* institutional
    accountability; judiciary; state
    building
ACHPR, 76–7, 78–9, 88
Adinkra symbols, 103, 117n16
AERG, 368, 372n20
AfCHPR, 84–5, 87–8
AFRC (Ghana), 318, 329, 331, 332
Africa: architecture for transitional
    justice, 75–6, 77–80, 81–3,
    90–2; Berlin conference (1884),
    14; colonialism, 13–14, 16–17,
    102; decolonization, 101–3, 121;
    human rights system, 81–2; insti-
    tutions of transitional justice,
    84–6; mechanisms of transitional
    justice, 86–90; shared values, 76,
    77–8, 80, 81, 85, 89, 91; state

building, 11–14; truth commis-
    sions, establishment of in, 4–5,
    14, 239, 252n1. *See also* African
    Union (AU); *specific countries
    (e.g., Liberia, Kenya)*
African (Banjul) Charter, 78–9, 83
African Charter on Human and
    Peoples' Rights (ACHPR), 76–7,
    78–9, 88
African Court on Human and
    Peoples' Rights (AfCHPR), 84–5,
    87–8
African National Congress (ANC),
    42, 122, 126, 130, 272, 287
African Peace and Security
    Architecture (APSA), 82, 84
African Peer Review Mechanism
    (APRM), 85, 156, 157
African Union (AU): African
    Charter on Human and Peoples'
    Rights (ACHPR), 76–7, 78–9, 88;
    *Agenda 2063: The Africa We
    Want,* 75, 77, 80, 81, 82;
    Constitutive Act, 76–7, 78, 83;
    hard law instruments for

transitional justice, 77–80;
institutions for transitional jus-
tice, 84–6, 91; Maputo Protocol
(on the Rights of Women in
Africa), 79; shared values, 76,
77–8, 80, 81, 85, 89, 91; soft
law instruments for transitional
justice, 80–3. *See also* Africa;
*specific countries (e.g., Liberia,
Kenya)*
African Union Transitional Justice
Policy (AUTJP), 77, 80, 81, 85–6
Afrikaner Weerstandsbeweging
(South Africa), 271
Agenda 2063: The Africa We Want,
75, 77, 80, 81, 82
Agyarko, Emmanuel Kyeremateng
(Ghana), 330
Akan cosmology, 103, 117n16
Algiers Peace Accord, 186, 188,
189, 202n2, 203n11
Alidu, Seidu, 20, 325
All Peoples' Congress (APC)
(Sierra Leone), 144–5, 148,
158, 160
Ame, Robert, 20
Ameh, Robert, 316, 317
amnesty: applications for, in South
Africa, 128–9, 132; Archbishop
Desmond Tutu on, 127, 128,
141n25, 267, 323; conditions of,
127–8, 131–2, 139n9; denials of,
130–1, 141n31; hearings, 269–
70; National Party (NP) efforts
for, 124; provisions in TRC, 7,
36, 124, 125, 141n25. *See also*
apartheid
Amnesty Committee (of the South
African TRC), 124, 125, 128,
132, 270

Amnesty International, 241
ANC, 42, 122, 126, 130, 272, 287
Anti-Corruption Commission
(Sierra Leone), 148
apartheid: amnesty applications,
127–33; Blacks, post-apartheid
challenges, 100, 259, 282; discrimination laws, 220; human
rights abuses, 13, 36, 42, 107,
110–11; Nobel Peace Prize,
108–9, 113; obligations of beneficiaries of, 3–4; prosecutions of
perpetrators, 129–30; reparations for victims of, 3, 126, 286;
roots of, 269; sexual violence
crimes, 60–1; whites, role of in,
121–2, 127, 134–5, 136–7, 138,
268. *See also* South African TRC
APC (Sierra Leone), 144–5, 148,
158, 160
APRM, 85, 156, 157
APSA, 82, 84
archives: access to, 282–3, 284–7,
288–90; as collective memory,
264, 277, 291–2, 367–8; disappearance of, 241, 245, 248–9,
251; gathering of, 242–3, 262–3;
importance of, 22, 25, 52, 240;
planning for, pre-TRC, 241, 244,
250. See also *Country of My
Skull* (Krog); records; *specific
truth commissions (e.g., South
African TRC)*
Argentina, 7, 169, 305
Armed Forces Revolutionary
Council (AFRC) (Ghana), 318,
329, 331, 332
Asare, Abena, 22, 99–100, 262,
334, 337n22
AU. *See* African Union (AU)

authoritarian rule: judiciary
    accountability, 208–9, 219–22,
    224–6, 226–8; Structural
    Adjustment Programs (SAPs)
    and, 14; transitions from, 4–5,
    11, 24, 36–7, 44, 123, 176–8.
    See also Burkina Faso; Gambia,
    The; judiciary; Nigeria
AUTJP, 77, 80, 81, 85–6
Avocats sans frontières (ASFC)
    (Canada), 186–7, 193–7, 198

Baba, Benson Tongo (Ghana),
    328–9
Babangida, Ibrahim (Nigeria),
    214–5
Bagosora, Théoneste (Rwanda),
    166
Barrow, Adama (The Gambia),
    298, 300
Basson, Wouter (South Africa),
    131, 287–8
Bawa, Sylvia, 21, 323
Benzien, Jeffrey (South Africa),
    270–1, 280n46
Bhabha, Homi, 262, 275–6
Bintumani-III (2019 conference).
    See Sierra Leone
Bio, Julius Maada (Sierra Leone),
    154–5, 158, 162n22
Blacks: majority rule, 121–2;
    post-apartheid challenges, 50,
    100, 115, 259, 282; South
    African TRC, response to, 137,
    287
Botha, P.W. (South Africa), 3–4, 129
Britain, 16, 17, 121
*Building Peace: Sustainable
    Reconciliation in Divided
    Societies* (Lederach), 152

Burkina Faso: Commission for
    National Reconciliation (CNR),
    171–2; Commission for National
    Reconciliation and Reforms
    (CNRR), 13, 20, 164, 172,
    173–4; Compaoré regime, 163,
    170–2, 173, 175, 176, 180n9;
    coups d'état, 170, 171, 174,
    175–6, 179, 180n9; final report
    (CNRR), 172; High Council for
    Reconciliation and National
    Unity (HCRNU), 164, 172,
    173–4; Kaboré regime, 164, 174,
    175–6, 177–8, 179; Norbert
    Zongo affair, 170–1; popular
    uprising (2014), 163, 165, 172,
    178, 179; reconciliation, mean-
    ing of, 176–7, 178; Sub-
    Commission on Truth, Justice,
    and National Reconciliation,
    164, 178–9; transitional justice
    process, 163, 164, 178–9, 179n1
Burton, Mary, 134, 135
Buthelezi, Mangosuthu Gatsha
    (South Africa), 271–2

Canada: archives (TRC), 284;
    Avocats sans frontières (ASFC),
    186–7, 193–7, 198; colonial
    history, 17; Indigenous peoples,
    6–7, 8, 41, 198–200, 206n44,
    207n48; National Centre for
    Truth and Reconciliation, 22;
    Truth and Reconciliation
    Commission, 7–8, 39, 41, 198–
    200, 207n46–47; voluntary par-
    ticipation in commission, 46
CEDAW, 79
children: participation in truth
    commissions, 47, 307; soldiers,

involuntary conscription as,
147–8; truth commissions to
address abuse of, 6
Chile: government influence on
reconciliation, 38; National
Commission for Truth and
Reconciliation, 7, 12, 36–7;
transitional justice, 169; TRC
records, 240, 251
civic engagement. *See* civic
participation
civic inclusion, 4, 25
civic participation: importance of,
43–4, 45, 48–51; and state building, 35–6, 37; in truth commissions, 43, 46–7
civil society organizations (CSOs):
partnerships with truth commissions, 45, 288, 300; peacebuilding, role in, 24, 155, 156, 157,
205n27, 361; pressure for TRC,
in Sierra Leone, 149; TRC
records, 288–9
CNLG, 364–5
CNR, 171–2
CNRR, 13, 20, 164, 172, 173–4
Coalition of Women's Human
Rights in Conflict Situations:
sexual violence, unaddressed in
TRCs, 60
collective rights, 79. *See also* rights
Colombian Commission for Truth,
Coexistence, and Non-repetition,
197
colonialism: Africa, 13–14; narratives to make sense of, 268, 273,
275; post-colonial societies, 9,
11, 13–14, 99–100, 101–2, 115;
truth commissions, as a

dominant theme of, 15, 16–17,
105, 189, 199–200
Commission for Dialogue,
Truth and Reconciliation
(Côte d'Ivoire), 243
Commission for Historical
Clarification (Guatemala), 62,
71n37
Commission for National
Reconciliation (CNR) (Burkina
Faso), 171–2
Commission for National
Reconciliation and Reforms
(CNRR) (Burkina Faso), 13, 20,
164, 172, 173–4
Commission for Reception, Truth
and Reconciliation (East Timor),
71n33
Commission nationale de lutte con-
tre le génocide (CNLG), 364–5
Commission of Inquiry into the
Disappearances of People in
Uganda, 315
Commission of Truth and
Friendship (CTF) (Indonesia –
Timor-Leste), 48
Commission on Human Rights and
Administrative Justice (Ghana),
330–1
commissions. *See* socio-historical
commissions; truth commissions
(non-specific); *specific commis-
sions (e.g., South African TRC)*
Commission Vérité, Justice et
Réconciliation. *See* Mali; Truth,
Justice, and Reconciliation
Commission
Communications and Outreach
Unit (TRRC) (The Gambia), 307

communist rule, 36, 123, 269, 273, 287

Compaoré, Blaise (Burkina Faso), 163, 170–2, 173, 175, 176

compensation, right to, 89, 169

Confiscated Assets Committee (NRC) (Ghana), 325

conflict-related sexual violence. See sexual violence

constitutional rights, 76. See also rights

Constitutive Act (of the AU), 76–7, 78, 83

Convention for the Protection and Assistance of Internally Displaced Persons in Africa (AU), 80

Convention on the Elimination of All Forms of Discrimination Against Women (CEDAW), 79

Convention on the Elimination of All Forms of Racial Discrimination, 89

Convention People's Party (Ghana), 318

Country of My Skull (Krog), 258, 261, 262, 264, 265–8, 275–7

courts: continental-level, 87–8; hybrid, 63, 87, 149, 151, 166–7, 344–5; international, 58, 66, 87, 166–7, 188, 327, 363, 370; national, 88–9. See also Gacaca courts (Rwanda)

Covid-19 pandemic, 342, 348

crimes against humanity, 17, 58–9, 78, 88, 151, 188, 203n11, 327, 362, 364

Cronje, Jack (South Africa), 267–8

CTF (Indonesia – Timor-Leste), 48

Dabo, Boukary, 171, 175

Dakuyo, Aboubacar, 20

Daniel, John, 126–7, 133, 134

DDR (Sierra Leone), 344

Declaration on Shared Values (AU), 81

decolonization: about, 102–3; Africa, challenges of, 101; gendered challenges of, 102, 115; resistance to, 121; *Sankofa* ("go back for"), 103–4; *Ubuntu* (indigenous social justice principles), 103, 105

de Dieu Sikulibo, Jean, 21

de Klerk, Frederik W. (South Africa): African National Congress (ANC), 122, 130; Nobel Peace Prize, 108–9, 113; South African TRC, 129, 141n28, 272

de Kock, Eugene, 130, 141n29

delegitimization of leaders, 166–7, 175–6

deliberative democracy, 168, 174

democracy: about, 165–6; contribution to by truth commissions, 49, 167–9; deliberative, 168, 174; reciprocity and, 177; rule of law, 166, 175–6; transitional justice and, 165–7; transitions to, 36, 123, 137–8

democratic participation: importance of, 43–4; truth commissions' role in, 25, 44–5

Democratic Republic of Congo, 85

Department of Justice (DOJ) (South Africa), 283, 285, 289–90. See South Africa

Diendere, Gilbert (Burkina Faso),
175
Disarmament, Demobilisation and
Reintegration (DDR) (Sierra
Leone), 344
Djan, Osahene Boakye, 329
documents. *See* archives; records
(TRC)
DOJ, 283, 285, 289–90

Ebola crisis (Sierra Leone), 342,
348
Economic Community of West-
African States (ECOWAS), 85, 88,
96n44
ECOWAS, 85, 88, 96n44
El Salvador: sexual violence
crimes unaddressed in TRC, 61;
truth commission, 48–9,
240, 250
engagement, civic. *See* civic
participation
EPR, 27, 343, 351–3
Equity and Reconciliation
Commission (Morocco), 7,
16–17
Ethnographic Peace Research
(EPR), 27, 343, 351–3
Extraordinary African Chambers,
87, 166

Fambul Tok process, 349
Fanon, Frantz, 272, 275
FARG (Rwanda), 24, 365–7, 370
Fawehinmi, Gani, 214, 215,
232n19
Foday-Musa, Teddy, 23
Fond d'Assistance aux rescapés du
Genocide (FARG) (Rwanda), 24,
365–7, 370

formation, identity. *See* identity
Francis, David (Sierra Leone), 158,
162n26
Freetown Mudslide (Sierra Leone),
342, 348

Gacaca courts (Rwanda):
challenges faced by, 364;
establishment of, 74n72, 362;
records, 368; restorative justice
model, 104–5, 371n8; reunifica-
tion of communities, 7; sexual
violence crimes, addressing of,
61, 66–7; success of, 362–4;
transitional justice, 23–4, 90.
See also National Unity and
Reconciliation Commission
(NURC) (Rwanda); Rwanda
Gallagher, Susan, 264–5, 268
Gambia, The: archives (TRRC),
251; authoritarian rule, 295–6;
elections, 298; impact of (TRRC),
301–3, 308–9; inclusivity in
TRRC process, 306–8. *See also*
Truth, Reconciliation and
Reparations Commission (TRRC)
(The Gambia)
gender: peacebuilding, role in,
157–8; sensitivity, in TRCs, 60,
63–4, 67; truth commissions,
experiences of, 21, 102. *See also*
women
gender-based violence, 60. *See also*
sexual violence
genocide: Genocide Survivors
Support and Assistance Fund
(FARG) (Rwanda), 24, 365–7,
370; ideology, 361–2, 364, 365;
memorialization efforts, 365,
367–8; National Commission for

the Fight Against Genocide,
364–5; truth commissions, 7;
Tutsis (Rwanda), 166, 358
Genocide Archive Rwanda, 368
Genocide Survivors Support and
Assistance Fund (FARG)
(Rwanda), 24, 365–7, 370
Germany: discrimination laws
(Nazi regime), 220; Federal
Constitutional Court, 76; West
Germany, postwar, 138
Ghana: archives, TRC, 247–8;
Ayawaso West Wuogon by-elec-
tion, 330, 331; de-confiscation,
325–6; documentaries (NRC),
332; exhumation of victims, 323–
4; human rights violations, his-
tory of, 315, 318–20, 319f, 329;
Plange file, 246–7, 251; regimes
(constitutional and unconstitu-
tional), 315–16, 329–30; repara-
tions for victims, 323–5; White
Paper, 322, 330–1, 337n20. See
also National Reconciliation
Commission (NRC) (Ghana)
Gibson, James L., 176, 281
Girinka program (Rwanda), 366
Giwa, Dele, 214
Global Truth and Reconciliation
Commission Collection of
Participedia, 25, 38
governments: influence on out-
comes of truth commissions, 37,
38. See also specific countries
(e.g., Ghana, Nigeria)
Graybill, Lyn, 326, 342, 349, 351
Green Paper (Sierra Leone), 155–6
Greensboro Truth and
Reconciliation Commission
(GTRC) (United States), 50–1

GTRC (United States), 50–1
Guatemala: Commission for
Historical Clarification, 62,
71n37, 250; government influence on commission, 38; Project
for the Recovery of Historical
Memory (REHMI) (truth commission), 40, 71n32; sexual violence crimes addressed in TRC,
61, 62

Habré, Hissène (Senegal), 87, 166
Hani, Chris (South Africa), 287
hate speech, 160
Haut conseil pour la réconciliation
et l'unité nationale. See Burkina
Faso
HCRNU (Burkina Faso), 164, 172,
173–4
Hechter, Jacques (South Africa),
266
High Council for Reconciliation
and National Unity (HCRNU)
(Burkina Faso), 164, 172, 173–4
Holocaust, 368
HRSA, 81–2
human rights: authoritarian rule
and, 209–10; protection of, in
Africa, 81–2, 92; and state-
building agendas, 42; truth com-
mission's role in, 6–7, 9, 13; vio-
lations, accountability for, 36, 89
Human Rights Commission of
Sierra Leone, 148, 155
Human Rights Strategy for Africa
(HRSA), 81–2
Human Rights Violations
Investigation Commission
(Oputa Panel) (Nigeria). See
Nigeria; Oputa Panel (Nigeria)

Human Rights Violations
Sub-committee (of the South
African TRC), 124, 125, 264
Humper, Joseph, 150, 161n14
hybrid courts, 63, 87. See also
courts

Ibhawoh, Bonny, 19–20, 26,
333
IBUKA (Remember) (Rwanda),
368, 372n19
ICTR, 58, 66, 87, 166, 363, 370
ICTY, 58
identity: cultural, 103, 258, 275–6,
360–1; formation, 4, 19;
national, 15, 38, 170, 268–9,
369, 372n21; of women in South
Africa, 110, 112, 114–15
IGAD (AU), 85, 96n43
Immorality Act (South Africa),
137
inclusion, civic. See civic inclusion
Independent Commission for Peace
and National Cohesion. See
Peace and National Cohesion
Commission
indigenization. See decolonization
Indigenous peoples (Canada):
reparations, 199; residential
schools, 8, 17, 198–9, 206n44,
207n48; Truth and
Reconciliation Commission, 6–7,
8, 41, 199
Inkatha Freedom Party, 271
Institute for Reconciliation and
Justice, 138
Institute of Research and Dialogue
for Peace, 367
institutional accountability, 220–1

Intergovernmental Authority on
Development (IGAD) (AU), 85,
96n43
International Center for
Transitional Justice, 148, 241
international courts, 58, 66, 87.
See also courts; International
Criminal Court (ICC)
International Covenant on Civil
and Political Rights, 89
International Criminal Court (ICC):
Mali conflict, 188; role in transi-
tional justice, 87, 327; sexual
violence, conflict-related, 58
International Criminal Tribunal for
Rwanda (ICTR), 58, 66, 87, 166,
363, 370. See also Gacaca courts
(Rwanda); Rwanda
International Criminal Tribunal
for the Former Yugoslavia
(ICTY), 58
International Day of Reflection,
367

Jalloh, Mohamed Juldeh (Sierra
Leone), 162n28
Jallow, Baba, 19
Jammeh, Yahya (The Gambia), 13,
295–8, 303, 305, 308
judiciary: about, 219–20; accountability, 208–9, 222, 223, 225–6,
229; authoritarian rule, 224–6;
corruption, 228; immunity,
223–4; independence, 221–3;
integrity, 222; post-authoritarian
rule, 226–8; and rule of law,
220–1
Junglers (The Gambia), 295–8,
301

justice. *See* restorative justice; retributive justice; transitional justice

Kabbah, Tejan (Sierra Leone), 148
Kaboré, Roch Marc Christian
  (Burkina Faso), 164, 174, 175–6,
  177–8, 179
Kagame, Paul (Rwanda), 363
Kallon, Foday Amara (Sierra
  Leone), 162n24
Kamara, Foday (Sierra Leone),
  147–8, 161n10
Kambanda, Jean (Rwanda), 166
Kampala Convention, 80
Kenosi, Lekoko, 285
Kenya: archives (TJRC), 248–9;
  Black majority rule, 121; Truth,
  Justice, and Reconciliation
  Commission, 15, 16, 47–8
Khan, Alpha (Sierra Leone), 158–9
knowledge exchange, international,
  196–7, 198–200
Koornhof, Piet (South Africa), 129
Koroma, Mohamed, 156
Krog, Antjie, 258, 262, 264–5,
  266–9, 271, 272, 274, 276–7
Kufuor, John Agyekum (Ghana),
  316, 325
Kukah, Matthew, 243
Ku Klux Klan, 50
Kven people (Norway), 8

Lavalie, Andrew, 154
Lawyers without Borders Canada
  (ASFC). *See* Avocats sans fron-
  tières (ASFC) (Canada)
Le Réseau national de lute anti-
  corruption (REN-LAC)
  (Burkina Faso), 172

Lespérance, Janine, 20, 23
Les voies du renouveau (CNRR
  report, Burkina Faso), 172
Liberia: Act to Establish the Truth
  and Reconciliation Commission,
  64; civic participation in TRC,
  47; Regional Economic
  Communities (RECs), 85;
  reparations, 89; sexual violence,
  truth seeking to address, 62–3,
  64; Truth and Reconciliation
  Commission, 7, 12, 13, 18,
  284
local justice initiatives, 90
Lomé Peace Agreement (Sierra
  Leone), 71n34, 71n39, 149,
  154–5

Madikizela-Mandela, Winifred. *See*
  Mandela, Winnie
Malan, Magnus (South Africa),
  131
Mali: Algiers Peace Accord, 186,
  188, 202n2, 203n11; Avocats
  sans frontières (ASFC), 186–7,
  193–6; conflict (past and present), 187–8, 191–2; criminal
  investigations, 188–9; knowledge
  exchange, truth commissions,
  196–7, 198–200; transitional
  justice, 188, 195–6. *See also*
  Truth, Justice, and
  Reconciliation Commission
  (CVJR) (Mali)
Mamdani, Mahmood, 101, 268,
  269, 272, 273
Mandela, Nelson: Winnie Mandela,
  marriage to, 110, 111; Nobel
  Peace Prize, 108, 113;

presidency, 122; South African
TRC, 7
Mandela, Winnie: about, 107;
gendered malignment of, 114,
115; on Nelson Mandela, wife
of, 110, 111; as mother of the
nation, 109–10; Soweto student
uprising, 112; torture of,
111–12; TRC testimony, 108–9,
274–5
Mandela United Football Club,
109, 274
Maputo Protocol (on the Rights of
Women in Africa), 79
Marfo, Isaac (Ghana), 333
Mauritius, 7, 15, 17, 244
Mbeki Report (*Report of the
African Union: High Level Panel
on Darfur*), 83
Mbeki, Thabo (South Africa), 126,
129
memorialization, 52, 87, 125, 256,
304, 365, 367–8
Mensa-Bonsu, Henrietta (Ghana),
328
Millar, Gearoid, 20–1, 26, 27, 282,
326
minority groups: colonialism,
impact on, 102; truth commis-
sions to address abuse of, 6, 9
Minow, Martha, 134, 135, 168,
343
Missing (Kani), 259
Mixed Marriages Act (South
Africa), 137
Momoh, Joseph Saidu (Sierra
Leone), 147
Morocco, 7, 16–17, 89
motherhood, notion of in Africa,
110, 114

Multidimensional Integrated
Stabilization Mission in Mali
(MINUSMA) (UN), 187
Mutase, Richard, 266

narratives: about, 265–6, 302, 375;
Afrikaner, 268–9, 273. *See also*
storytelling
narrativity, 257. *See also*
storytelling
National Archives of South Africa,
TRC Collection, 22, 283, 284–5,
286, 289–90. *See also* South
African TRC
National Centre for Historical
Memory (Colombia), 197
National Centre for Truth and
Reconciliation (Canada), 22, 198
National Commission for
Democracy (Sierra Leone), 157
National Commission for the Fight
against Genocide (CNLG), 364–5
National Commission for Truth
and Reconciliation (Chile), 7, 12,
36–7, 240
National Commission of Inquiry
into Disappearances, 315
National Commission on the
Disappeared (Argentina), 7
national courts, 88–9. *See also*
courts
National Itorero Commission
(Rwanda), 369
National Party (NP) (South Africa),
38, 123, 132, 133, 137
National Prosecution Authority
(South Africa), 289
National Reconciliation
Commission (NRC) (Ghana):
archives, 245, 247–8;

establishment of, 316, 320; findings, 318–20, 319f, 321f; human
rights abuses, 47, 317, 318, 325,
331–3; legacy, 20, 327, 331–3,
334–5; mandate, 317–18; Plange
file, 246–7; recommendations,
321–2; reparations, 323–5;
report, 318, 319f, 323, 329,
330–1; state building, 11–12,
334–5; testimonies, 320, 321f,
324, 328–9. See also Ghana

National Services of Gacaca Courts
(NSGC) (Rwanda), 364

National Unity and Reconciliation
Commission (NURC) (Rwanda):
establishment of, 360; mandate, 7,
18, 360; reconciliation, 360–1;
state building, 12. See also Gacaca
courts (Rwanda); Rwanda

nation building: about, 11, 12, 13,
30n17, 38; truth commissions'
role in, 4, 19. See also state
building

nation (re)building. See nation
building; state building

nations: defined, 12–13;
institutions, importance of, 85–6

Ndahimana, Jean Nepo, 23–24

New Patriotic Party (NPP)
(Ghana), 316, 320, 326, 327,
329–30

Ngwaba, Uchechukwu, 26

Nigeria: Abacha regime
(1993–1998), 210; Abubakar
regime (1998–1999), 210–11;
authoritarian past, 209–10, 224,
225–6, 231n6; Constitution
(1999), 216, 217, 218; Dele
Giwa petition, 214–5; governance, post-authoritarian,

226–8; government influence on
Oputa Panel, 38, 216–7;
judiciary accountability, 224–6,
228, 229; Olusegun Obasanjo, ,
211, 212; Presidential Elections
Petition Tribunal, 228, 236n72;
on reclamation, 104; state
building, 11; Supreme Court
ruling, Oputa Panel case, 215–6,
217, 218; Tribunals of Inquiry
Act (TIA), 211, 214, 215, 216.
See also Oputa Panel (Nigeria)

Nkrumah, Kwame (Ghana), 102,
318, 325

non-governmental organizations
(NGOs): TRC records, 289; truth
commissions, role in, 187, 193–5

non-recurrence. See non-repetition

non-repetition: goal of TRCs,
305–7; right to, 89, 163, 169

Norbert Zongo affair, 170–1

NP (South Africa), 38, 123, 132,
133, 137

NPP (Ghana), 316, 320, 326, 327,
329–30

NSGC, 364

Nuremberg war crimes tribunal, 40

Nuttall, Sarah (South Africa), 260,
263

OAU, 78

Obasanjo, Olusegun (Nigeria),
211, 212, 232n17, 243

Ofosu-Ampofo, Samuel (Ghana),
330

Ogoni Nine, 210

Okafor, Obiora, 26

Omar, Dullah (South Africa), 124

Oputa Panel (Nigeria): establishment of, 211; evidence by proxy,

215–6; final report, 243; judicial
accountability, lack of, 215–7,
226; mandate, 212, 213–4;
Oputa Panel case, 215, 216,
217, 218–9, 229; state building,
11; truth seeking, 89, 213. *See
also* Nigeria
Organization of African Unity
(OAU), 78. *See also* African
Union (AU)
Osei Tutu II, Asantehene Otumfuo,
331

Panel of the Wise (AU), 84
participatory governance. *See*
democratic participation
patron-client governance model,
146, 147
PCRD *(Policy Framework for Post-
Conflict Reconstruction and
Development)* (AU), 82–3
Peace and National Cohesion
Commission (Sierra Leone), 144,
145, 155–6, 158, 159, 160,
162n22. *See also* Sierra Leone
Peace and Security Council (AU),
84
peacebuilding: about, 163–4;
national ownership, 144; Sierra
Leone, 144–6, 152–3, 155–6,
160, 341–3, 345–6, 349–51;
truth commissions' role in,
186–7
Peace Fund (AU), 84
peace infrastructures, 152–3, 155
Peace Museum (Sierra Leone), 22
People's National Party (Ghana),
318
peoples' rights, 79. *See also* rights

perpetrators: amnesty for, 3, 7, 36,
124, 125, 127–8; prosecution of,
129–30, 131–2, 141n30,
141n31, 166, 175–6; records,
identified in TRC, 285, 318–20,
319f; role of in truth commissions, 106; as victims, 270–1
Peru: final TRC report, 48, 50;
sexual violence crimes addressed
in TRC, 61, 62; Truth and
Reconciliation Commission, 36,
46, 71n31, 71n35, 168
Pinochet, Augusto (Chile), 240
Plange file (Ghana), 246–7, 251
Plange, Nii Ayi (Ghana), 246–7
PNDC (Ghana), 318, 326, 328,
331, 332
*Policy Framework for Post-Conflict
Reconstruction and
Development (PCRD)* (AU), 82–3
political participation. *See*
democratic participation
post-authoritarian societies:
democracy, transition to, 36;
truth commissions, 4, 5, 11, 13.
See also Burkina Faso;
Gambia, The
post-colonial societies, 4, 5, 9, 11,
12–14, 99–100, 101–2, 115
post-conflict societies: truth
commissions, 4, 5, 11, 12, 13.
See also Liberia; Mali; Sierra
Leone
post-genocide societies, 18, 23–4.
See also Rwanda
Presidential Elections Petition
Tribunal (Nigeria), 228, 236n72
*Principles for the Protection and
Promotion of Human Rights*

through Action to Combat Impunity (UN), 23, 45, 376, 377
Project for the Recovery of Historical Memory (REMHI) (Guatemala), 40
Promotion of Access to Information Act (South Africa), 289
Promotion of National Unity and Reconciliation Act (South Africa), 18, 60, 124, 127, 129, 281
Protocol to the Establishment of the Peace and Security Council of the African Union, 80
Provisional National Defense Council (PNDC) (Ghana), 318, 326, 328, 331, 332
public participation. *See* civic participation

Rawling, Jerry J. (Ghana), 318, 332
(re)building. *See* nation building; state building
reclamation, 103–5
reconciliation: about, 176–7, 360–1; achievement of, 284, 290; as goal of truth commissions, 42, 133–4, 281–2, 301–3; importance of, 123–4; Indigenous/non-Indigenous peoples (Canada), 199–200
Reconciliation Unit (TRRC) (The Gambia), 307, 308
records: about, 242–3; access to, 22–3, 282–3, 284–7, 288–90; closed, 22, 241, 250; final reports (general), 16, 22, 39, 40, 48, 243–4; open, 22. *See also* archives; *specific truth commissions (e.g., South African TRC)*
RECs (Africa), 81, 82, 85, 92
Regional Economic Communities (RECs) (Africa), 81, 82, 85, 92
rehabilitation rights, 89, 169. *See also* rights
REMHI (Guatemala), 40
REN-LAC (Burkina Faso), 172
reparations: apartheid victims, 3, 124–5, 126, 140n16, 140n17; genocide survivors, 365–7; Indigenous peoples (Canada), 199; individual vs collective, 105, 114–15; as mandate of truth commissions, 191, 286; memorialization, 52, 87, 125, 256, 304, 365, 367–8; right to, 89, 163, 169; types of, 125. *See also specific countries (e.g., Ghana, Rwanda); specific truth commissions (e.g., TRRC)*
Reparations and Rehabilitation Committee (RRC) (of the TRC), 124, 125
Report of the African Union: High Level Panel on Darfur (Mbeki Report), 83
Research and Investigation Unit (TRRC) (The Gambia), 307
restitution, right to, 89, 169
restorative justice: about, 40–1; Desmond Tutu on, 3, 41; and state building, 42; and truth commissions, 4, 40, 133–4, 376
retributive justice: about, 40–1; and state building, 42

Revolutionary United Front (RUF)
  (Sierra Leone), 147, 161n10
rights, 36, 76, 79, 89, 163, 169,
  376–7. *See also* human rights
Rodrigues, Joao (South Africa),
  141n31
RUF (Sierra Leone), 147, 161n10
rule of law, 166, 175–6, 220–1
Rwanda: curriculum, revision of
  history, 368–9; genocide (1994),
  166, 358; genocide ideology,
  361–2, 364, 365, 369;
  International Criminal Tribunal
  (ICTR), 58, 66, 166; memorialization efforts, 367–8; prosecution of genocide criminals, 166;
  reparations for genocide survivors, 365–7; security system
  reform, 369; sexual violence
  crimes, addressing of, 61, 66–7;
  transitional justice experience,
  23–4, 178, 359, 360. *See also*
  Gacaca courts (Rwanda);
  International Criminal Tribunal
  for Rwanda (ICTR); National
  Unity and Reconciliation
  Commission (NURC) (Rwanda)

SACP, 141n30, 141n31
SAHA, 245, 288–9
Sankara, Thomas (Burkina Faso),
  102, 170, 175
Sankofa ("go back for"), 103–4,
  117n16
Sankoh, Foday (Sierra Leone), 147
satisfaction, right to, 89, 169
Saunders, Rebecca, 259, 271, 277
SCSL, 63, 87, 149, 151, 166, 344–5
Seipei, Stompie (South Africa), 113,
  114, 274

Sessouma, Guillaume (Burkina
  Faso), 171
sexual violence: conflict-related,
  58–9, 102, 188; truth commissions, 59–61, 274; truth seeking
  processes, 62–5
Sidibé, Ousmane Oumarou (Mali),
  189
Sierra Leone: Bintumani-III (2019
  conference), 23, 145, 152, 156,
  158–60; civil war, 147–8, 149;
  community response to TRC,
  149, 150–1, 344–7; consultations, nationwide, 156–8; Ebola
  crisis, 342, 348; Freetown
  Mudslide, 342, 348; Green
  Paper, 155–6; Lomé Peace
  Agreement, 71n35, 71n39, 149,
  154–5; natural resources, 146–7;
  peacebuilding, 144–6, 152–3,
  155–6, 160, 341–3, 345–6,
  349–51; Peace Museum, 22;
  postwar reconstructions, 148; on
  reclamation, 104; reparations,
  89; sexual violence crimes, 61,
  62, 63–4, 65; Special Court for
  Sierra Leone (SCSL), 63, 149,
  151, 166. *See also* Peace and
  National Cohesion Commission
  (Sierra Leone); Sierra Leone
  Truth and Reconciliation
  Commission
Sierra Leone Peoples' Party (SLPP),
  144–5, 148, 160
Sierra Leone Truth and
  Reconciliation Commission:
  challenges faced, 150, 151–2,
  344–5, 346–7; documents,
  244–5, 284; establishment of,
  71n34, 148–9; legacy, 20–1,

152–3, 326, 341–2, 345–6;
publicity campaign, 150–1, 151*t*,
344, 345; recommendations, 23,
143–4, 152, 159; report, 48, 64,
143; state building, 12, 13. *See
also* Sierra Leone
Sinclair, Murray, 7–8, 199
SLPP, 144–5, 148, 160
social media: as platform for
hate speech/violence, 154, 160,
365; TRC campaigns, 190, 307,
308, 310
socio-historical commissions, 39
socio-historical transitions, 11,
13–14, 41
South Africa: Apartheid Museum,
22; cultural critiques of, 257–60;
democracy, transition to, 123–4,
137–8, 168; Department of
Justice (DOJ), 283, 285, 289–90;
discrimination laws (apartheid
regime), 220; judiciary resistance
to TRC, 222; National Party
(NP), 38, 123, 132, 133, 137;
Promotion of National Unity
and Reconciliation Act (1995),
18, 60, 124, 127; reconciliation,
meaning of, 176; records, public
access to TRC, 22, 282–3, 284–7,
288–90; state building, 17–18;
transitional justice experience,
178; whites, role in apartheid,
121–2, 131–5, 136–7, 138.
See also amnesty; South
African TRC
South African Broadcasting
Corporation, 245, 264
South African Communist Party
(SACP), 141n30, 141n31
South African Defence Force, 129

South African History Archive
(SAHA), 245, 288–9
South African Human Rights
Commission, 291
South African TRC: committees of,
124, 125, 128, 132, 264;
criticisms of, 36, 42, 61, 115,
126, 134, 282–3, 287–8;
democracy, role in transition,
122–4, 168; establishment of,
124; goals of, 7, 124–5; Winnie
Mandela, 108–9, 115, 274–5;
recommendations from, 284,
286, 288, 291; records, 22, 245,
284–7, 288–90; Register of
Reconciliation (TRC), 135–6;
report, 3–4, 125, 126, 129, 135,
281, 343–4; sexual violence
crimes overlooked, 60–1; and
state building, 17–18, 52, 133,
284; testimonies, 266, 267, 268,
270–3; as transitional justice
mechanism, 89; transparency of,
125, 285; voluntary participation in, 46–7. *See also* amnesty;
South Africa
Southall, Roger, 26
South Korea, 7, 17
Soweto student uprising, 109, 112
Special Court for Sierra Leone
(SCSL) (hybrid court), 63, 87,
149, 151, 166, 344–5
Special Jurisdiction for Peace
(Colombia), 197
state building: about, 12, 13, 15,
30n17, 38; and accountability
(judicial, institutional), 208–9,
220–1; and archivization, 262;
as implicit goal of truth commissions, 35–6, 37, 41, 50–1;

participatory, 37; and storytelling (narrativity), 275–7; truth commissions as a mechanism for, 17–19, 21, 25, 28; violence in the name of, 268, 269–72, 273, 275, 277. *See also* nation building

state (re)building. *See* nation building; state building

Stevens, Siaka (Sierra Leone), 146–7

storytelling: and historical truth, 266; and South African TRC, 260–1; and transitional justice, 256–7, 327–8. *See also* narratives; narrativity

Student Survivors Association (AERG) (Rwanda), 368, 372n20

Sub-Commission on Truth, Justice, and National Reconciliation (Burkina Faso), 164, 178–9

survivors. *See* victim-survivors

Svärd, Proscovia, 22

Tambadou, Abubacarr (The Gambia), 297–8, 299

Taylor, Charles (Liberia), 166

Teitel, Ruti, 41, 169

Terre'Blanche, Eugene (South Africa), 271–2

Theissen, Gunnar, 136, 137–8, 142n45

Timor-Leste: Commission of Truth and Friendship (CTF), 48–9, 51, 71n33, 71n38; sexual violence crimes addressed in TRC, 61, 62

torture: authorization of, 129, 136, 272, 328–9; as colonial practice, 16; investigations of by TRCs, 171, 188–9, 190, 240, 270–1,

297, 302, 318; of prisoners/detainees, 61, 107, 110, 111–12, 274; transitional justice mechanisms against, 80, 89, 376; as weapon of war, 147–8, 188

transitional justice: about, 5, 40–1, 163–4; architecture for (in Africa), 77–80, 81–3, 90–2; challenges faced by, 92, 270–1, 301; democracy, transition to, 123, 163, 165–7; faith-based organizations, 86; institutions of, 84–6, 91, 148; judicial accountability, 208–9, 229; mechanisms of (in Africa), 86–90; as a political field, 169–70; sexual violence, addressing conflict-related, 63; and storytelling (narrativity), 256–7, 265, 275–7; truth commissions' role in, 4, 24, 37, 51, 89, 375–6. See also *specific countries (e.g., Burkina Faso, Rwanda)*

TRC report. *See* South African TRC

Truth, Justice, and Reconciliation Commission (CVJR) (Mali): archives, 23; ASFC, 186, 193–8, 205n31, 206n33; challenges, 20, 191–3, 203n15, 204n21; communication strategy, 190; composition of, 189, 201–2, 204n16; establishment of, 186–7, 189, 202n1; international learning, 196–200; reparations mandate, 191, 205n27; state building, 13, 18; transitional justice mechanism, 188; truth seeking mandate, 189–90; victims' statements, 190, 191–2, 196. *See also* Mali

Truth, Justice, and Reconciliation
   Commission (Kenya), 15, 16,
   47–8
Truth, Reconciliation and
   Reparations Commission (TRRC)
   (The Gambia): archives, 251;
   challenges, 301–2, 303–4;
   effectiveness of, 308–9; establish-
   ment of, 300–1, 306; mandate,
   7, 298–9; reconciliation, 301–3,
   308; reparations, 7, 303–4;
   specialized units, 307, 308; state
   building, 13, 18; study tour of
   TRCs, 299–300; testimonies,
   295. See also Gambia, The
Truth and Dignity Commission
   (Tunisia), 46, 48
Truth and Justice Commission
   (Mauritius), 7, 15, 17, 244
Truth and Reconciliation
   Commission (TRC) (South
   Africa). See South African TRC
Truth and Reconciliation
   Commission of Sierra Leone Act
   (2000), 143
Truth and Reconciliation
   Commissions (non-specific). See
   truth commissions (non-specific)
truth commissions (non-specific):
   about, 6–7, 39–40, 99, 167–8,
   252n1; challenges faced by,
   150–2, 246–7; communication
   strategies, 23, 25, 46–7, 125,
   190, 245; democracy, contributions to, 167–9, 174, 281; effectiveness of, 45, 49–51, 52, 166,
   308–10; establishment of
   (global), 4–5, 9, 10f, 11f, 45;
   final reports (general), 16, 22,
   39, 40, 48, 243–4; global

experiences, 196–7, 198–200,
   239, 343; goals of, 7–9, 35–6,
   133–4, 143, 374–5; governments, influence of, 37, 38;
   limitations of, 100, 106–7, 115,
   305–6, 327; non-governmental
   organizations (NGOs), role in,
   193–5; participation in, voluntary, 46; proxy, evidence by,
   215–6, 233n21; recommendations from, 48–9, 64–5, 200;
   reparation policies, 89, 140n16,
   140n17; and state failure, 13–14,
   15. See also amnesty; archives;
   civic inclusion; civic participation; democratic participation;
   records; restorative justice; sexual violence; state building; torture; transitional justice;
   victim-survivors; women; specific
   countries (e.g., Canada, Sierra
   Leone); specific truth commissions (e.g., South African TRC)
truth finding. See truth seeking
truth seeking: and accountability
   (judicial, institutional), 220–1;
   democratization, role in, 167–9,
   173, 284; as mandate of truth
   commission, 189–90; proxy,
   evidence by, 215–6, 233n21;
   reparation policies, 89; restriction of, 36–7; right to, 163,
   376–7; truth commissions' role
   in, 24, 25, 42–3, 106, 134, 377;
   truth telling, versus, 106, 343.
   See also truth telling
truth telling: community-based
   methods of, 21, 256, 257, 258;
   as healing, 51, 99, 125, 148,
   149–50, 257, 346; sexual

violence, conflict-related, 62–5; South African TRC model of, 7–8, 18, 139n9, 271, 343–4; and storytelling, 260–1, 267, 327; truth seeking, *versus*, 106, 343. *See also* truth seeking

Tunisia, 46, 48

Tutsis (Rwanda): genocide, 166, 358, 371n8; reparations, 365–7; women, sexual violence against, 62, 65–6, 67

Tutu, Desmond (Archbishop): on amnesty, 127, 128, 141n25, 267, 323; on the impact of the South African TRC, 50, 257, 281–2; Winnie Mandela trial, 108; Register of Reconciliation (South African TRC), 135; on restorative justice, 3, 4, 41, 323; role in South African TRC, 124; on *Ubuntu*, 103

Ubuntu, 103, 105, 108, 115, 177

Ugor, Paul, 23, 327–8

Umkhonto we Sizwe, 287

UN. *See* United Nations (UN)

UNDP, 152–3

Unidad Revolucionaria Nacional Guatemalteca, 71n37

United Nations (UN): *Declaration on the Rights of Indigenous Peoples*, 376; High Commissioner for Human Rights, 60, 148, 204n18, 244–5, 299; Multidimensional Integrated Stabilization Mission in Mali (MINUSMA), 187; on national ownership, 144; on peacebuilding, 163–4; *Principles for the Protection and Promotion of Human Rights through Action to Combat Impunity*, 23, 45; resolution 2467 (sexual violence in conflict situations), 58; right to remedy and reparation for human rights violations, 89, 169; Security Council Resolution 1315, 72n46; study of truth commissions, 52

United Nations Development Program (UNDP), 152–3

United States: Commission on Truth, Racial Justice, Healing and Transformation, 8; Greensboro Truth and Reconciliation Commission (GTRC), 50–1

unity, national, 18, 99–100, 144, 157, 160, 172, 281, 360

van der Merwe, Johan (South Africa), 267

Victim Support Unit (TRRC) (The Gambia), 307

victim-survivors: impact of truth commissions on, 49–51; perpetrators as, 270–1; reparations for, 3, 65–7, 124–5, 140n16, 140n17, 191, 286, 365–7; rights of, 36; role of in truth commissions, 106, 190, 191–2; of sexual violence, conflict-related, 59–61, 62–5; of violence, 318–20, 319f; voluntary participation in truth commissions, 16, 46, 168. *See also* human rights; torture; violence

Viljoen, Constand (South Africa), 267, 273

Villa-Vicencio, Charles, 124, 128, 133–4
violence: investigations by TRCs, 318–20, 319f; social media as platform for, 160; state building, in the name of, 268, 269–72, 273, 275, 277. See also torture; victim-survivors
Vlakplaas, 130, 266, 267–8

Wachira, George, 92
Wallace, Jennifer, 19–20, 26
war crimes: sexual violence as, 58–9; tribunals, 40. See also torture
White Paper, 322, 330–1, 337n20
whites: amnesty hearings, 127, 267–8; apartheid, role of in, 127, 131–7, 138, 268; Black majority rule, 121–2; Register of Reconciliation (TRC), 135–6; TRC, acceptance of, 137–8, 142n45

Who Killed the Judges? (documentary), 332
women: colonialism, impact on, 102; gendered experience, truth commissions, 21, 59–61, 62–5, 102; identity of in Africa, 110, 114–15; participation in truth commissions, 6, 47, 191, 273–5, 307, 308; peacebuilding, role in, 157–8; rights of, 79; social justice struggle, role in, 111; TRC, acceptance of, 142n45
Women's Affairs Unit (TRRC) (The Gambia), 307, 308

youth. See children
Youth and Children's Network Coordination (TRRC) The Gambia), 307
Zalaquett, José, 324
Zongo, Norbert (Burkina Faso), 170–1, 175